# Teach Yourself VISUALLY™

## Windows® 7

by Paul McFedries

Wiley Publishing, Inc.

# Teach Yourself VISUALLY™ Windows® 7

Published by
**Wiley Publishing, Inc.**
10475 Crosspoint Boulevard
Indianapolis, IN 46256

www.wiley.com

Published simultaneously in Canada



Library of Congress Control Number: 2009932711

ISBN: 978-0-470-50386-7

Manufactured in the United States of America

10 9 8 7 6 5 4

## Trademark Acknowledgments



## Contact Us

For general information on our other products and services please contact our Customer Care Department within the U.S. at 877-762-2974, outside the U.S. at 317-572-3993 or fax 317-572-4002.

For technical support please visit www.wiley.com/techsupport.

Wiley Publishing, Inc.

**Sales**

Contact Wiley
at (877) 762-2974 or
fax (317) 572-4002.

# Praise for Visual Books

***"Like a lot of other people, I understand things best when I see them visually. Your books really make learning easy and life more fun."***

John T. Frey (Cadillac, MI)

***"I have quite a few of your Visual books and have been very pleased with all of them. I love the way the lessons are presented!"***

Mary Jane Newman (Yorba Linda, CA)

***"I just purchased my third Visual book (my first two are dog-eared now!), and, once again, your product has surpassed my expectations."***

Tracey Moore (Memphis, TN)

***"I am an avid fan of your Visual books. If I need to learn anything, I just buy one of your books and learn the topic in no time. Wonders! I have even trained my friends to give me Visual books as gifts."***

Illona Bergstrom (Aventura, FL)

***"Thank you for making it so clear. I appreciate it. I will buy many more Visual books."***

J.P. Sangdong (North York, Ontario, Canada)

***"I have several books from the Visual series and have always found them to be valuable resources."***

Stephen P. Miller (Ballston Spa, NY)

***"Thank you for the wonderful books you produce. It wasn't until I was an adult that I discovered how I learn — visually. Nothing compares to Visual books. I love the simple layout. I can just grab a book and use it at my computer, lesson by lesson. And I understand the material! You really know the way I think and learn. Thanks so much!"***

Stacey Han (Avondale, AZ)

***"I absolutely admire your company's work. Your books are terrific. The format is perfect, especially for visual learners like me. Keep them coming!"***

Frederick A. Taylor, Jr. (New Port Richey, FL)

***"I have several of your Visual books and they are the best I have ever used."***

Stanley Clark (Crawfordville, FL)

***"I bought my first Teach Yourself VISUALLY book last month. Wow. Now I want to learn everything in this easy format!"***

Tom Vial (New York, NY)

***"Thank you, thank you, thank you...for making it so easy for me to break into this high-tech world. I now own four of your books. I recommend them to anyone who is a beginner like myself."***

Gay O'Donnell (Calgary, Alberta, Canada)

***"I write to extend my thanks and appreciation for your books. They are clear, easy to follow, and straight to the point. Keep up the good work! I bought several of your books and they are just right! No regrets! I will always buy your books because they are the best."***

Seward Kollie (Dakar, Senegal)

***"Compliments to the chef!! Your books are extraordinary! Or, simply put, extra-ordinary, meaning way above the rest! THANK YOU THANK YOU THANK YOU! I buy them for friends, family, and colleagues."***

Christine J. Manfrin (Castle Rock, CO)

***"What fantastic teaching books you have produced! Congratulations to you and your staff. You deserve the Nobel Prize in Education in the Software category. Thanks for helping me understand computers."***

Bruno Tonon (Melbourne, Australia)

***"Over time, I have bought a number of your 'Read Less - Learn More' books. For me, they are THE way to learn anything easily. I learn easiest using your method of teaching."***

José A. Mazón (Cuba, NY)

***"I am an avid purchaser and reader of the Visual series, and they are the greatest computer books I've seen. The Visual books are perfect for people like myself who enjoy the computer, but want to know how to use it more efficiently. Your books have definitely given me a greater understanding of my computer, and have taught me to use it more effectively. Thank you very much for the hard work, effort, and dedication that you put into this series."***

Alex Diaz (Las Vegas, NV)

**July 05**

# Credits

**Executive Editor**
Jody Lefevere

**Project Editor**
Sarah Hellert

**Technical Editor**
Vince Averello

**Copy Editor**
Scott Tullis

**Editorial Director**
Robyn Siesky

**Editorial Manager**
Cricket Krengel

**Business Manager**
Amy Knies

**Sr. Marketing Manager**
Sandy Smith

**Vice President and Executive Group Publisher**
Richard Swadley

**Vice President and Executive Publisher**
Barry Pruett

**Project Coordinator**
Lynsey Stanford

**Graphics and Production Specialists**
Joyce Haughey
Andrea Hornberger
Jennifer Mayberry
Julie Trippetti
Christine Williams

**Quality Control Technician**
Melissa Cossell

**Proofreader**
Cindy Ballew

**Indexer**
Potomac Indexing, LLC

**Screen Artists**
Ana Carrillo
Jill A. Proll

**Illustrators**
Ronda David-Burroughs
Cheryl Grubbs
Mark Pinto

# About the Author

**Paul McFedries** is a full-time technical writer. Paul has been authoring computer books since 1991 and he has more than 60 books to his credit. Paul's books have sold more than three million copies worldwide. These books include the Wiley titles *Windows 7 Visual Quick Tips, Switching to a Mac Portable Genius, iPhone 3G Portable Genius, Teach Yourself VISUALLY Office 2008 for Mac*, and *Internet Simplified*. Paul is also the proprietor of Word Spy (www.wordspy.com and twitter.com/wordspy), a Web site that tracks new words and phrases as they enter the language. Paul invites you to drop by his personal Web site at www.mcfedries.com, or to follow him on Twitter at twitter.com/paulmcf.

# Author's Acknowledgments

It goes without saying that writers focus on text, and I certainly enjoyed focusing on the text that you'll read in this book. However, this book is more than just the usual collection of words and phrases. A quick thumb through the pages will show you that this book is also chock full of images, from sharp screen shots to fun and informative illustrations. Those colorful images sure make for a beautiful book, and that beauty comes from a lot of hard work by Wiley's immensely talented group of designers and layout artists. They are all listed in the Credits section on the previous page, and I thank them for creating another gem. Of course, what you read in this book must also be accurate, logically presented, and free of errors. Ensuring all of this was an excellent group of editors that included project editor Sarah Hellert, copy editor Scott Tullis, and technical editor Vince Averello. Thanks to all of you for your exceptional competence and hard work. Thanks, as well, to acquisitions editor Jody Lefevere for asking me to write this book.

# Table of Contents

## Getting Started with Windows 7

## Launching and Working with Programs

## ...diting Documents

## ...h Images

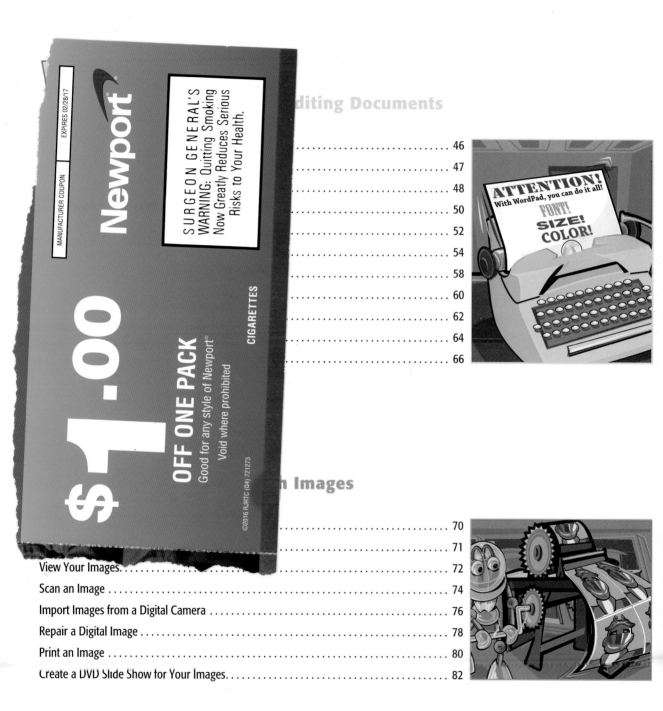

# Table of Contents

## chapter 5 Playing Music and Other Media

## chapter 6 Working with Files

## chapter 7 Sharing Your Computer with Others

# Table of Contents

## Using Windows 7's Notebook Features

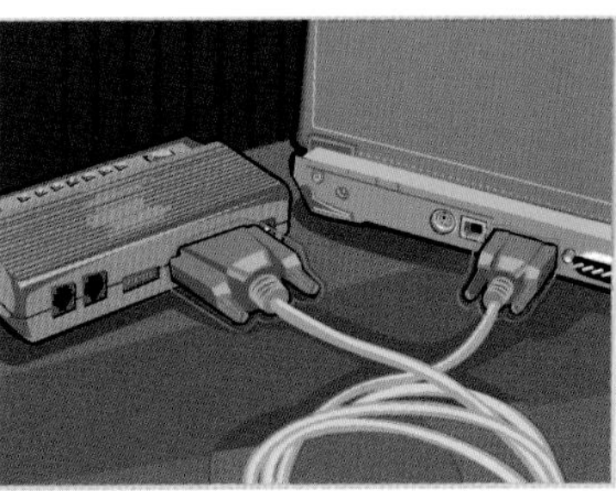

## chapter 9 Getting Connected to the Internet

## chapter 10 Surfing the World Wide Web

## chapter 11 Working with E-mail, Contacts, and Events



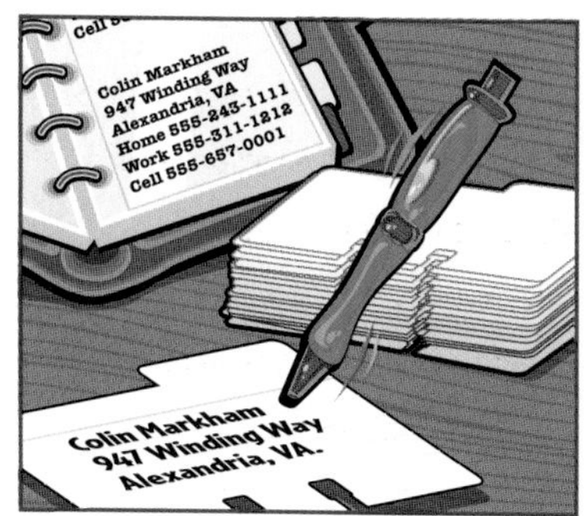

# Table of Contents

## chapter 12 Implementing Security in Windows 7

## chapter 13 Customizing Windows 7

## chapter 14 Maintaining Windows 7

# How to use this book

Do you look at the pictures in a book or newspaper before anything else on a page? Would you rather see an image instead of read about how to do something? Search no further. This book is for you. Opening *Teach Yourself VISUALLY Windows 7* allows you to read less and learn more about the Windows operating system.

### Who Needs This Book

This book is for a reader who has never used this particular technology or software application. It is also for more computer literate individuals who want to expand their knowledge of the different features that *Windows 7* has to offer.

### Book Organization

*Teach Yourself VISUALLY Windows 7* has 14 chapters.

Chapter 1, "Getting Started with Windows 7," gives you the basics of starting and stopping Windows 7, understanding the Windows 7 screen, and using a mouse.

In Chapter 2, "Launching and Working with Programs," you learn how to install and start programs, how to use menus, toolbars, and dialog boxes, and how to switch between program windows.

In Chapter 3, "Creating and Editing Documents," you learn how to create and open documents, edit document text, and save and print your work.

Chapter 4, "Working with Images," shows you how to work with images in Windows 7, load images from the digital camera or scanner, and create a DVD-based slide show.

With Chapter 5, "Playing Music and Other Media," you learn how to use Windows Media Player to play music, sound, and video files, audio CDs, and DVDs.

Chapter 6, "Working with Files," gives you the details on how to view, select, copy, and move files, burn files to a recordable CD, rename and delete files, and search for files.

Chapter 7, "Sharing Your Computer with Others," shows you how to use Windows 7's User Accounts feature to enable multiple people to share a single computer, and introduces you to some basic networking techniques.

In Chapter 8, "Using Windows 7's Notebook Features," you find out how to use Windows 7's notebook computer features.

Chapter 9, "Getting Connected to the Internet," shows you how to configure Windows Vista to connect to the Internet.

In Chapter 10, "Surfing the World Wide Web," you learn how to use the Internet Explorer program to browse the World Wide Web.

With Chapter 11, "Working with E-mail, Contacts, and Events," you learn how to use the Windows Live Mail program to send and receive e-mail messages and track your appointments, events, and tasks.

Chapter 12, "Implementing Security in Windows 7," gives you information on the Windows 7 security features, including the new Action Center, passwords, parental controls, and more.

Chapter 13, "Customizing Windows 7," shows you various ways to customize Windows 7 to suit the way you work.

In Chapter 14, "Maintaining Windows 7," you learn about some programs that enable you to perform routine maintenance that will keep your system running smoothly.

### Chapter Organization

This book consists of sections, all listed in the book's table of contents. A *section* is a set of steps that show you how to complete a specific computer task.

Each section, usually contained on two facing pages, has an introduction to the task at hand, a set of full-color screen shots and steps that walk you through the task, and a set of tips. This format allows you to quickly look at a topic of interest and learn it instantly.

Chapters group together three or more sections with a common theme. A chapter may also contain pages that give you the background information needed to understand the sections in a chapter.

## Using the Mouse

This book uses the following conventions to describe the actions you perform when using the mouse:

### Click

Press your left mouse button once. You generally click your mouse on something to select something on the screen.

### Double-click

Press your left mouse button twice. Double-clicking something on the computer screen generally opens whatever item you have double-clicked.

### Right-click

Press your right mouse button. When you right-click anything on the computer screen, the program displays a shortcut menu containing commands specific to the selected item.

### Click and Drag, and Release the Mouse

Move your mouse pointer and hover it over an item on the screen. Press and hold down the left mouse button. Now, move the mouse to where you want to place the item and then release the button. You use this method to move an item from one area of the computer screen to another.

## The Conventions in This Book

A number of typographic and layout styles have been used throughout *Teach Yourself VISUALLY Windows 7* to distinguish different types of information.

### Bold

Bold type represents the names of commands and options that you interact with. Bold type also indicates text and numbers that you must type into a dialog box or window.

### Italics

Italic words introduce a new term and are followed by a definition.

### Numbered Steps

You must perform the instructions in numbered steps in order to successfully complete a section and achieve the final results.

### Bulleted Steps

These steps point out various optional features. You do not have to perform these steps; they simply give additional information about a feature.

### Indented Text

Indented text tells you what the program does in response to you following a numbered step. For example, if you click a certain menu command, a dialog box may appear or a window may open. Indented text may also tell you what the final result is when you follow a set of numbered steps.

### Notes

Notes give additional information. They may describe special conditions that may occur during an operation. They may warn you of a situation that you want to avoid — for example, the loss of data. A note may also cross reference a related area of the book. A cross reference may guide you to another chapter or another section within the current chapter.

### Icons and buttons

Icons and buttons are graphical representations within the text. They show you exactly what you need to click to perform a step.

You can easily identify the tips in any section by looking for the TIPS icon. Tips offer additional information, including tips, hints, and tricks. You can use the TIPS information to go beyond what you have learned in the steps.

CHAPTER 1

# Getting Started with Windows 7

Are you ready to learn about Windows 7? In this chapter, you learn the basics of starting and activating Windows 7, getting help, and shutting down your system.

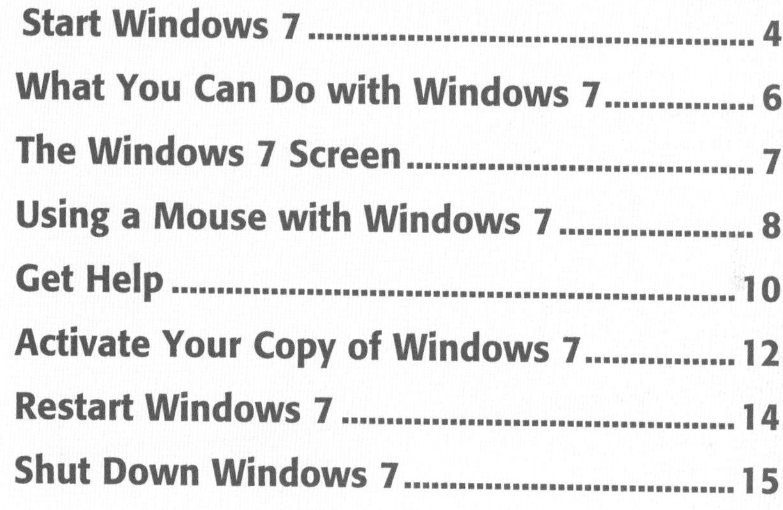

# Start Windows 7

When you turn on your computer, Windows 7 starts automatically, but you may have to navigate the Welcome screen along the way.

**The first time you start your computer, you may need to run through a series of configuration steps.**

## Start Windows 7

1. Turn on your computer.

- The Windows 7 Welcome screen appears.

***Note:*** *If your version of Windows 7 is configured with just a single user and no password, then you bypass the Welcome screen and go directly to the desktop.*

2. Click the icon that corresponds to your Windows 7 user name.

   Windows 7 prompts you to enter your password.

***Note:*** *If you are the only user on your computer, Windows 7 prompts you for your password right away, so you can skip Step* **2**.

3 Type your password.

***Note:** The password characters appear as dots as you type them so that no one else can read your password.*

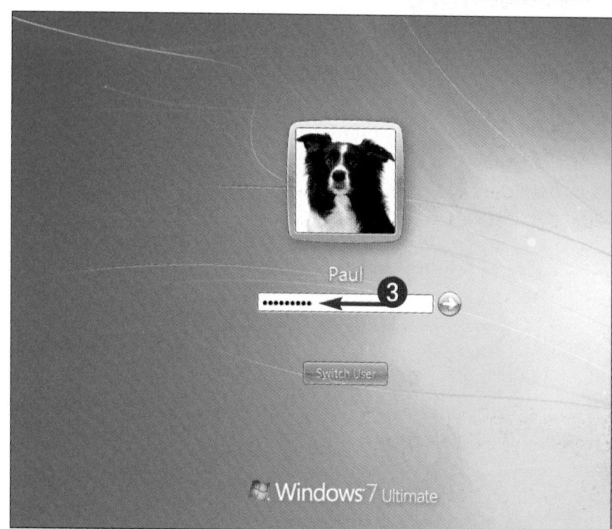


4 Click the **Go** arrow ( ) or press Enter.

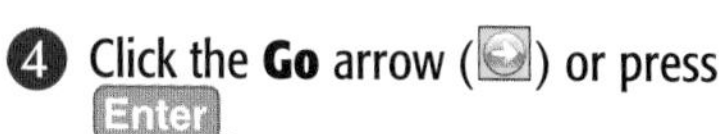

The Windows 7 desktop appears after a few moments.

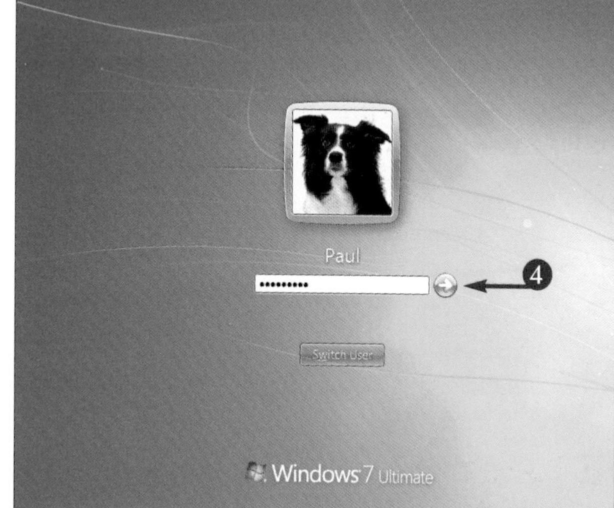


TIP

**What happens if I forget my Windows 7 password?**

Most Windows 7 user accounts that are password protected are also set up with a password *hint* — usually a word or phrase designed to jog your memory. You choose the question when you set your password, as explained in the "Protect an Account with a Password" section in Chapter 12. If you forget your password, click the **Go** arrow ( ) and then click **OK** to see the password hint.

# What You Can Do with Windows 7

**Windows 7 is an operating system that contains a collection of tools, programs, and resources. Here is a sampling of what you can do with them.**

## Get Work Done

With Windows 7, you can run programs that enable you to get your work done more efficiently, such as a word processor for writing memos and letters, a spreadsheet for making calculations, and a database for storing information. Windows 7 comes with some of these programs (such as the WordPad program you learn about in Chapter 3), and you can purchase and install others separately.

## Create and Edit Pictures

Windows 7 comes with a lot of features that let you work with images. You can create your own pictures from scratch, import images from a scanner or digital camera, or download images from the Internet. After you create or acquire an image, you can edit it, print it, or send it via e-mail. You learn about these and other picture tasks in Chapter 4.

## Play Music and Other Media

Windows 7 has treats for your ears as well as your eyes. You can listen to audio CDs, play digital sound and video clips, watch DVD movies, tune in to Internet radio stations, and copy audio files to a recordable CD. You learn about these multimedia tasks in Chapter 5.

## Get on the Internet

Windows 7 makes connecting to the Internet easy (see Chapter 9). And after you are on the Net, Windows 7 has all the tools you need to get the most out of your experience. For example, you can use Internet Explorer to surf the World Wide Web (see Chapter 10) and Windows Live Mail to send and receive e-mail (see Chapter 11).

# The Windows 7 Screen

Before getting to the specifics of working with Windows 7, take a few seconds to familiarize yourself with the basic screen elements.

### Desktop Icon

An icon on the desktop represents a program or Windows 7 feature. A program you install often adds its own icon on the desktop.

### Mouse Pointer

When you move your mouse, this pointer moves along with it.

### Desktop

This is the Windows 7 "work area," meaning that it is where you work with your programs and documents.

### Time and Date

This is the current time and date on your computer. To see the full date, position the mouse over the time. To change the date or time, click the time.

### Notification Area

This area displays small icons that notify you about things that are happening on your computer. For example, you see notifications if your printer runs out of paper or if an update to Windows 7 is available over the Internet.

### Taskbar

The programs you have open appear in the taskbar. You use this area to switch between programs if you have more than one running at a time.

### Taskbar Icons

You use these icons to launch some Windows 7 features with just a mouse click.

### Start Button

You use this button to start programs and launch many of Windows 7's features.

# Using a Mouse with Windows 7

Windows 7 was built with the mouse in mind, so it pays to learn the basic mouse techniques early on because you will use them for as long as you use Windows.

**If you have never used a mouse before, remember to keep all your movements slow and deliberate, and practice the techniques in this section as much as you can.**

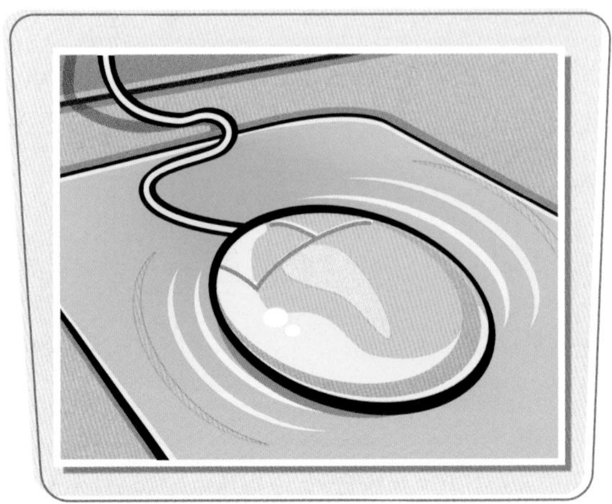

## Using a Mouse with Windows 7

### CLICK THE MOUSE

1. Position the mouse over the object you want to work with.
2. Click the left mouse button.

- Depending on the object, Windows 7 either selects the object or performs some operation in response to the click (such as displaying the Start menu).

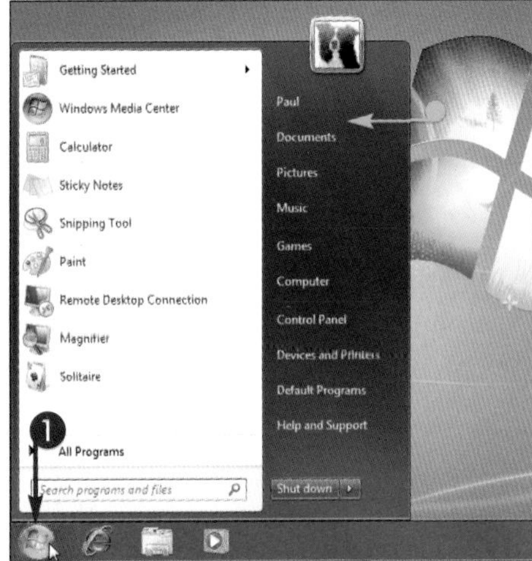


### DOUBLE-CLICK THE MOUSE

1. Position the mouse over the object you want to work with.
2. Click the left mouse button twice in quick succession.

- Windows 7 usually performs some operation in response to the double-click action (such as displaying the Recycle Bin window).

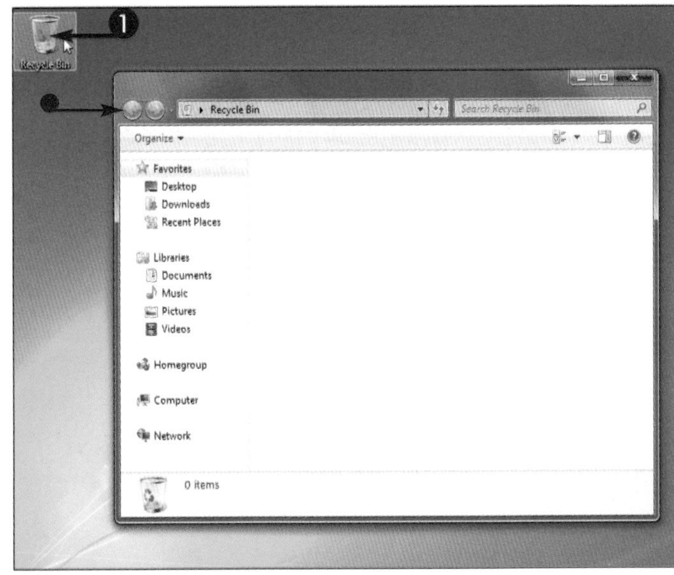

## RIGHT-CLICK THE MOUSE

1. Position the mouse over the object you want to work with.
2. Click the right mouse button.

- Windows 7 displays a shortcut menu when you right-click something.

**Note:** *The contents of the shortcut menu depend on the object you right-clicked.*

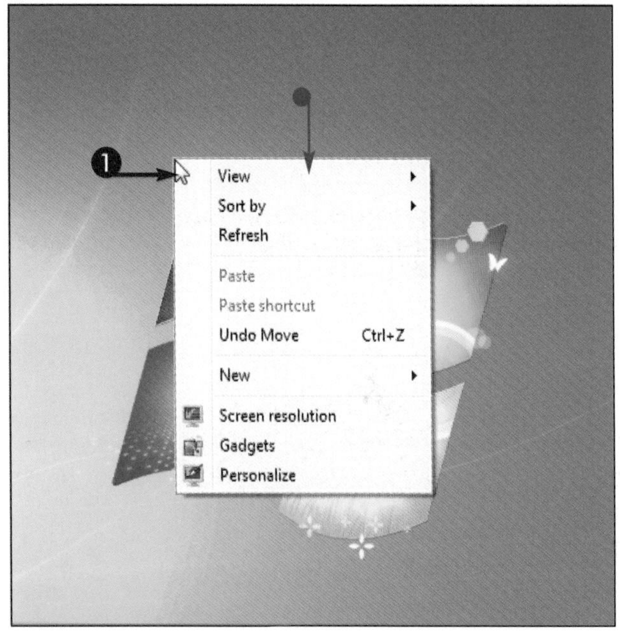


## CLICK AND DRAG THE MOUSE

1. Position the mouse over the object you want to work with.
2. Click and hold the left mouse button.
3. Move the mouse to drag the selected object.

- In most cases, the object moves along with the mouse.

4. Release the mouse button when the selected object is repositioned.

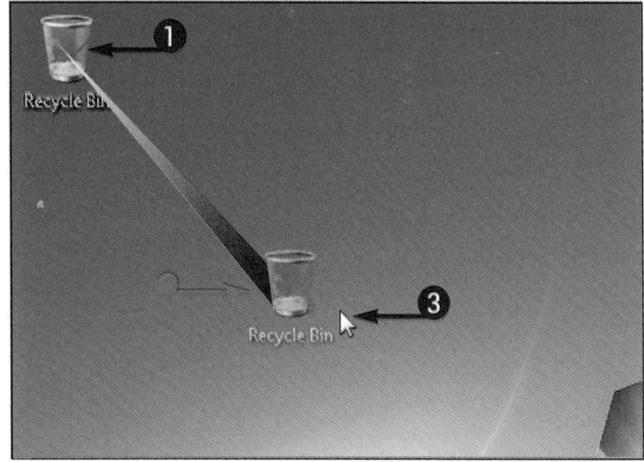

### Why does Windows 7 sometimes not recognize my double-clicks?

Try to double-click as quickly as you can, and be sure not to move the mouse between clicks. If you continue to have trouble, click **Start**, **Control Panel**, **Hardware and Sound**, and then **Mouse** to open the Mouse Properties dialog box. Click the **Buttons** tab. In the Double-click Speed group, click and drag the slider to the left (toward Slow).

### How can I set up my mouse for a left-hander?

Click **Start**, **Control Panel**, **Hardware and Sound**, and then **Mouse** to open the Mouse Properties dialog box. Click the **Buttons** tab. Click **Switch primary and secondary buttons** ( changes to ).

# Get Help

You can find out more about Windows 7, learn how to perform a task, or troubleshoot problems by accessing the Help system.

**Most of the Help system is arranged into various categories, such as "Security and privacy" and "Files, folders, and libraries." Each category offers a number of subcategories, and each category and subcategory contains a collection of related topics.**

## Get Help

1. Click **Start**.

   The Start menu appears.

2. Click **Help and Support**.

   The Windows Help and Support window appears.

3. Click the **Browse Help** button ( ).

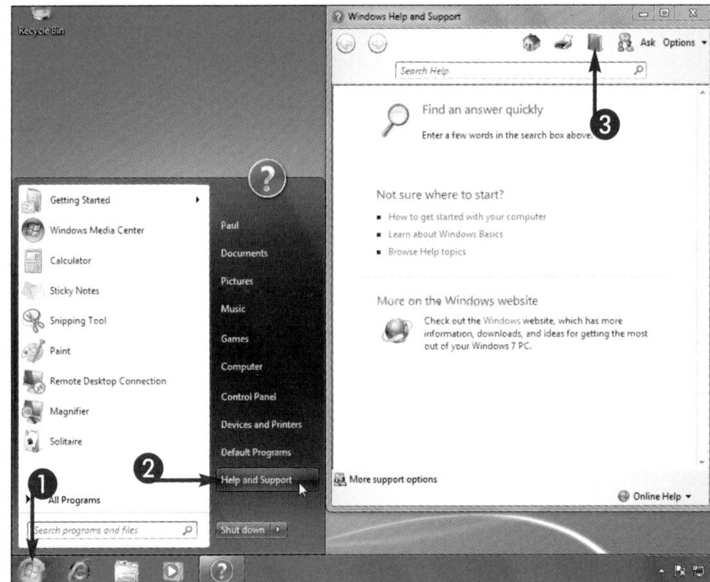

   The Table of Contents appears.

4. Click a category.

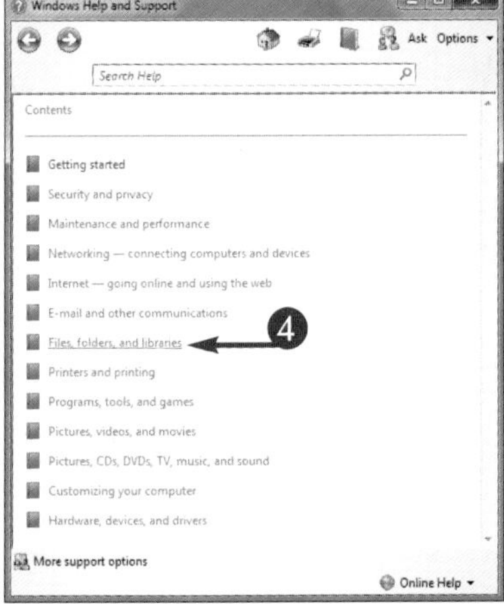

- A list of Help topics appears for the category you selected.
- A list of subcategories appears for the category you selected.

5 Click a topic.

***Note:*** *If the topic you want is part of a subcategory, click the subcategory to display the list of topics it contains, and then click the topic.*

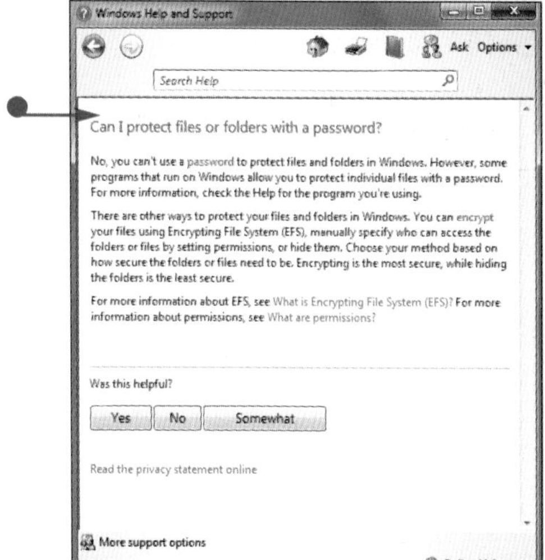


- The item you selected appears in the Windows Help and Support Center window.

6 Read the article.

***Note:*** *To return to a previous Windows Help and Support Center screen, click the **Back** button ( ) until you get to the screen you want.*

## How do I get help for a specific program?

Almost all Windows programs have their own Help features. You can access Help in a specific program one of three main ways:

- Click **Help** from the menu, and then click the command that runs the Help features (it may be called **Help Contents**, **Help Topics**, or ***Program* Help**, where *Program* is the name of the program (for example, **Microsoft Word Help**).
- Press F1.
- In a dialog box or program window, click the **Help** button ( ).

# Activate Your Copy of Windows 7

To avoid piracy, Microsoft requires that each copy of Windows 7 be activated. Otherwise, your copy of Windows 7 will refuse to run after the activation period has expired.

**This section assumes that Windows 7 has not yet prompted you to start the activation. If you see an icon in the notification area with the message "Activate Windows now," click that message and then skip to Step 5.**

## Activate Your Copy of Windows 7

1. Click **Start**.

   The Start menu appears.

2. Right-click **Computer**.
3. Click **Properties**.

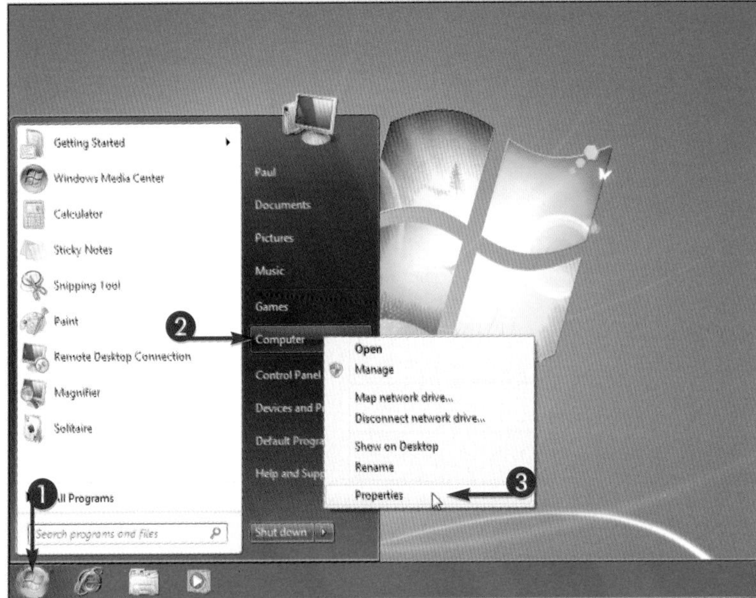


The System window appears.

***Note:** If the System window shows the Ask for Genuine Microsoft Software logo in the Windows Activation area, then you do not need to perform the rest of the steps in this section. Click the **Close** button (☒) to close the System window.*

4. Click the **Activate Windows now** link.

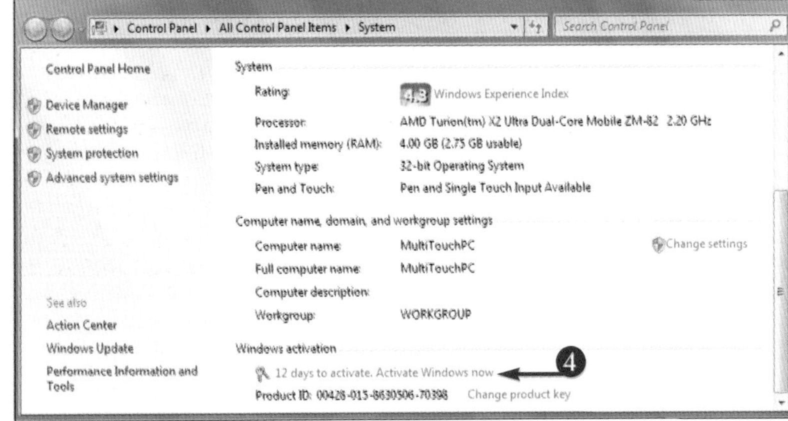

The Windows Activation dialog box appears.

5 Click **Activate Windows online now**.

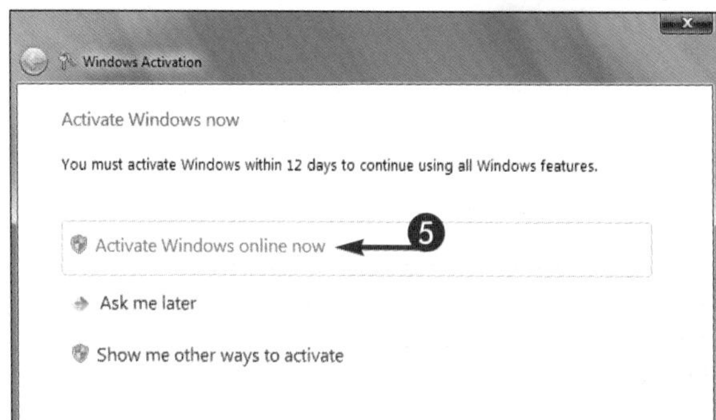


Windows 7 confirms that it has been activated.

6 Click **Close**.

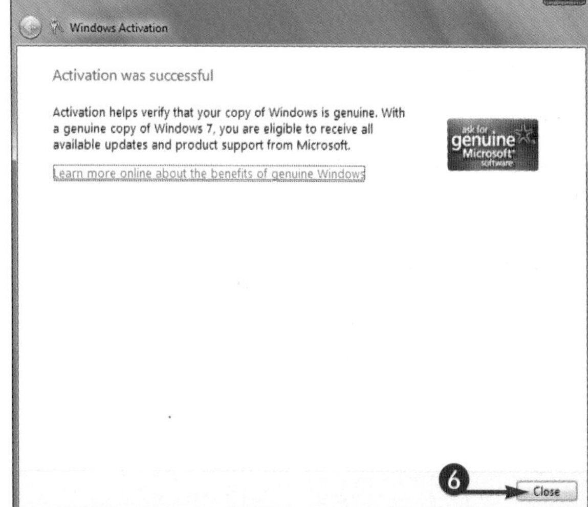

**Can I activate Windows 7 on more than one computer?**

No, not usually. The activation process creates a special value unique to your computer's hardware configuration. When you activate Windows 7, your copy of the program is associated with this unique hardware value, which means your copy works only with that one computer. However, if that computer breaks down, you can telephone Microsoft to let them know, and they should allow you to activate Windows 7 on another computer.

**How can I activate my copy of Windows 7 if I do not have Internet access?**

If you do not have Internet access, perform Steps **1** to **5** anyway. After a few moments, Windows Activation displays a list of options. Click **Show me other ways to activate**. If your computer has a modem attached, click **Use my modem to connect directly to the activation service**. If you do not have a modem, click **Use the automated phone system**, instead.

# Restart Windows 7

You can restart Windows 7, which means it shuts down and starts up again immediately. This is useful if your computer is running slow or acting funny. Sometimes a restart solves the problem.

**Knowing how to restart Windows 7 also comes in handy when you install a program or device that requires a restart to function properly. If you are busy right now, you can always opt to restart your computer yourself later, when it is more convenient.**

## Restart Windows 7

1. Shut down all your running programs.

*Note: Be sure to save your work as you close your programs.*

2. Click **Start**.

   The Start menu appears.

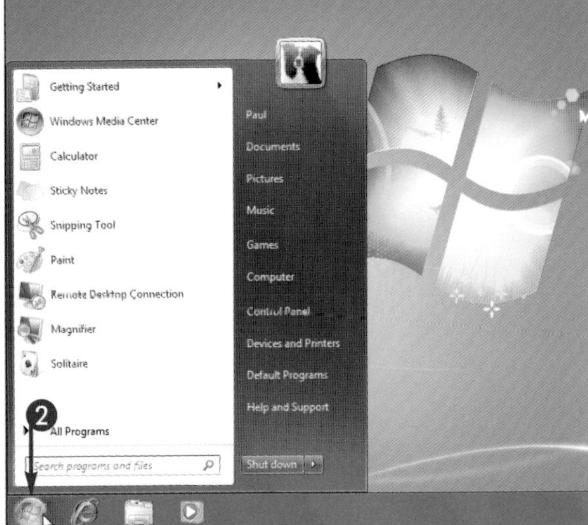


3. Click the power button arrow (▸).
4. Click **Restart**.

   Windows 7 shuts down and your computer restarts.

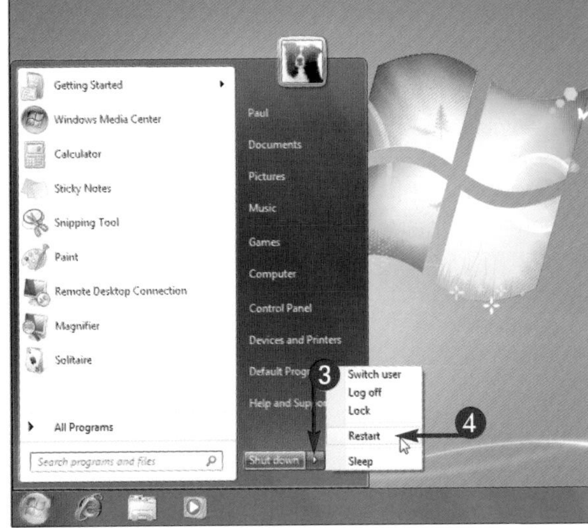

# Shut Down Windows 7

When you complete your work for the day, you should shut down Windows 7. However, do not just shut off your computer's power. Follow the proper steps to avoid damaging files on your system.

**Shutting off the computer's power without properly exiting Windows 7 can cause two problems. First, if you have unsaved changes in some open documents, you may lose those changes. Second, you could damage one or more Windows 7 system files, which could make your system unstable.**

## Shut Down Windows 7

1. Shut down all your running programs.

***Note:*** *Be sure to save your work as you close your programs.*

2. Click **Start**.

   The Start menu appears.

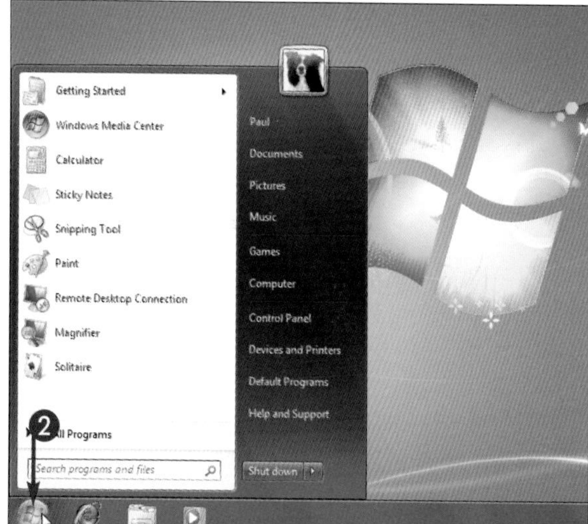

3. Click **Shut Down**.

   Windows 7 shuts down and turns off your computer.

- If you want Windows 7 to automatically reopen all the programs and documents currently on your screen, click the power button arrow (▶) and then click **Sleep**, instead.

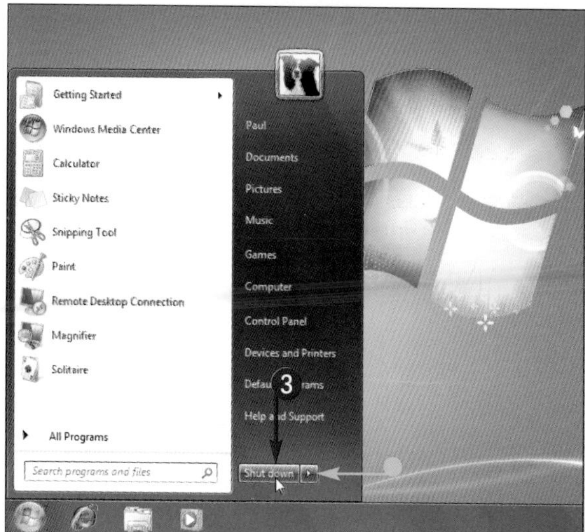

# Launching and Working with Programs

On its own, Windows 7 does not do very much. To do something useful with your computer, you need to work with a program, either one that comes with Windows 7 or one that you install yourself. In this chapter, you learn how to install, launch, and work with programs.

# Install a Program

If Windows 7 does not come with a program that you need, you can obtain the program yourself and then install it on your computer.

**How you start the installation process depends on whether the program comes on a CD or DVD disc, or from the Internet.**

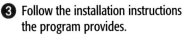

## Install a Program

### INSTALL FROM A CD OR DVD

1. Insert the program's disc into your computer's CD or DVD drive.

- The AutoPlay dialog box appears.

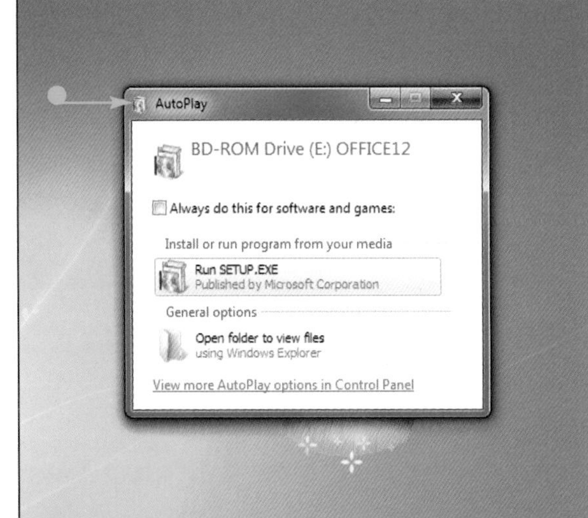


2. Click **Run *file***, where *file* is the name of the installation program (usually SETUP.EXE).
3. Follow the installation instructions the program provides.

***Note:*** *Installation steps vary from program to program.*

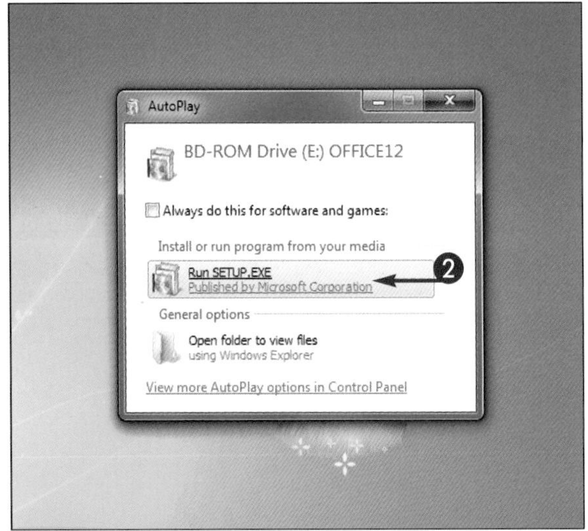

### INSTALL FROM A FILE DOWNLOADED FROM THE INTERNET

1. Click **Start**.
2. Type **downloads**.
3. Click **Downloads**.

***Note:*** *If you saved the downloaded file in a folder other than Downloads, use Windows Explorer to find the downloaded file. To view a file with Windows Explorer, see the "View Your Files" section in Chapter 6.*

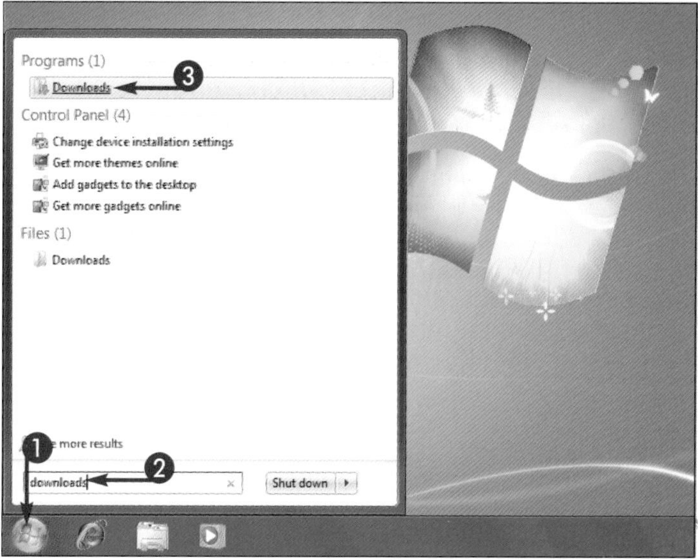


The Downloads folder appears.

4. Double-click the file.

   The software's installation program begins.

***Note:*** *For compressed files, extract the files, and then double-click the setup file. See the "Extract Files from a Compressed Folder" section in Chapter 6.*

5. Follow the installation instructions the program provides.

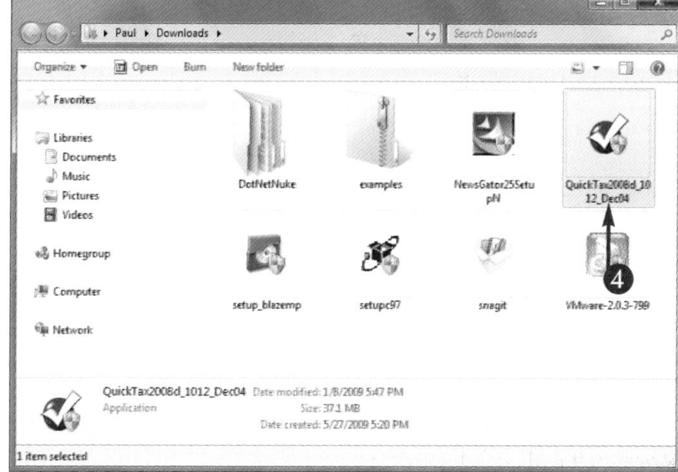

**How do I find my software's product key or serial number?**

The product key or serial number is crucial because many programs do not install until you enter the number. Look for a sticker attached to the back or inside of the CD case. Also look on the registration card, the CD itself, or the back of the box. If you downloaded the program, the number should appear on the download screen and on the e-mail receipt you receive.

# Change or Repair a Program Installation

When you install a program, you can choose the "custom" installation option to install only some of the program's components. If you decide later on to install more components or remove installed components, you can rerun the install program to make these changes.

**If an installed program does not start or is behaving erratically, it may have one or more missing or corrupt files. Many programs come with a repair option that can fix such problems.**

## Change or Repair a Program Installation

1. Click **Start**.
2. Click **Control Panel**.

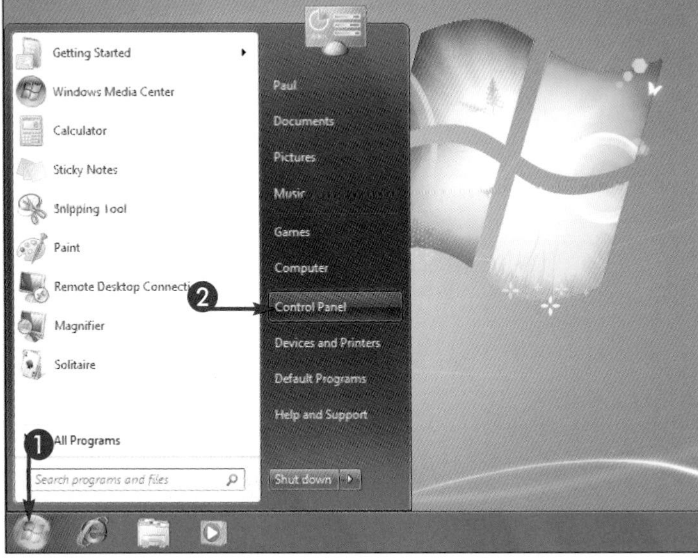


The Control Panel window appears.

3. Click **Uninstall a program**.

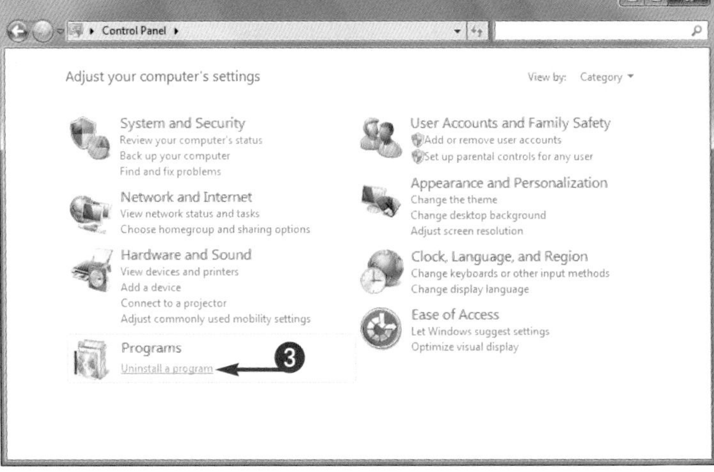

The Programs and Features window appears.

- Windows 7 displays a list of the programs installed on your computer.

4 Click the program you want to work with.

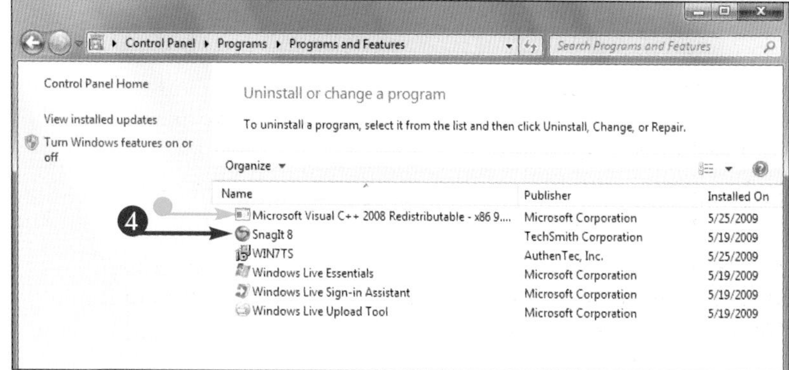

5 Click **Change**.

***Note:*** *For some programs, you click **Uninstall/ Change**, instead.*

- If you want to repair the program, click **Repair** instead.

6 Follow the installation instructions the program provides.

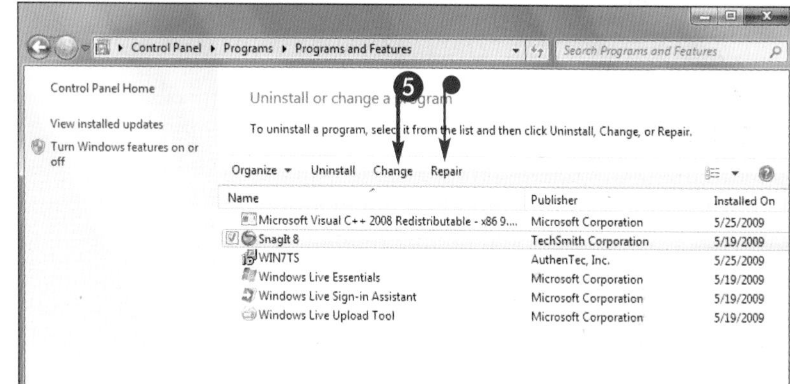


## TIPS

### What is the difference between a "typical" and "custom" installation?

A "typical" installation automatically installs only those program components that people use most often. In a "custom" installation, you select which components are installed, where they are installed, and so on. The custom option is best suited for experienced users, so you are usually better off choosing the typical install.

### Is it dangerous to repair a program?

Generally speaking, no it is not dangerous to repair a program. In almost all cases, what the repair tool does is copy fresh copies of the program's original files to your hard disk. However, in some rare cases repairing a program could cause you to lose data that you created using the program. For this reason, it is a good idea to back up your data before repairing any program. See Chapter 14 to learn how to perform backups in Windows 7.

# Start a Program

To work with any program, you must first tell Windows 7 which program you want to run. Windows 7 then launches the program and displays it on the desktop.

## Start a Program

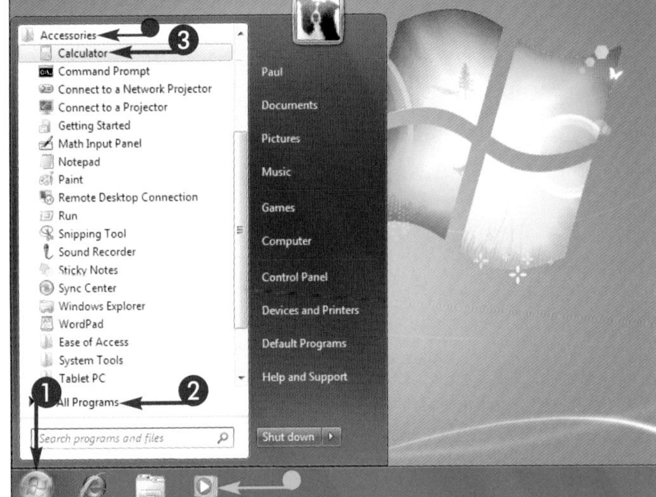


1. Click **Start**.

- If the program you want to use has a taskbar button, you can click the button to launch the program.

2. Click **All Programs**.

***Note:*** *When you click* ***All Programs****, the command name changes to Back.*

3. Click the icon for the program you want to launch.

- If your program icon is in a submenu, click the submenu and then click the program icon.

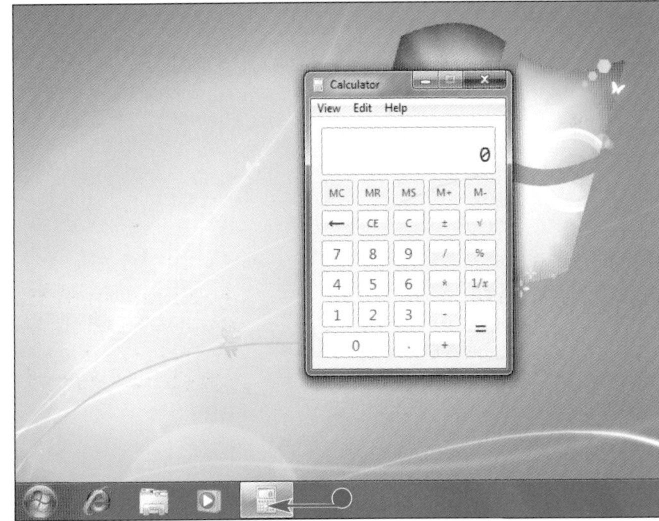


The program appears on the desktop.

- Windows 7 adds a button for the program to the taskbar.

***Note:*** *After you have used a program a few times, it may appear on the main Start menu. If so, you can launch the program by clicking its Start menu icon.*

# Understanding Program Windows

You work with a program by manipulating the various features of its window.

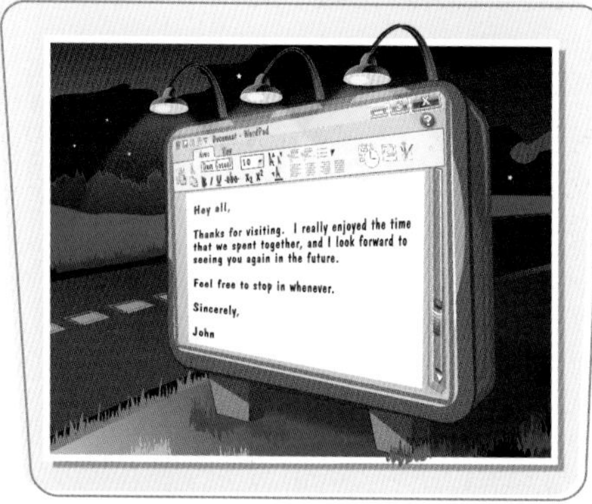

### System Menu Icon

Clicking this icon or pressing Alt + Spacebar displays a menu that enables you to work with program windows via the keyboard.

### Title Bar

The title bar displays the name of the program. In some programs, the title bar also displays the name of the open document. You can also use the title bar to move the window.

### Menu Bar

The menu bar contains the pull-down menus for Windows 7 and most Windows 7 software. In some programs you must press Alt to see the menu bar.

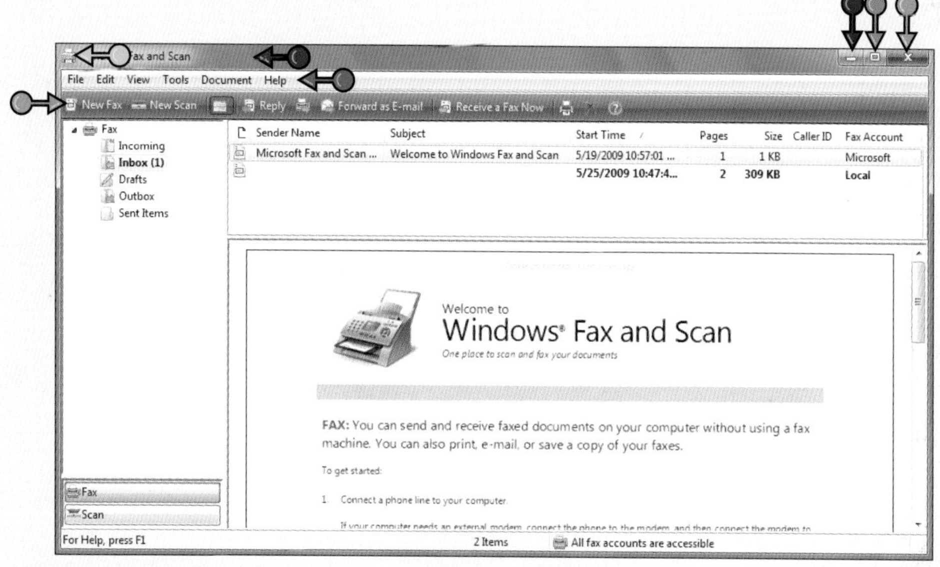

### Toolbar

Buttons that offer easy access to common program commands and features appear in the toolbar. Some buttons are commands and some have lists from which you can make a choice.

### Minimize Button

You click the **Minimize** button (▭) to remove the window from the desktop and display only the window's taskbar button. The window is still open, but not active.

### Maximize Button

To enlarge the window either from the taskbar or so that it takes up the entire desktop, you click the **Maximize** button (▢).

### Close Button

When you click the **Close** button (✕), the program shuts down.

# Using Pull-Down Menus

When you are ready to work with a program, use the pull-down menus to access the program's commands and features.

**The items in a pull-down menu are either commands that execute some action in the program, or features that you turn on and off. If you do not see any menus, you can often display them by pressing Alt.**

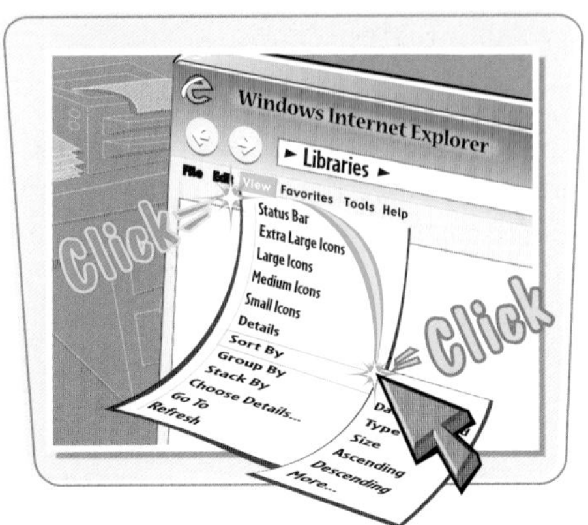


## Using Pull-Down Menus

### RUN COMMANDS

1. Click the name of the menu you want to display.

- The program displays the menu.

  You can also display a menu by pressing and holding Alt and pressing the underlined letter in the menu name.

2. Click the command you want to run.

   The program runs the command.

- If your command is in a submenu, click the submenu and then click the desired command.

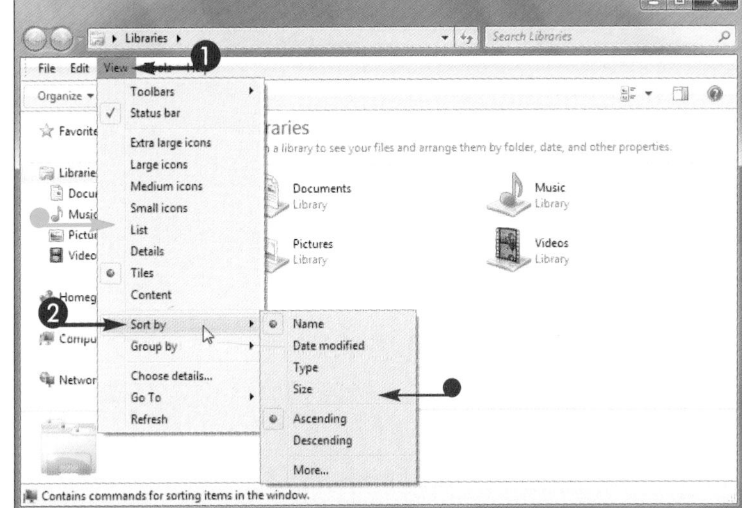


### TURN FEATURES ON AND OFF

1. Click the name of the menu you want to display.

- The program displays the menu.

2. Click the menu item.

   Click a submenu if your command is not on the main menu.

- Toggle features are either turned on (indicated by ✓) or off (no check mark appears).

- Click an option feature to turn it on (indicated by ●) and turn off the previously activated item.

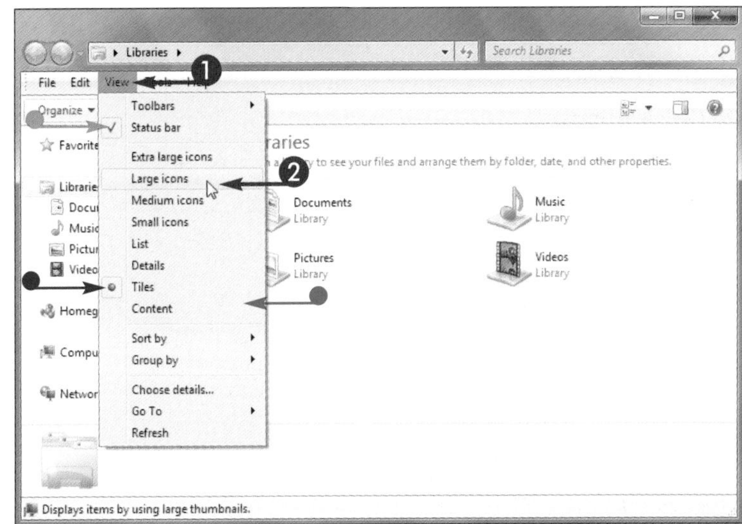

# Using Toolbars

You can use the toolbar to access commands faster than using the menus. Most programs come with one or more toolbars, which are collections of buttons that in most cases give you one-click access to the program's most common features.

## Using Toolbars

### EXECUTE COMMANDS

1. Click the toolbar button that represents the command or list.

*Note: If the toolbar button remains "pressed" after you click it, the button toggles a feature on and off and the feature is now on. To turn the feature off, click the button to "unpress" it.*

- The program executes the command or, as shown here, drops down the list.

2. If a list appears, click the list item that represents the command.

   The program runs the command.

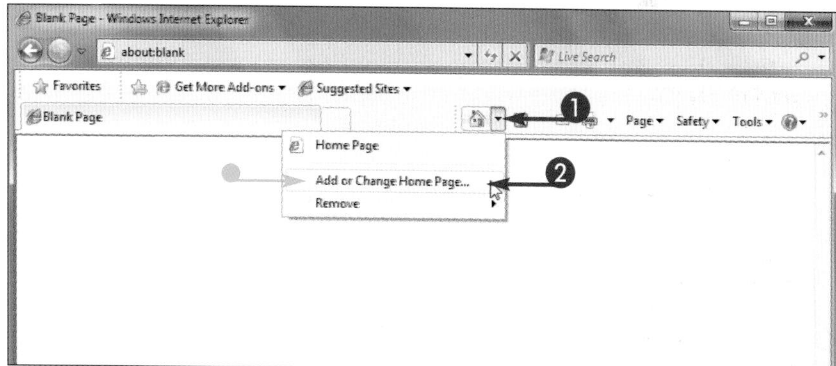


### DISPLAY AND HIDE TOOLBARS

1. Click **View**.
2. Click **Toolbars**.
3. Click a toolbar.

- If the toolbar is currently displayed (indicated by ☑ in the View menu), the program hides the toolbar.

  If the toolbar is currently hidden, the program displays the toolbar (indicated by ☑ in the View menu).

***Note:*** *Some programs have only a single toolbar. In this case, you click* ***View*** *and then click* ***Toolbar*** *to toggle the toolbar on and off.*

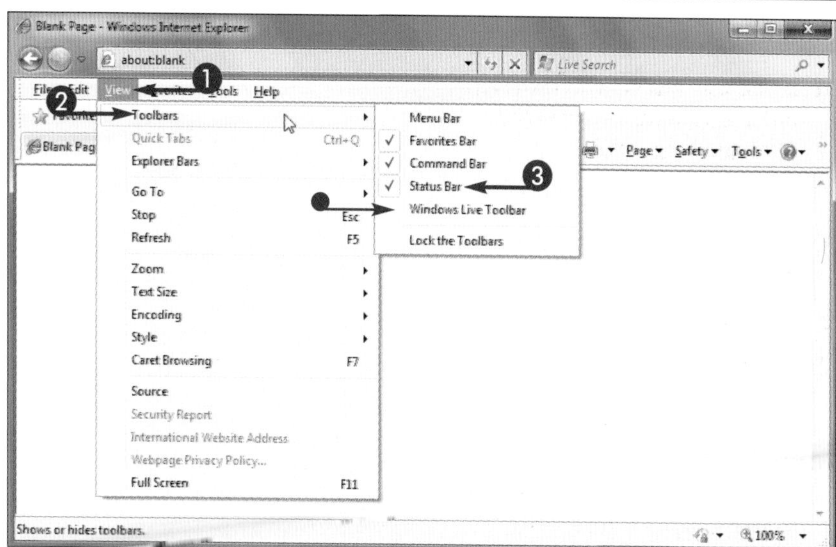

# Understanding Dialog Box Controls

**Dialog boxes appear when a program needs you to provide information. You provide that information my manipulating various types of controls.**

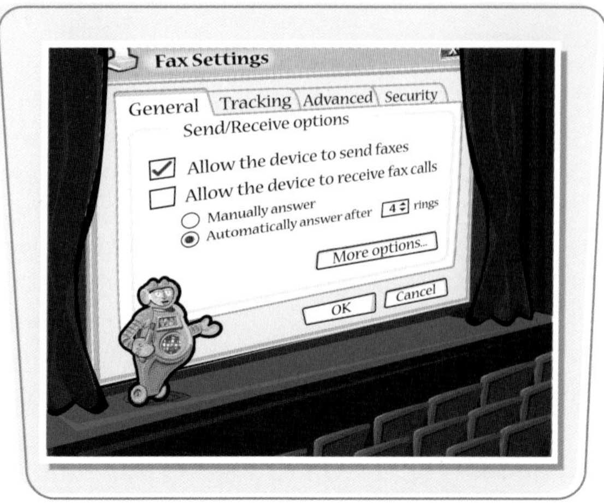


### Option Button

Clicking an option button turns on a program feature. Only one option button in a group can be turned on at a time. When you click an option button, it changes from ○ to ◉.

### Check Box

Clicking a check box toggles a program feature on and off. If you are turning a feature on, the check box changes from ☐ to ☑; if you are turning the feature off, the check box changes from ☑ to ☐.

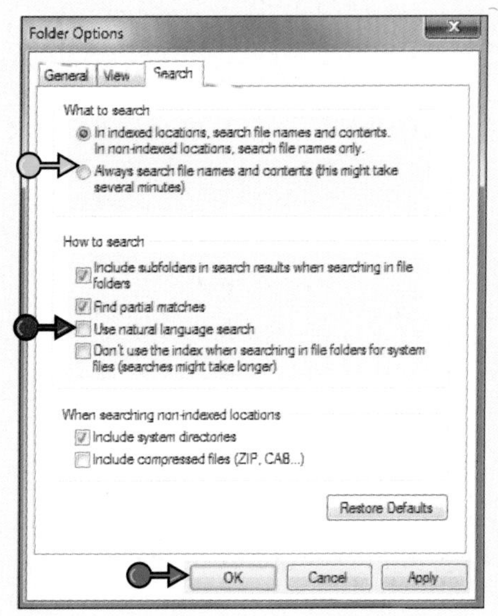


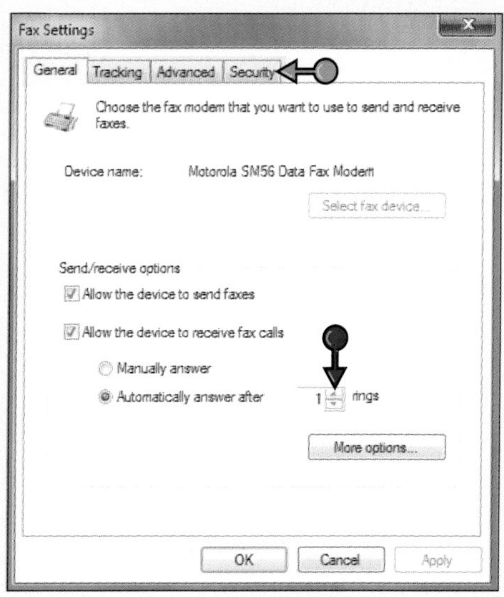


### Command Button

Clicking a command button executes the command written on the button face. For example, you can click **OK** to put settings you choose in a dialog box into effect and close the dialog box; you can click **Apply** to put the settings into effect and leave the dialog box open; or you can click **Cancel** to close the dialog box without changing the settings.

### Tab

The various tabs in a dialog box display different sets of controls. You can choose from these settings in a dialog box to achieve a variety of results.

### Spin Button

The spin button (⬍) enables you to choose a numeric value.

### Text Box

A text box enables you to enter typed text.

### List Box

A list box displays a relatively large number of choices, and you click the item you want. If you do not see the item you want, you can use the scrollbar to bring the item into view; see "Using Scrollbars," later in this chapter.

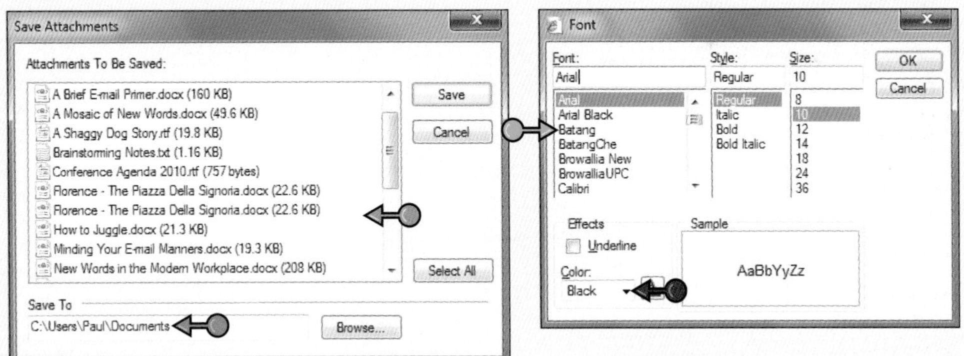


### Combo Box

The combo box combines both a text box and a list box. This means that you can either type the value you want into the text box, or you can use the list to click the value you want.

### Drop-Down List Box

A drop-down list box displays only the selected item from a list. You can open the list to select a different item.

# Using Dialog Boxes

You use dialog boxes to control how a program works. Dialog boxes appear frequently, so you need to know how to use them to get the most out of any program.

**For example, when you print a document, you use the Print dialog box to specify the number of copies you want printed.**

## Using Dialog Boxes

### USING A TEXT BOX

1. Click inside the text box.

- A blinking, vertical bar (called a *cursor* or an *insertion point*) appears inside the text box.

2. Use Backspace or Delete to delete any existing characters.

3. Type your text.

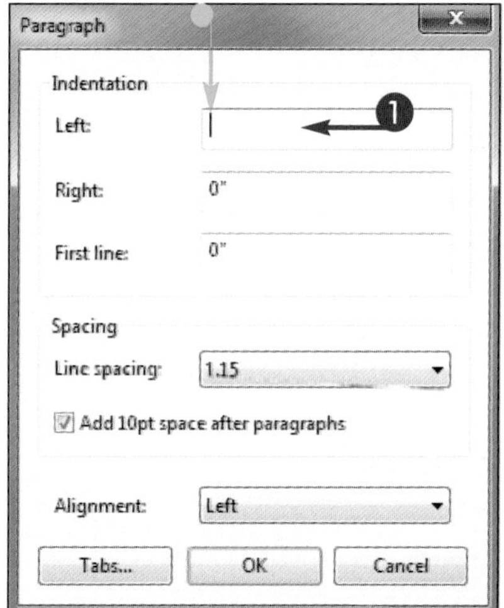


### ENTER A VALUE WITH A SPIN BUTTON

1. Click the top arrow on the spin button (⬍) to increase the value.

2. Click the bottom arrow on the spin button (⬍) to decrease the value.

- You can also type the value in the text box.

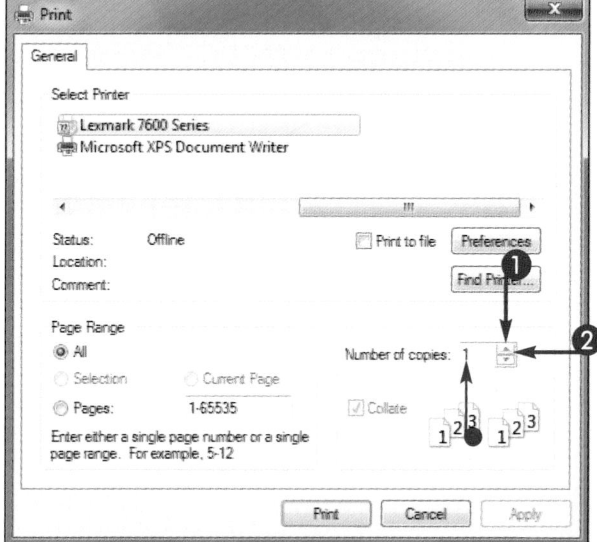

### SELECT A LIST BOX ITEM

1. If necessary, click the down arrow (▾) to scroll down the list and bring the item you want to select into view.

***Note:*** *See the "Using Scrollbars" section to learn how to use scrollbars.*

2. Click the item.

- Click the up arrow (▴) to scroll back up through the list.

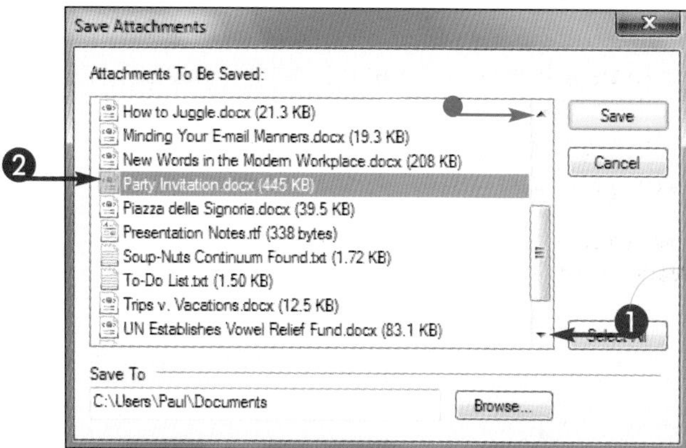


### SELECT AN ITEM USING A COMBO BOX

- Click the item in the list box to select it.
- You can also type the item name in the text box.

### SELECT AN ITEM FROM A DROP-DOWN LIST BOX

1. Click the drop-down arrow (▾).

- The list appears.

2. Click the item in the list that you want to select.

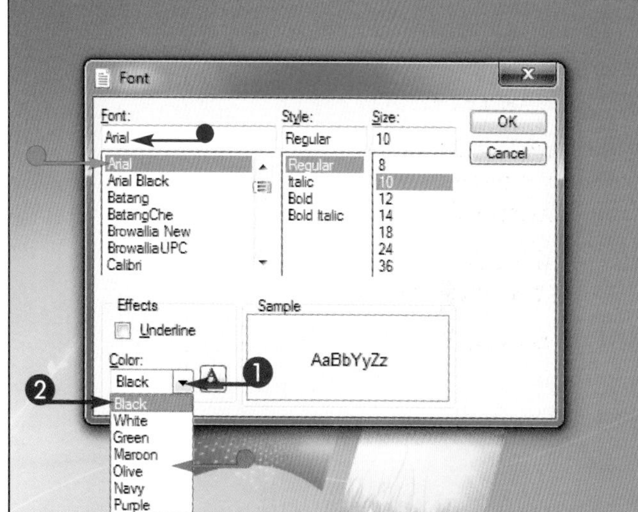

**Are there keyboard shortcuts I can use to make dialog boxes easier to work with?**

| Key | Action |
|---|---|
| Enter | Selects the default command button (which is indicated with a highlight around it). |
| Esc | Cancels the dialog box (which is the same as clicking **Cancel**). |
| Alt + *letter* | Selects the control that has the *letter* underlined. |
| Tab | Moves forward through the dialog box controls. |
| Shift + Tab | Moves backward through the dialog box controls. |
| ↑ and ↓ | Moves up and down within the current option button group. |
| Alt + ↓ | Drops down the selected combo box or drop-down list box. |

# Work with Program Windows

You need to know how to work with program windows so that you can keep your desktop neat and your programs easier to find.

**For example, you can minimize a window to clear it from the desktop. Similarly, you can move or resize windows so that they do not overlap each other.**

## Work with Program Windows

### MINIMIZE A WINDOW

1. Click the **Minimize** button (▭).

- The window disappears from the screen, but its taskbar button remains visible.

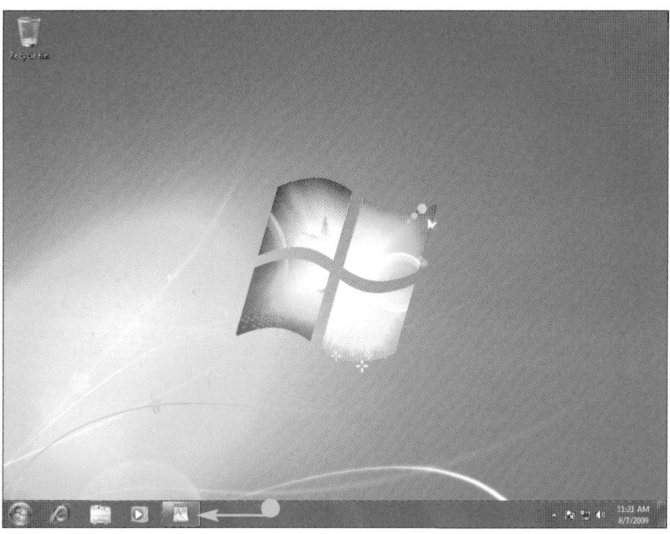

## MAXIMIZE A WINDOW

1 Click the **Maximize** button (▣).

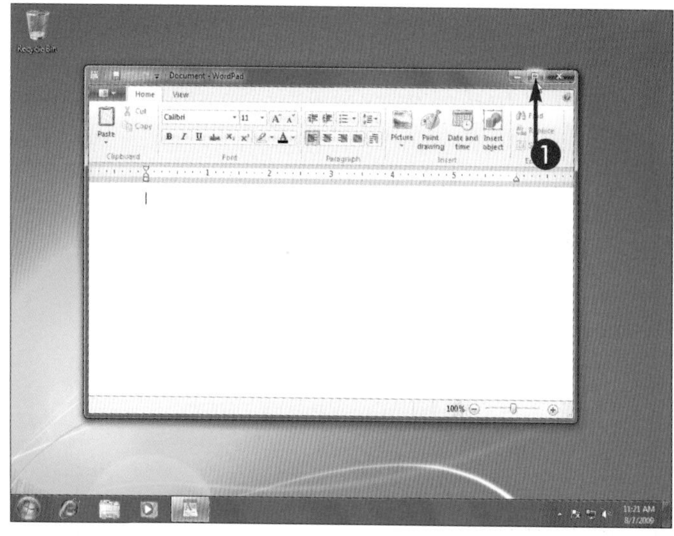

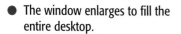

- The window enlarges to fill the entire desktop.

*Note: You can also maximize a window by double-clicking its title bar.*

*Note: Another way to maximize a window is to drag its title bar to the top of the screen. When you release the mouse button, Windows 7 maximizes the window.*

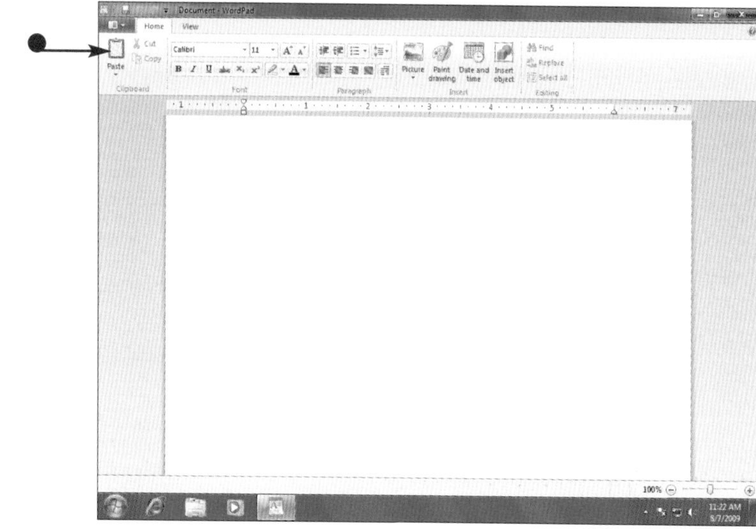

TIPS

**Is there a faster way to minimize all my open windows?**

To see your desktop without minimizing, position the mouse over the **Show desktop** bar on the right edge of the taskbar. To minimize all your open windows, click the **Show desktop** bar, or right-click the taskbar and then click **Show the desktop**.

**Is it possible to maximize a minimized window?**

Yes. To do this, press and hold the Shift key and then right-click the window's taskbar button. In the menu that appears, click **Maximize**.

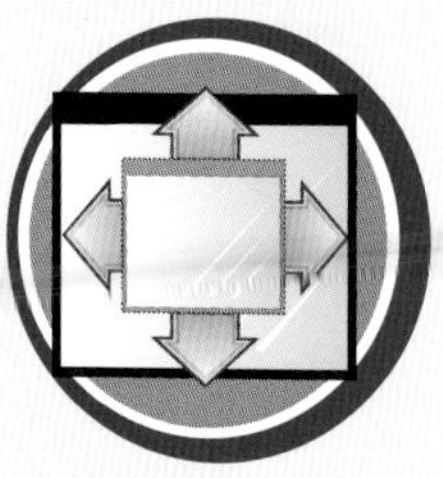

continued

# Work with Program Windows *(continued)*

Are you ready for more window techniques? Windows 7 uses many windows, so the more you know, the faster and more efficiently you can work.

**For example, you should know how to *restore* a window. This means that you return the window to its original size and location after you have either minimized it or maximized it.**

## Work with Program Windows *(continued)*

### RESTORE A WINDOW

1. If the window is maximized, click the **Restore** button (□).

   If the window is minimized, click its taskbar button instead.

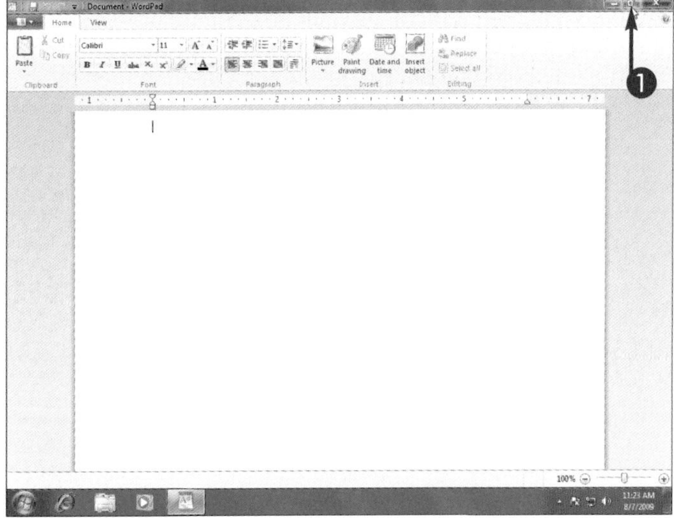


- The window returns to its previous size and location.

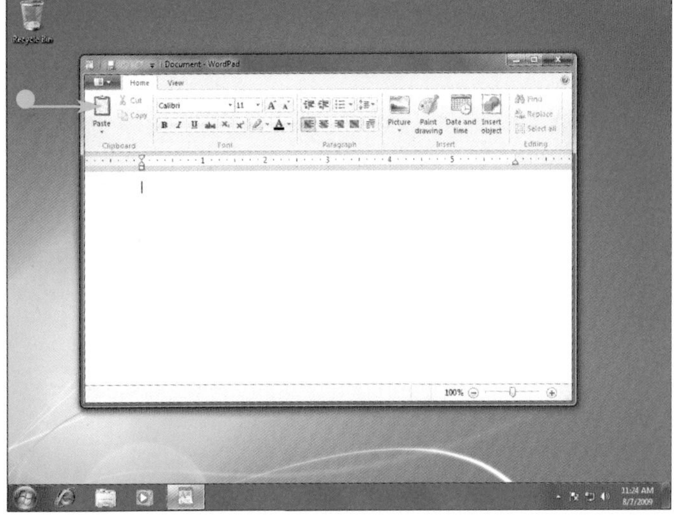

## CLOSE A WINDOW

1. Click the **Close** button (☒).

   The window disappears from the screen.

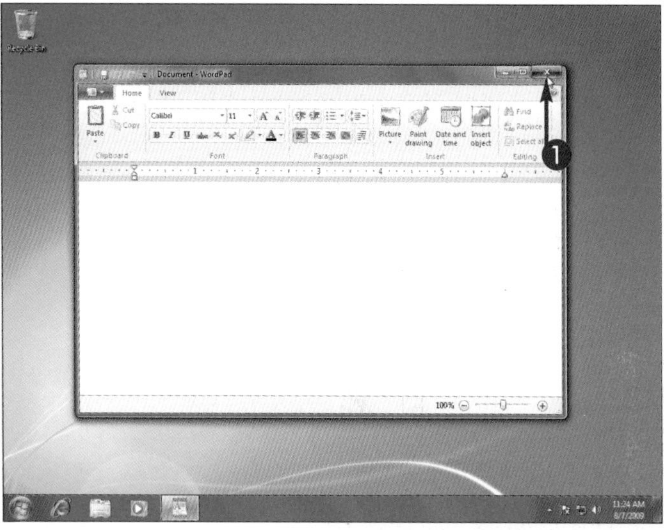

- If the window has a taskbar button, the button disappears from the taskbar.

***Note:*** *If the window contains a document, the program may ask if you want to save any changes you made in the document before closing.*

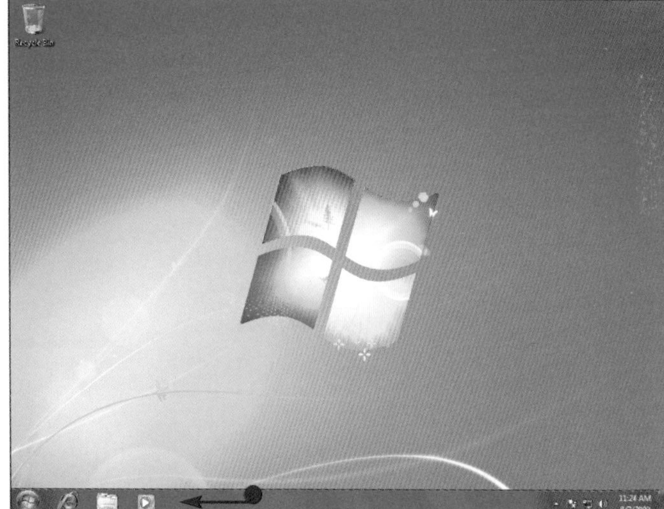

TIP

### Can I work with program windows via the keyboard?

Yes, you do this by using the *system menu* that comes with each window. Press Alt + Spacebar or click the system menu icon in the upper left corner to display the menu, press ↑ and ↓ on the keyboard to highlight the command you want, and then press Enter. If you choose **Move** or **Size** from the system menu, use the keyboard ↑, ↓, ←, and → to move or size the window, and then press Enter.

continued

# Work with Program Windows *(continued)*

If your windows overlap each other, making it hard to read what is in other windows, you can move the windows around or resize them.

## Work with Program Windows *(continued)*

### CHANGE THE WINDOW SIZE

1. Position the mouse over the window border that you want to move.

- The changes to a two-headed arrow (⇕).

***Note:*** *If the pointer does not change, it means the window cannot be resized.*

2. Click and drag the ⇕ to make the window larger or smaller.

   Windows 7 moves the border along with the ⇕.

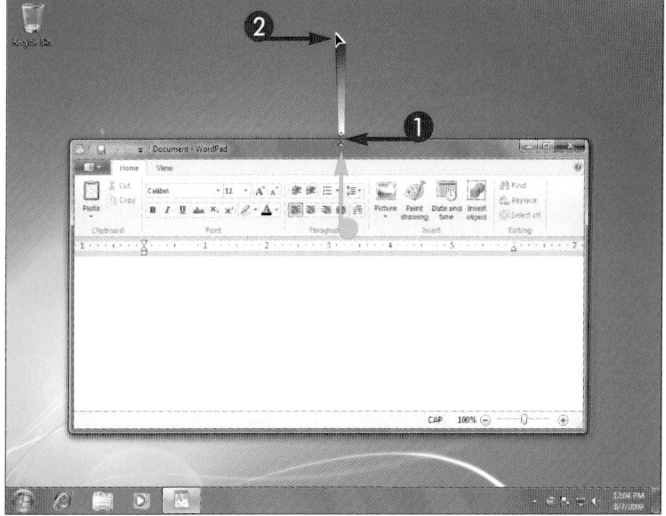

3. Release the mouse button.

- Windows 7 resizes the window.

***Note:*** *To resize two borders at once, click and drag any corner of the window.*

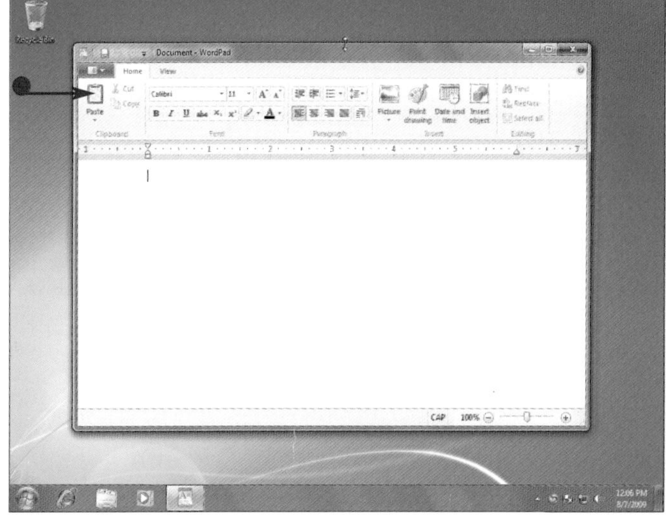

### MOVE A WINDOW

1. Position the mouse over an empty section of the window's title bar.
2. Click and drag the mouse in the direction you want the window to move.

   Windows 7 moves the window along with the mouse.

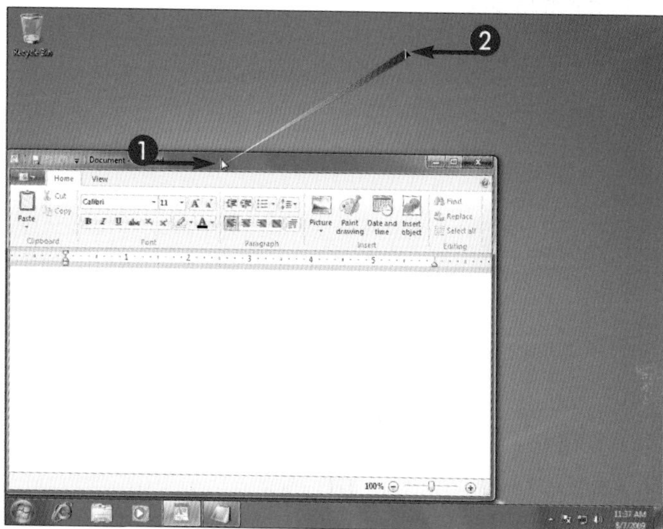

3. Release the mouse button.

- Windows 7 moves the window.

### TIPS

**When I have several windows open, is there an easier way to size them so that none of the windows overlap?**

Use Windows 7's Side by Side feature: Right-click an empty section of the taskbar and then click **Show windows side by side**. Windows 7 divides the desktop to give each window an equal amount of space.

**When I have several windows open, is there an easier way to move them so that the windows are arranged neatly?**

Use Windows 7's Stack feature: Right-click an empty section of the taskbar and then click **Show windows stacked**. Windows 7 arranges the windows in a tidy diagonal pattern from the top left corner of the desktop.

# Using Scrollbars

If the entire content of a document does not fit inside a window, you can see the rest of the document by using the window's scrollbars to move vertically or horizontally.

**Scrollbars also appear in many list boxes, so knowing how to work with scrollbars also helps you use dialog boxes.**

## Using Scrollbars

### SCROLL UP OR DOWN IN A WINDOW

1. Click and drag the vertical scroll box down or up to scroll through a window.

   You can also click the up arrow (▲) or down arrow (▼).

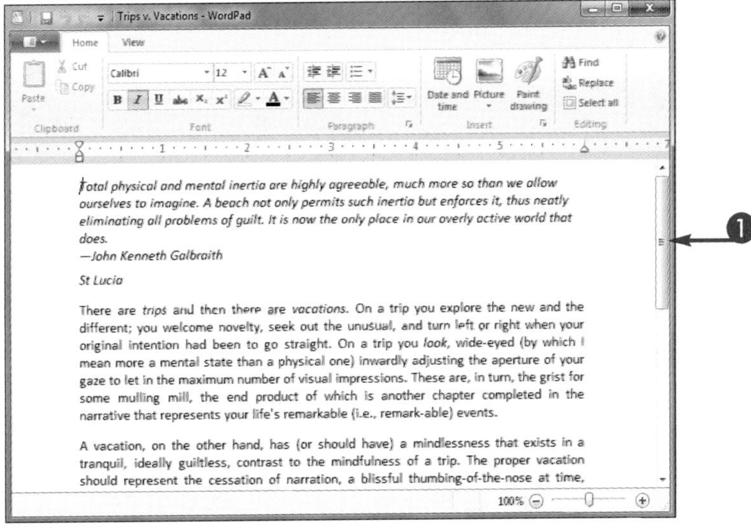


- The text scrolls down or up.

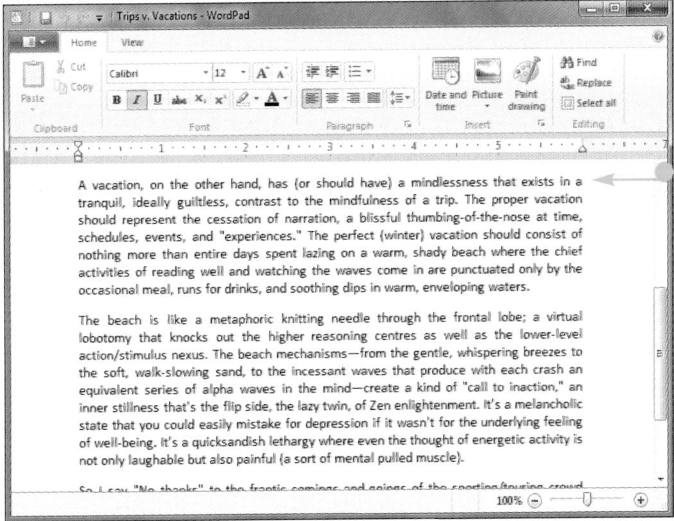

## SCROLL RIGHT OR LEFT IN A WINDOW

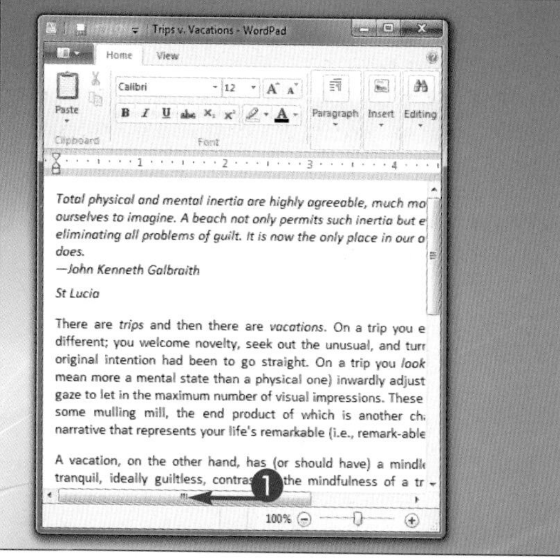


1. Click and drag the horizontal scroll box.

   You can also click the right arrow (▸) or the left arrow (◂).

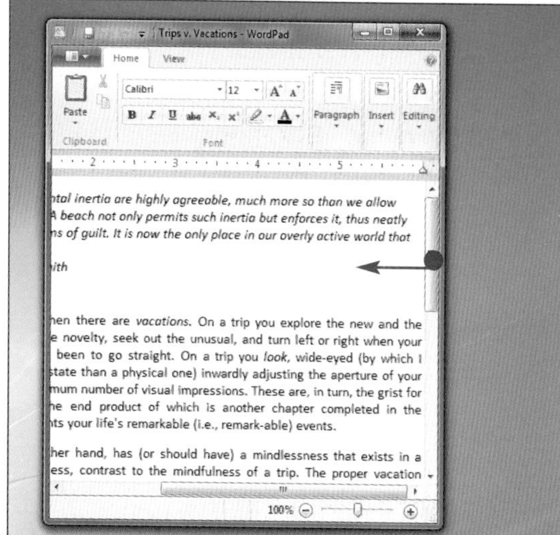


- The text scrolls left or right.

**TIP**

**What is the wheel on my mouse used for?**

Not everyone's mouse has a wheel, but if yours does, you can use the wheel for scrolling up or down in a document. It works the same way as clicking the up arrow (▴) or the down arrow (▾) does. Move the wheel backward, toward your arm, and the document scrolls down; move the wheel forward, toward your computer, and the document scrolls up.

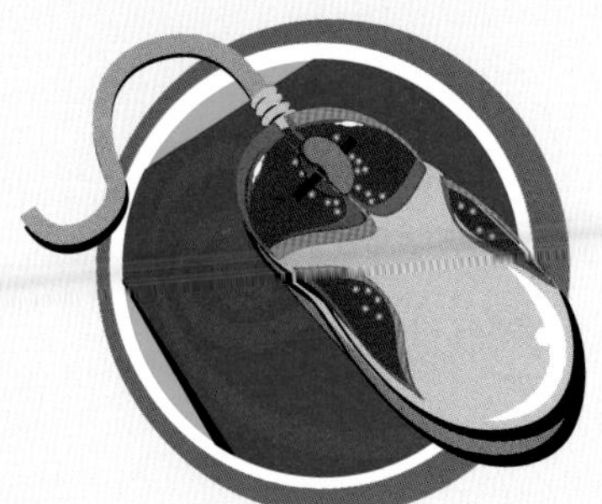

# Switch Between Programs

With Windows 7, if you are *multitasking* — running two or more programs at once — you need to know how to switch from one to another.

**You can switch from one program to another using either the taskbar or the keyboard.**

## Switch Between Programs

### SWITCH PROGRAMS USING THE TASKBAR

1. Click the taskbar button of the program to which you want to switch.

***Note:*** *A program does not have to be minimized to the taskbar for you to use the program's taskbar button.*

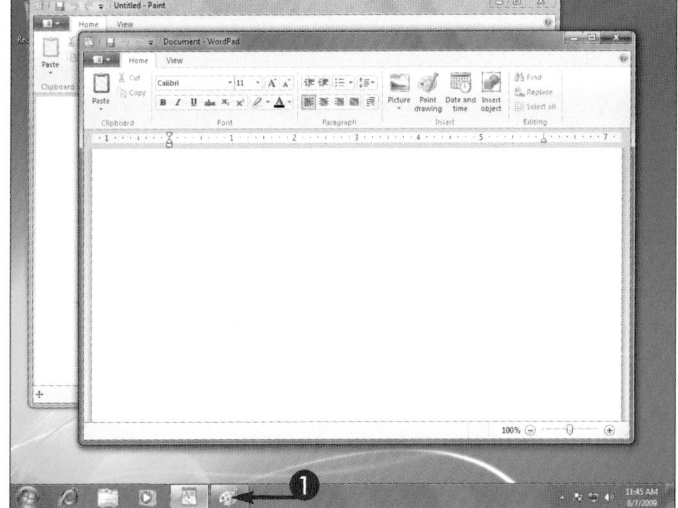

- Windows 7 brings the program's window to the foreground.

***Note:*** *You can also switch to another window by clicking the window, even if it is the background.*

## SWITCH PROGRAMS USING THE KEYBOARD

1. Press and hold Alt and press Tab.
   - Windows 7 displays thumbnail versions of the open windows and the desktop.
2. Press Tab until the window in which you want to work is selected.
3. Release Alt.

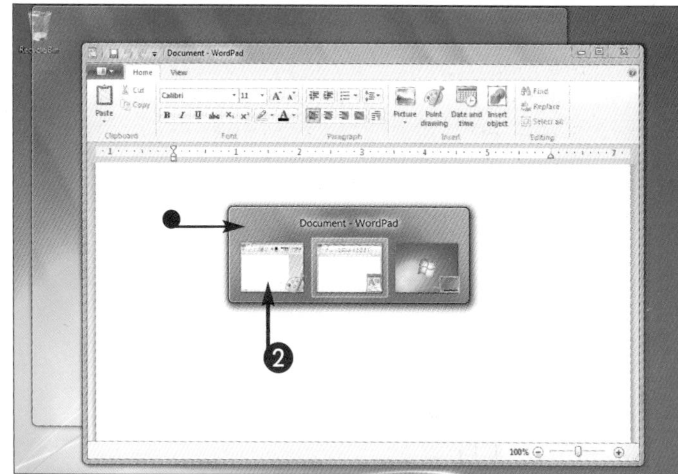


- Windows 7 brings the program's window to the foreground.

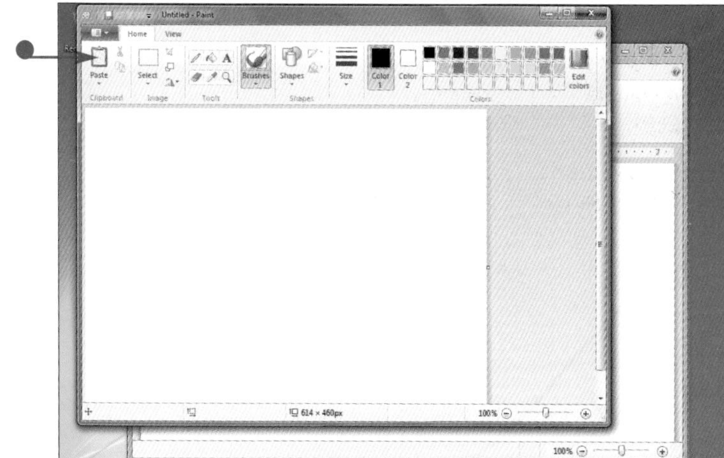

### Can I see what is in a window before switching to it?

Yes. In fact, Windows 7 gives you three different ways to do this:

- Position the mouse over a program's taskbar button. Windows 7 displays a thumbnail version of the program window.
- Press and hold Alt and repeatedly press Esc. Each time you press Esc, Windows 7 brings a program window to the foreground. When you see the window you want, release Alt.
- On some systems, you can press and hold the Windows key and repeatedly press Tab. Windows 7 displays the open windows as a 3-D stack and each time you press Tab, Windows 7 brings a program window to the foreground. When you see the window you want, release the Windows key.

# Take Advantage of Program Jump Lists

You can use the new jump list feature in Windows 7 to open files or run program tasks. A *jump list* is a list associated with each program that supports this feature. Most jump lists consist of items you most recently used in the program, but some jump lists also include common program tasks.

**The recent items you see on a program's jump list are called *destinations*, and they can be files, folders, Web sites, or whatever type of data the program supports.**

## Take Advantage of Program Jump Lists

### OPEN A DESTINATION

1. Right-click the program's taskbar icon.
2. Click the destination.

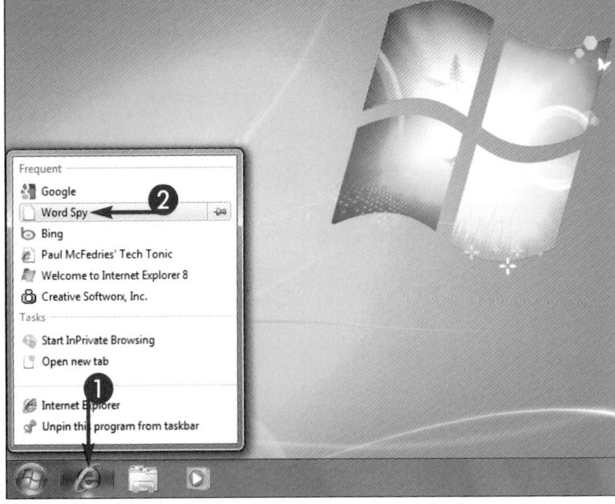


Windows 7 launches the program if it is not already running and opens the destination.

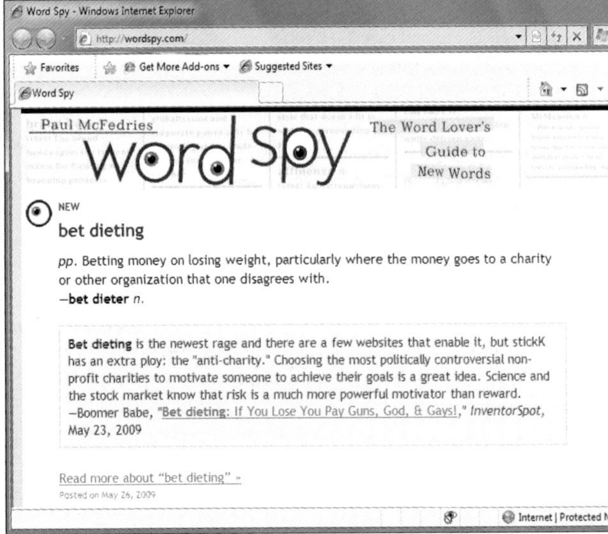

RUN A TASK

1. Right-click the program's taskbar icon.
2. Click the task.

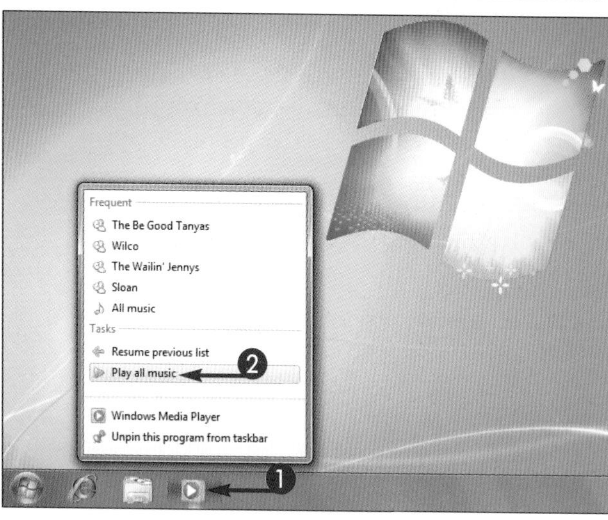


Windows 7 launches the program if it is not already running and runs the task.

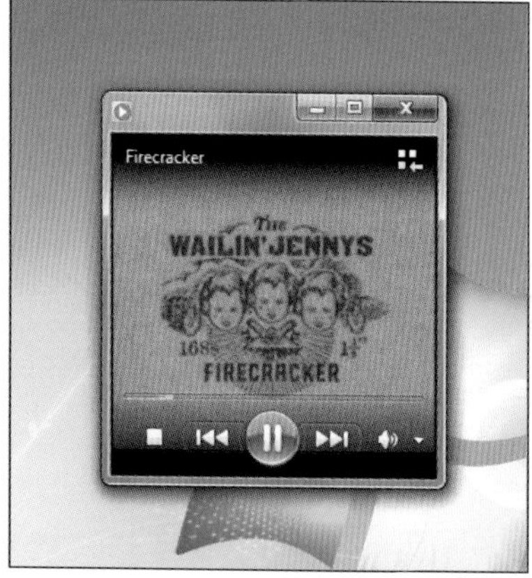


TIPS

**Is there a way to ensure that a particular destination always appears on a program's jump list?**

Yes, you can *pin* the destination to the jump list, which means an icon for the destination always appears in the Pinned section of the jump list. If the destination is already on the jump list, right-click the destination and then click **Pin to this list**. Otherwise, locate the file in Windows Explorer, click and drag the file and then drop it on the program's taskbar icon.

**Can I remove a destination from a jump list?**

Yes. Right-click the program's taskbar icon to display the jump list. Right-click the destination you want to remove and then click **Remove from this list**. If you pinned a destination as described in the previous tip, you can remove the destination from the pinned area. Right-click the pinned destination and then click **Unpin from this list**.

# Uninstall a Program

When you plan to no longer use a program, you should uninstall it from your computer.

**Removing unused programs frees up disk space and makes your All Programs menu easier to navigate.**

## Uninstall a Program

1. Click **Start**.
2. Click **Control Panel**.

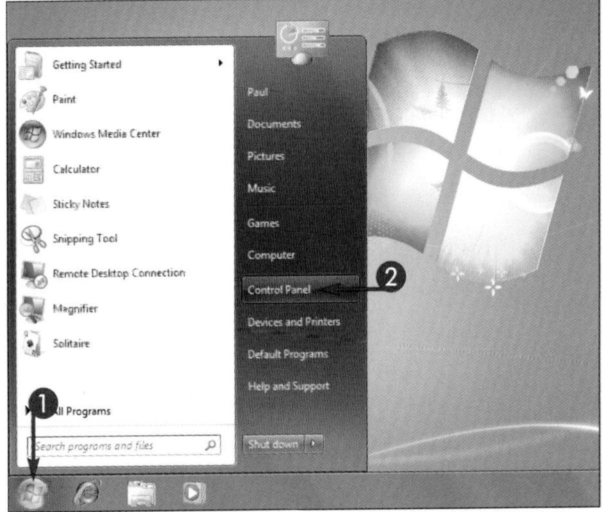

The Control Panel window appears.

3. Click **Uninstall a program**.

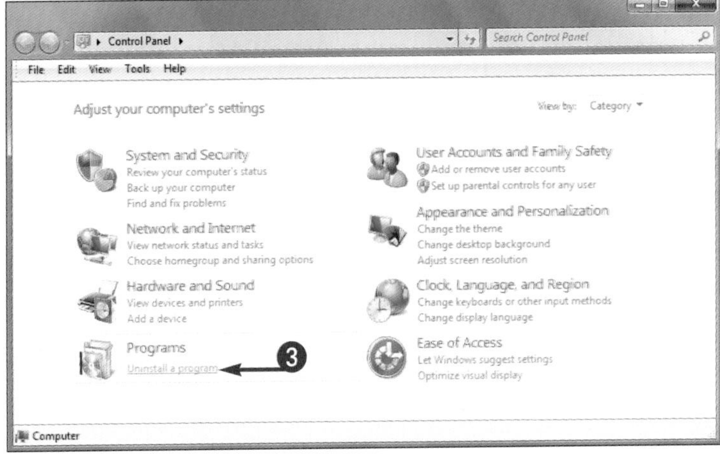

The Installed Programs window appears.

4. Click the program you want to uninstall.

5. Click **Uninstall** (or **Uninstall/ Change**).

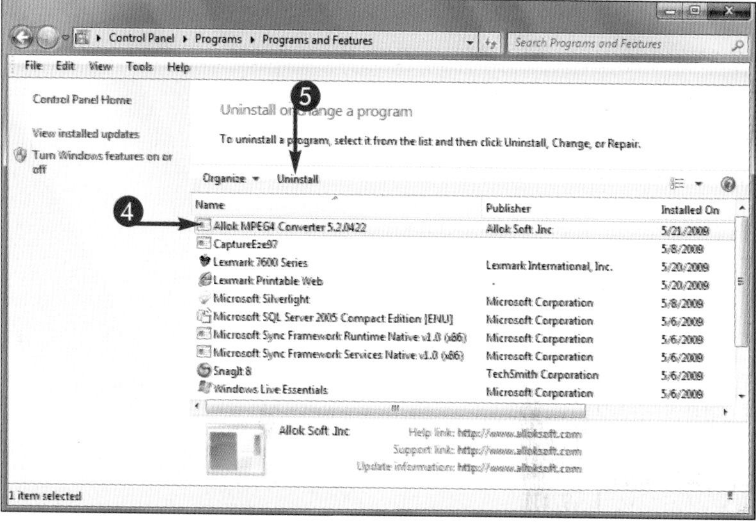

- In most cases, the program asks you to confirm that you want to uninstall it.

6. Click **Yes**.

The program's uninstall procedure begins.

7. Follow the instructions on the screen, which vary from program to program.

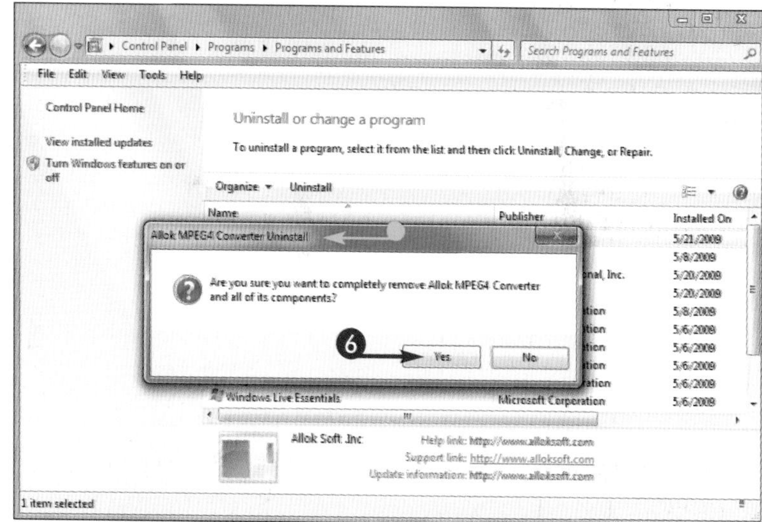

TIPS

**Is there a quicker way to uninstall a program?**

Yes. Many programs come with their own uninstall command. Click **Start**, click **All Programs**, and then click the program name. If you see a command that includes the word ***Uninstall***, click that command to begin the uninstall procedure.

**What is the difference between an Automatic and a Custom uninstall?**

Some programs give you a choice of uninstall procedures. The Automatic uninstall requires no input from you. It is the easiest, safest choice and therefore the one you should choose. The Custom uninstall gives you more control, but is more complex and suitable only for experienced users.

CHAPTER

# 3

# Creating and Editing Documents

To get productive with Windows 7, you need to know how to work with documents. In this chapter, you learn what documents are, and you learn how to create, save, open, edit, and print documents.

# Understanding Documents

**Documents are files that you create or edit yourself. The four examples shown here are the basic document types that you can create using the programs that come with Windows 7.**

### Text Document

A text document is one that includes only the characters that you see on your keyboard, plus a few others (see the "Insert Special Symbols" section in this chapter). A text document contains no special formatting, such as colored text or bold formatting, although you can change the font. In Windows 7 you normally use the Notepad program to create text documents (although you can also use WordPad).

### Word Processing Document

A word processing document contains text and other symbols, but you can format those characters to improve the look of the document. For example, you can change the size, color, and typeface, and you can make words bold or italic. In Windows 7, you use the WordPad program to create word processing — or Rich Text Format — documents.

### Drawing

A drawing in this context is a digital image you create using special "tools" that create lines, boxes, polygons, special effects, and free-form shapes. In Windows 7, you use the Paint program to create drawings.

### E-mail Message

An e-mail message is a document that you send to another person via the Internet. Most e-mail messages use plain text, but some programs support formatted text, images, and other effects. In Windows 7, you must download and install the Windows Live Mail program to create and send e-mail messages (see Chapter 11).

# Create a Document



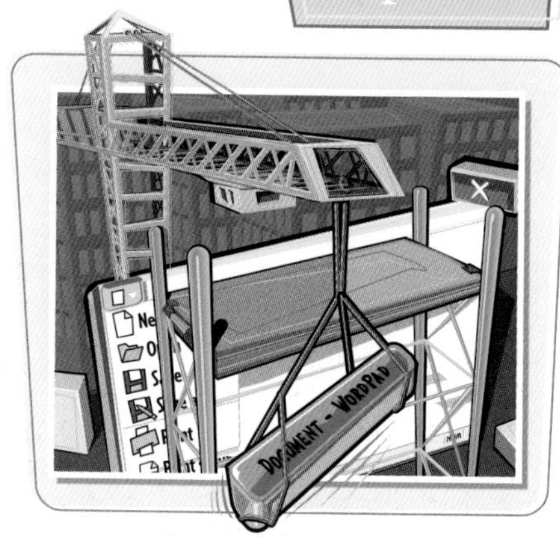

When you are ready to create something using Windows 7, in most cases you begin by creating a new document to hold your work.

**Many Windows 7 programs (such as WordPad and Paint) create a new document for you automatically when you begin the program.**

## Create a Document

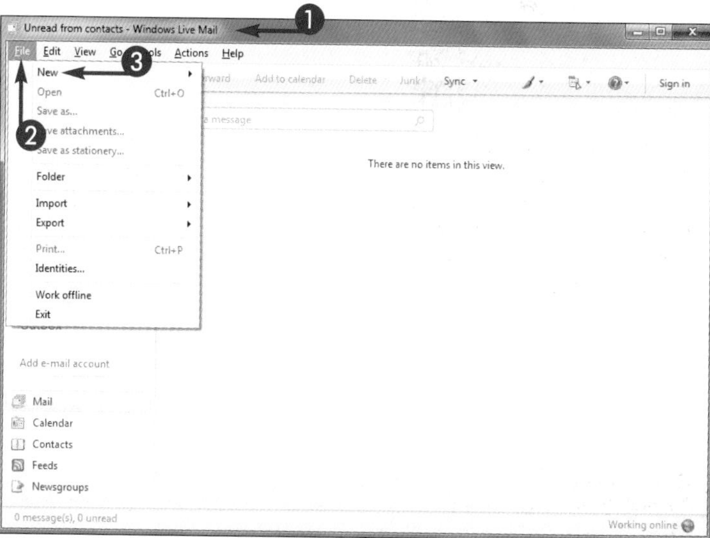

1. Start the program you want to work with.
2. Click **File**.
3. Click **New**.

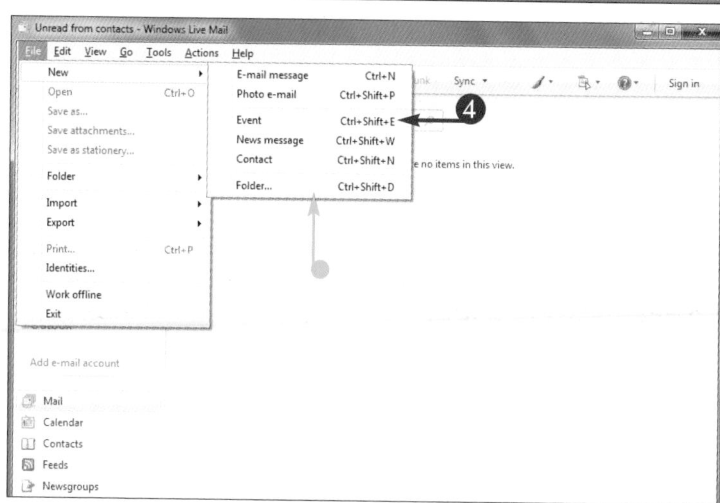

- If the program supports more than one type of file, the program asks which type you want to create.

***Note:*** *Some programs display a dialog box with a list of document types.*

4. Click the document type you want.

   The program creates the new document.

***Note:*** *In some programs you can also create a document by clicking the* ***New Document*** *toolbar button ( ).*

***Note:*** *In most programs, you can also press* Ctrl + N *to create a new document.*

# Save a Document

After you create a document and make any changes to it, you can save the document to preserve your work.

**When you work on a document, Windows 7 stores the changes in your computer's memory, which is erased each time you shut down your computer. Saving the document preserves your changes on your computer's hard drive.**

## Save a Document

1. Click **File** (▤).
2. Click **Save**.

***Note:*** *In most programs, you can also press* Ctrl + S *or click the* ***Save*** *button (💾).*

***Note:*** *If you saved the document previously, your changes are now preserved. You do not need to follow the rest of the steps in this section.*

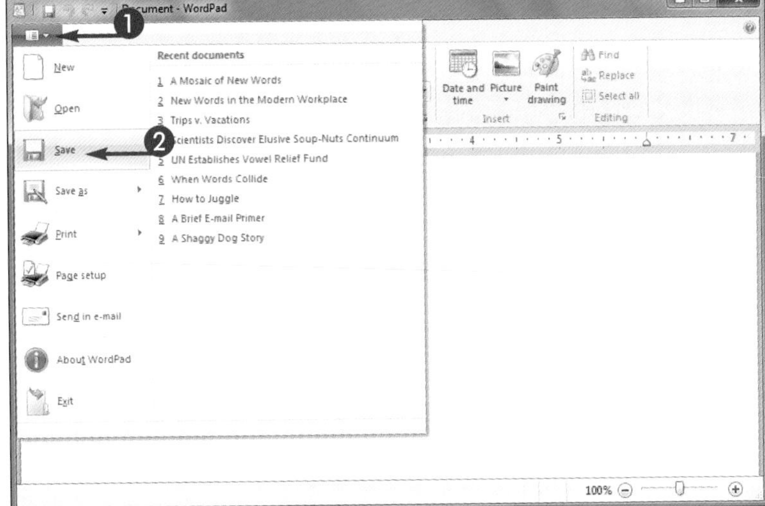


If this is a new document that you have never saved before, the Save As dialog box appears.

3. Click here to see a list of your folders.
4. Click **Documents**.

***Note:*** *In most programs, the Documents folder is selected automatically when you save a document.*

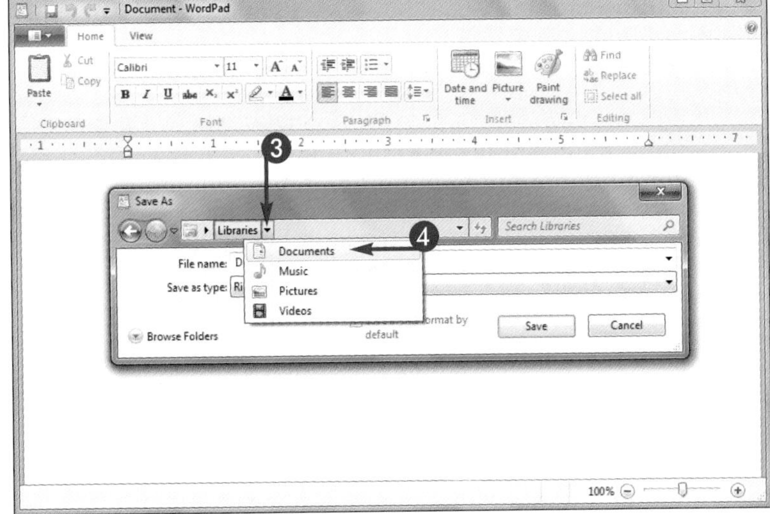

- Windows 7 opens the Documents folder.

5. Click in the File Name text box and type the name you want to use for the document.

***Note:*** *The name you type can be up to 255 characters long, but it cannot include the following characters: < > , ? : " \ *.*

6. Click **Save**.

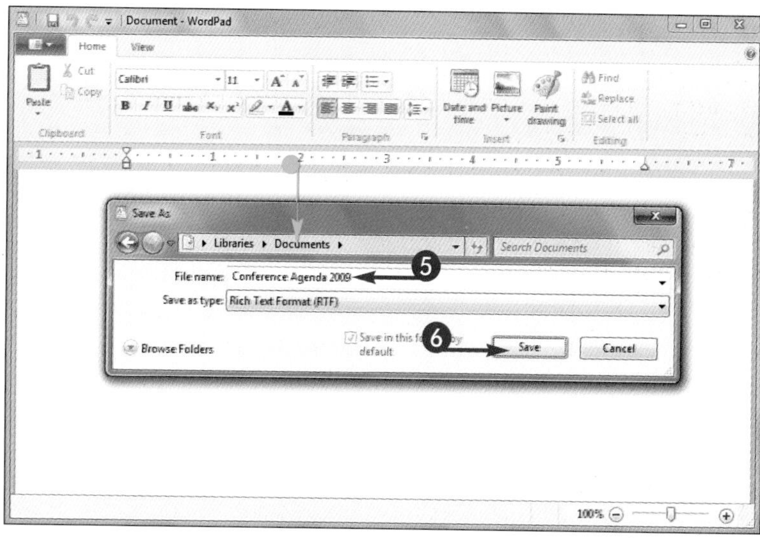


- The file name you typed appears in the program's title bar.

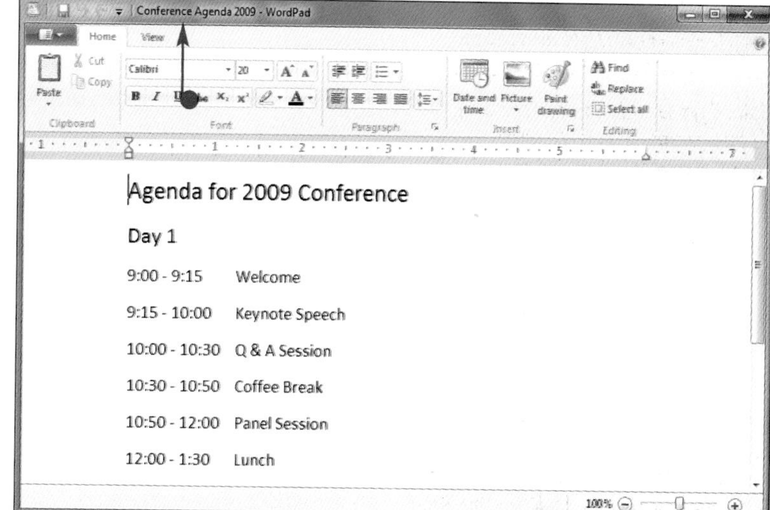

### Can I create different types of documents in a program?

Yes, in most programs. With WordPad, for example, you can create both word processing documents and text documents. However, a program such as Notepad supports only text documents. If the program supports multiple document types, the Save As dialog box includes a drop-down list named Save As Type (or something similar). Use that list to choose the document type you want.

# Open a Document

To work with a document that you have saved in the past, you need to open the document in the program that you used to create it.

## Open a Document

❶ Start the program you want to work with.

❷ Click **File** ( ).

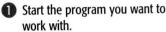

***Note:** If you see the document you want in a list of the most recently used documents on the File menu, click the name to open it. You can skip the rest of the steps in this section.*

❸ Click **Open**.

***Note:** In most programs, you can also press Ctrl + O or click the **Open** button ( ).*

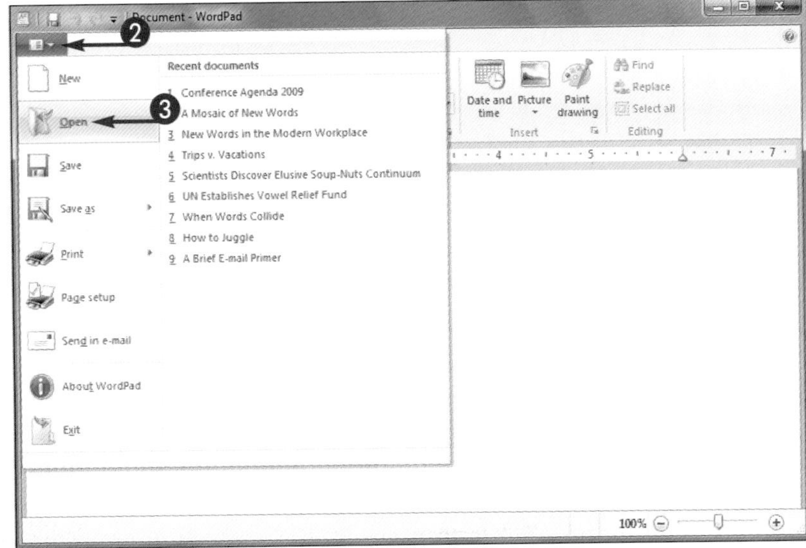


The Open dialog box appears.

❹ Double-click **Documents**.

***Note:** In most programs, the Documents folder is selected automatically when you open a document.*

- If you want to open the document from some other folder, click here, click your user name, and then double-click the folder.

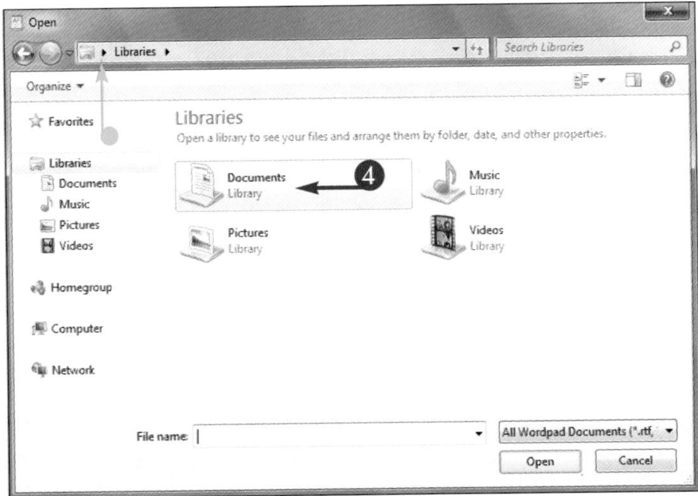

- Windows 7 opens the Documents folder.

5 Click the document name.

6 Click **Open**.

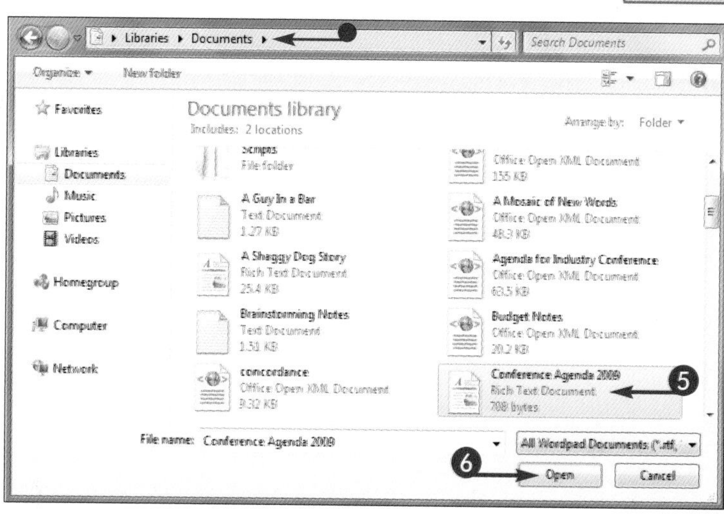


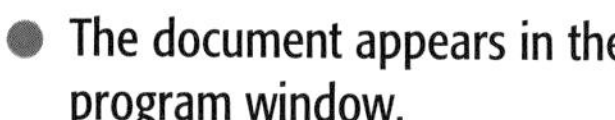

- The document appears in the program window.

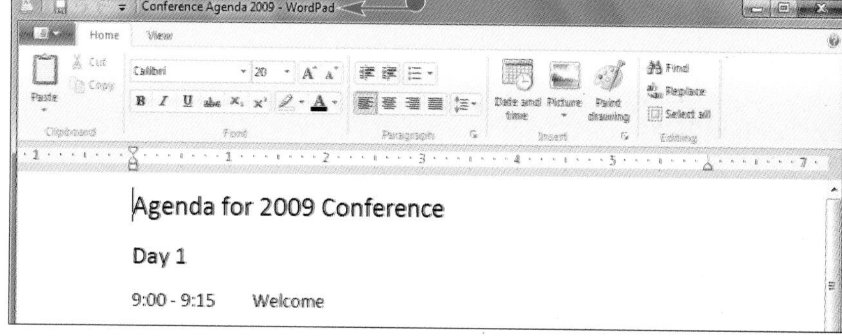


TIP

## Is there a more direct way to open a document?

Yes there is. You do not always need to open the program first. Instead, open the folder that contains the document and then double-click the document. Windows 7 automatically launches the program and opens the document.

1 Click **Start**.

2 Click **Documents**.

The Documents folder appears.

3 Double-click the document.

Windows 7 starts the program in which you created the document and then opens the document.

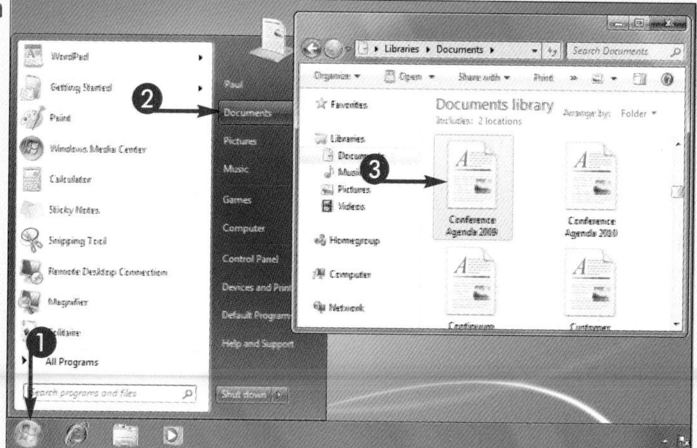

# Make a Copy of a Document

When you need to create a document that is nearly identical to an existing document instead of creating the new document from scratch, you can save time by making a copy of the existing document and then modifying the copy as needed.

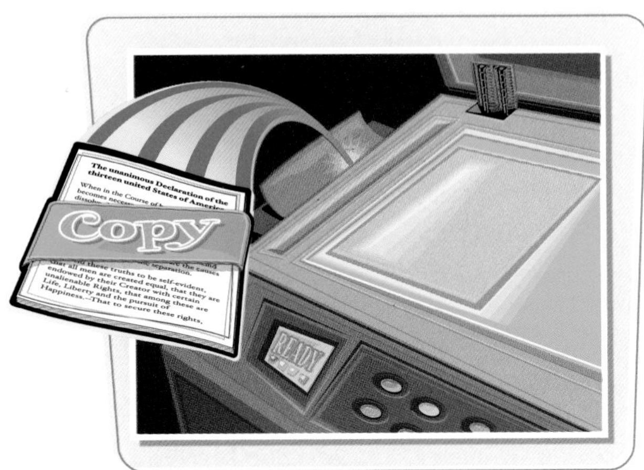


## Make a Copy of a Document

1. Start the program you want to work with and open the original document.
2. Click **File** (▤).
3. Click **Save As**.

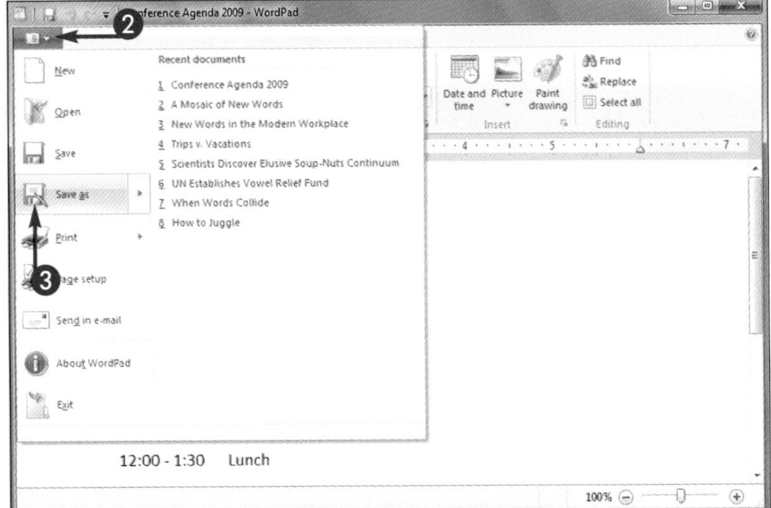


The Save As dialog box appears.

4. Click here to display a list of your folders.
5. Click **Documents**.

***Note:*** *In most programs, the Documents folder is selected automatically when you run the Save As command.*

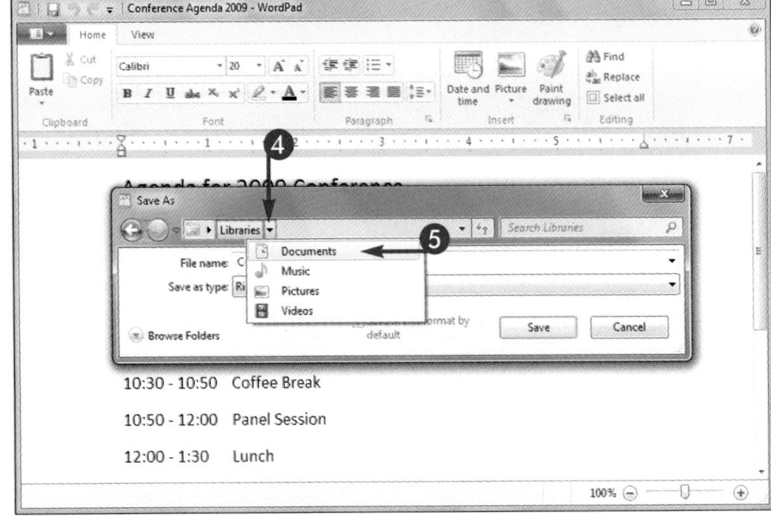

- Windows 7 opens the Documents folder.

6. Click in the File Name text box and type the name you want to use for the copy.

***Note:** The name you type can be up to 255 characters long, but it cannot include the following characters: < > , ? : " \ *.*

7. Click **Save**.

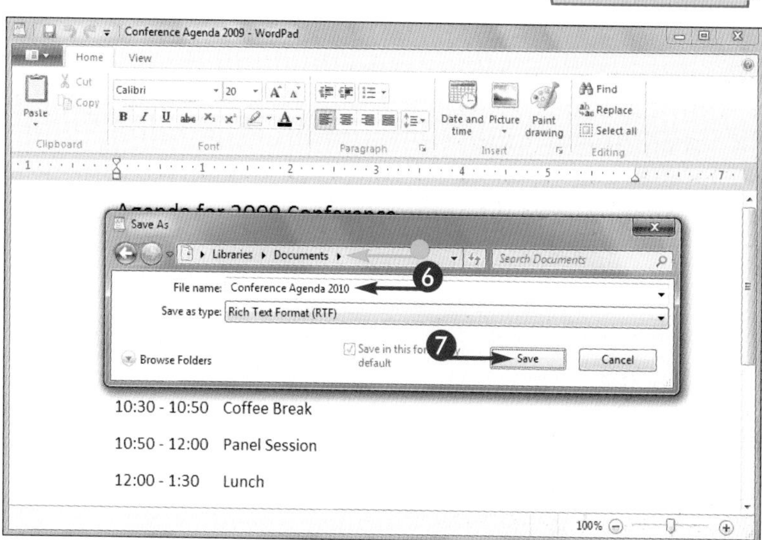


The program closes the original document and opens the copy you just created.

- The file name you typed appears in the program's title bar.

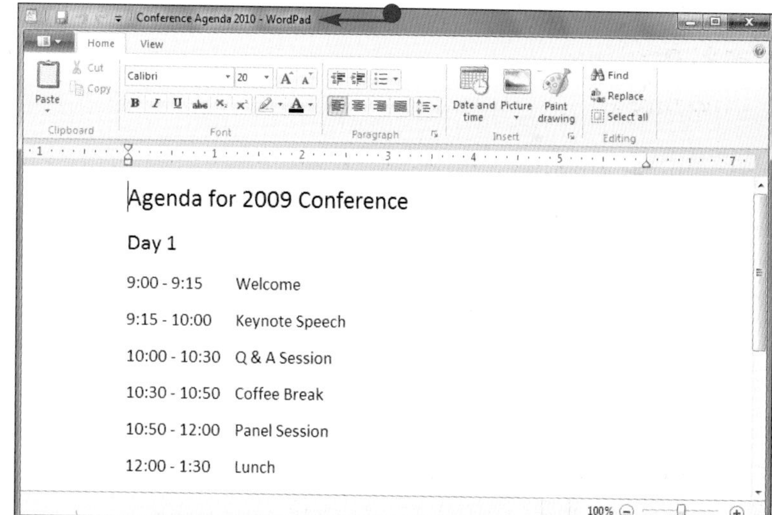

## Can I use the Save As command to make a backup copy of a document?

Yes, Save As can operate as a rudimentary backup procedure. (For a better solution, see the "Back Up Files" section in Chapter 14.) Create a copy with the same name as the original, but store the copy in a different location. Good places to choose are a second hard drive, a USB flash drive, or a memory card. Remember, too, that after you complete the Save As steps, the *backup copy* will be open in the program. Be sure to close the copy and then reopen the original.

# Edit Document Text

When you work with a character-based file, such as a text or word processing document or an e-mail message, you need to know the basic techniques for editing, selecting, copying, and moving text.

## Edit Document Text

### DELETE CHARACTERS

1. Click immediately to the left of the first character you want to delete.
   - The cursor appears before the character.

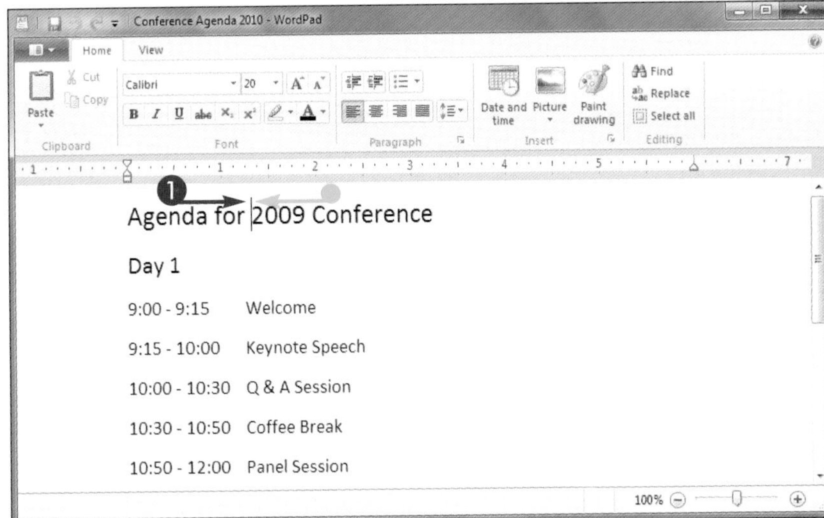


2. Press Delete until you have deleted all the characters you want.

***Note:** An alternative method is to click immediately to the right of the last character you want to delete and then press Backspace until you have deleted all the characters you want.*

***Note:** If you make a mistake, immediately press Ctrl + Z or click the **Undo** button ( ). Alternatively, click **Edit**, and then click **Undo**.*

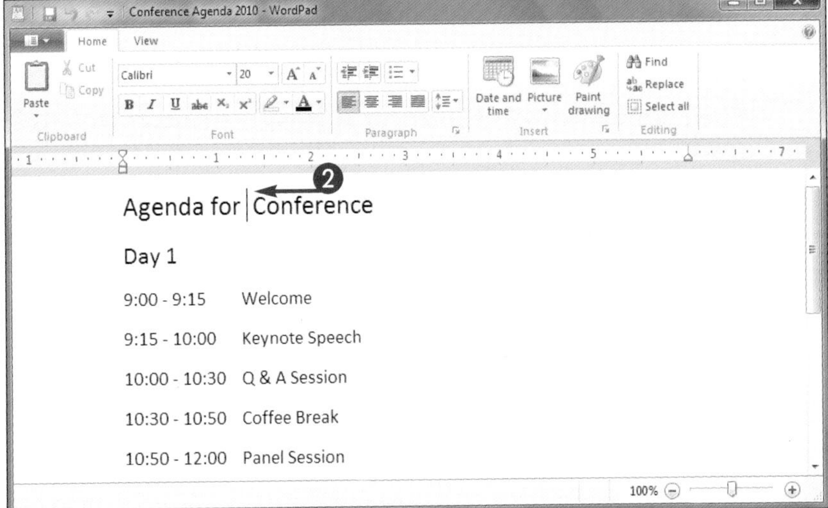

## SELECT TEXT FOR EDITING

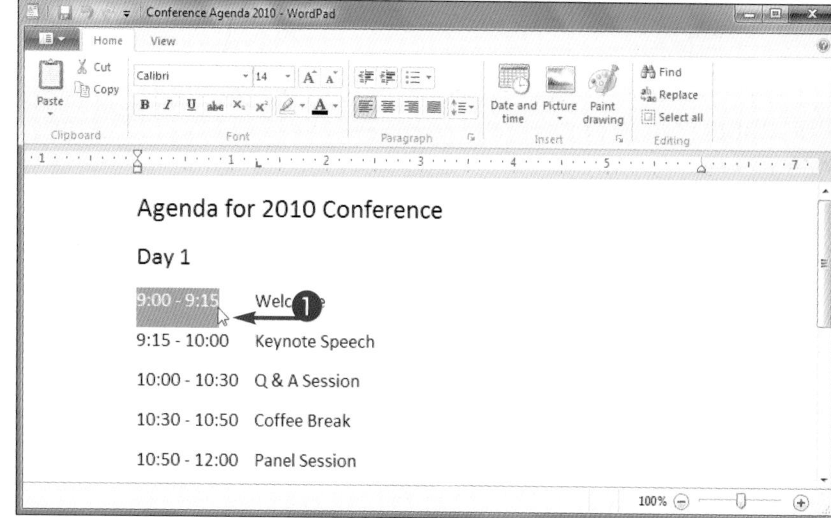

1. Click and drag across the text you want to select.

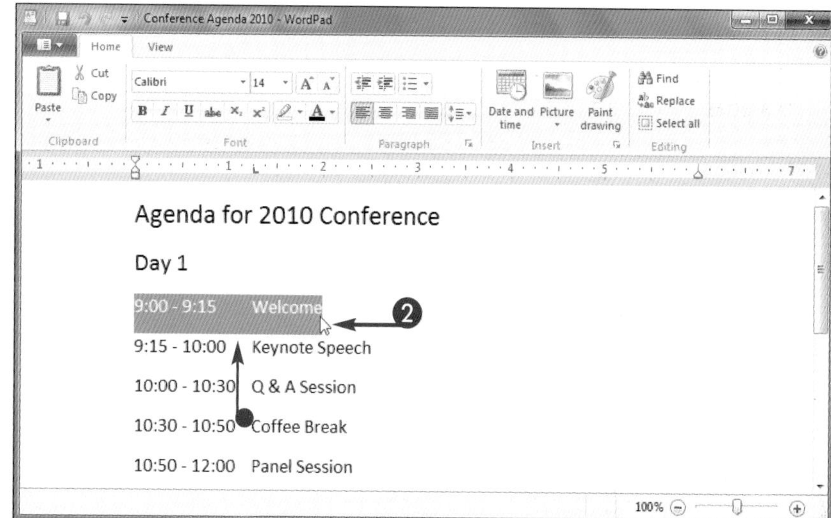

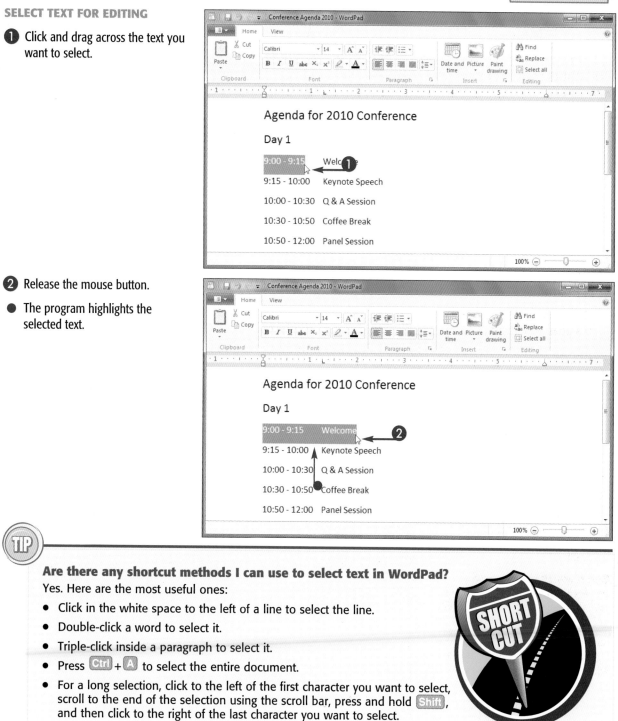

2. Release the mouse button.

- The program highlights the selected text.

**Are there any shortcut methods I can use to select text in WordPad?**

Yes. Here are the most useful ones:

- Click in the white space to the left of a line to select the line.
- Double-click a word to select it.
- Triple-click inside a paragraph to select it.
- Press Ctrl + A to select the entire document.
- For a long selection, click to the left of the first character you want to select, scroll to the end of the selection using the scroll bar, press and hold Shift, and then click to the right of the last character you want to select.

continued

# Edit Document Text *(continued)*

Once you select some text, you can work with all of the selected characters together, which is much faster than working with one character at a time. You will find some examples in the rest of this section.

**COPY TEXT**

1. Select the text you want to copy.
2. Click **Copy** ( ).

***Note:*** *In most programs, you can also press* Ctrl + C *or click the **Edit** menu and then click **Copy**.*

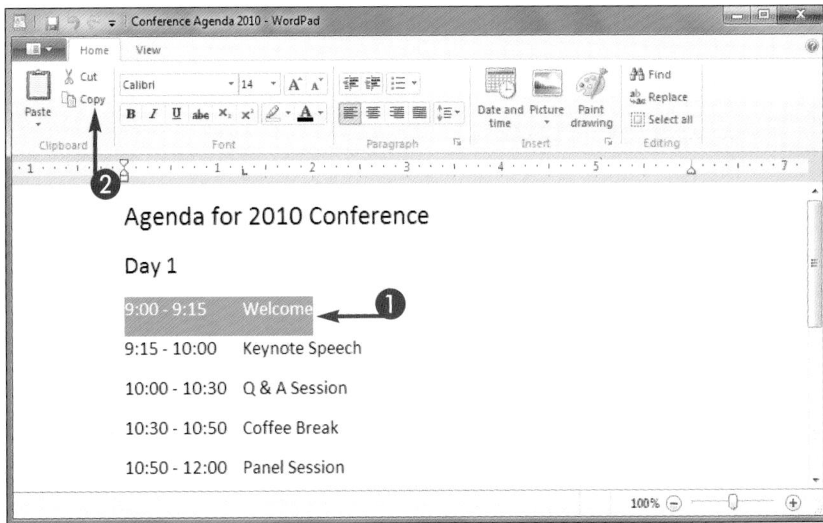


3. Click inside the document at the position where you want the copy of the text to appear.

   The cursor appears in the position you clicked.

4. Click **Paste** ( ).

***Note:*** *In most programs, you can also press* Ctrl + V *or click the **Edit** menu and then click **Paste**.*

- The program inserts a copy of the selected text at the cursor position.

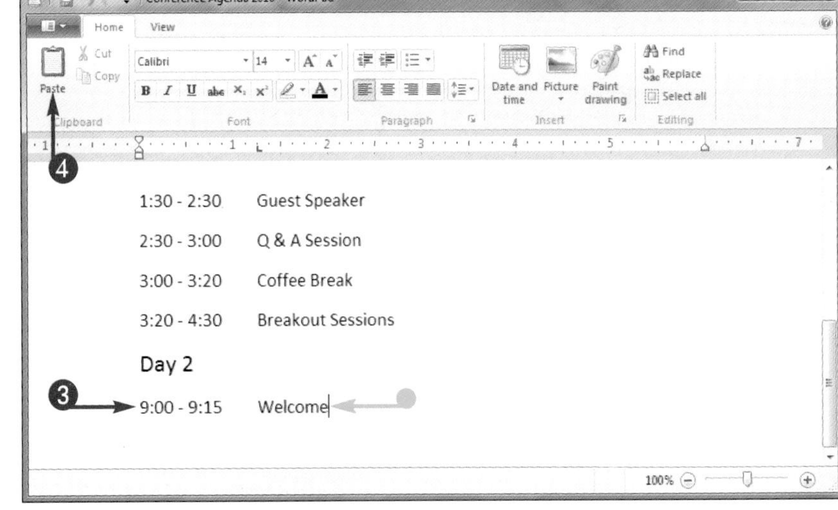

## MOVE TEXT

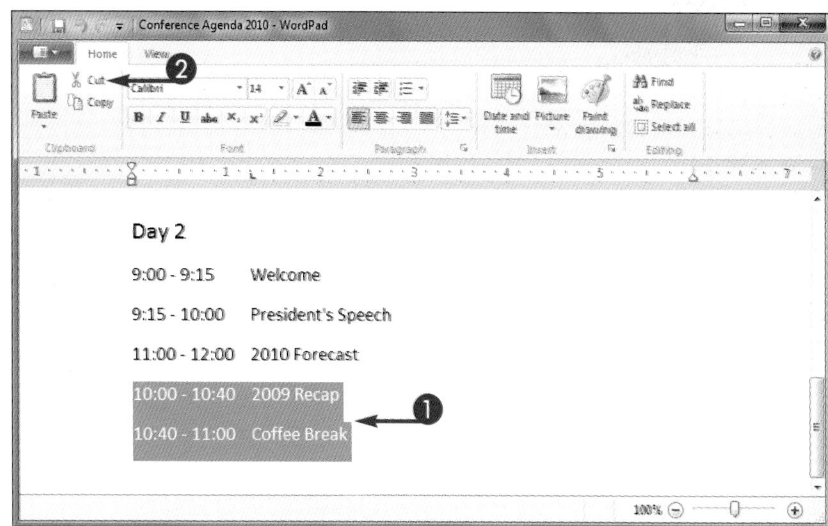


1. Select the text you want to move.
2. Click **Cut** (✂).

***Note:** In most programs, you can also press Ctrl + X or click the **Edit** menu and then click **Cut**.*

The program removes the text from the document.

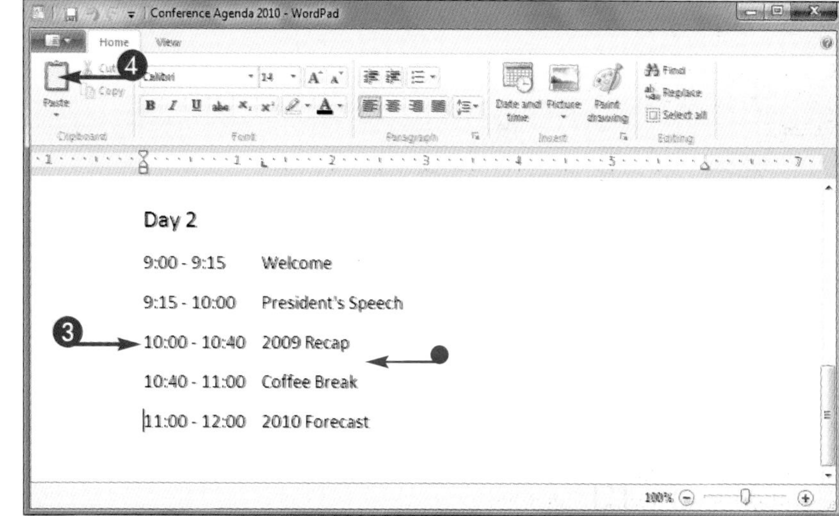


3. Click inside the document at the position where you want to move the text.

The cursor appears at the position you clicked.

4. Click **Paste** (📋).

***Note:** In most programs, you can also press Ctrl + V or click the **Edit** menu and then click **Paste**.*

- The program inserts the text at the cursor position.

TIP

### How do I move and copy text with my mouse?

First, select the text you want to work with. To move the selected text, position the mouse over the selection, and then click and drag the text to the new position within the document.

To copy the selected text, position the mouse over the selection, press and hold Ctrl, and then click and drag the text to the desired position within the document.

# Change the Text Font

When you work in a word processing document, you can add visual appeal by changing the font formatting.

**The font formatting includes attributes such as the typeface (the overall look of each character), style (bold or italic), size, or special effects (such as underline or colors).**

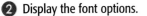

## Change the Text Font

1. Select the text you want to format.

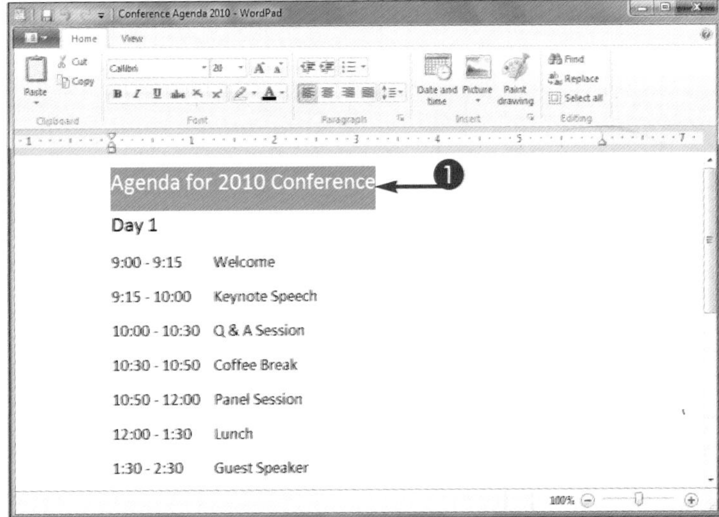


2. Display the font options.

- In WordPad, you display the font options by clicking the **Home** tab.

*Note: In many other programs, you display the font options by clicking* ***Format*** *in the menu bar and then clicking the* ***Font*** *command.*

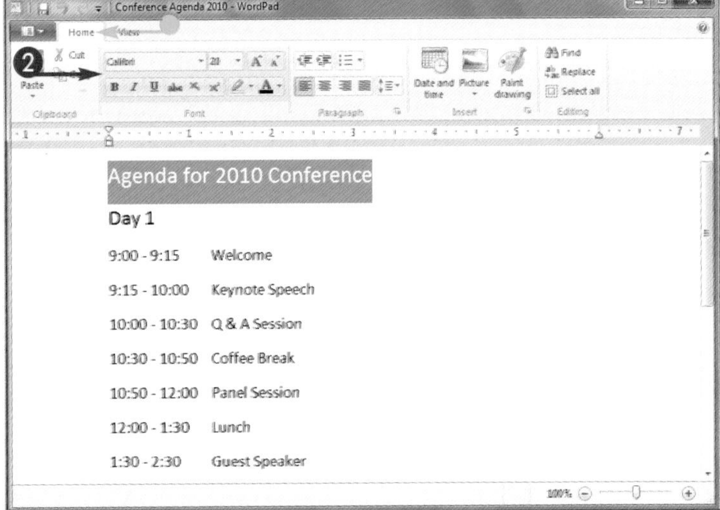

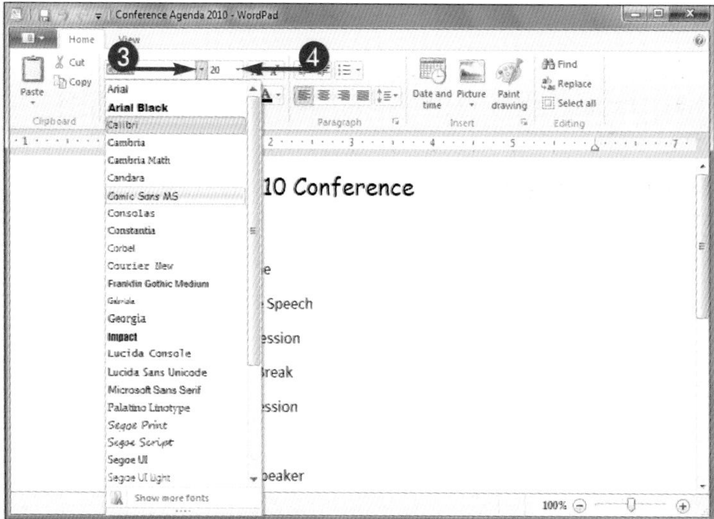


3. In the Font list, click ▾ and then click the typeface you want.
4. In the Size list, click the type size you want.

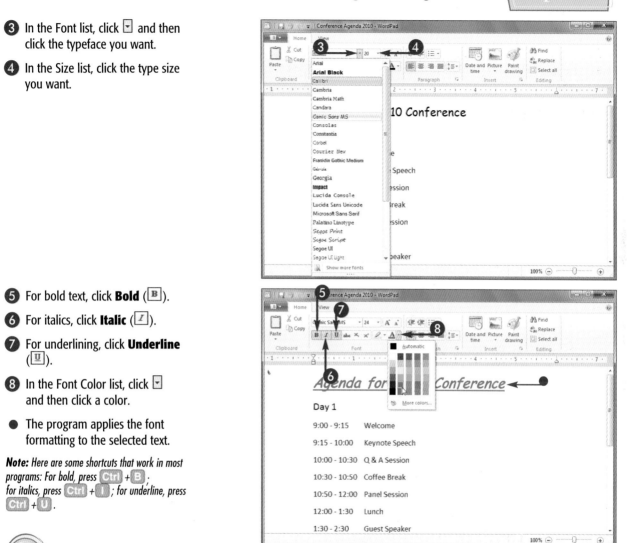

5. For bold text, click **Bold** (B).
6. For italics, click **Italic** (*I*).
7. For underlining, click **Underline** (U).
8. In the Font Color list, click ▾ and then click a color.

- The program applies the font formatting to the selected text.

***Note:*** *Here are some shortcuts that work in most programs: For bold, press* Ctrl + B*; for italics, press* Ctrl + I*; for underline, press* Ctrl + U.

### How can I make the best use of fonts in my documents?

- Do not use many different typefaces in a single document. Stick to one or at most two typefaces to avoid the "ransom note look."
- Avoid overly decorative typefaces because they are often difficult to read.
- Use bold only for document titles, subtitles, and headings.
- Use italics only to emphasize words and phrases, or for the titles of books and magazines.
- Use larger type sizes only for document titles, subtitles, and, possibly, the headings.
- If you change the text color, be sure to leave enough contrast between the text and the background. In general, dark text on a light background is the easiest to read.

# Find Text

In large documents, when you need to find specific text, you can save a lot of time by using the program's Find feature, which searches the entire document in the blink of an eye.

**Most programs that work with text — including Windows 7's WordPad and Notepad programs — have the Find feature.**

## Find Text

1. Click **Find** (binoculars icon).

***Note:** In many programs, you run the Find command by clicking **Edit** in the menu bar and then clicking the **Find** command, or by pressing Ctrl + F.*

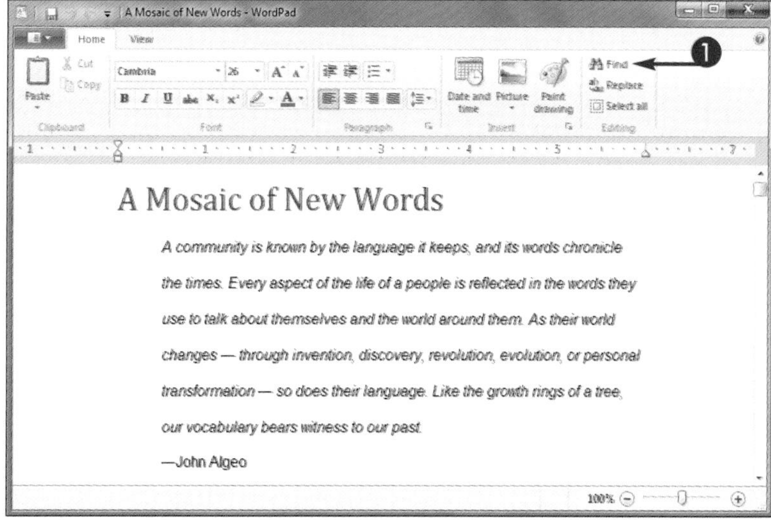


The Find dialog box appears.

2. Click in the Find What text box and type the text you want to find.
3. Click **Find Next**.

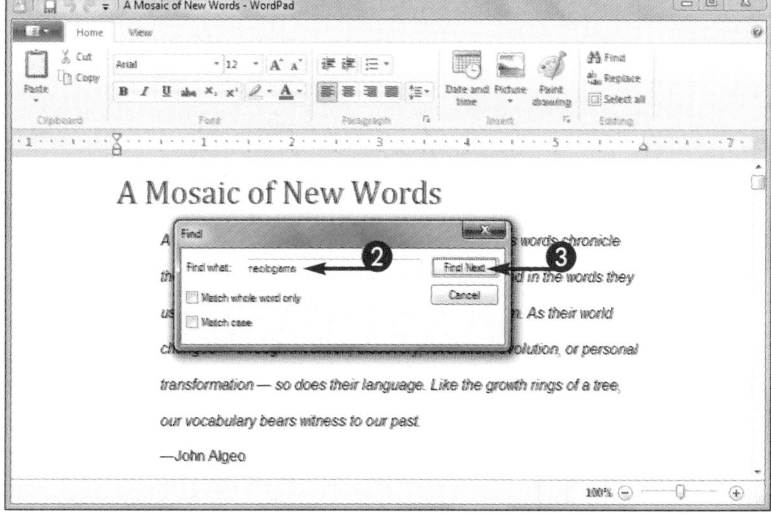

- The program selects the next instance of the search text.

***Note:*** *If the search text does not exist in the document, the program displays a dialog box to let you know.*

4. If the selected instance is not the one you want, click **Find Next** until the program finds the correct instance.

5. Click the **Close** button (✖) to close the Find dialog box.

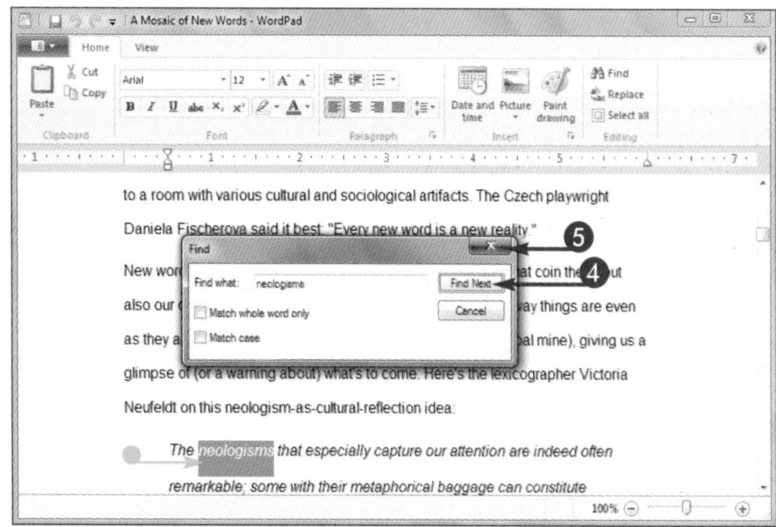


- The program leaves the found text selected.

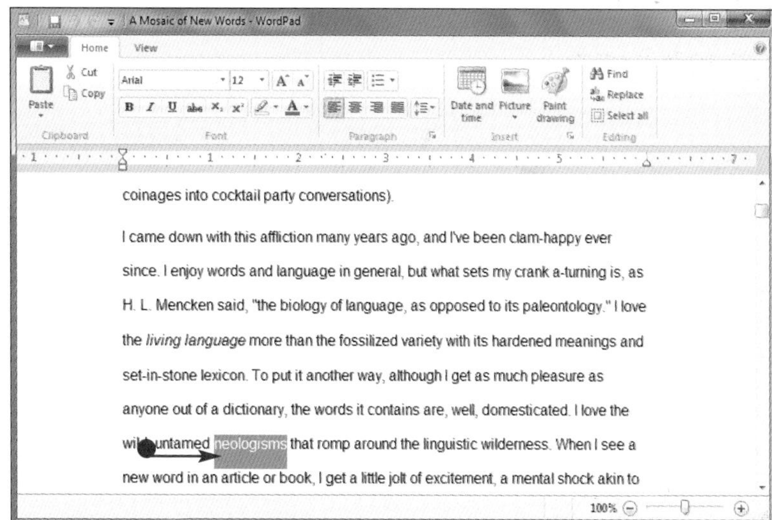


## TIPS

**When I search for a small word such as the, the program matches it in larger words such as theme and bother. How can I avoid this?**

In the Find dialog box, click **Match whole word only** (☐ changes to ☑). This tells the program to match the search text only if it is a word on its own and not part of another word.

**When I search for a name such as Bill, the program also matches the non-name bill. Is there a way to fix this?**

In the Find dialog box, click **Match case** (☐ changes to ☑). This tells the program to match the search text only if it has the same mix of uppercase and lowercase letters that you specify in the Find What text box. If you type **Bill**, for example, the program matches only *Bill* and not *bill*.

# Replace Text

Do you need to replace a word or part of a word with some other text? If you have several instances to replace, you can save time and do a more accurate job if you let the program's Replace feature replace the word for you.

**Most programs that work with text – including Windows 7's WordPad and Notepad programs – have the Replace feature.**

## Replace Text

1. Click **Replace** (ab/ac).

***Note:*** *In many programs, you run the Find command by clicking* ***Edit*** *in the menu bar and then clicking the* ***Replace*** *command, or by pressing* Ctrl + H.

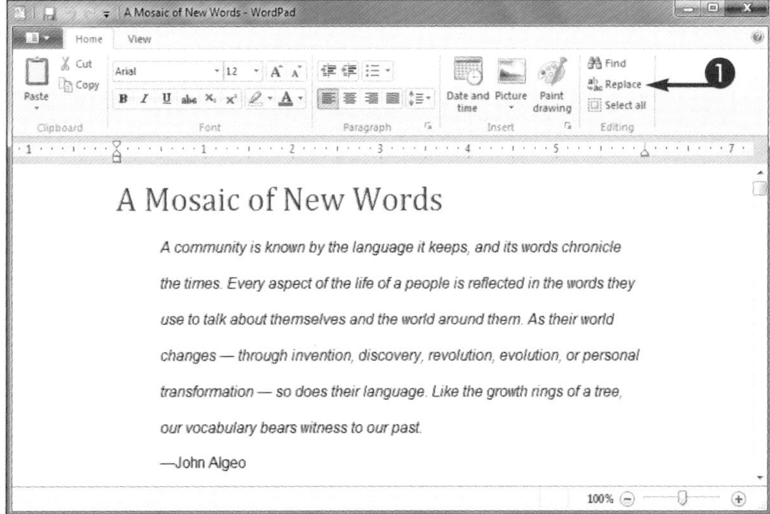


The Replace dialog box appears.

2. In the Find What text box, enter the text you want to find.
3. Click in the Replace With text box and type the text you want to use as the replacement.
4. Click **Find Next**.

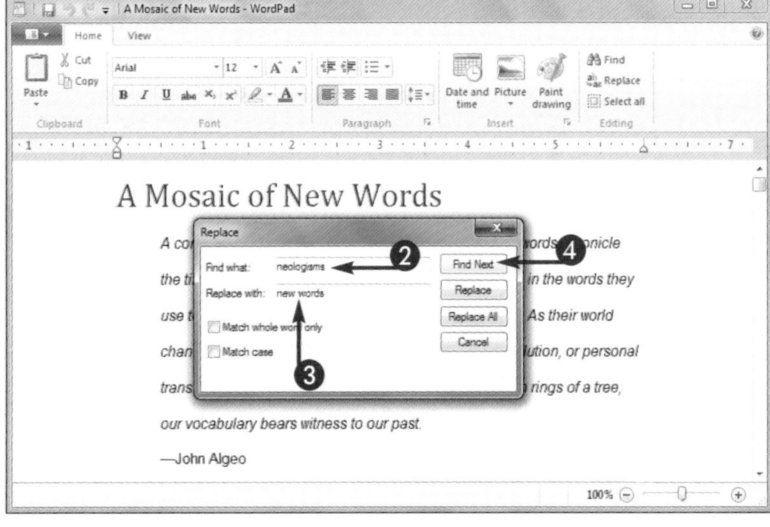

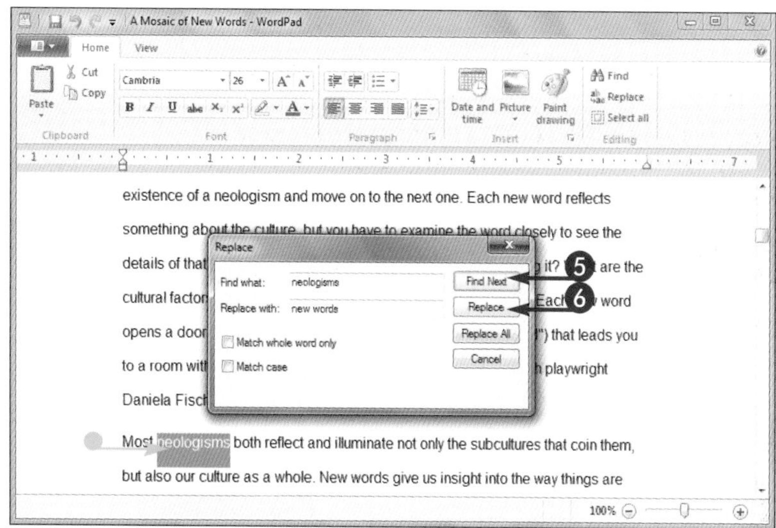

- The program selects the next instance of the search text.

***Note:*** *If the search text does not exist in the document, the program displays a dialog box to let you know.*

5. If the selected instance is not the one you want, click **Find Next** until the program finds the correct instance.
6. Click **Replace**.

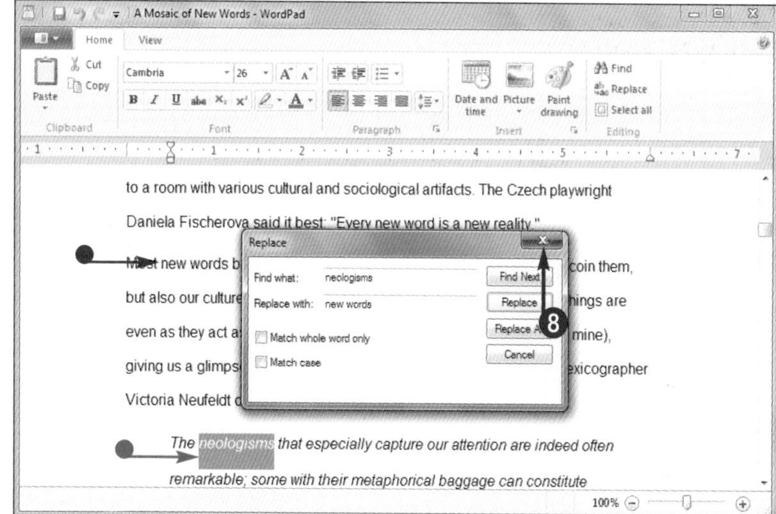

- The program replaces the selected text with the replacement text.
- The program selects the next instance of the search text.

7. Repeat Steps **5** and **6** until you have replaced all of the instances you want to replace.
8. Click the **Close** button () to close the Replace dialog box.

TIP

## Is there a faster way to replace every instance of the search text with the replacement text?

Yes. In the Replace dialog box, click **Replace All**. This tells the program to replace every instance of the search text with the replacement text. However, you should exercise some caution with this feature because it may make some replacements that you did not intend. Click **Find Next** a few times to make sure the matches are correct. Also, consider clicking the **Match whole word only** and **Match case** check boxes (☐ changes to ☑), as described in the "Find Text" section in this chapter.

# Insert Special Symbols

You can make your documents more readable and more useful by inserting special symbols that are not available via your keyboard.

**These special symbols include foreign characters such as ö and é, mathematical symbols such as $ and ½, financial symbols such as ¢ and ¥, commercial symbols such as © and ®, and many more.**

## Insert Special Symbols

1. Click **Start**.
2. Click **All Programs**.

*Note: When you click **All Programs**, the command name changes to Back.*

3. Click **Accessories**.
4. Click **System Tools**.
5. Click **Character Map**.

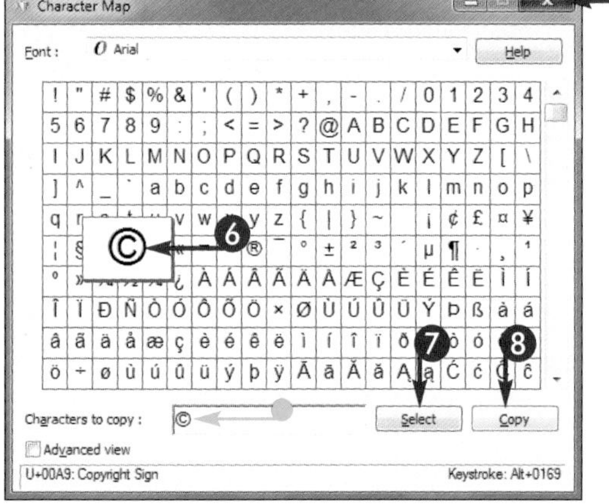


The Character Map window appears.

6. Click the symbol you want

*Note: Many other symbols are available in the Webdings and Wingdings typefaces. To see these symbols, click the **Font** ▾, and then click either **Webdings** or **Wingdings**.*

7. Click **Select**.

- Character Map adds the symbol to the Characters to Copy text box.

8. Click **Copy**.
9. Click the **Close** button (✕) to shut down Character Map after you choose all the characters you want.

⑩ In your document, position the cursor where you want to insert the symbol.

⑪ Click **Paste** (📋).

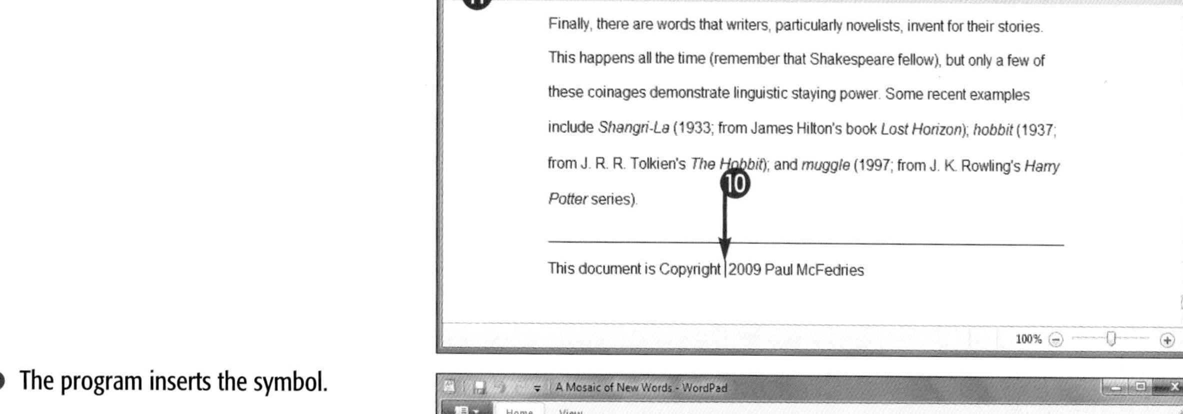


- The program inserts the symbol.

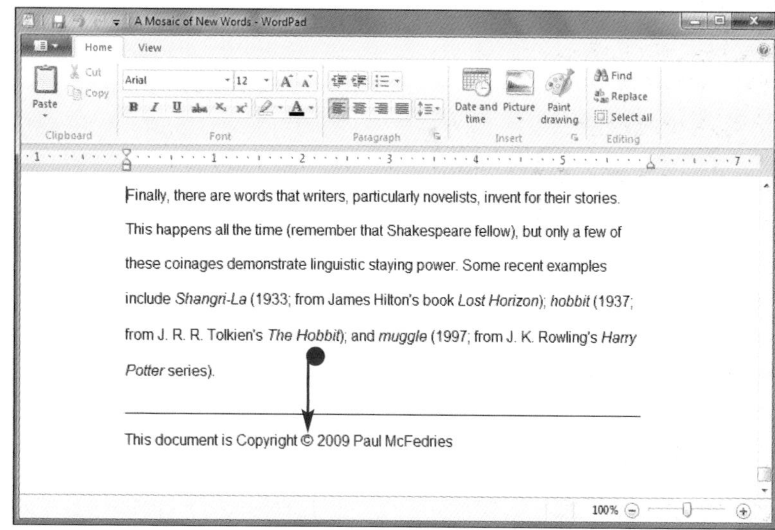


TIP

**When I click a symbol, Character Map sometimes displays a "Keystroke" in the status bar. What does this mean?**

This tells you that you can insert the symbol directly into your document by pressing the keystroke shown. For example, you can insert the copyright symbol (©) by pressing Alt + 0 1 6 9. When you type the numbers, be sure to use your keyboard's numeric keypad.

# Print a Document

When you need a hard copy of your document, either for your files or to distribute to someone else, you can get a hard copy by sending the document to your printer.

## Print a Document

❶ Turn on your printer.

❷ Open the document you want to print.

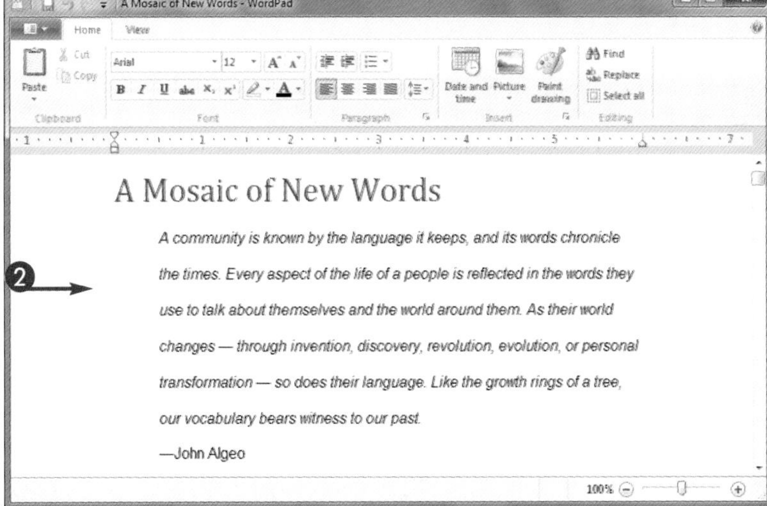

❸ Click **File** (▤).

❹ Click **Print**.

***Note:*** *In many programs, you can select the Print command by pressing* Ctrl + P *or by clicking the* ***Print*** *button (🖨).*

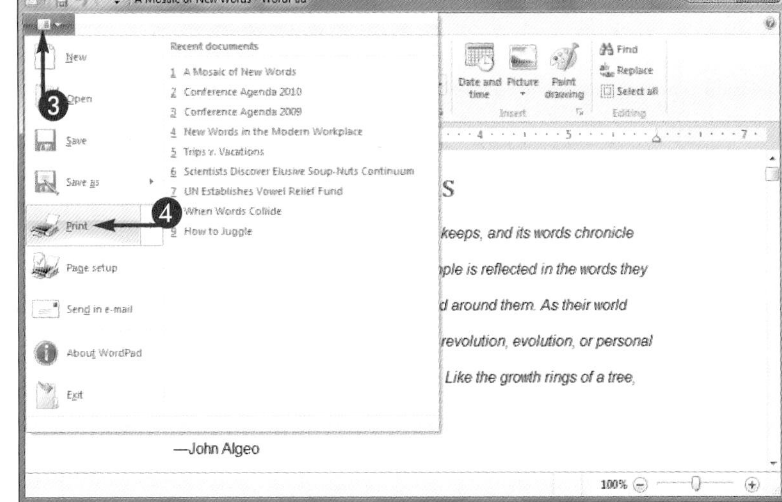

The Print dialog box appears.

***Note:** The layout of the Print dialog box varies from program to program. The WordPad version shown here is a typical example.*

5. If you have more than one printer, click the printer you want to use.

6. Use the **Number of copies** spinner to specify the number of copies to print.

7. Click **Print**.

- Windows 7 prints the document. The print icon (printer icon) appears in the taskbar's notification area while the document prints.

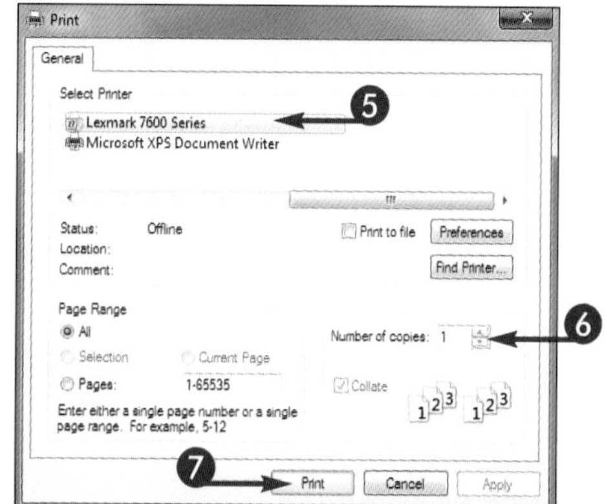


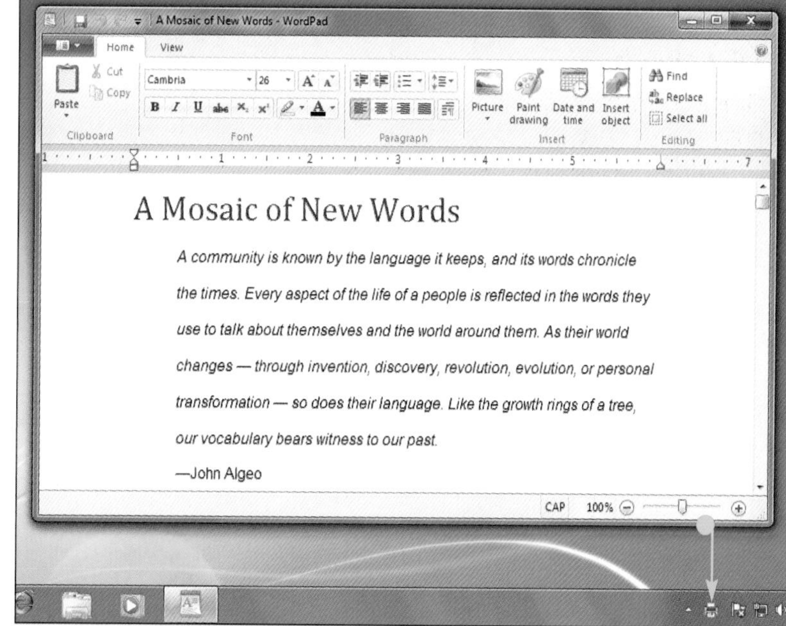

### How do I print only part of a document?

Most programs enable you to use the following methods to print only part of the document:

- Print selected text: Select the text you want to print. In the Print dialog box, click **Selection** (○ changes to ◉).
- Print a specific page: Place the cursor on the page you want to print. In the Print dialog box, click **Current Page** (○ changes to ◉).
- Print a range of pages: In the Print dialog box, click **Pages** (○ changes to ◉). In the text box, type the first page number, a dash (–), and the last page number (for example, 1–5).

# CHAPTER 4

# Working with Images

Whether you load your images from a digital camera or a scanner, download them from the Internet, or draw them yourself, Windows 7 comes with a number of useful tools for working with those images.

# Open the Pictures Library

Before you can work with your images, you need to view them on your computer. You do that by opening Windows 7's Pictures library, which is a special folder designed specifically for storing images.

## Open the Pictures Library

❶ Click **Start**.

❷ Click **Pictures**.

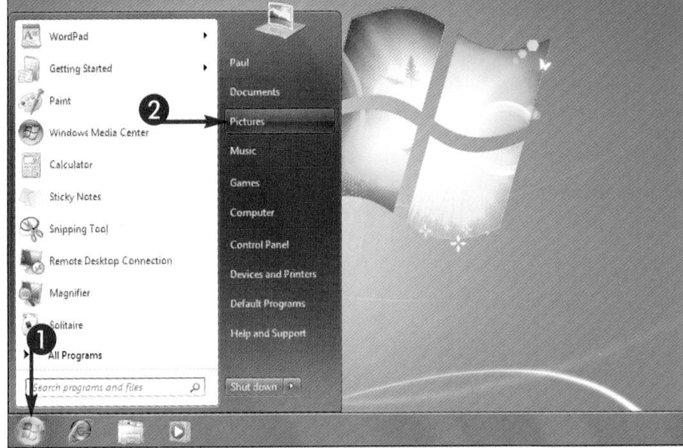


The Pictures library appears.

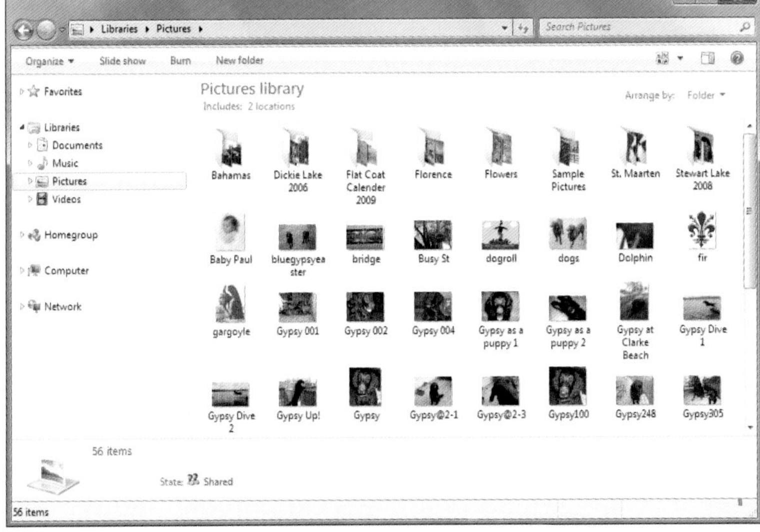

# Preview an Image

You can preview any saved image file using either the Details pane or the Preview pane in the Pictures library. The Details pane, located at the bottom of the window, also displays details about the file, such as the file type, dimensions, and size. The Preview pane, which appears on the right side of the window, shows a larger preview of the image.

**You can also use the Preview pane to preview images stored in *subfolders* – folders stored within the main Pictures library.**

## Preview an Image

1. Click the image file you want to preview.
   - The Details pane shows a small preview of the image.
   - Details about the image file appear here.
2. Click **Show the Preview Pane** (▢).

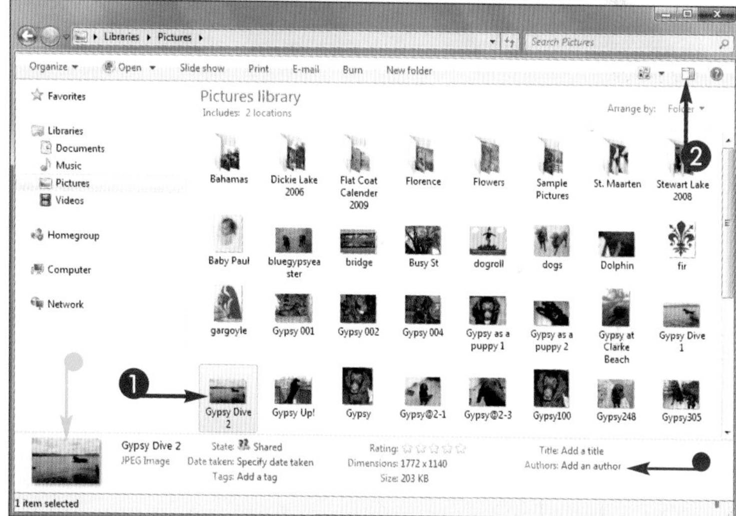


- Windows 7 opens the Preview pane and displays a larger preview of the image.

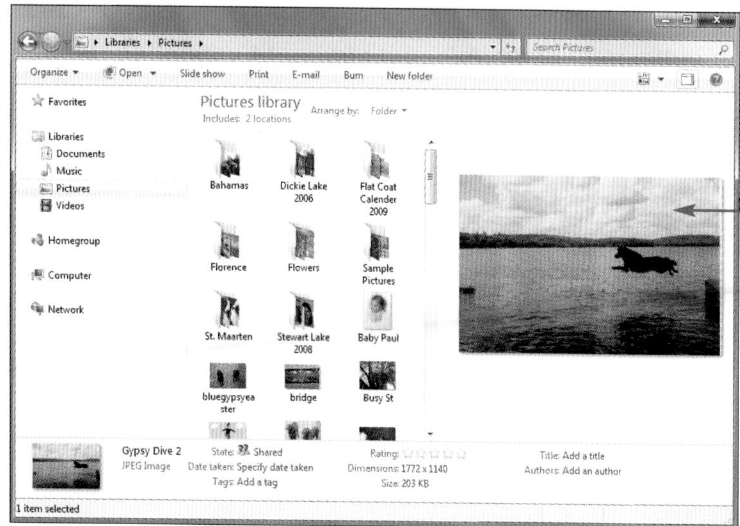

# View Your Images

If you want to look at several images, you can use either Windows Photo Viewer or Windows Live Photo Gallery to navigate backwards and forwards through the images in the Pictures library.

**You can also use either program to zoom in and out of an image and to run an image slide show. See Chapter 11 to learn how to install Windows Live Photo Gallery.**

## View Your Images

### VIEW IMAGES USING WINDOWS PHOTO VIEWER

1. Click the image.
2. Click the **Open** ▾.
3. Click **Windows Photo Viewer**.

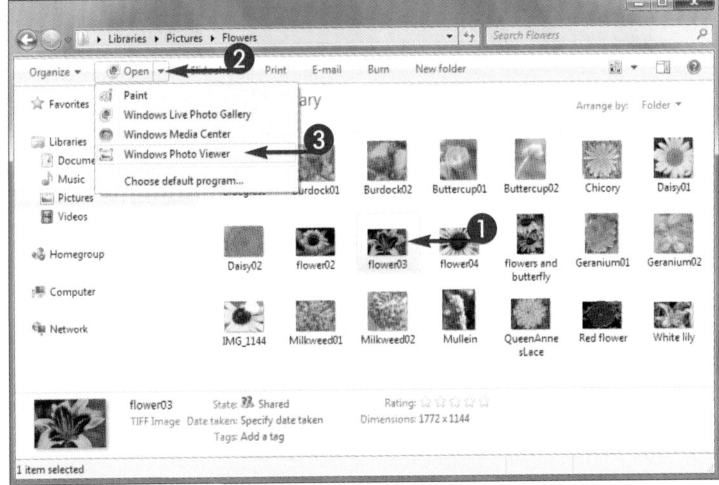


The image opens in Windows Photo Viewer.

4. To get a closer look at the image, click the magnifying glass and then click and drag the slider up.
5. To view the next image in the folder, click the **Next** button (▶|).
6. To view the previous image in the folder, click the **Previous** button (|◀).
7. To start a slide show of all the images in the folder, click the **Play Slide Show** button (▭).

***Note:*** *To stop the slide show, press* Esc.

## VIEW IMAGES USING WINDOWS LIVE PHOTO GALLERY

❶ Click the image.

❷ Click the **Open** ▾.

❸ Click **Windows Live Photo Gallery**.

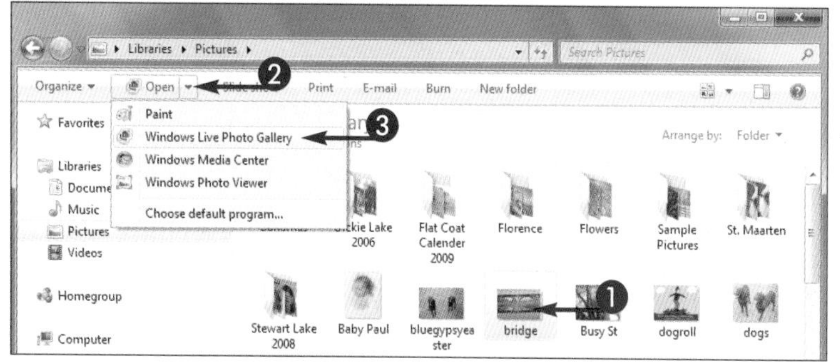


The image opens in Windows Live Photo Gallery.

❹ To see more of the image, click and drag the slider to the right.

❺ To view the next image in the folder, click the **Next** button (▶|).

❻ To view the previous image in the folder, click the **Previous** button (|◀).

❼ To start a slide show of all the images in the folder, click the **Play Slide Show** button (▭).

***Note:*** *To stop the slide show, press* Esc.

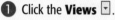

**Is there a way I can view my pictures without using the Photo Gallery Viewer?**

Yes, you can change the Picture folder's view to display large *thumbnails* — scaled-down versions of the actual images:

❶ Click the **Views** ▾.

❷ Click **Extra Large Icons**.

● Windows 7 displays the images as thumbnails.

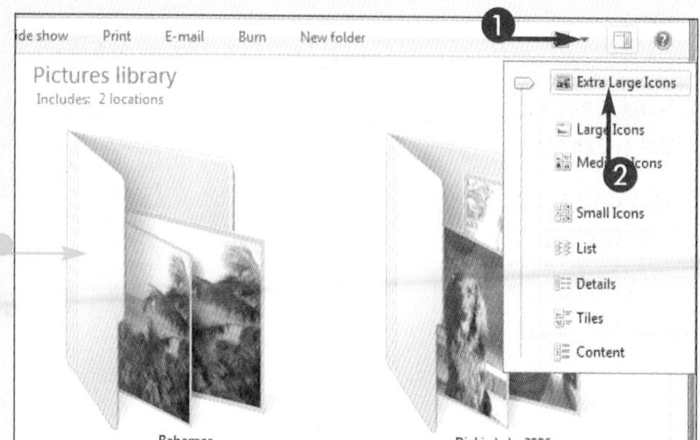

# Scan an Image

You can create a digital copy of a photo or other image by using a document scanner, or the scanner component of an all-in-one printer. The scanner copies the image to your computer, where you can then store it as a file on your hard drive.

**There are many ways you can use a scanned image. For example, you can scan a photo to e-mail to friends or publish on a Web page. You can also scan a logo or other image to use in a document.**

## Scan an Image

1. Turn on your scanner or all-in-one printer and position a photo or other image on the scanner bed.
2. Click **Start**.
3. Click **Devices and Printers**.

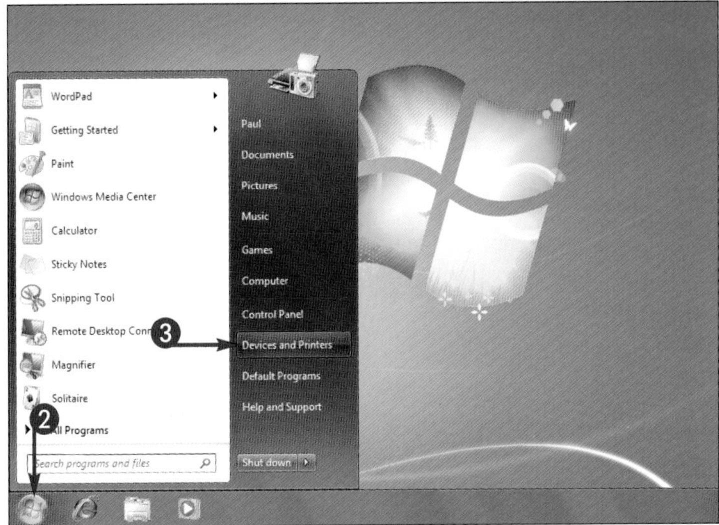


The Devices and Printers window appears.

4. Click the device you want to use to perform the scan.
5. Click **Start scan**.

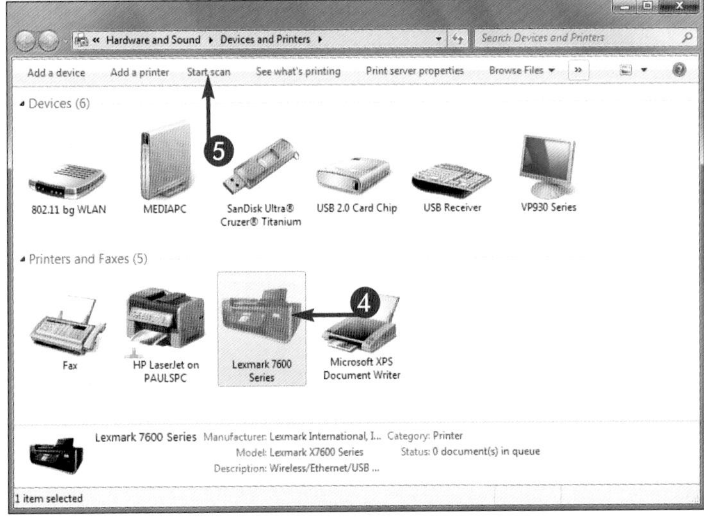

The New Scan dialog box appears.

6 Click the **Profile** ▾ and then click **Photo**.

7 Click the **Resolution** ⬍ to specify the scan resolution.

***Note:*** *The higher the resolution, the sharper the image, but the larger the resulting file.*

8 Click **Preview**.

- A preview of the scan appears here.

9 Click and drag the edges of the dashed rectangle to set the scan area.

10 Click **Scan**.

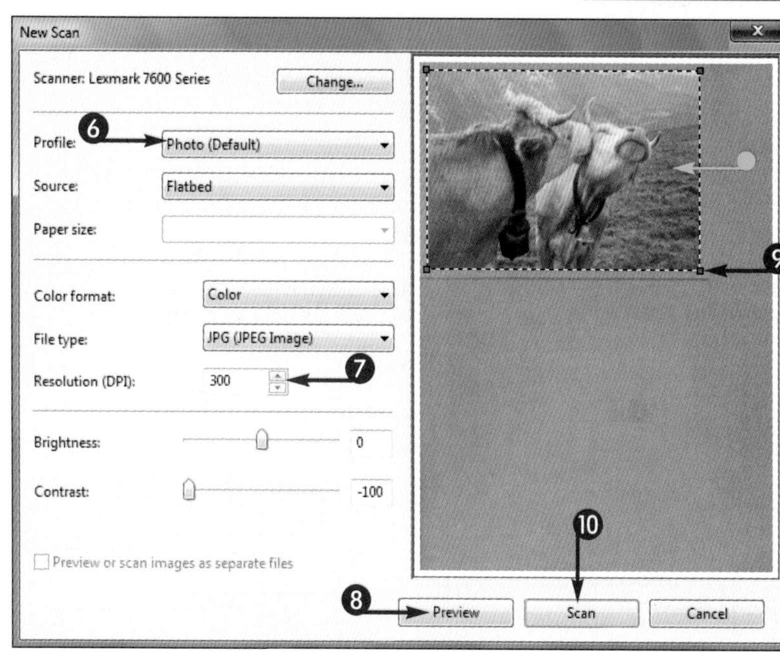


Windows 7 scans the image.

The Importing Pictures and Videos dialog box appears.

11 Type a word or phrase that describes the scan.

12 Click **Import**.

Windows 7 imports the image to your computer.

### How do I view a picture I have previously scanned?

Windows 7 stores the image in the Pictures library. It creates a new folder, the name of which is the current date followed by whatever word or phrase you type in the Importing Pictures and Videos dialog box; for example, 2009-08-23 Flower. Open the subfolder to see your scanned picture.

### Are there other methods I can use to scan an image?

Yes. Most scanners or all-in-one printers come with a Scan button that you can push to start a new scan. You can also click **Start**, **All Programs**, **Windows Fax and Scan**, and then **New Scan**. In Paint (click **Start**, **All Programs**, **Accessories**, and then **Paint**), click the **File** menu and then click **From scanner or camera**. In Windows Live Photo Gallery (click **Start**, **All Programs**, **Windows Live**, and then **Windows Live Photo Gallery**), click **File** and then click **Import from a camera or scanner**.

# Import Images from a Digital Camera

You can import photos from a digital camera and save them on your computer. If your camera stores the photos on a memory card, you can also use a memory card reader attached to your computer to upload the digital photos from the removable drive that Windows 7 sets up.

**Once you have the digital photos on your system, you can view, make repairs to, or print the images.**

## Import Images from a Digital Camera

1. Plug in your camera or memory storage card reader.

   The AutoPlay dialog box appears.

2. Click **Import Pictures and Videos using Windows**.

The Import Pictures and Videos dialog box appears.

3. Type a word or phrase that describes the photos.
4. Click **Import**.

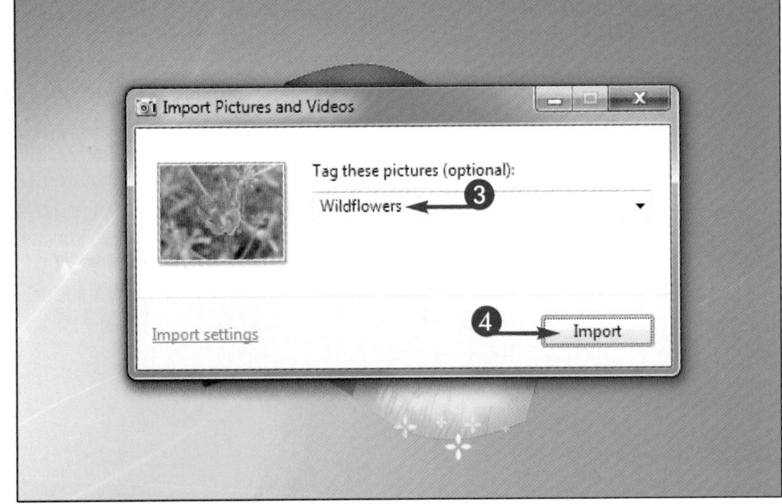

Windows 7 begins importing the digital photos.

5 To have Windows 7 erase the photos from the camera or card, click **Erase after importing** (☐ changes to ☑).

The Imported Pictures and Videos window appears and displays the recently imported photos.

6 When you have finished looking at your photos, click the **Close** button (☒) to close the window.

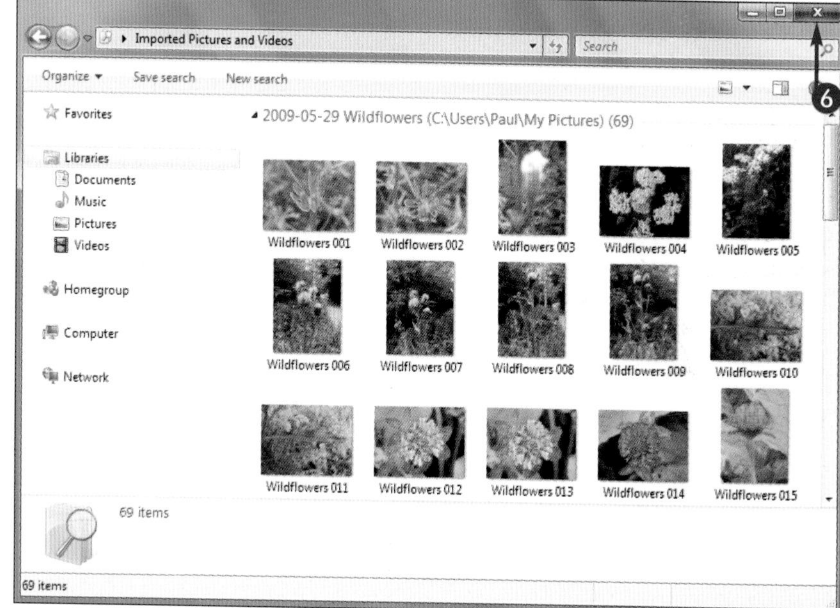


TIP

## How do I view the imported photos?

If you have closed the Imported Pictures and Videos window, note that Windows 7 stores the imported digital photos in the Pictures library. It creates a new subfolder, the name of which is the current date followed by whatever word or phrase you type in the Importing Pictures and Videos dialog box. For example, if the current date is August 23, 2009 and you typed **Nassau Vacation** in the text box, the new subfolder will be named 2009-08-23 Nassau Vacation. Open the subfolder to see your imported digital photos.

# Repair a Digital Image

You can use Windows Live Photo Gallery to improve the look of digital photos and other images. Windows Live Photo Gallery includes a special Fix window that offers a number of tools for repairing various image attributes.

**The Fix window enables you to adjust an image's brightness, contrast, color temperature, tint, and saturation. You can also crop and rotate an image and fix red eye. See Chapter 11 to learn how to download and install Windows Live Photo Gallery.**

## Repair a Digital Image

1. Click **Start**.
2. Click **All Programs**.

*Note: When you click* ***All Programs****, the command name changes to Back.*

3. Click **Windows Live**.
4. Click **Windows Live Photo Gallery**.

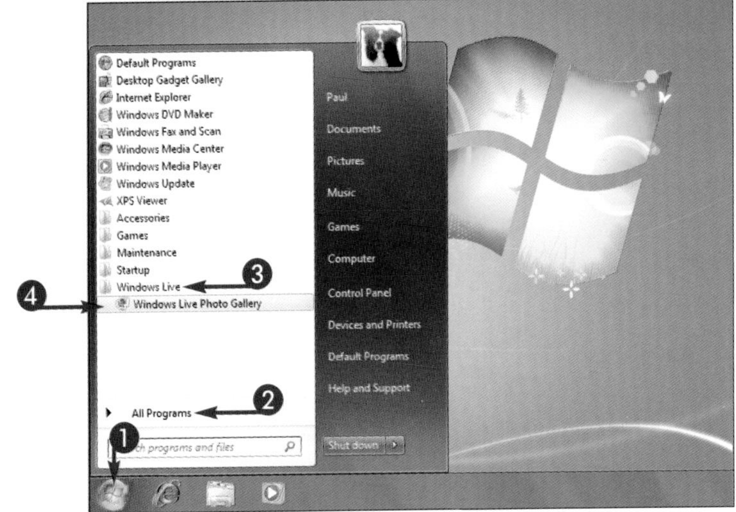


- Windows Live Photo Gallery appears.

5. Click the image you want to repair.
6. Click **Fix** to open the Fix window.

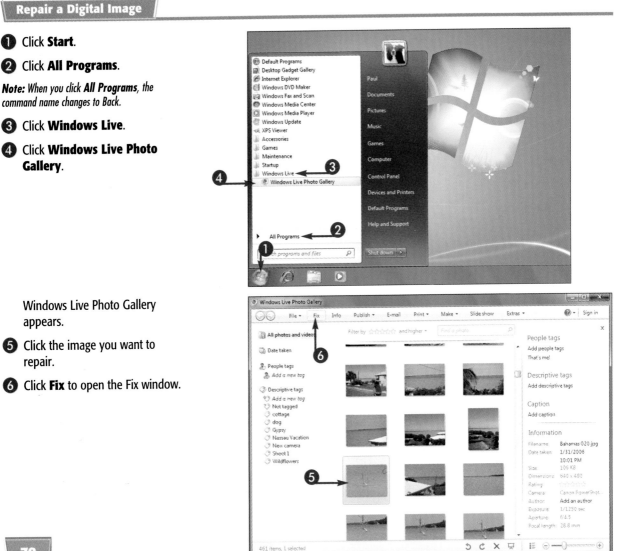

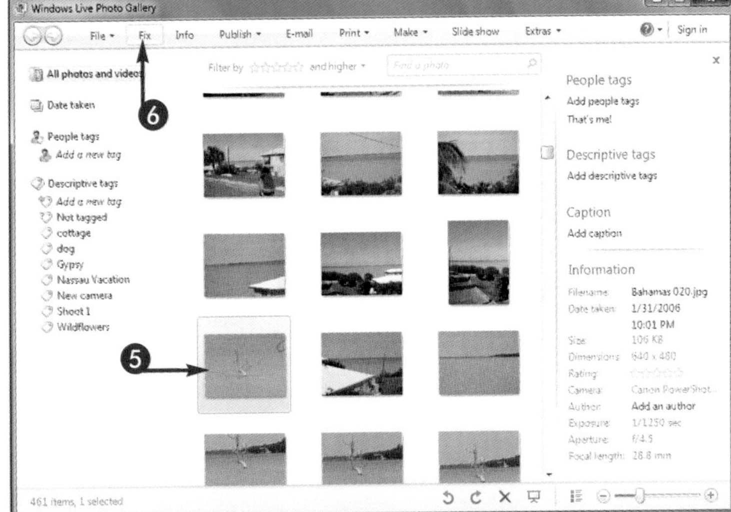

7. To change the exposure, click **Adjust exposure** and then click and drag the **Brightness** and **Contrast** sliders.

8. To change the color, click **Adjust color** and then click and drag the **Color temperature**, **Tint**, and **Saturation** sliders.

- If you are not sure how to use these tools, click **Auto adjust** to have Photo Gallery make the adjustments for you.

9. To remove red eye from a photo, click **Fix red eye**.

10. To crop the picture, first click **Crop photo**.

11. Click the **Proportion** ▾ and choose a dimension.

***Note:** Click **Original** to keep the same relative height and width; click **Custom** to crop to any height and width.*

12. Click and drag the handles to set the new size.

13. Click **Apply**.

14. When you are done, click **Back to gallery**.

    Windows Live Photo Gallery applies the repairs.

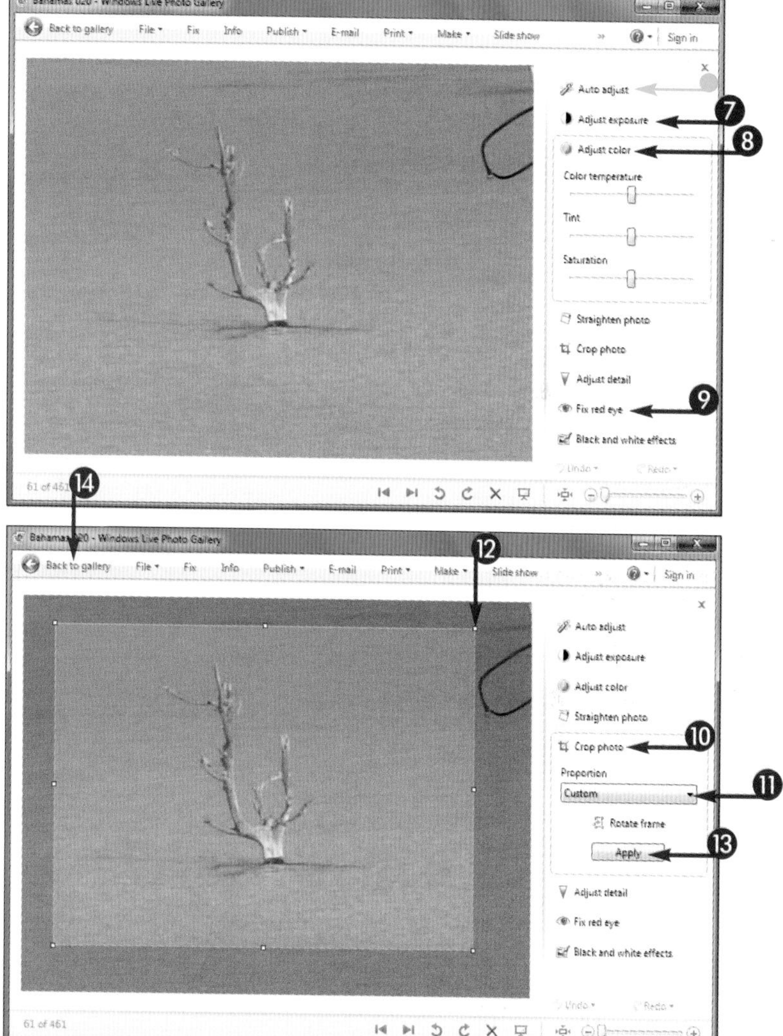

### How did my photo end up sideways?

When you take a vertical shot with your digital camera, your photo appears sideways when you download the image to your computer. You may also have scanned the image vertically instead of horizontally. In the Fix window, click ↺ to rotate the image counterclockwise; click ↻ to rotate the image clockwise.

### I do not like the repairs I made to my image. Can I get the original image back?

Yes, you can. Windows Live Photo Gallery always keeps a backup copy of the original image, just in case. To undo all your changes and get the original image back, click the image and then click **Fix**. In the Fix window, click **Revert** and then click **Revert to Original** (or press Ctrl + R).

# Print an Image

You can print an image from the Pictures library, or from any subfolder in the Pictures library. When you activate the Print task, the Print Pictures dialog box appears. You can use this dialog box to choose a printer and a layout, and to send the image to the printer.

**You can print a single image or multiple images. If you work with multiple images, you can print them individually or print two or more images per sheet.**

## Print an Image

1. In the Pictures library, select the image or images you want to print.

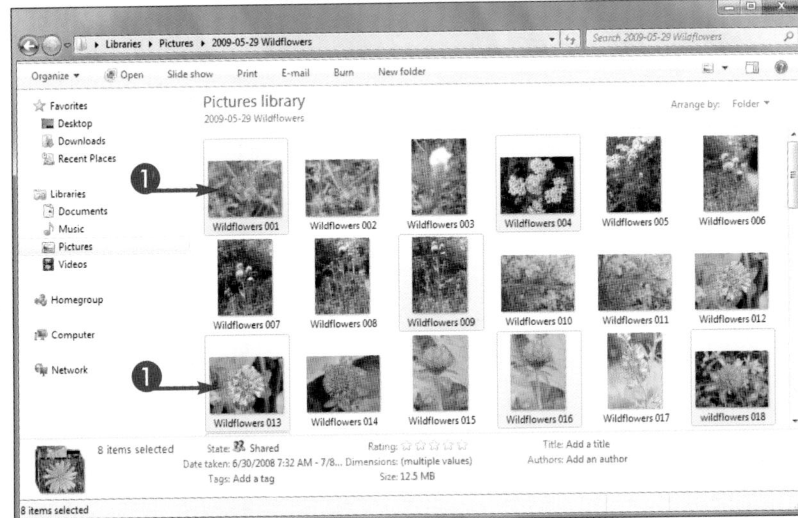


2. Click **Print**.

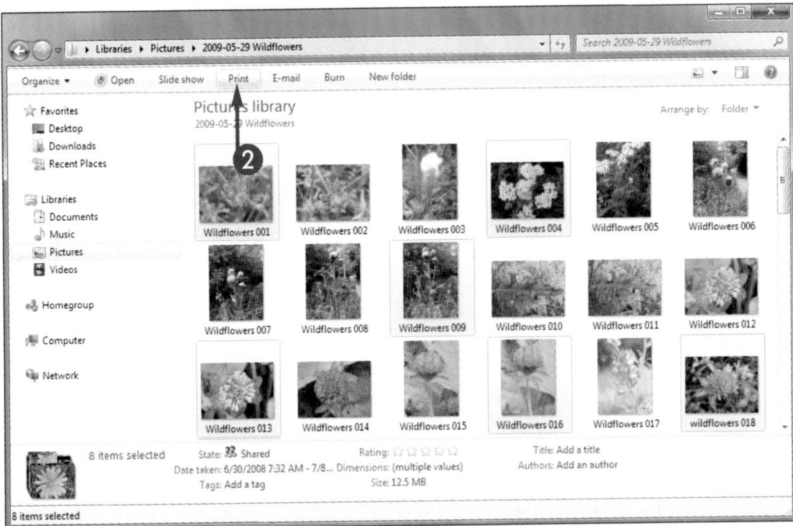

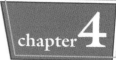

The Print Pictures dialog box appears.

3. If you use more than one printer with your computer, click ▾ and click the printer you want to use.
4. Click ▾ and click the size of paper you are using.
5. Click ▾ and click the printout quality you prefer.

***Note:** Print quality is measured in dots per inch (dpi). The higher the dpi value, the better the print quality.*

6. Click the layout you want to use for the printed image.

- The wizard displays a preview of the printout.
- Click the **Next** button (▶) to see previews of other pages.

7. Click ⬍ to select the number of copies you want.
8. Click **Print**.

The wizard sends your image or images to the printer.

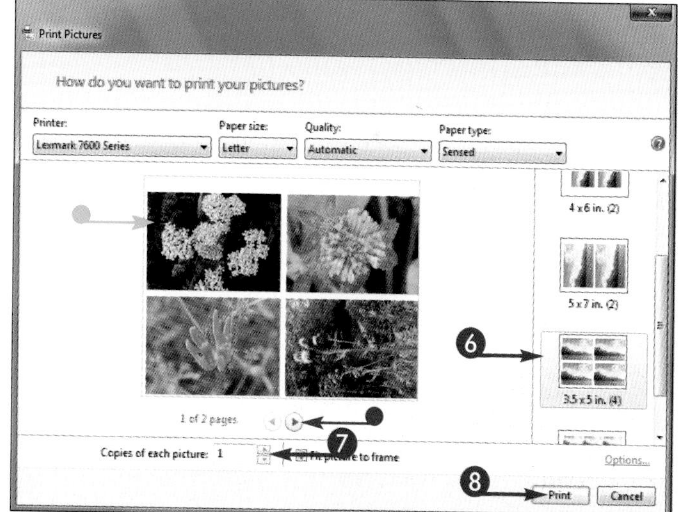

**What type of paper should I use for my photo printouts?**

Depending on the kind of printer you are using, you can find a variety of photo-quality paper types for printing out your digital photographs. Photo-quality paper, though more expensive than multipurpose paper, is designed to create a more permanent image and improve the resolution and color of the printed images. Photo-quality paper comes in glossy and matte finishes, as well as variations of each. Be sure to select a photo-quality paper that your printer manufacturer recommends.

# Create a DVD Slide Show for Your Images

You can create a slide show of images and burn it to a recordable DVD disc for playback on your computer or home or portable DVD player. After you start the slide show, the feature automatically advances and displays each image on the disc as a slide.

**By default, each image is displayed for seven seconds, so you can add up to about 800 images to a disc.**

## Create a DVD Slide Show for Your Images

1. Insert a recordable DVD in your DVD burner.
2. Click **Start**.
3. Click **All Programs**.

*Note: When you click **All Programs**, the command name changes to Back.*

4. Click **Windows DVD Maker**.

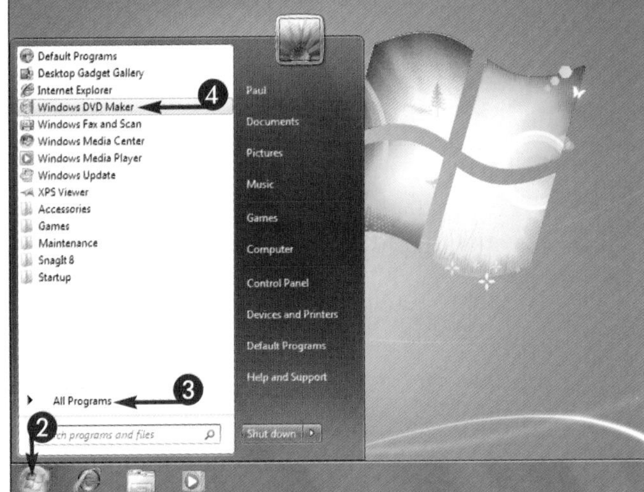


The Windows DVD Maker window appears.

5. Click **Choose Photos and Videos**.

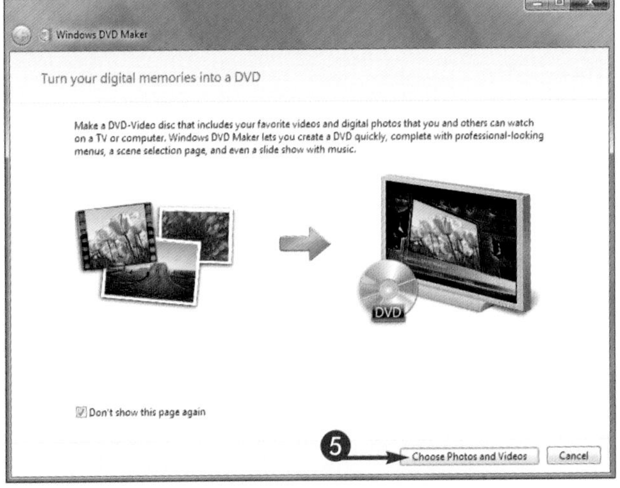

The Add Pictures and Video to the DVD window appears.

6 Click **Add items**.

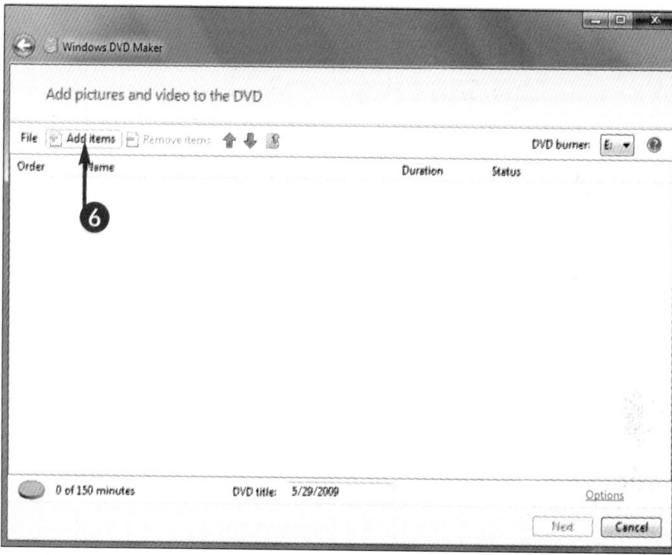


The Add Items to DVD dialog box appears.

7 Select the images you want to include on the DVD.

8 Click **Add**.

9 Repeat Steps **5** to **7** to specify any other images you want on the DVD.

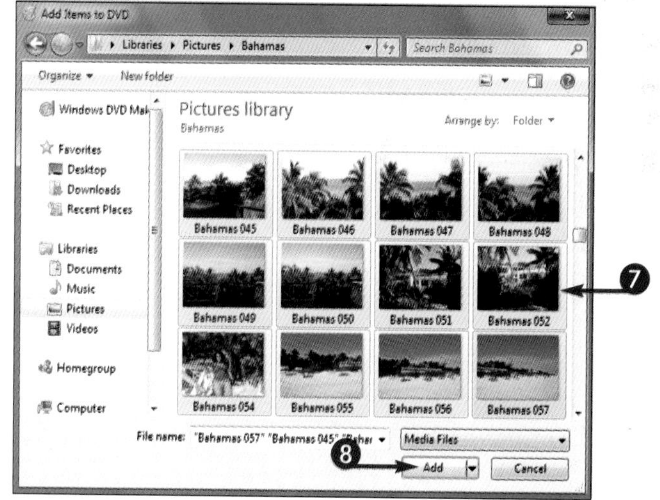


TIPS

**How can I get my images to play in a continuous loop?**

In the DVD Maker window, click **Options** to display the DVD Options dialog box. Click **Play video in a continuous loop** (◎ changes to ◉), and then click **OK**.

**I added an image by mistake. How do I remove it from my slide show?**

In the Windows DVD Maker window, double-click the **Pictures** icon to display the individual images. Click the image you do not want and then click **Remove items**. Note, too, that you can also reorder your images. Click an image and then click either **Move up** or **Move down**.

# Create a DVD Slide Show for Your Images *(continued)*

Windows DVD Maker offers a number of options for displaying slide show images. For example, you can change the duration that each image is displayed (the longer the duration, the fewer images you can place on the disc), and you can specify a transition effect between each image.

**You can also "pan and zoom" each image, which gives the slides an animated effect where the "camera" appears to move along (pan) and into and out of (zoom) each image.**

## Create a DVD Slide Show for Your Images *(continued)*

⑩ Type a name for the DVD disc.

⑪ Click **Next**.

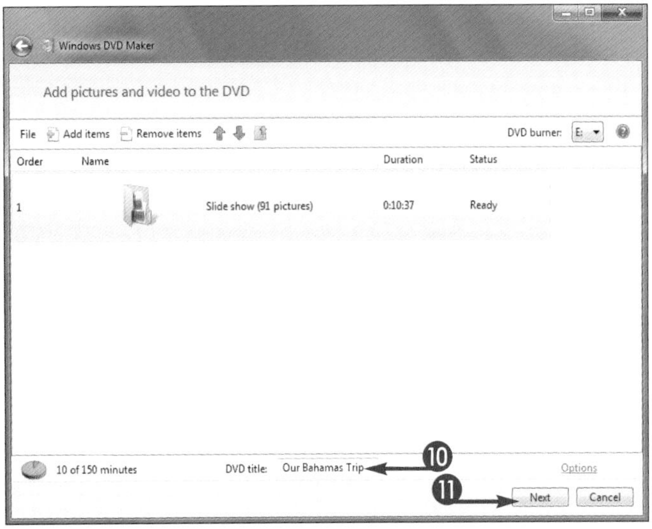

The Ready to Burn DVD window appears.

⑫ Click the menu style you want to use.

⑬ Click **Slide show**.

The Change Your Slide Show Settings window appears.

14 Click the **Picture length** ▾ and then click the length of time, in seconds, that you want each photo displayed.

15 Click the **Transition** ▾ and then click the type of transition you want between each photo.

16 To display each image with pan and zoom effect, click this option (☐ changes to ☑).

17 Click **Change Slide Show**.

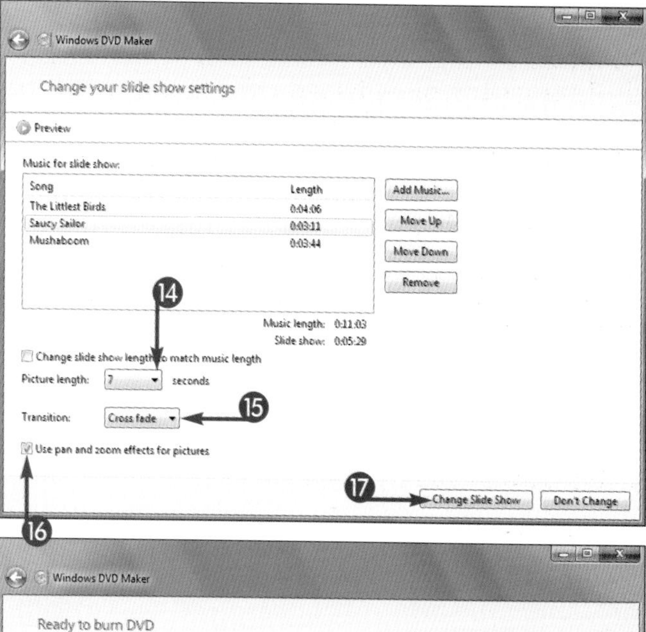


- If you want to see a preview of the disc before burning the slide show, click **Preview**.

18 Click **Burn**.

DVD Maker burns the slide show to the disc.

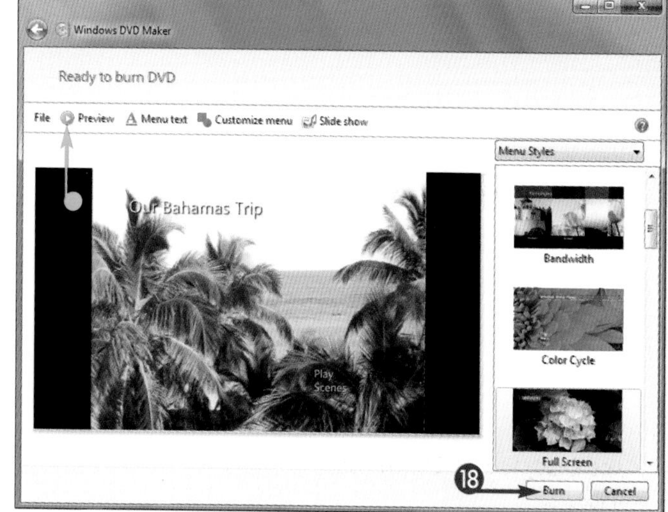

### Can I add a music soundtrack to my slide show?

Yes. In the Ready to Burn DVD window, click **Slide show** and then click **Add Music**. Use the Add Music to Slide Show dialog box to select the music file you want to play while the slide show is running, and then click **Add**.

### I do not need the Scenes button in the initial slide show window. How do I delete it?

In the Ready to Burn DVD window, click **Menu text** to display the Change the DVD Menu Text window. Delete the text in the Scenes button text box. You can also use this window to change the other button text and change the menu font. Click **Change Text** when you are finished.

CHAPTER 5

# Playing Music and Other Media

Using Windows Media Player, you can listen to audio files and music CDs, watch video files, play DVD discs, and even create your own music CDs. Using Windows Media Center, you can view pictures and videos on your TV, and listen to audio files through your stereo.

# Open and Close Windows Media Player

Windows 7 includes Windows Media Player to enable you to play back and record audio as well as view video. To begin using the program, you must first learn how to open the Windows Media Player window. When you finish using the program, you can close the Windows Media Player window to free up computer processing power.

## Open and Close Windows Media Player

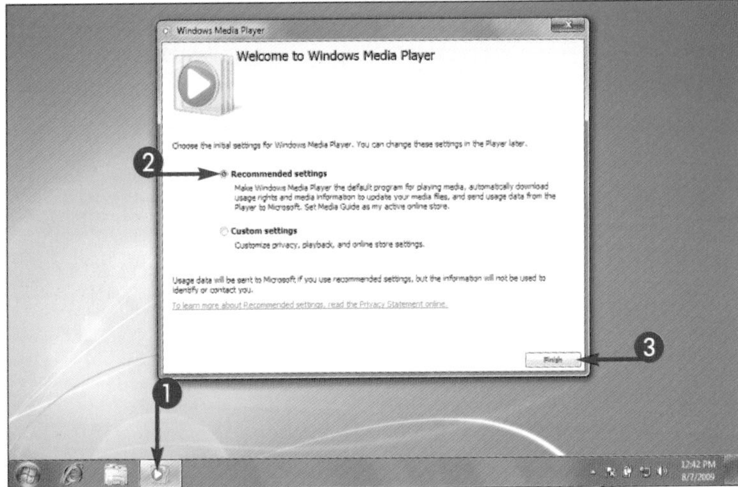


1. Click **Windows Media Player** (▢) in the taskbar.

*Note: If you do not see the Media Player icon, you can also click **Start**, click **All Programs**, and then click **Windows Media Player**.*

The first time you start the program, the Welcome to Windows Media Player dialog box appears.

2. Click **Recommended settings** (◯ changes to ◉).
3. Click **Finish**.

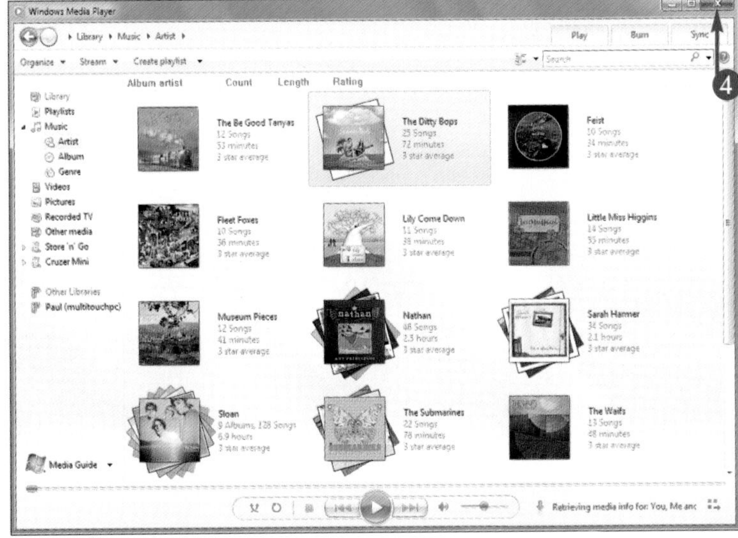


The Windows Media Player window appears.

4. When you have finished with Media Player, click the **Close** button (☒) to close the window.

The Windows Media Player window closes.

# Navigate the Media Player Window



Familiarizing yourself with the various elements of the Windows Media Player window is a good idea so that you can easily navigate and activate elements when you are ready to play audio files or view videos and DVDs.

### Address Bar

This area shows your current location in the Media Player library.

### Tabs

The tabs are links to the key features of Windows Media Player.

### Toolbar

You can use the Media Player toolbar to access commands, change the view, and search for media.

### Navigation Pane

You use this pane to navigate the Media Player library's categories.

### Playback Controls

These buttons control how a video or music file plays, and enable you to make adjustments to the sound.

### Details Pane

This pane displays information about the contents of the current library location, such as the album art and title, and the title and length of the song or video.

# Using the Library

You can use the library feature in Windows Media Player to manage all of the media files on your computer, including audio files and videos. The library also enables you to organize other digital content, such as music CDs.

**When you first start using Windows Media Player, the program automatically updates the library with the files already in your computer's media folders, such as Music and Videos.**

## Using the Library

### NAVIGATE THE LIBRARY

1. In the Navigation pane, click the category you want to use.
2. If the category includes subcategories, click a subcategory to see its contents.
3. Double-click the item you want to use.

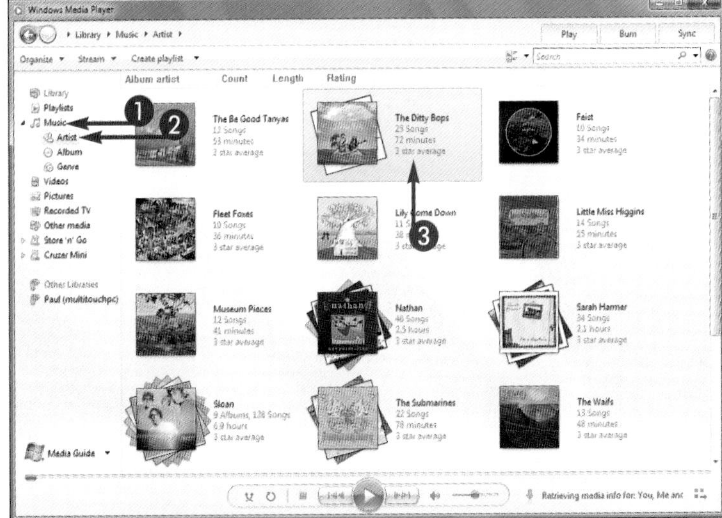


Media Player displays the contents of the item in the details pane.

- You can also click the items in the address bar to return to a category or subcategory.
- Click an arrow to see the contents of any address bar item.

## CHANGE THE LIBRARY VIEW

1. Click the **View options** ▾.
2. Click the view you want to use.

Media Player changes the view.

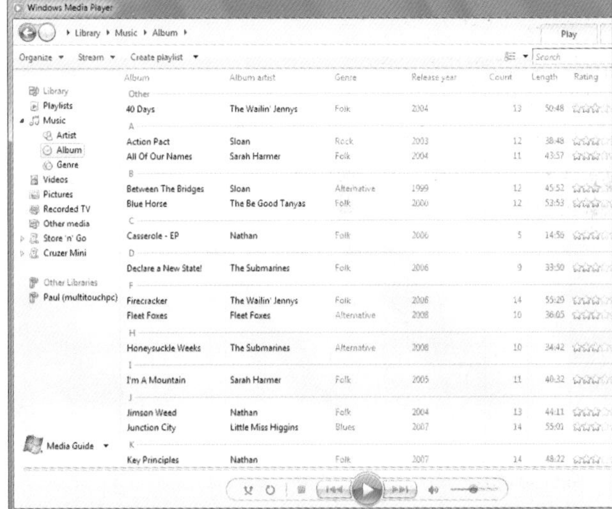

### My library is quite large. How do I search for a specific file?

If you want to search the entire library, click **Library** in the address bar. Otherwise, click the category you want to search, such as **Music**. Click in the search box on the right side of the toolbar. Type a word or phrase that represents the media you want to find. The matching media appear in the library.

### How does the library create its folders and subfolders?

The library automatically groups music into the categories based on their media content information. Media content information, also called *metadata* or *tags*, includes information such as the artist name, song title, rating, play count, and composer. Media content information also identifies the file type.

# Play an Audio or a Video File

Windows Media Player uses the library to play audio files that you store on your computer. When you select an audio file from a library folder and play it in Windows Media Player, you can also switch to the Now Playing view to see a visualization along with the song.

## Play an Audio or a Video File

1. Use the library to navigate to the folder that contains the audio or video file that you want to play.

***Note:*** *See "Using the Library" to learn more about working with the library's folder.*

2. Click the audio or video file.
3. Click the **Play** button (▶).
4. Click **Switch to Now Playing** (⊞) to view the album art while an audio file plays.

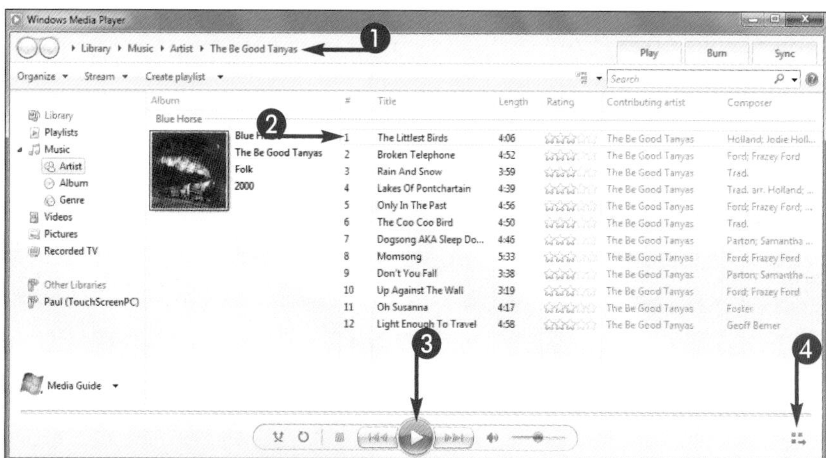


Windows Media Player begins playing the audio or video file.

5. Move the mouse ↖ into the Now Playing window.

- The playback buttons appear, which enable you to control how the song or video plays.

***Note:*** *See "Play a Music CD" to learn more about the playback buttons.*

- You can click **Switch to Library** (⊞) to return to the Media Player library.

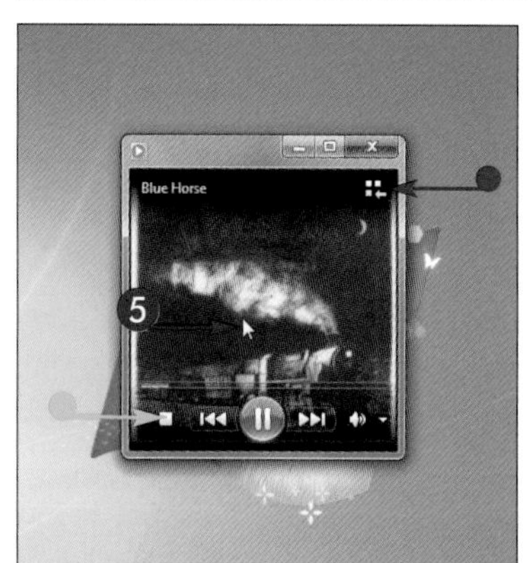

# Adjust the Volume

While an audio or video file is playing, you can adjust the volume in Windows Media Player up or down to get the audio just right. If you need to silence the media temporarily, you can mute the playback.

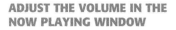

## Adjust the Volume

### ADJUST THE VOLUME USING THE LIBRARY

1. Click and drag the **Volume** slider left (to reduce the volume) or right (to increase the volume).

- If you want to silence the playback, click the **Mute** button ( ).

***Note:** To restore the volume, click the **Sound** button ( ).*

### ADJUST THE VOLUME IN THE NOW PLAYING WINDOW

1. Move the mouse within the Now Playing window.

   The playback controls appear.

2. Click here and then drag the **Volume** slider left (to reduce the volume) or right (to increase the volume).

- To silence the playback, click the **Mute** button ( ).

***Note:** To restore the volume, click the **Sound** button ( ).*

# Play a Music CD

You can play your favorite music CDs in Windows Media Player. You can control some playback options using the Now Playing window, but you can also switch to the Media Player library for more options.

## Play a Music CD

### PLAY A CD

1. Insert a music CD into your computer's CD or DVD drive.

   If Media Player is not already running, the Now Playing window appears and the CD begins playing.

- On commercial CDs, the album cover appears here.

2. Move the mouse within the Now Playing window.

- The playback controls appear.

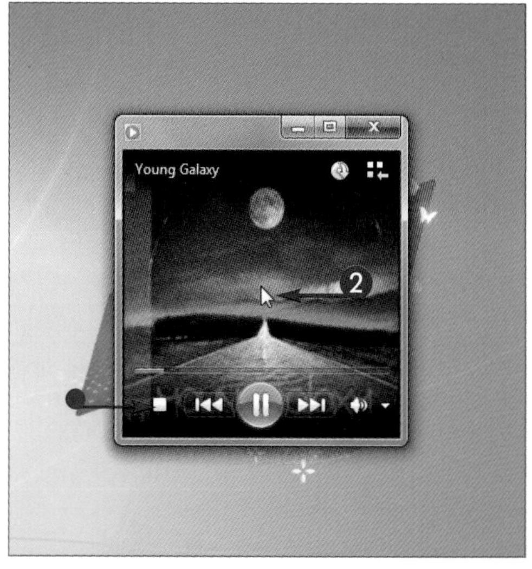

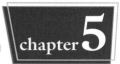

### SKIP A TRACK

3. Click the **Next** button (⏭) to skip to the next track.
4. Click the **Previous** button (⏮) to skip to the previous track.

### PAUSE AND RESUME PLAY

5. Click the **Pause** button (⏸).

   Windows Media Player pauses playback.
6. Click the **Play** button (▶).

   Windows Media Player resumes playback where you left off.

**Can I change the CD's audio levels?**

Yes, Windows Media Player has a graphic equalizer component you can work with. To display it, right-click the **Now Playing** window, click **Enhancements**, and then click **Graphic Equalizer**. To choose a predefined set of levels, click **Default**, and then click a preset value such as Rock or Classical. Alternatively, use the sliders to set your own audio levels.

**Can I display something other than album art during playback?**

Yes. Right-click the **Now Playing** window and then click **Visualizations** to see a list of visualization categories. Click a category and then click the visualization you want to view. The visualizations in the Battery category are fun to play with, as their names suggest: Dance of the Freaky Circles, Green Is Not Your Enemy, Spider's Last Moment, and My Tornado Is Resting.

continued

# Play a Music CD *(continued)*

You can use the playback buttons at the bottom of the Windows Media Player library to control how a CD plays. For example, you can stop a CD and then select another song to play, you can repeat the entire CD, or you can play the songs randomly.

## Play a Music CD *(continued)*

### STOP PLAY

7. Click the **Stop** button (■).

   Windows Media Player stops playback.

   If you click the **Play** button (▶) after clicking the **Stop** button (■), the current song starts over again.

8. Click **Switch to Library** (⊞) to open the Media Player library window.

### PLAY ANOTHER SONG

9. In the Details pane, double-click the song you want to play.

   Windows Media Player begins playing the song.

- This area displays the current song title, the album title, and the song composer.

## REPEAT THE CD

⑩ Click the **Turn Repeat On** button (⟳).

Windows Media Player restarts the CD after the last track finishes playing.

***Note:** To turn on Repeat from the Now Playing window, press Ctrl + T.*

## PLAY SONGS RANDOMLY

⑪ Click the **Turn Shuffle On** button (⤮).

Windows Media Player shuffles the order of play.

***Note:** To turn on Shuffle from the Now Playing window, press Ctrl + H.*

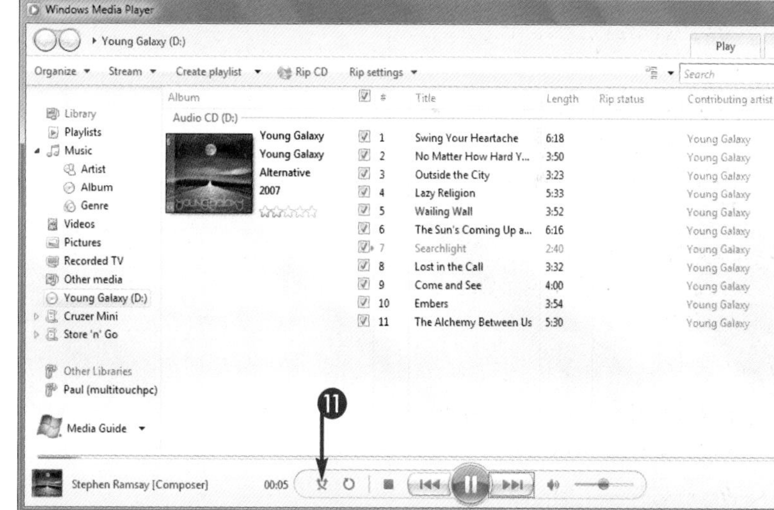

### My Details pane does not list the song titles. Why not?

Windows Media Player tries to gather information about the album from the Internet. If it cannot ascertain song titles, then it displays track numbers instead. To add your own titles, right-click the song title you want to change and click **Edit**. Type your text and press Enter. You can also press F2 and then Tab to edit a song title.

### Is there a way to keep the Now Playing window in view at all times?

Yes. You can configure the Now Playing window so that it stays on top of any other window that you have open on your desktop. This enables you to control the playback no matter what other programs are running on your PC. Right-click the Now Playing window and then click **Always show Now Playing on top**.

# Copy Tracks from a Music CD

You can add tracks from a music CD to the library in Windows Media Player. This enables you to listen to an album without having to put the CD into your CD or DVD drive each time. The process of adding tracks from a CD is called *copying*, or *ripping*, in Windows 7.

**You can either rip an entire CD directly from the Now Playing window, or you can rip selected tracks using the library.**

## Copy Tracks from a Music CD

### RIP AN ENTIRE CD USING THE NOW PLAYING WINDOW

1. Insert a CD into your computer's CD or DVD drive.

   The Now Playing window appears.

2. Click **Rip CD** ( ).

   Media Player begins ripping the entire CD.

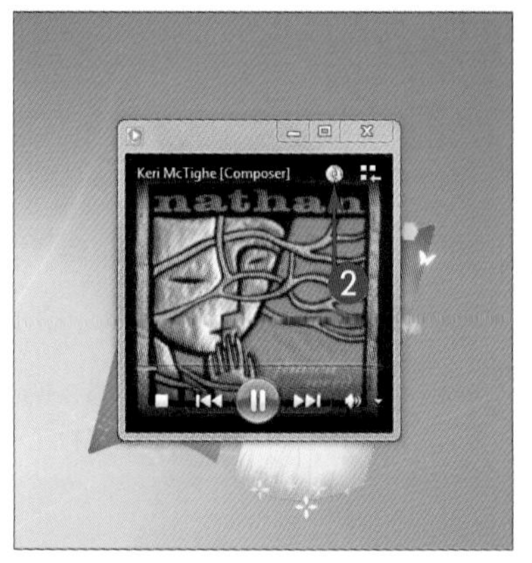


### RIP SELECTED TRACKS USING THE LIBRARY

1. Insert a CD into your computer's CD or DVD drive.

   If the Now Playing window appears, click **Switch to Library**.

- Media Player displays a list of the CD's tracks.

2. Click the CD tracks that you do not want to copy ( changes to ).

3. Click **Rip CD**.

Windows Media Player begins copying the track or tracks.

- The Rip Status column displays the copy progress.

- After each file is copied, the Rip Status column displays a Ripped to Library message.
- The copy is complete when all the tracks you selected display the Ripped to Library status.

## TIPS

### I ripped a track by accident. How do I remove it from the library?

In the library, click **Music**, click **Album**, and then double-click the album that you ripped to display a list of the tracks. Right-click the track that you want to remove, and then click **Delete** from the menu that appears.

### Can I adjust the quality of the copies?

Yes. You do that by changing the *bit rate*, which is a measure of how much of the CD's original data gets copied to your computer. This is measured in kilobits per second (Kbps): the higher the value the higher the quality, but the more disk space each track takes up. Click **Rip Settings**, click **Audio Quality** from the menu that appears, and then click the value you want.

# Create a Playlist

A *playlist* is a collection of songs, or music tracks you copy from a music CD, store on your computer hard drive, or download from the Internet. You can create customized playlists in Windows Media Player that play only the songs that you want to hear.

## Create a Playlist

❶ Click **Create playlist**.

- Windows Media Player creates a new playlist folder.

❷ Type a name for the new playlist.

❸ Press Enter.

4 Click and drag items from the library and drop them on the playlist.

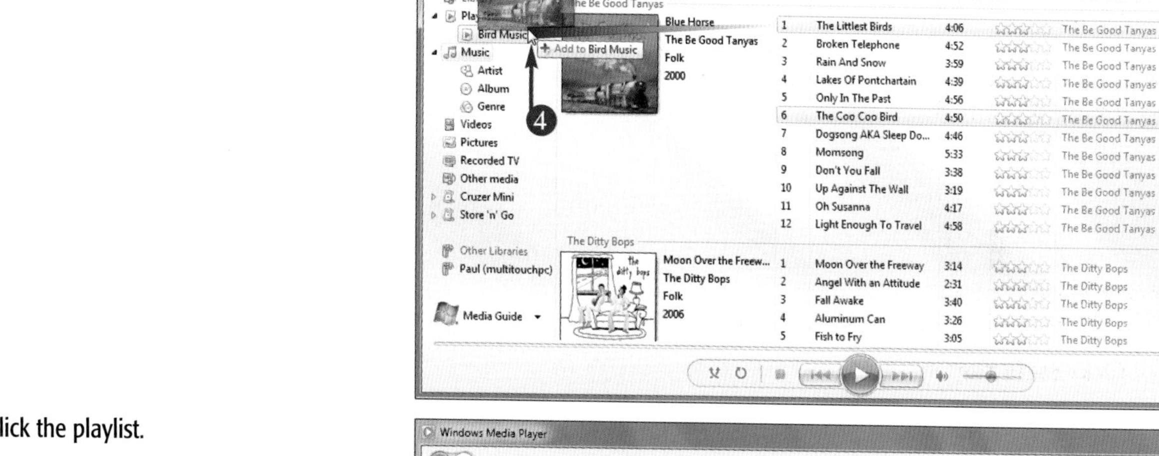

5 Click the playlist.

The Details pane shows the songs you added.

6 Click and drag the songs to change the playlist order.

7 Click **Play** (▶) to listen to the playlist.

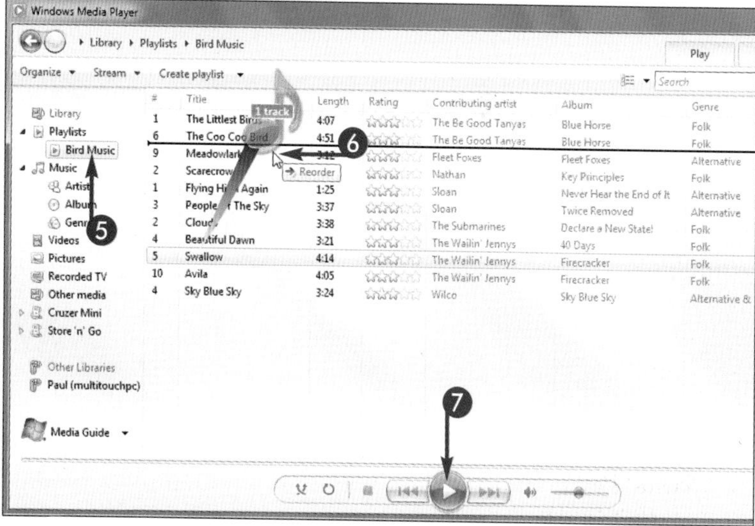

### Can I add items to an existing playlist?

Yes, there are a couple of methods you can use. The first method is to repeat Step **4** for any other items you want to add to the playlist. The second method is to locate the song you want to add, right-click the song, click **Add to**, and then click the name of the playlist in the menu that appears.

### Why does Media Player show only my most recently created playlists in the Navigation pane?

By default, Media Player's Navigation pane is configured to show only the five most recent playlists. If you prefer to see all your playlists, right-click any item in the Navigation pane and then click **Customize navigation pane**. In the Customize Navigation Pane dialog box, click the **All** check box that appears under the Playlists branch (☐ changes to ☑).

# Burn Music Files to a CD

You can copy, or *burn*, music files from your computer onto a CD. Burning CDs is a great way to create customized CDs that you can listen to on the computer or in a portable device. You can burn music files from within the Windows Media Player window.

## Burn Music Files to a CD

1. Insert a blank CD into your computer's recordable CD drive.
2. Click the **Burn** tab.
   - The Burn list appears.

3. Click and drag items from the library and drop them inside the Burn list.
4. Repeat Step **3** to add more files to the Burn list.

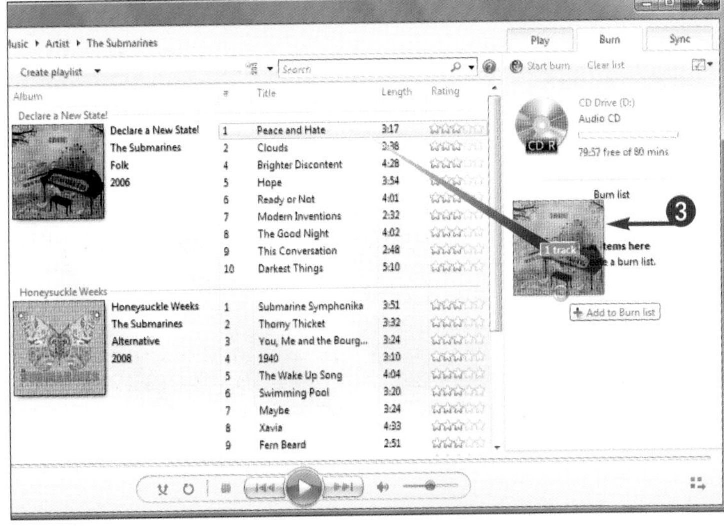

- Windows Media Player adds the files to the Burn list.
- Windows Media Player updates the approximate time remaining on the disc.

5 Click **Start burn**.

Windows Media Player converts the files to CD tracks and copies them to the CD.

- The Burn tab shows the progress of the burn.

***Note:** When the recording is complete, Windows Media Player automatically ejects the disc. Do not attempt to eject the disc yourself before the burn is finished.*

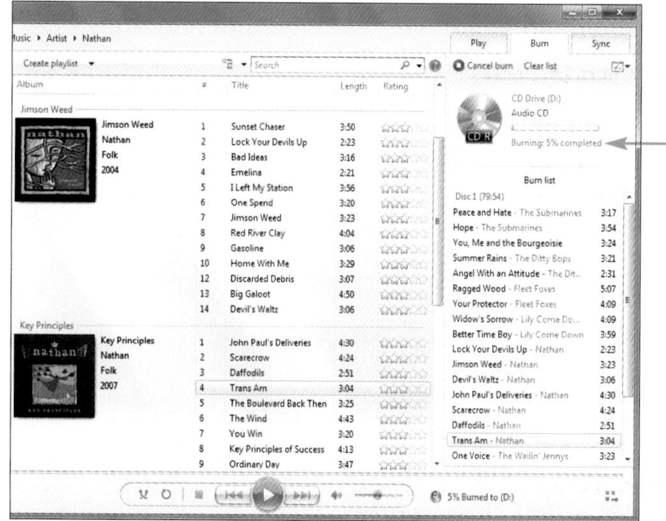

### Do I have to burn the songs in the order they appear in the list?

No, Media Player offers several options for rearranging the tracks before burning. Perhaps the easiest method is to click and drag a track and then drop it in the list location you prefer. You can also click **Burn options** (▾) and then click either **Shuffle list** or **Sort list by** and then click a sort order.

### What happens if I have more music than can fit on a single disc?

You can still add all the music you want to burn to the Burn list. Windows Media Player fills the first disc and then starts on a second disk (look for Disc 2 in the Burn list). After the program finishes burning the first disc, it prompts you to insert the next one.

# Play a DVD

You can use Windows Media Player to play DVDs. Windows Media Player enables you to watch any multimedia items stored on a DVD, such as movies and video footage.

**Depending on how you set up your DVD drive and Windows Media Player, your DVD may begin playing as soon as you insert it. If it does not, you can follow the steps in this section to initiate playback.**

## Play a DVD

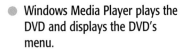

1. Insert a DVD into your computer's DVD drive.
2. In Windows Media Player, click the DVD in the Navigation pane.
3. Click **Play** (▶).

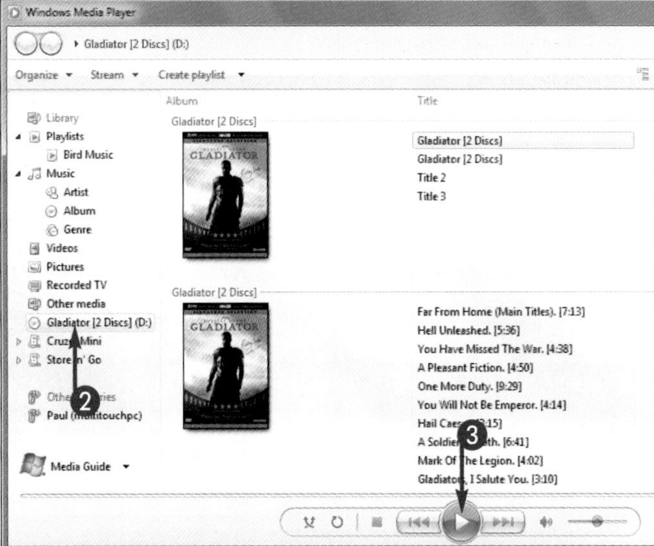


- Windows Media Player plays the DVD and displays the DVD's menu.

  DVD menu items can vary in appearance and use different layouts.

4. Click the menu item or feature you want to access.

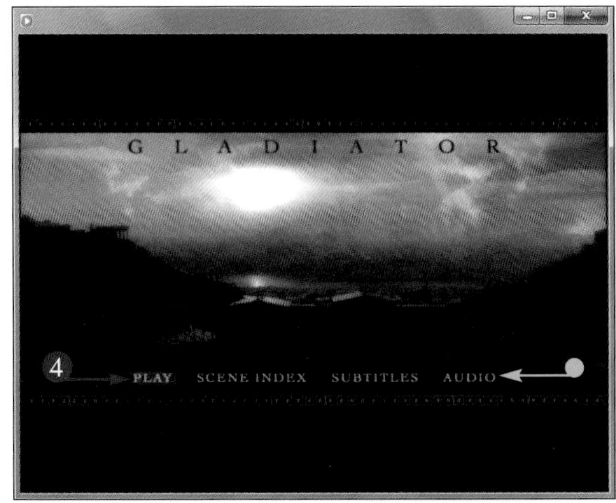

Windows Media Player begins playback.

5 To control playback, position the mouse within the DVD window.

- Media Player displays the playback controls.
- You can click the **DVD** ▾ to see a list of DVD options.

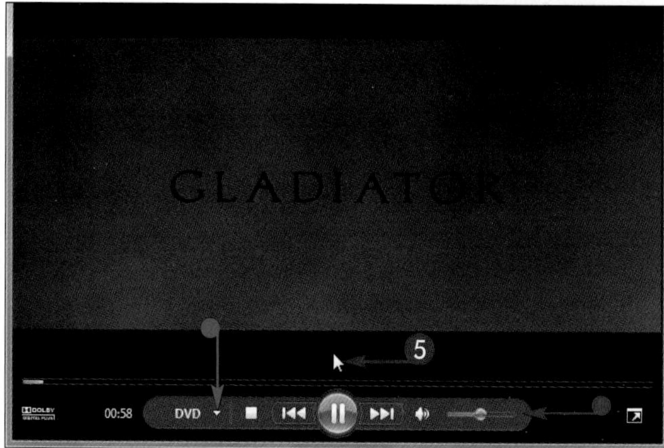


- You can use the DVD options to return to the main menu, select special features, and display the DVD full-screen.

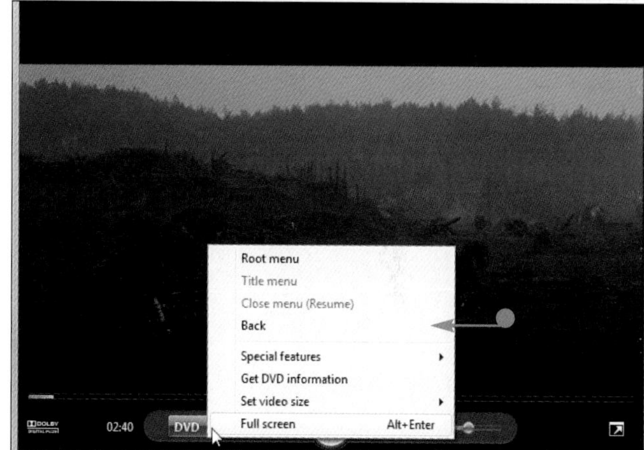

## Can I restrict the DVDs my kids watch?

Yes. First, set up your kids with Standard user accounts (Chapter 7). Then, in Windows Media Player:

1. Click **Organize** and then click **Options**.
2. In the Options dialog box, click the **DVD** tab.
3. Click **Change**.
4. In the Change Rating Restriction dialog box, click ▾ and then click the maximum rating you want.
5. Click **OK**, and click **OK** again in the **Options** dialog box.

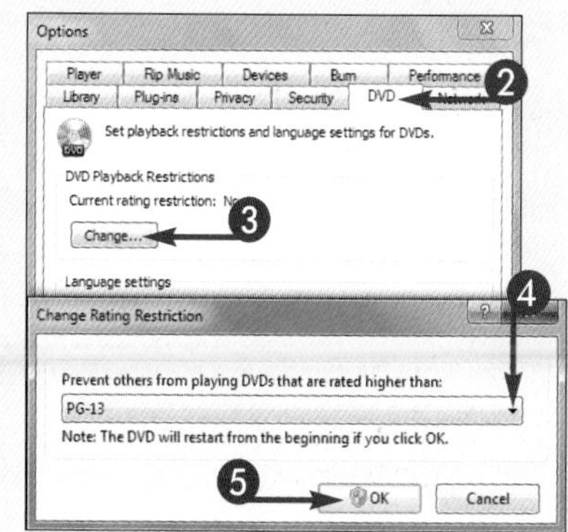

# Navigate a DVD

You can control how a DVD plays by using the various navigation controls in the Windows Media Player window. The window includes volume and playback controls. You can also navigate to different scenes using the list of tracks in the Playlist pane. All scenes, or tracks, stem from a root menu that directs you to the DVD's contents.

**Throughout this section, note that you must position the mouse within the DVD window to display the playback controls.**

## Navigate a DVD

### STOP AND START A DVD

1. Click the **Stop** button (■).

   Windows Media Player stops the DVD playback.

2. Click the **Play** button (▶).

   Windows Media Player restarts the playback from the beginning.

   You can also click the **Pause** button (⏸) to pause the playback if you want to resume playing in the same scene.

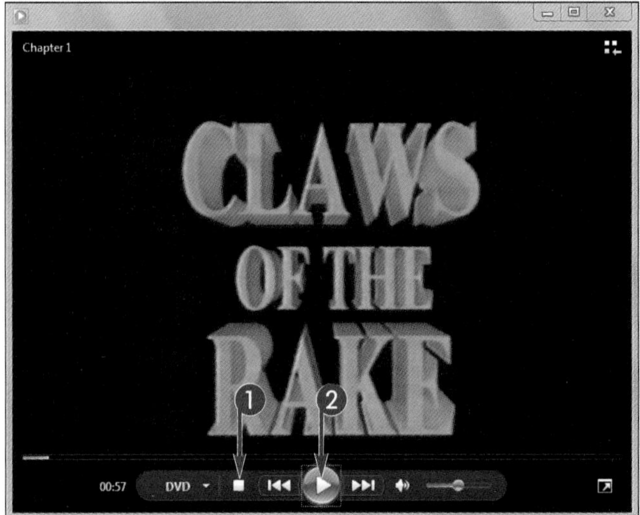


### NAVIGATE SCENES

1. Click the **Previous** button (⏮).

   Windows Media Player jumps to the previous scene.

2. Click the **Next** button (⏭).

   Windows Media Player jumps to the next scene.

- You can also rewind or fast-forward the DVD by clicking and dragging the **Seek** slider.

### RETURN TO THE ROOT MENU

1. Click the **DVD** .
2. Click **Root menu**.

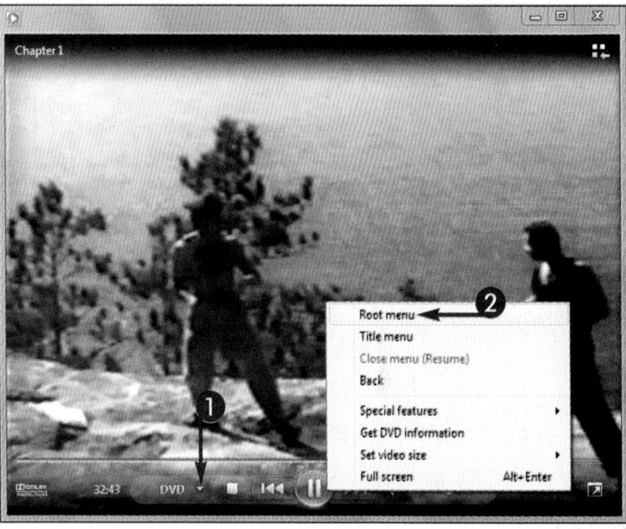


The DVD's opening menu appears in the Windows Media Player window.

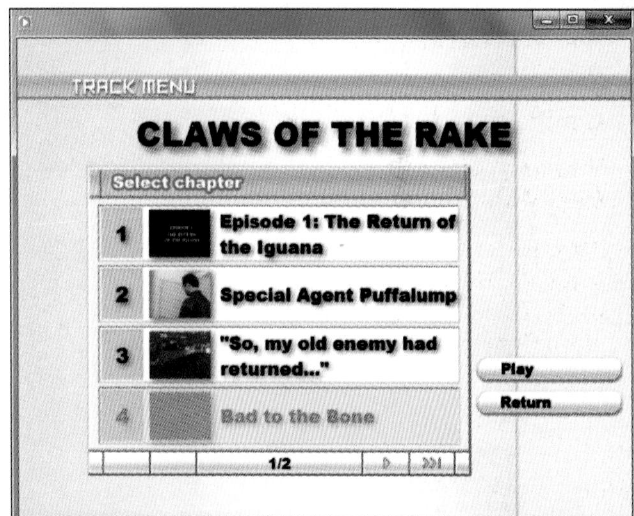

#### What is a root menu?

The *root menu* is the opening menu of a DVD, and it typically displays links to the various segments, features, or clips on the DVD. You can return to the root menu at any time to access other DVD elements. On full-screen view, you can quickly access the root menu with a shortcut menu. Right-click over the DVD screen, click **DVD features**, and then click **Root menu**.

#### Can I adjust the DVD's play speed?

Yes, you can choose from three settings: Slow, Normal, or Fast. The Slow setting plays the DVD in slow motion. The Normal setting plays the DVD at normal speed. The Fast setting accelerates the play. To change the play speed, right-click the **Play** button ( ), and then click **Slow playback** (or press Ctrl + Shift + S), **Normal playback** (or press Ctrl + Shift + N), or **Fast playback** (or press Ctrl + Shift + G).

# Connect Your PC and Your Home Theater

With the appropriate hardware, you can connect your computer to your television and stereo system. You can then use the Media Center program to display DVDs and pictures on your TV and play music on your stereo.

**In some cases, you can also attach a television cable to your computer and then watch and record TV shows on your PC.**

### TV Connection

To view computer-based DVDs, images, and video files on your TV, run an HDMI cable from the HDMI output port on the back of your computer's video card to the HDMI input port on the back of your TV. (Older computers and TVs may require an S-Video connection, instead.)

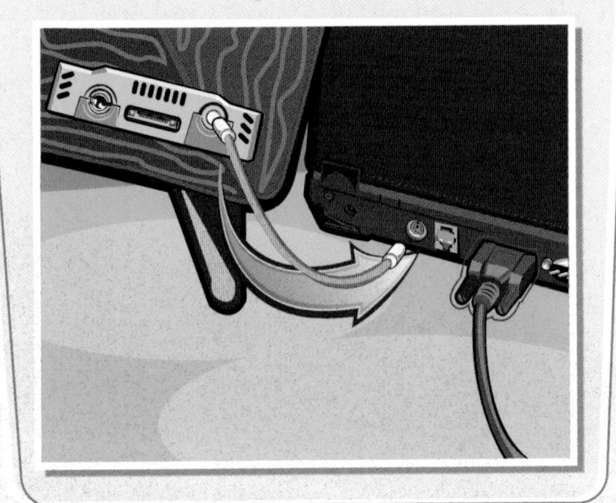

### Stereo Connection

To listen to computer-based music and sound files through your stereo system, run audio cables (red and white connectors) from the appropriate ports in the back of your computer's sound card to the corresponding input jacks on the back of your stereo receiver.

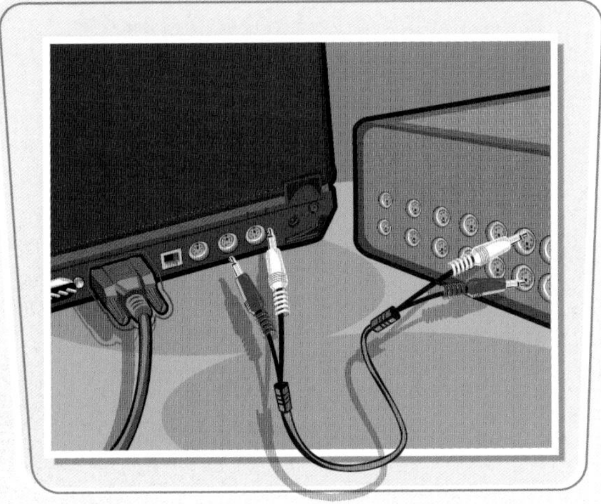

### TV-to-PC

A *TV tuner* is an internal or external device that captures an incoming TV signal. You can use it to watch and record TV on your computer. Attach a TV cable to the TV tuner's cable jack. Alternatively, you can run RCA cables or an S-Video cable from your TV's output jacks (if it has them) to the corresponding ports on the TV tuner.

### Remote Control

You can purchase a special remote control that enables you to use the Media Center program on your TV. This enables you to use Media Center from your couch because you do not need to use the computer directly. For those times when you must use the computer, you can also add a wireless keyboard and mouse to your system.

### Media Extender

A *media extender* is a wireless device that takes the signal from a remote PC and relays it to your TV. This saves you from having a PC in the same room as your TV. An example of a media extender is the Xbox 360 gaming console.

# What You Can Do with Media Center

The Media Center program is designed to be a hub around which you can view and work with all the media files on your computer as well as view and work with your TV and stereo system.

### Play DVDs

If your computer has a DVD drive, you can insert a DVD movie and then start the movie for playback on your computer monitor or on your TV.

### Play Music

Media Player picks up the music files in your Music folder. You can view the music by title, artist, or genre, edit file data, and delete files. You also have many options for playing music, including shuffle and repeat.

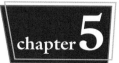

### View Pictures

Media Player picks up the images you have in your Pictures folder. You can manipulate the images and then display them in a slide show using animated transitions. You can also listen to music during the slide show.

### Listen to Internet Audio

Media Player offers links to a number of online sites that offer music, news, sports, and other audio content. You can also listen to some Internet-based radio stations.

### Burn CDs and DVDs

Media Player enables you to burn files to a disc. If you have a recordable CD drive, you can burn music to an audio CD or any files to a data CD. If you have a recordable DVD drive, you can burn music, images, video, or recorded TV to a DVD.

### Record TV

You can use Media Player as a *digital video recorder*, which enables you to record TV programs to your hard drive as you watch them, or at scheduled times. You can also pause, rewind, and fast-forward live TV, as well as watch instant replays.

# Open and Close Media Center

To begin using Media Center, you must first learn how to find and open the Media Center window. When you finish using the program, you can close the Media Center window to free up computer processing power.

## Open and Close Media Center

1. Click **Start**.
2. Click **All Programs**.

***Note:*** *When you click All Programs, the command changes to Back.*

3. Click **Windows Media Center**.

***Note:*** *The first time you start Media Center, you must run through a set of screens designed to configure the program.*

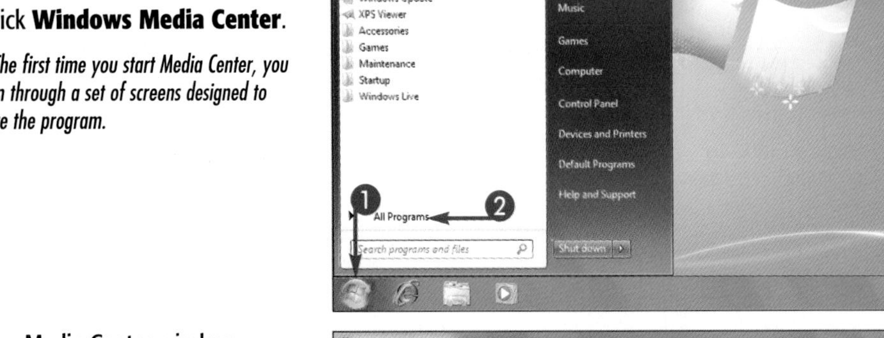


The Media Center window appears.

4. When you have finished with Media Center, click the **Close** button (✕) to close the window.

The Media Center window closes.

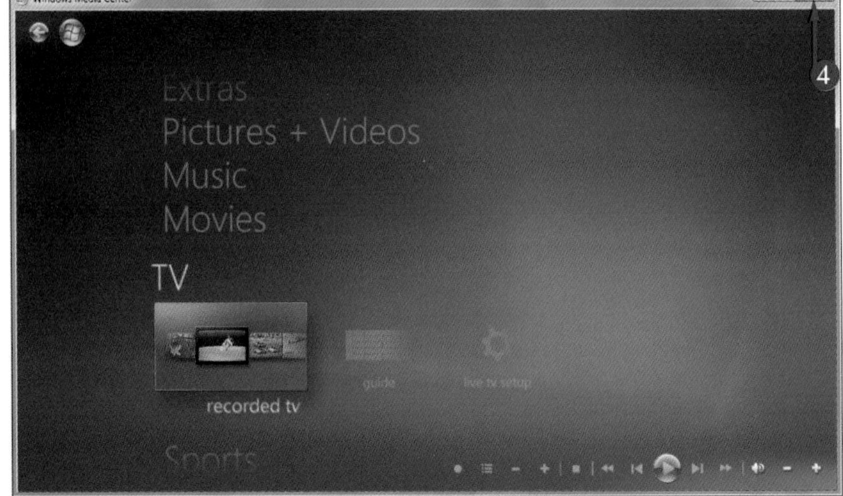

# Navigate the Media Center Window

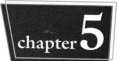

Familiarizing yourself with the various elements of the Media Center window is a good idea so that you can easily navigate and activate elements when you are ready to play audio files or view videos and DVDs.

**Back**

Click this button to return to the previous Media Center screen.

**Main Menu**

These items represent the main Media Center features.

**Tasks**

Each main menu item has one or more tasks that you can perform.

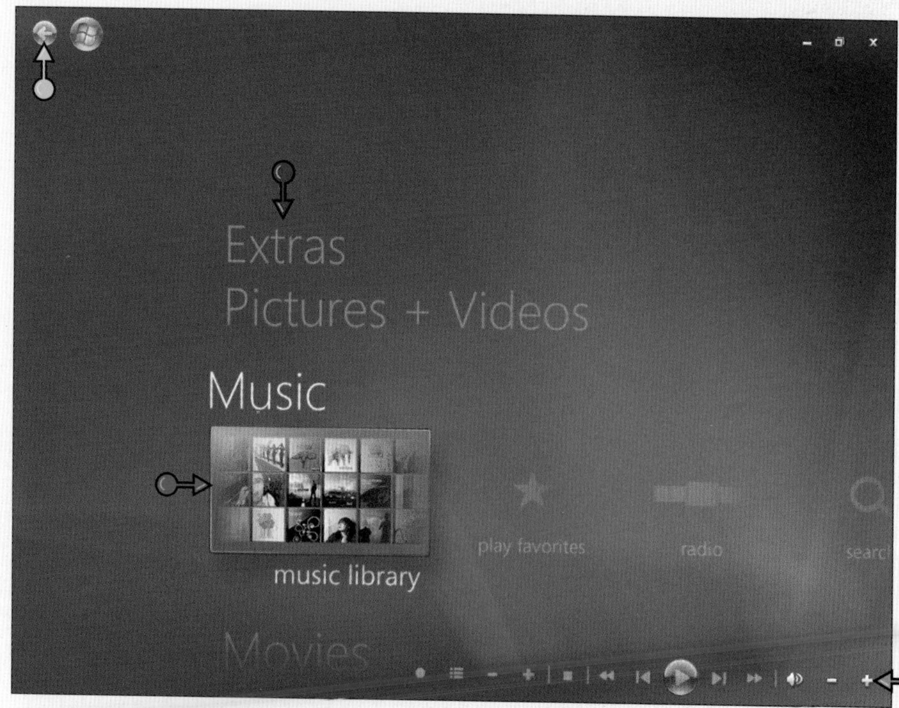


**Playback Controls**

These buttons control how a DVD or music file plays, and they enable you to make adjustments to the sound.

# Run a Media Center Slide Show

You can use Media Player to run a slide show of images in your Pictures folder. After you start the slide show, the feature automatically advances and displays each image in the folder as a slide.

**Each image is displayed for 12 seconds, and Media Center uses an animated transition between images.**

## Run a Media Center Slide Show

1. In Media Center, navigate to the Pictures + Videos section.
2. Click **picture library**.

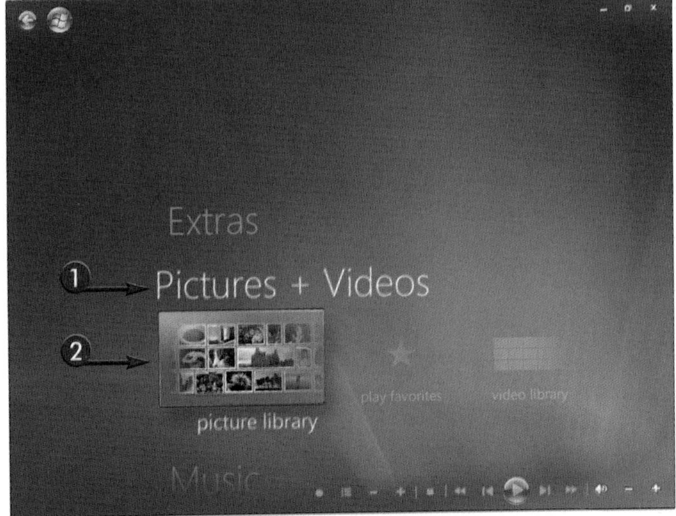


The Media Center picture library appears.

3. Click **play slide show**.

The slide show begins.

4. Click the **Next** button (▶) to advance to the next picture.
5. Click the **Previous** button (◀) to return to the previous picture.
6. Click the **Pause** button (⏸) to pause the slide show.

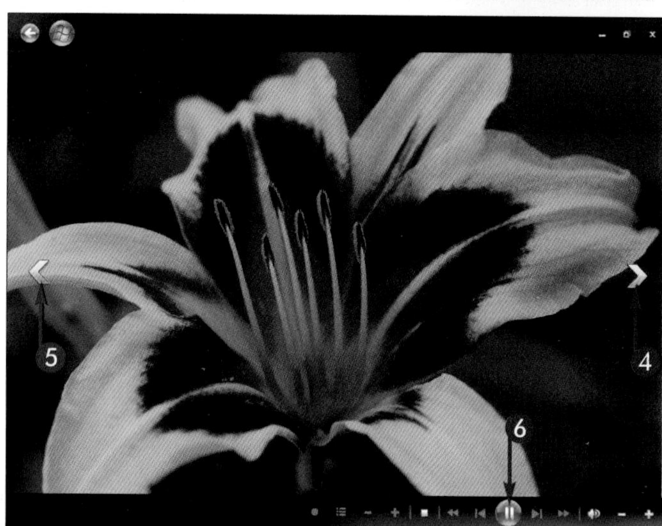


7. Click the **Play** button (▶) to resume the slide show.
8. Click the **Stop** button (■) to stop the slide show.

**Can I display the slide show images in random order?**

Yes, in the main Media Center menu, navigate to **Tools** and then click **settings**. Click **Pictures** to display the picture settings. Click **Show pictures in random order** (☐ changes to ☑). If you also want to see the name of the each picture and the date it was created, click **Show caption** (☐ changes to ☑). Click **Save**.

**How do I change the amount of time that Media Center displays each image?**

In the main Media Center menu, navigate to **Tasks** and then click **settings**. Click **Pictures** and then use the **Transition time** controls to set the time each image is displayed: click **plus** (+) to increase the time; click **minus** (–) to decrease the time. Click **Save** when you are done.

CHAPTER

# Working with Files

This chapter shows you how to work with the files on your computer. These easy and efficient methods show you how to view, select, copy, move, rename, and delete files, as well as how to copy files to a CD and how to create new folders to hold your files.

# View Your Files

You can view the files you create, as well as those stored on your hard drive that you download and copy to your computer. If you want to open or work with those files, you first need to view them.

## View Your Files

❶ Click **Start**.

❷ Click your user name.

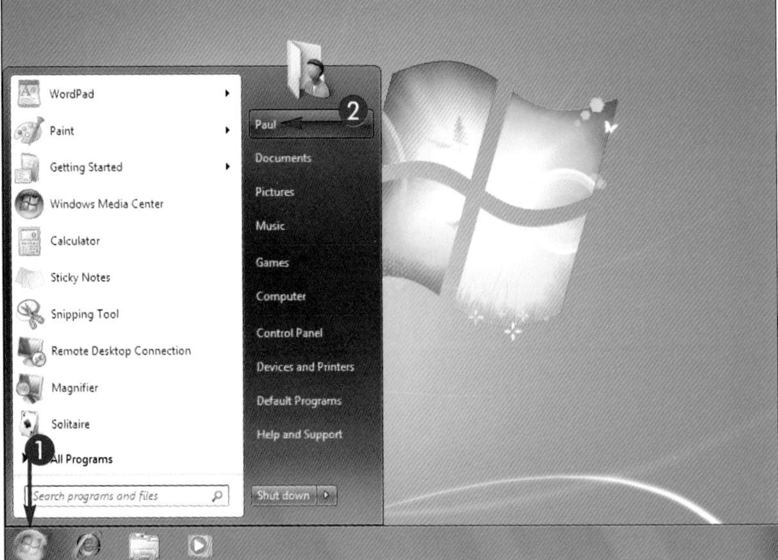


- Windows 7 displays your user folder.

❸ Double-click the folder you want to view.

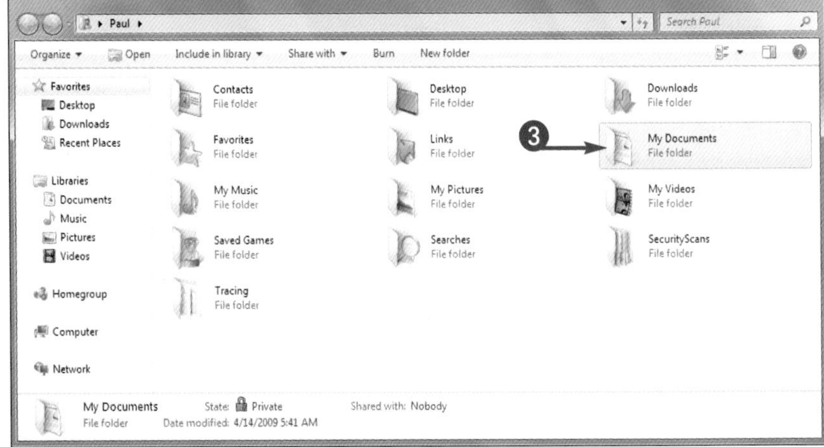

Windows 7 displays the contents of the folder including subfolders.

4 If the files you want to view are stored in a subfolder, double-click the subfolder.

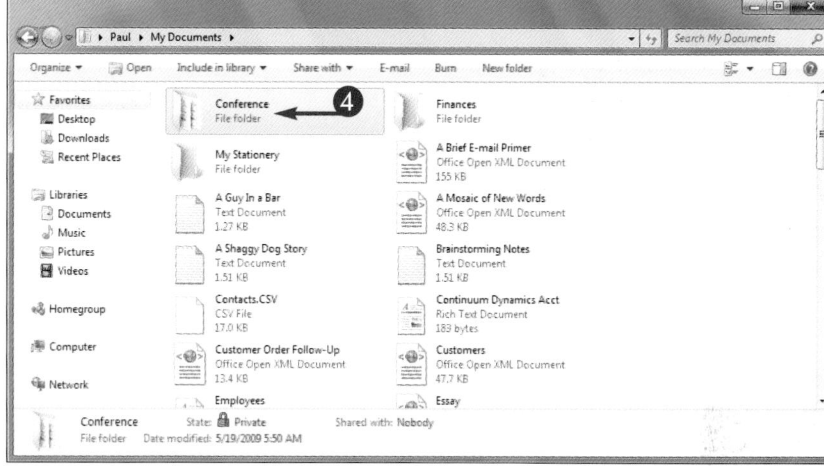


Windows 7 displays the contents of the subfolder.

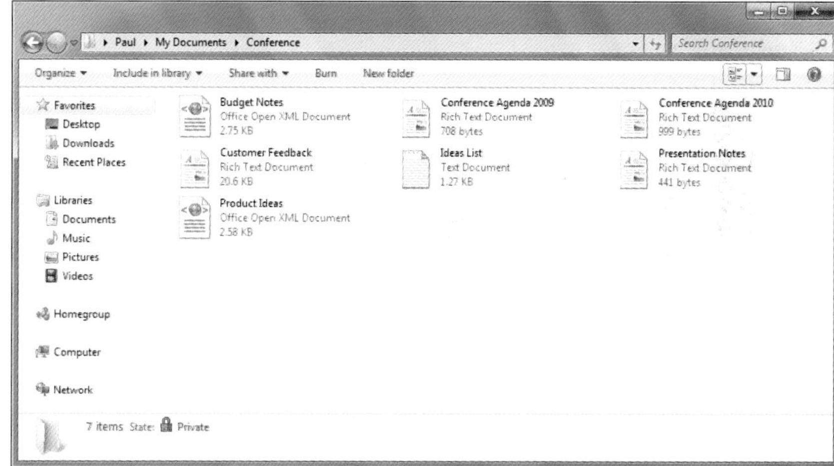

**How do I view the files I have on a CD, Flash drive, memory card, or other media?**

Insert the media into the appropriate drive or slot on your computer. If you see the AutoPlay window, click **Open folder to view files**. Otherwise, click **Start** and then click **Computer** to display the Computer window, and then double-click the disk drive or device that contains the files you want to view. Windows 7 displays the contents of the media.

**What is a file library?**

In Windows 7, the four main document storage areas — Documents, Music, Pictures, and Videos — are set up as *libraries*, where each library consists of two or more folders. For example, the Documents library consists of your My Documents folder and the Public Documents folder. To add a folder to a library, click the **locations** link and then click **Add**.

# Select a File

Whether you want to rename a file, move several files to a new location, or delete some files, you first have to select the files so that Windows 7 knows exactly the ones you want to work with.

**Although you learn specifically about selecting files in this section, the technique for selecting folders is exactly the same.**

## Select a File

### SELECT A SINGLE FILE

1. Open the folder containing the file.
2. Click the file.

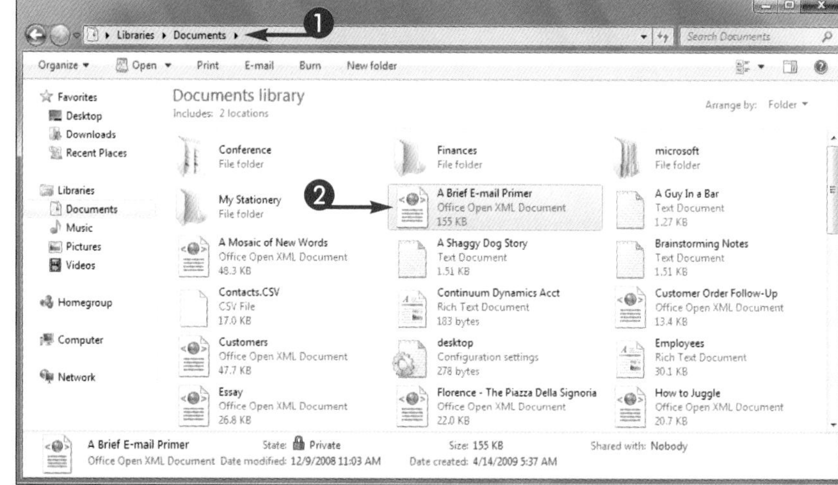


### SELECT MULTIPLE FILES

1. Open the folder containing the files.
2. Click the first file you want to select.
3. Press and hold Ctrl and click each of the other files you want to select.

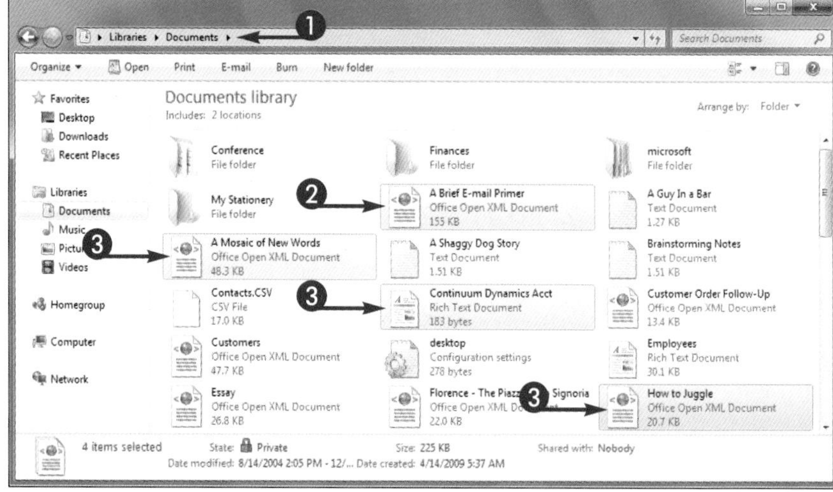

## SELECT A GROUP OF FILES

1. Open the folder containing the files.
2. Position the mouse slightly above and slightly to the left of the first file in the group.
3. Click and drag the mouse down and to the right until all the files in the group are selected.

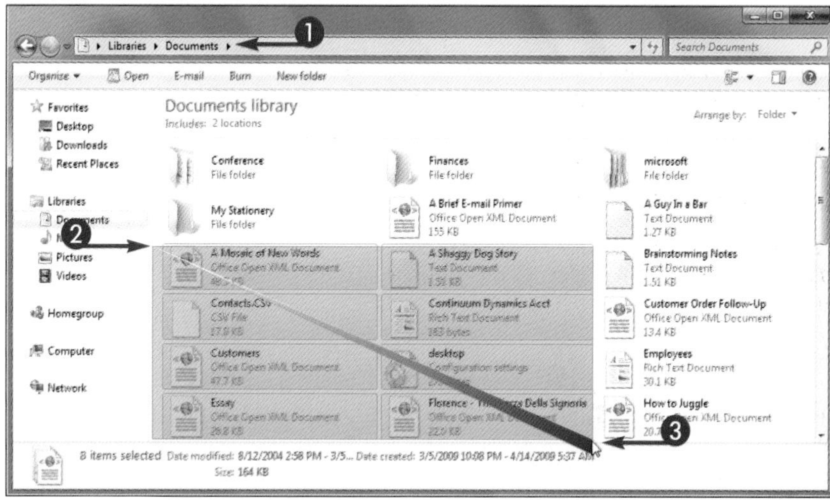


## SELECT ALL FILES

1. Open the folder containing the files.
2. Click **Organize**.
3. Click **Select all**.

- Windows Explorer selects all the files in the folder.

***Note:*** *A quick way to select all the files in a folder is to press* Ctrl *+* A.

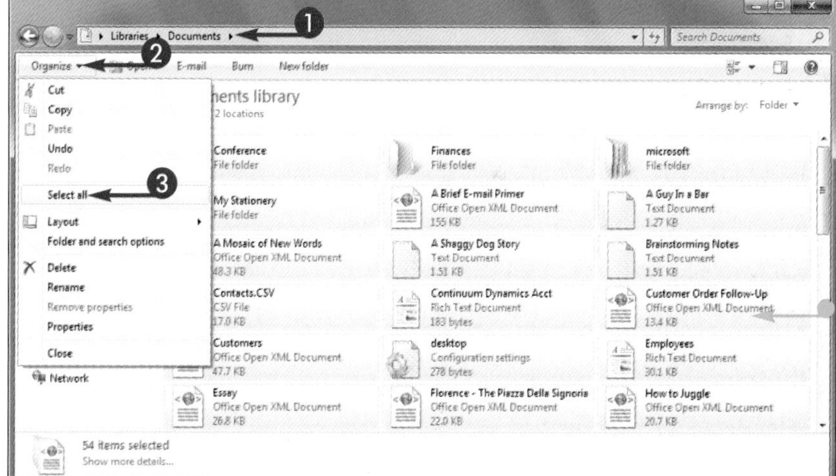

### How do I deselect a file?

- To deselect a single file from a multiple-file selection, press and hold Ctrl and click the file you want to deselect.
- To deselect all files, click an empty area within the folder.
- To reverse the selection — deselect the selected files and select the deselected files — press Alt, click **Edit**, and then click **Invert Selection**.

# Change the File View

You can configure how Windows 7 displays the files in a folder by changing the file view. This enables you to see larger or smaller icons or the details of each file.

**Choose a view such as Small Icons to see more files in the folder window. If you want to see more information about the files, choose either the Tiles view or Details view.**

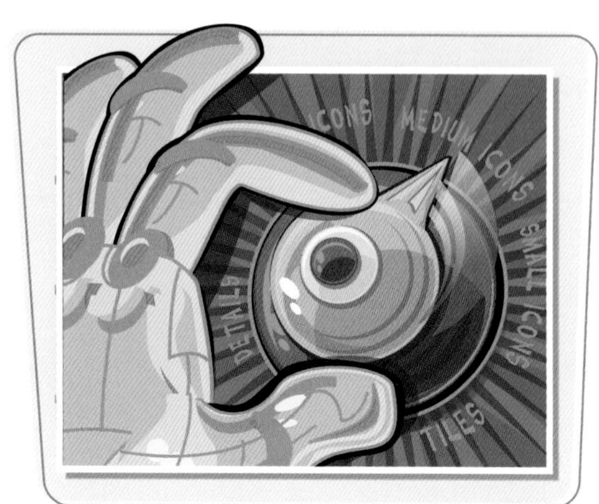


## Change the File View

1. Open the folder containing the files you want to view.
2. Click the **Views** ▾ to open the Views list.

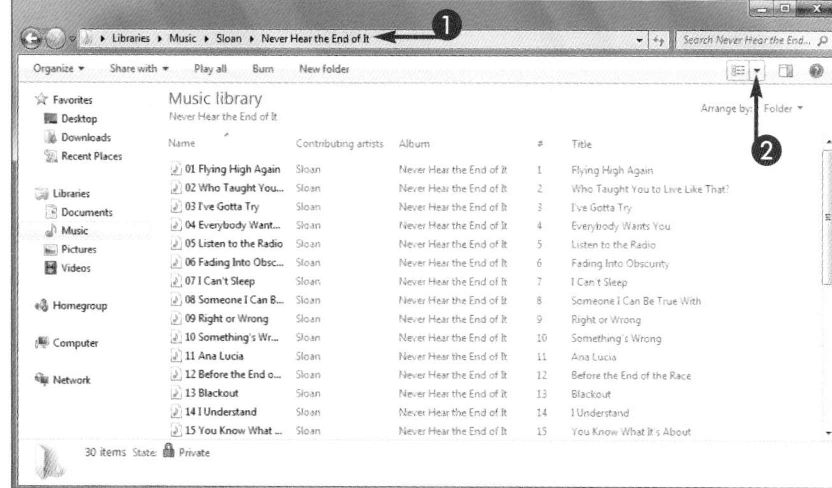


3. Click the view you want.

- The slider points to the current view. You can also click and drag the slider to select a view.
- Windows Explorer changes the file view (to Tiles, in this example).

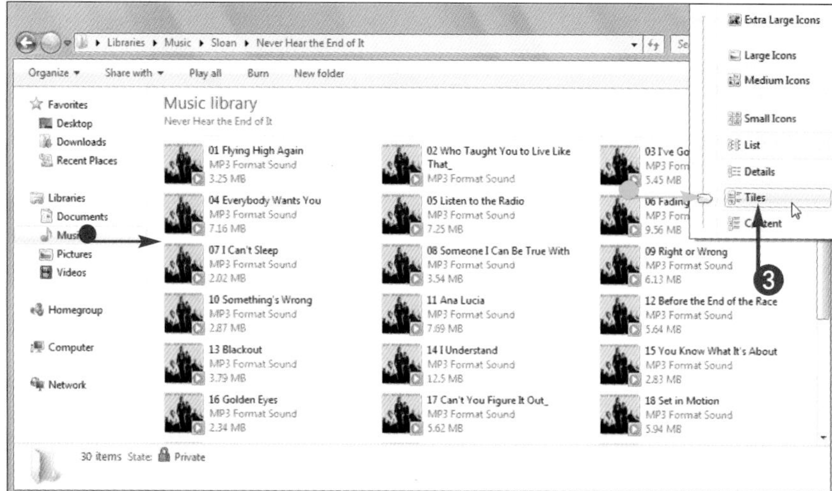

# Preview a File

Windows 7 enables you to view the contents of some files without opening them. This makes it easier to select the file you want to work with.

**Windows 7 only previews certain types of files, such as text documents, rich text documents, Web pages, images, and videos.**

## Preview a File

1. Open the folder containing the file you want to preview.
2. Click the **Preview pane** icon (▯).

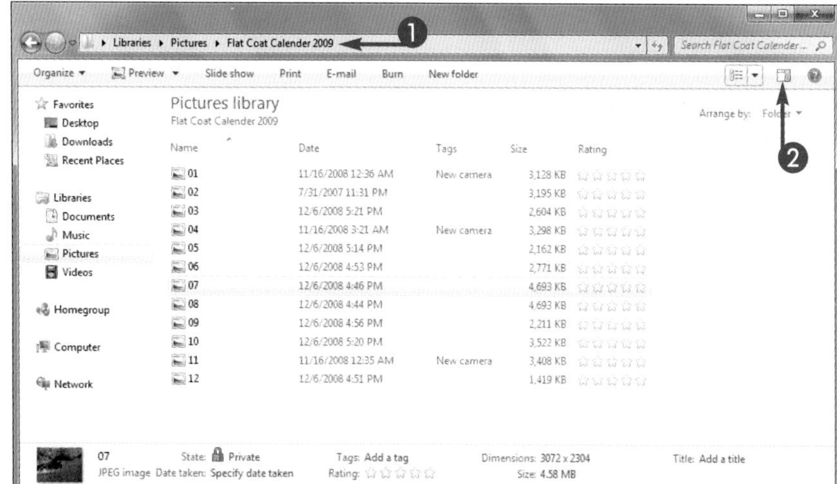


- The Preview pane appears.
- The file's contents appear in the Preview pane.
- You can click and drag the left border of the Preview pane to change its size.
- When you are finished with the Preview pane, click ▯ to close it.

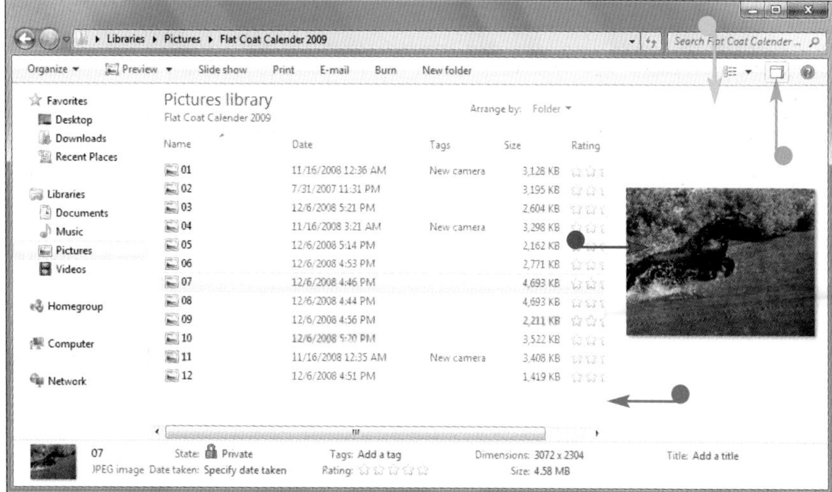

# Copy a File

You can make an exact copy of a file, which is useful if you want to make a backup of an important file on a flash drive, memory card, or other removable disk, or if you want to send the copy on a disk to another person.

**This section shows you how to copy a single file, but the steps also work if you select multiple files. You can also use these steps to copy a folder.**

## Copy a File

1. Open the folder containing the file you want to copy.
2. Select the file.
3. Click **Organize**.
4. Click **Copy**.

   Windows 7 places a copy of the file in a special memory location called the *clipboard*.

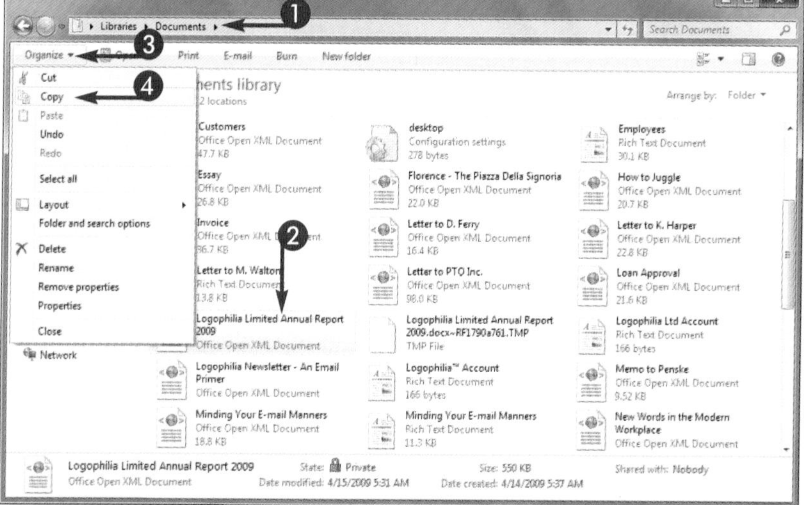


5. Open the location you want to use to store the copy.
6. Click **Organize**.
7. Click **Paste**.

- Windows 7 inserts a copy of the file in the location.

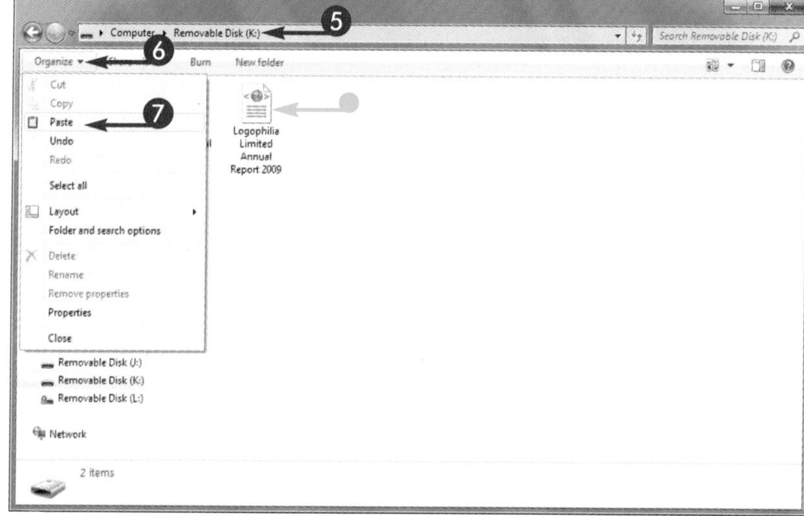

# Move a File

When you need to store a file in a new location, the easiest way is to move the file from its current folder to another folder on your computer.

**This section shows you how to move a single file, but the steps also work if you select multiple files. You can also use these steps to move a folder.**

## Move a File

1. Open the folder containing the file you want to move.
2. Select the file.
3. Click **Organize**.
4. Click **Cut**.

   Windows 7 removes the file from the folder and places it in a special memory location called the *clipboard*.

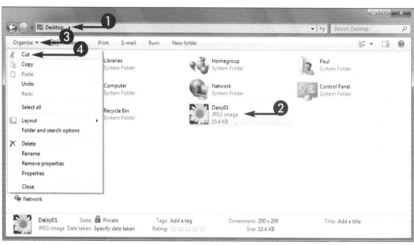

5. Click the new location you want to use for the file.
6. Click **Organize**.
7. Click **Paste**.

- Windows 7 inserts the file in the new location.

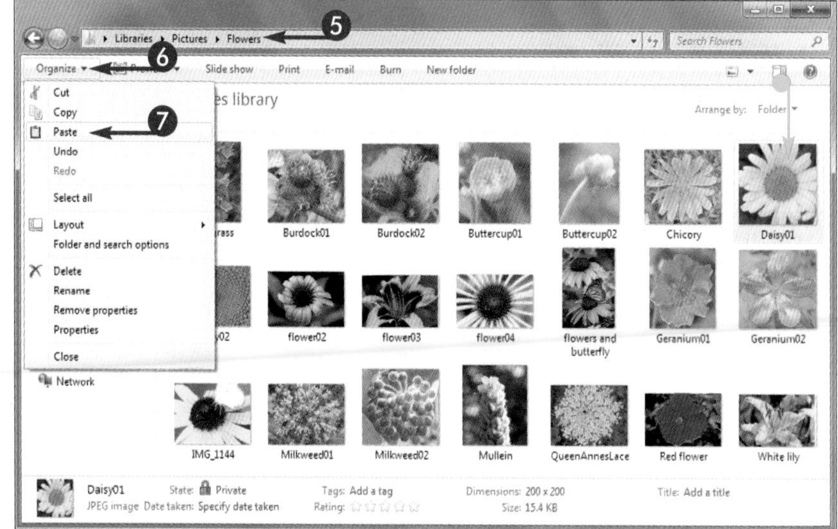

# Burn Files to a CD or DVD

If your computer has a recordable CD or DVD drive, you can copy — or *burn* — files and folders to a recordable disc. This enables you to store a large amount of data in a single place for convenient transport, storage, or backup.

**If you want to copy music files to a CD, see the "Burn Music Files to a CD" section in Chapter 5.**

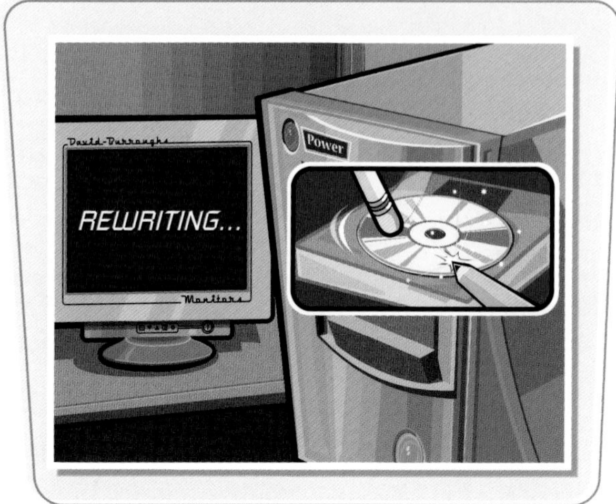


## Burn Files to a CD or DVD

1. Insert a recordable disc into your recordable CD or DVD drive.

   The AutoPlay dialog box appears.

2. Click **Burn files to disc**.

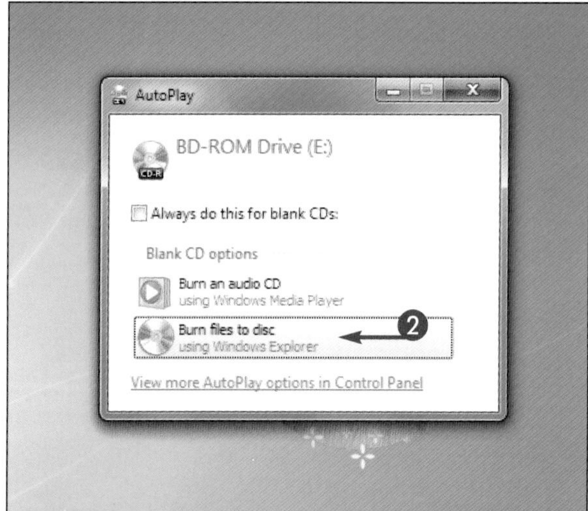


   If you have never used the disc for burning files, the Burn a Disc dialog box appears.

3. Type a title for the disc.
4. Click **Like a USB flash drive** (◎ changes to ◉).
5. Click **Next**.

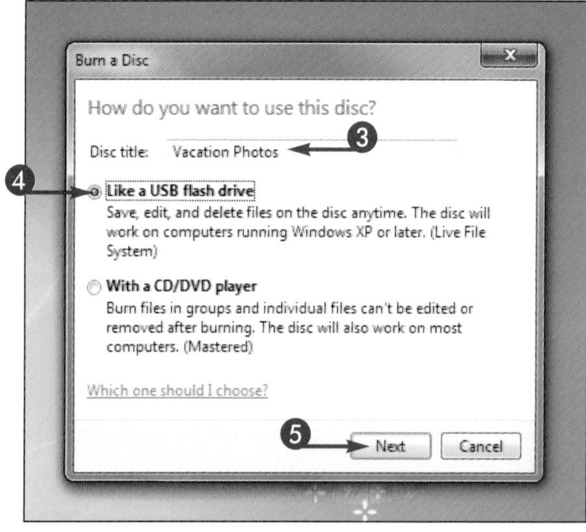

Windows 7 formats the disc and displays a dialog box to show you the progress.

When the format is complete, the AutoPlay dialog box appears.

6. Click **Close** (☒).

7. Open the folder containing the files you want to copy to the disc.
8. Select the files.

- If you selected more than 15 files and you want to see the total size of the selection, first click **Show more details**.

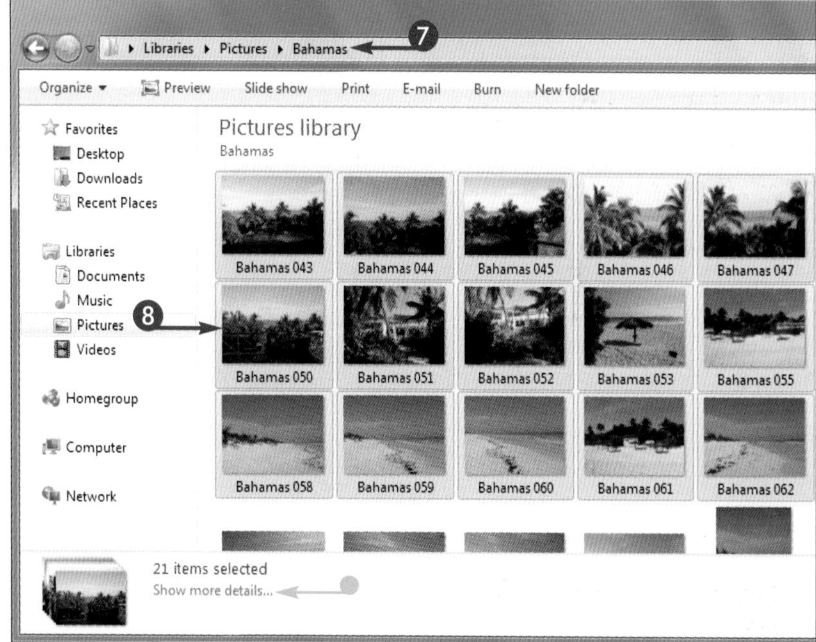


## TIPS

### Does it matter what type of recordable CD or DVD I use?

Not in Windows 7. Normally, CD-R and DVD-R discs allow to copy files to the disc only After you finalize the disc, it is locked and you cannot copy more files to the disc, or deletes files from the disc. However, Windows 7 uses a new system that enables you to copy, recopy, and delete files with any type of recordable disc.

### How much data can I store on a recordable CD?

Most recordable CDs can hold about 650MB (megabytes) of information. If a typical word processing document is about 50KB (kilobytes), this means you can store about 13,000 files on a recordable CD. For larger files, such as images, you can store about 650 1MB files on the disc.

continued

# Burn Files to a CD or DVD *(continued)*

With Windows 7's new method for burning files to a CD or DVD, you only need to format the disc once. After that, you can burn more files to the disc, delete files from the disc, and more.

## Burn Files to a CD or DVD *(continued)*

- If you clicked Show More Details, the Size number shows the total size of the selected files.

9. Click **Burn**.

***Note:** If you want to copy everything in the folder to the disc, do not select any file or folder and click **Burn**.*

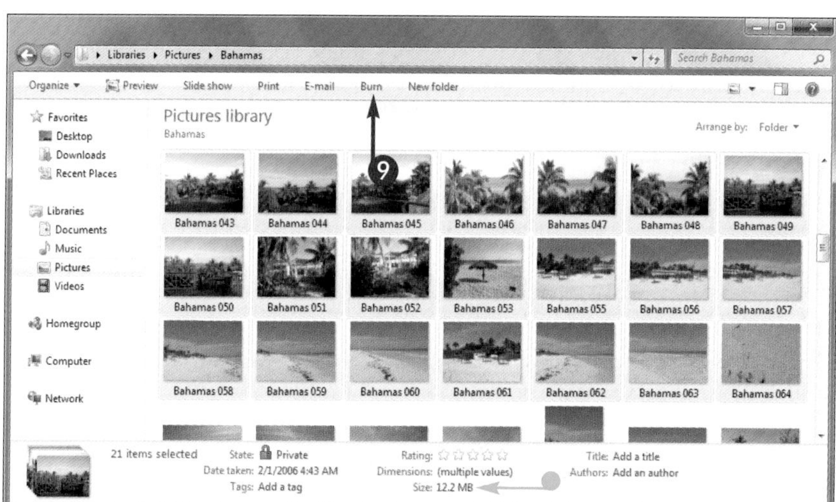


Windows 7 burns the files to the disc.

- Windows 7 opens the disc and displays the copied files.

10. Repeat Steps **7** to **9** to burn more files to the disc.

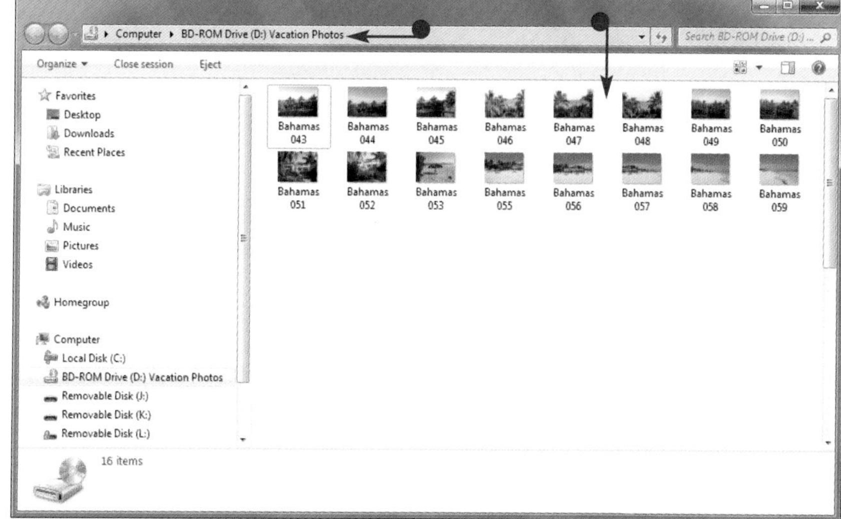

11. Open the disc folder.
12. Click **Close session**.

    Windows 7 closes the disc session to allow the disc to be used on other computers.

- This message appears while the disc is being closed.

13. When the Closing Session message disappears, click **Eject**.

    Windows 7 ejects the disc.

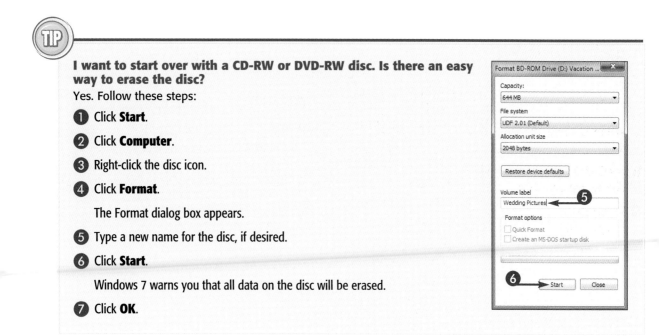

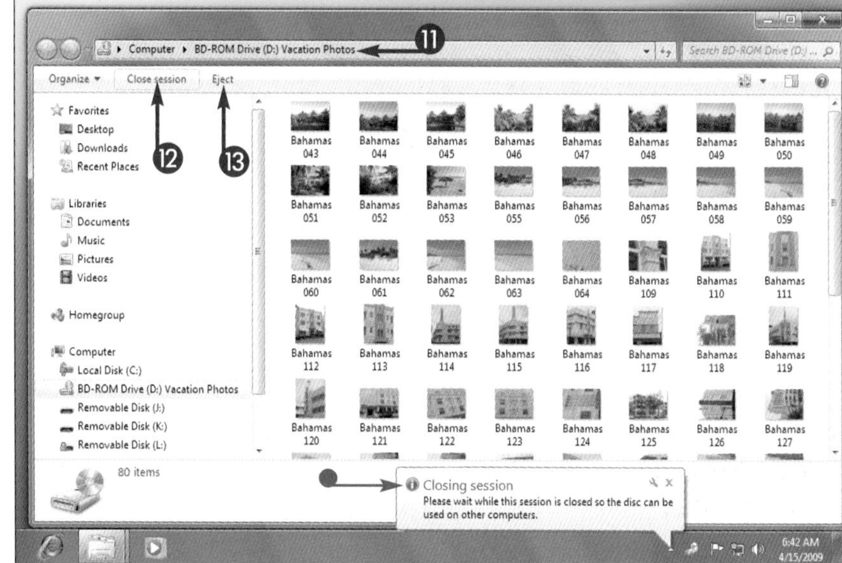

**I want to start over with a CD-RW or DVD-RW disc. Is there an easy way to erase the disc?**

Yes. Follow these steps:

1. Click **Start**.
2. Click **Computer**.
3. Right-click the disc icon.
4. Click **Format**.

   The Format dialog box appears.

5. Type a new name for the disc, if desired.
6. Click **Start**.

   Windows 7 warns you that all data on the disc will be erased.

7. Click **OK**.

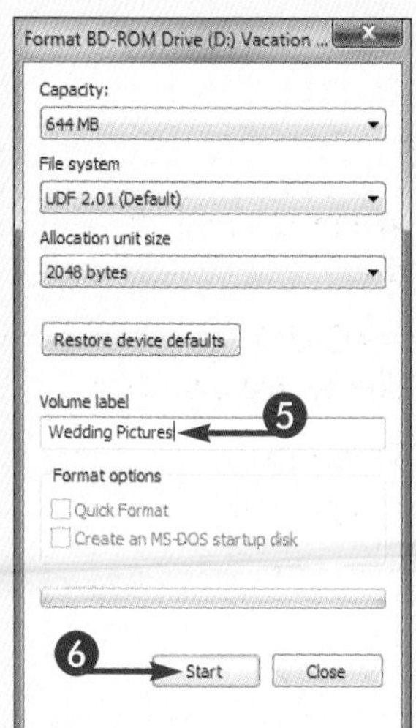

# Rename a File

You can change the names of your files, which is useful if the current name of the file does not accurately describe its contents. By giving your documents descriptive names, you make it easier to later find the file you want.

**Make sure that you rename only those documents that you have created yourself or that have been given to you by someone else. Do not rename any of the Windows 7 system files or any files associated with your programs, or your computer may behave erratically or crash.**

## Rename a File

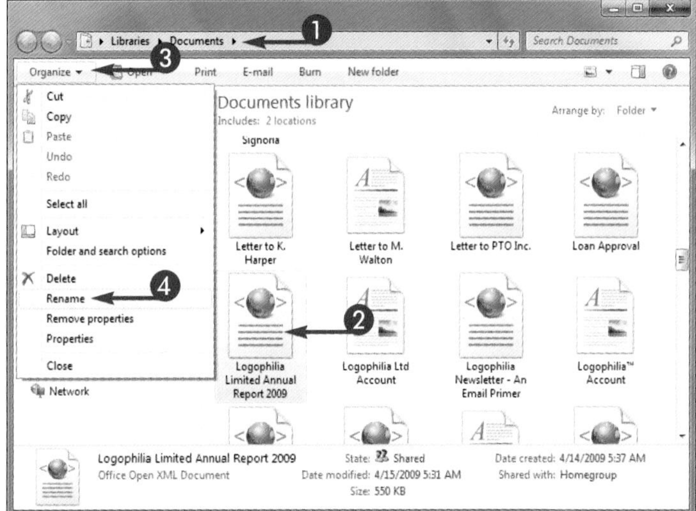


1. Open the folder that contains the file you want to rename.
2. Click the file.
3. Click **Organize**.

***Note:*** *In addition to renaming files, you can also rename any folders that you created yourself.*

4. Click **Rename**.

   A text box appears around the file name.

***Note:*** *You can also select the Rename command by clicking the file and then pressing* F2.

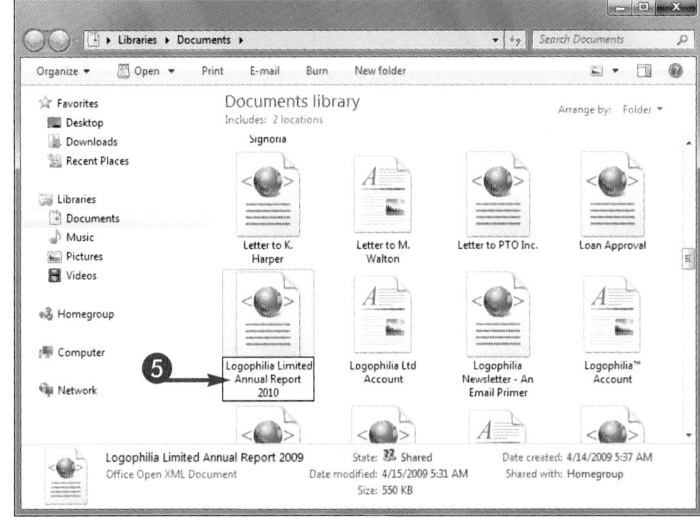


5. Type the new name you want to use for the file.

***Note:*** *If you decide that you do not want to rename the file after all, press* Esc *to cancel the operation.*

***Note:*** *The name you type can be up to 255 characters long, but it cannot include the following characters: < > , ? : " \ *.*

6. Press Enter or click an empty section of the folder.

   The new name appears under the file's icon.

# Create a New File



You can quickly create a new file directly within a file folder. This method is faster, and often more convenient, than running a program's New command, as explained in the "Create a Document" section in Chapter 3.

## Create a New File

1. Open the folder in which you want to create the file.
2. Right-click an empty section of the folder.
3. Click **New**.
4. Click the type of file you want to create.

***Note:*** *If you click* ***Folder****, Windows 7 creates a new subfolder.*

***Note:*** *The New menu on your system may contain more items than you see here because some programs install their own file types.*

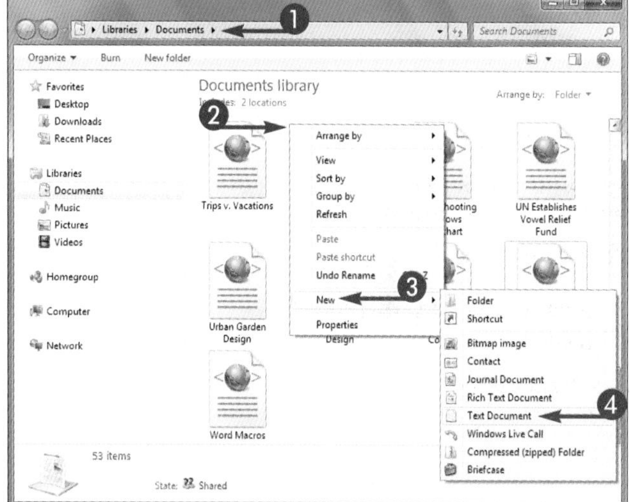

An icon for the new file appears in the folder.

5. Type the name you want to use for the new file.
6. Press Enter.

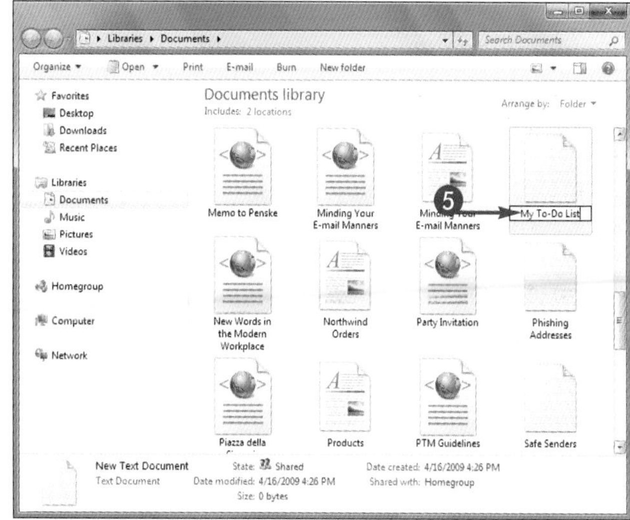

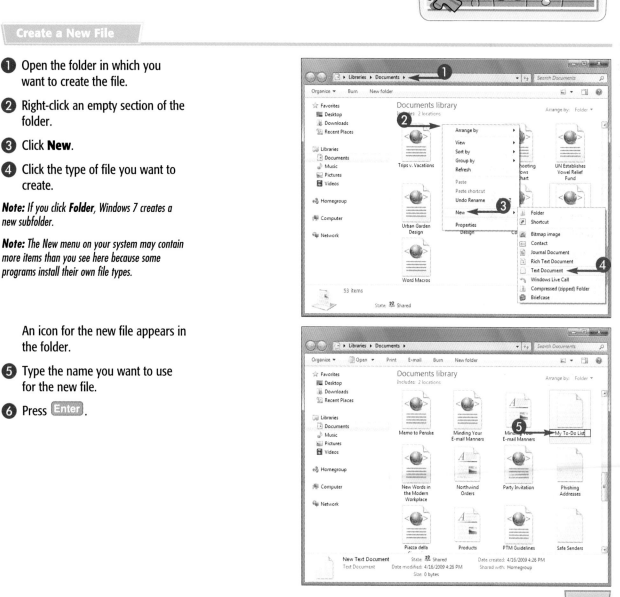

# Delete a File

When you have a file that you no longer need, instead of leaving the file to clutter your hard drive, you can delete it.

**Make sure that you delete only those documents that you have created yourself or that have been given to you by someone else. Do not delete any of the Windows 7 system files or any files associated with your programs, or your computer may behave erratically or crash.**

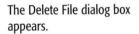

## Delete a File

1. Open the folder that contains the file you want to delete.
2. Click the file you want to delete.

***Note:*** *If you need to remove more than one file, select all the files you want to delete.*

3. Click **Organize**.
4. Click **Delete**.

***Note:*** *Another way to select the Delete command is to press* Delete.

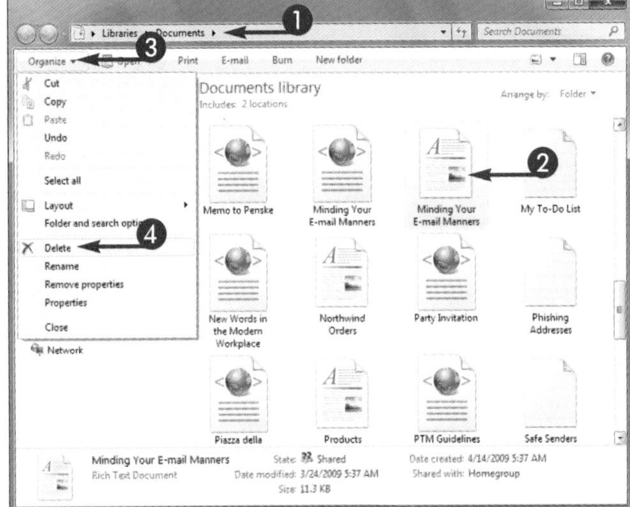


The Delete File dialog box appears.

5. Click **Yes**.

The file disappears from the folder.

***Note:*** *Another way to delete a file is to click and drag it to the desktop's Recycle Bin icon.*

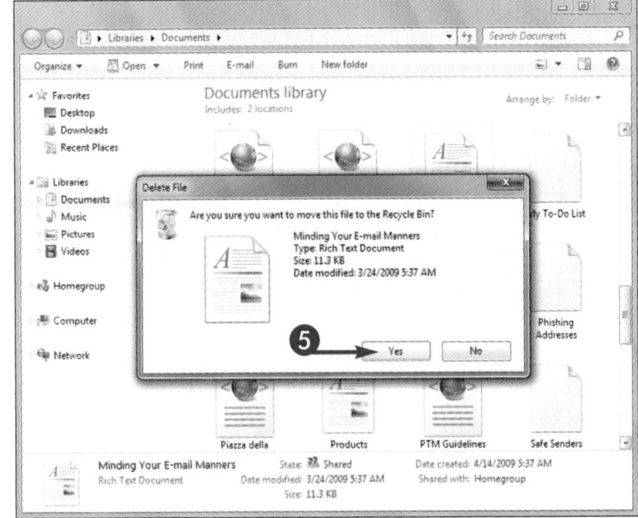

# Restore a Deleted File

If you delete a file in error, Windows 7 enables you to restore the file by placing it back in the folder from which you deleted it.

**You can restore a deleted file because Windows 7 stores each deleted file in a special folder called the Recycle Bin, where the file stays for a few days or a few weeks, depending on how often you empty the bin or how full the folder becomes.**

## Restore a Deleted File

1. Double-click the desktop **Recycle Bin** icon.

The Recycle Bin folder appears.

2. Click the file you want to restore.
3. Click **Restore this item**.

The file disappears from the Recycle Bin and reappears in its original folder.

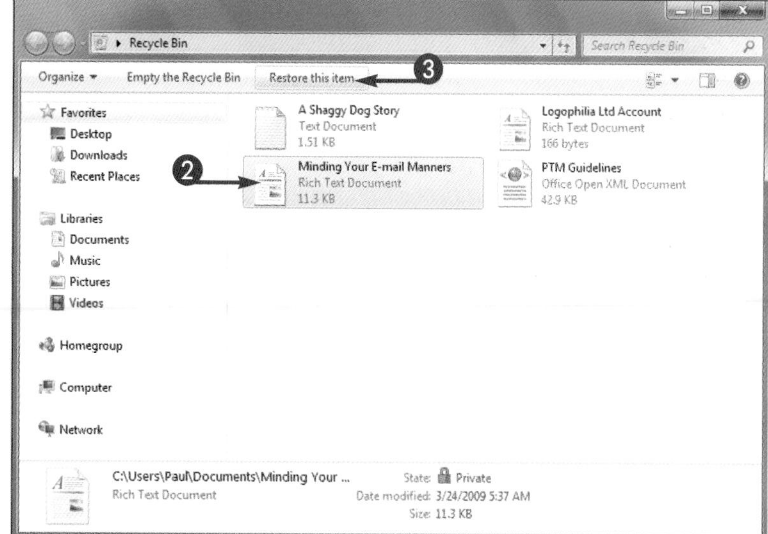

# Add Tags to a File

You can describe many of your files to Windows 7 by adding one or more tags that indicate the content or subject matter of the file. Adding tags to files makes it easier to search and organize your documents.

**A *tag* is a word or short phrase that describes some aspect of a file. You can add as many tags as you need. Note, however, that some types of files do not support tags.**

## Add Tags to a File

1. Click the file you want to work with.
2. Click **Organize**.
3. Click **Properties**.

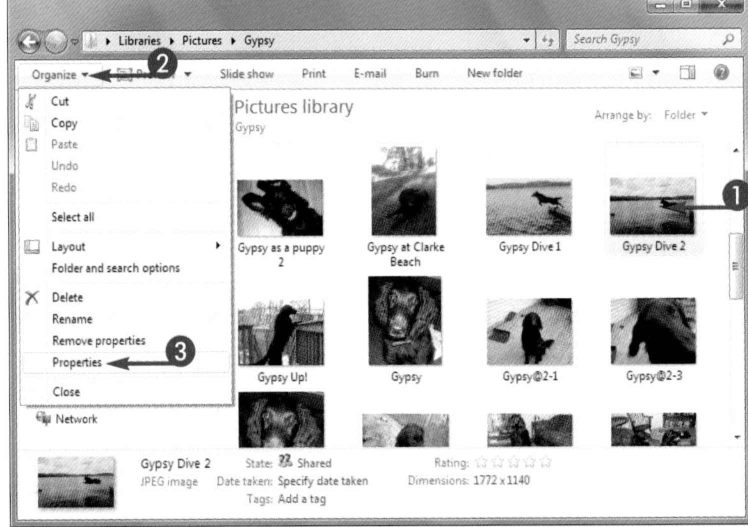


The file's Properties dialog box appears.

4. Click the **Details** tab.
5. Click the Tags text box.

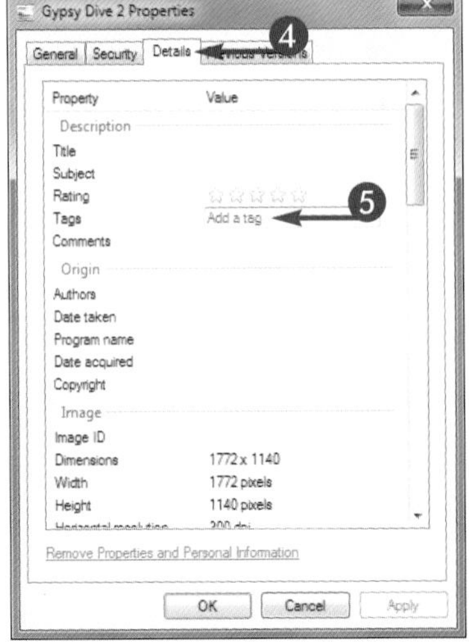

6 Type each tag, followed by a semicolon (**;**).

- As you type a tag, Windows 7 displays existing tags that match; click a tag check box to add it (☐ changes to ☑).

7 Click **OK**.

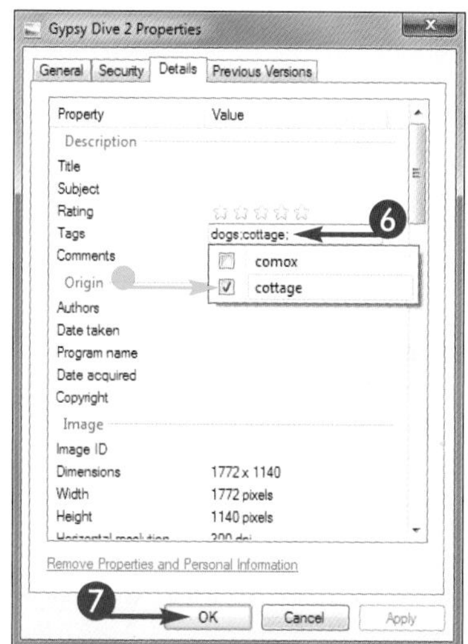

Windows 7 applies the tags to the file.

- The first few tags appear in the Details pane when you select the file.

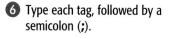

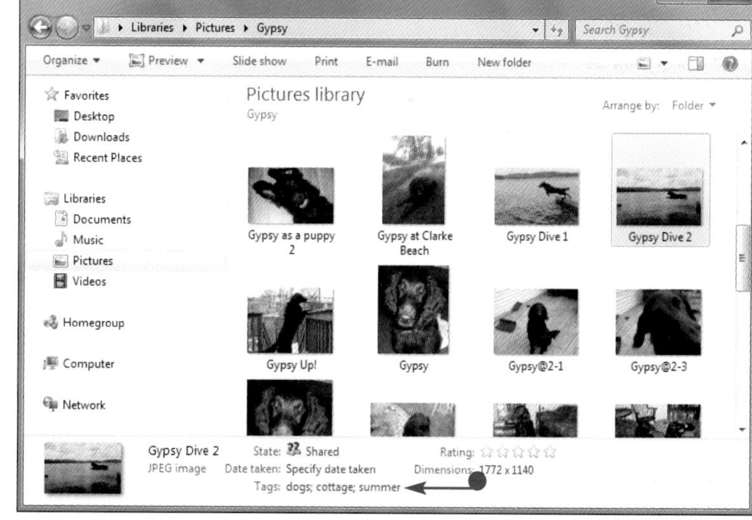

### Why does the Tags field not appear in my Details pane?

You need to enlarge the Details pane to show more file details. Right-click an empty section of the Details pane, click **Size**, and then click **Large**. Alternatively, click and drag the top edge of the Details pane up until the Tags field appears.

### Can I add other details to a file?

Yes, the Details tab has quite a few fields where you can add or edit data. These fields include Title, Subject, Rating (one star to five stars), Comments, and Authors.

# Search for a File

After you have used your computer for a while and have created many documents, you might have trouble locating a specific file. You can save a great deal of time by having Windows 7 search for your document.

**You can search from the Start menu or use the Search box in a folder window.**

## Search for a File

### SEARCH FROM THE START MENU

1. Click **Start**.
2. Click the Search box.

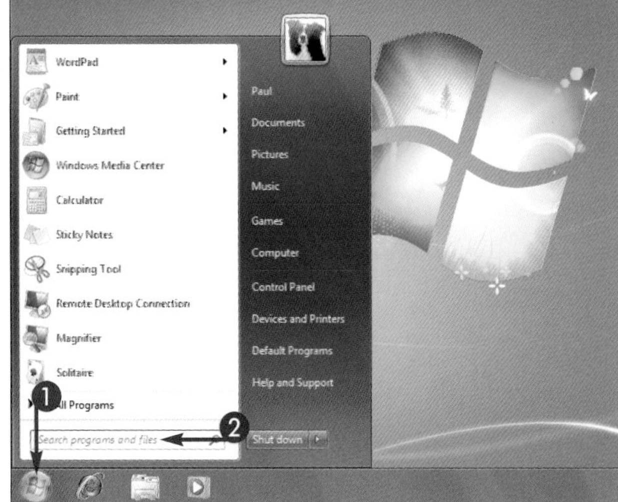


3. Type your search text.
   - As you type, Windows 7 displays the programs, documents, and other data on your system with a name that matches your search text.
4. If you see the program or document you want, click it to open it.

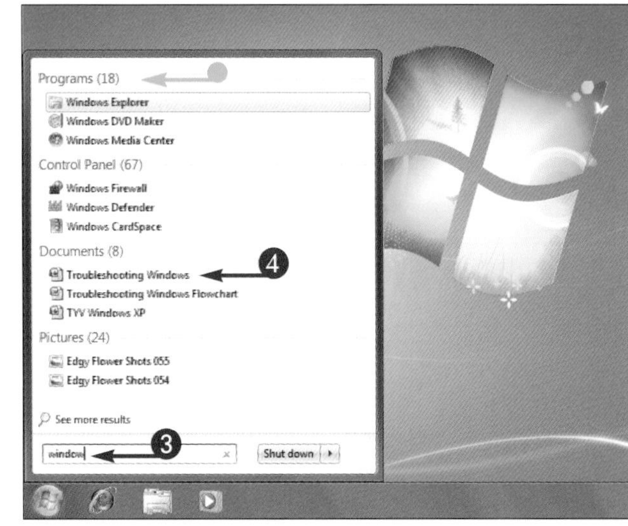

## SEARCH FROM A FOLDER WINDOW

1. Open the folder in which you want to search.
2. Click the Search box.

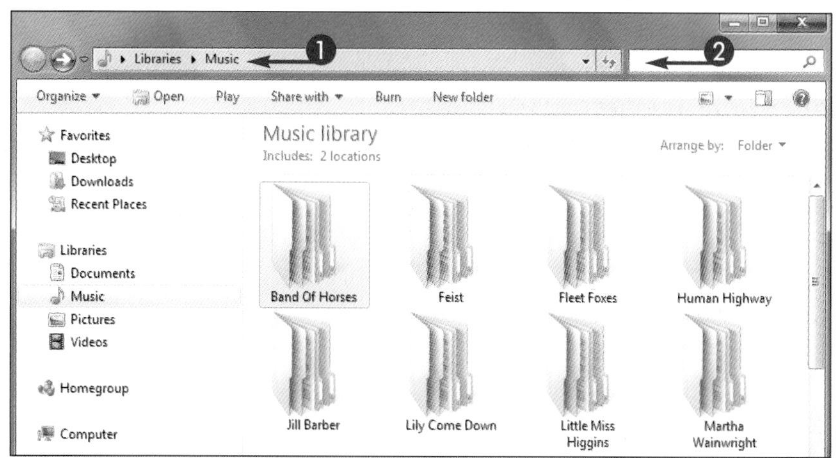

3. Type your search text.

- As you type, Windows 7 displays the folders and documents in the current folder with names, contents, or keywords that match your search text.

4. If you see the folder or document you want, double-click it to open it.

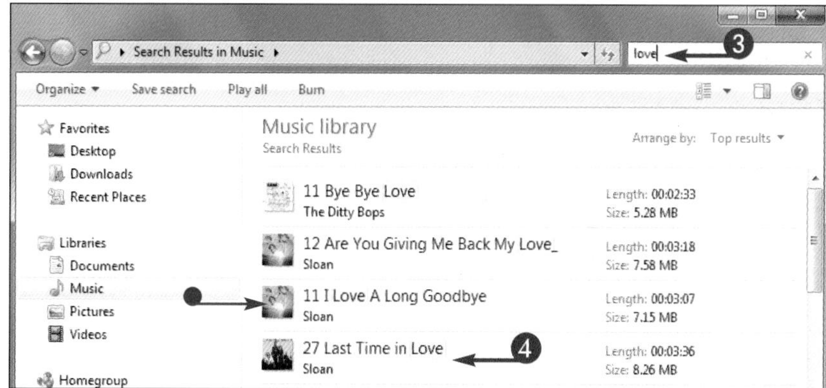

**I want to run the same search frequently. Can I save it?**

1. Run the search you want to save.
2. Click **Save Search**.
3. In the Save As dialog box, type a file name for the search.
4. Click **Save**.

- Windows 7 saves the search file in the Favorites area. Click the file to rerun your search.

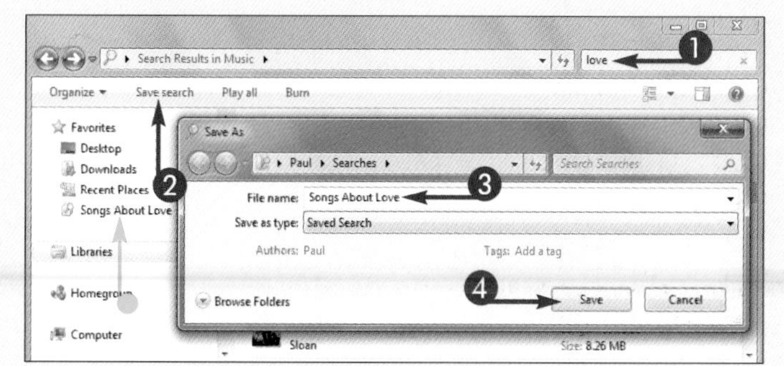

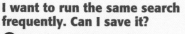

# Extract Files from a Compressed Folder

If someone sends you a file via e-mail, or if you download a file from the Internet, the file often arrives in a *compressed* form, which means the file actually contains one or more files that have been compressed to save space. To use the files on your computer, you need to extract them from the compressed file.

**Because a compressed file can contain one or more files, it acts like a kind of folder. Therefore, Windows 7 calls such files *compressed folders, zipped folders,* or *ZIP archives.***

## Extract Files from a Compressed Folder

1. Open the folder containing the compressed folder.

- The compressed folder usually appears as a folder icon with a zipper.

2. Right-click the compressed folder.
3. Click **Extract All**.

***Note:*** *You may not see the Extract All command if you have installed some other compression program such as WinZip.*

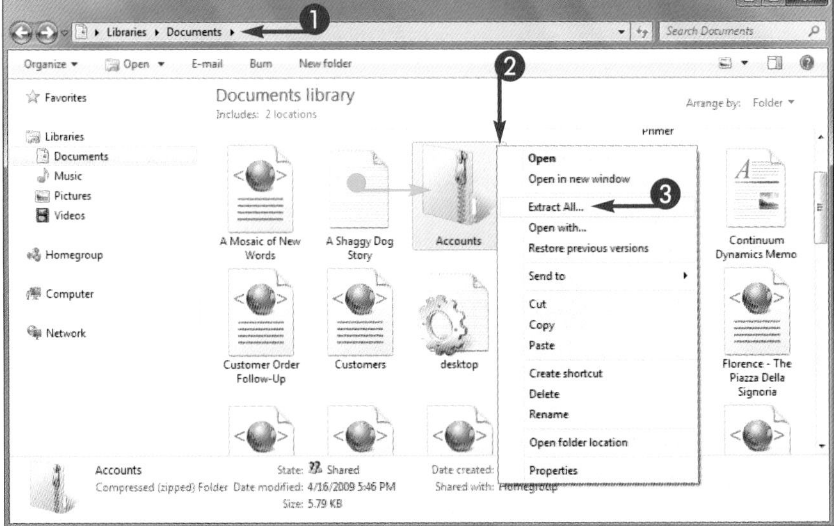


The Select a Destination and Extract Files dialog box of the Extract Wizard appears.

4. Type the location of the folder into which you want the files extracted.

- You can also click **Browse** and choose the folder using the Select a Destination dialog box.

5. If you want to open the folder into which you extracted the files, click **Show extracted files when complete** (☐ changes to ☑).
6. Click **Extract**.

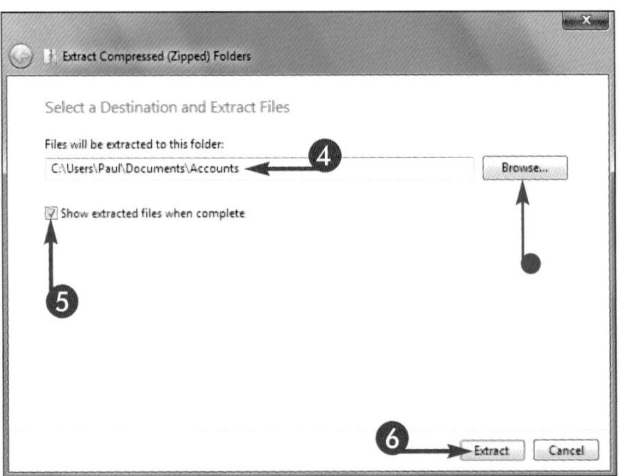

Windows 7 extracts the files.

***Note:** You can view the contents of a compressed folder before you extract the files. Double-click the compressed folder to open it. Windows 7 treats the compressed folder just like a regular subfolder, which means it displays the files in the window. In that window, you can click **Extract all files** to launch the Extract Wizard.*

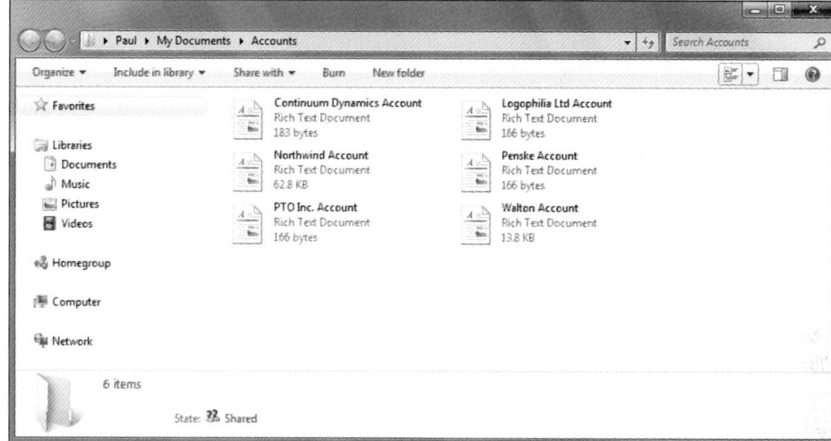

**How can I create a compressed folder?**

Follow these steps:

1. Select the files and folders you want to store in the compressed folder.
2. Right-click any selected file.
3. Click **Send to**.
4. Click **Compressed (zipped) folder**.

   The compressed folder appears.

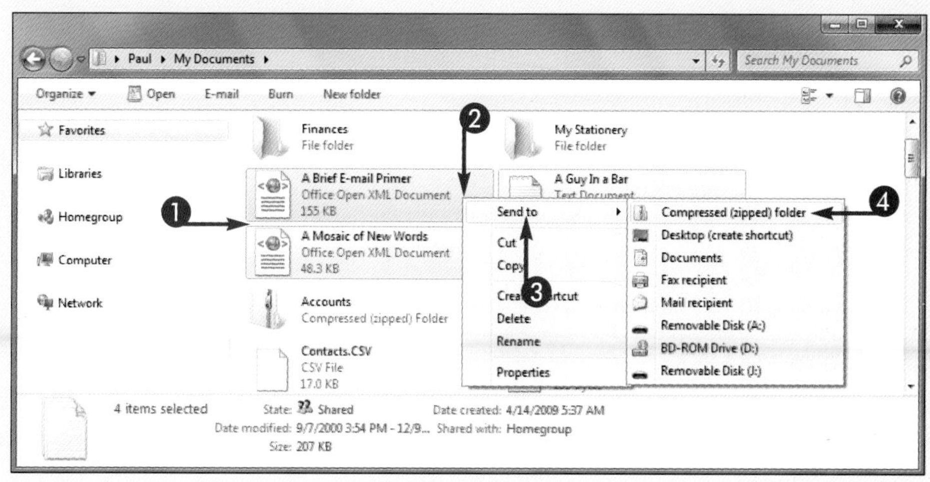

CHAPTER 7

# Sharing Your Computer with Others

If you share your computer with other people, you can create separate user accounts so that each person works only with his own documents, programs, and Windows 7 settings. This chapter shows you how to create and change user accounts, how to log on and off different accounts, how to share documents between accounts, and how to connect and work with a network and homegroup.

# Display User Accounts

To create, change, or delete user accounts, you need to display Windows 7's Manage Accounts window.

**A *user account* is a collection of Windows 7 folders and settings associated with one person.**

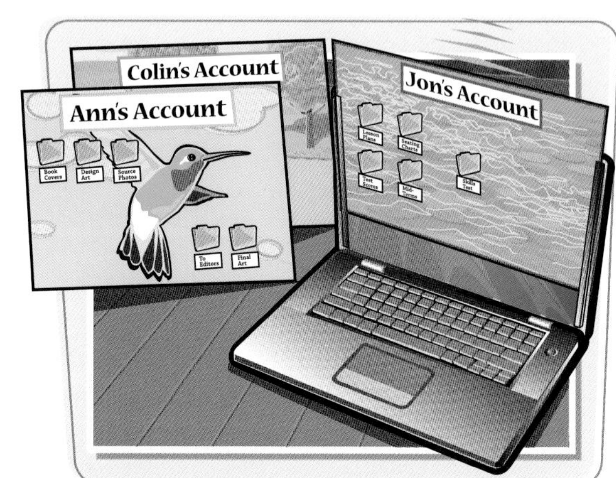


## Display User Accounts

1. Click **Start**.
2. Click **Control Panel**.

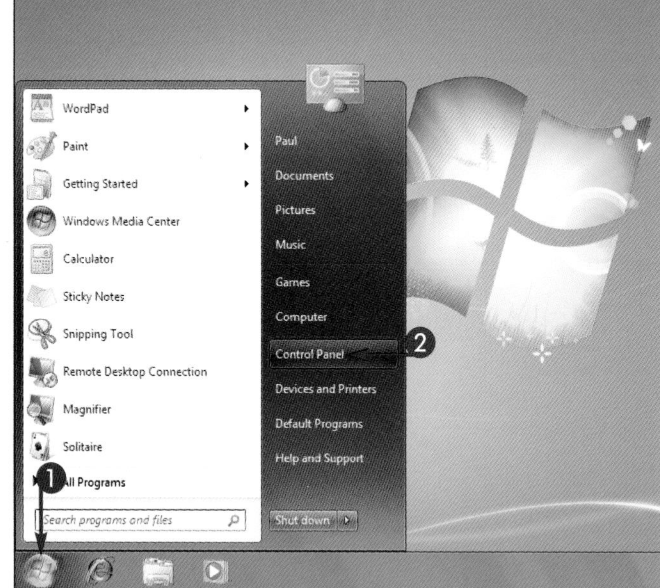


The Control Panel window appears.

3. Click **Add or remove user accounts**.

***Note:*** *If the User Account Control dialog box appears, click* ***Continue*** *or type an administrator password and click* ***Submit****.*

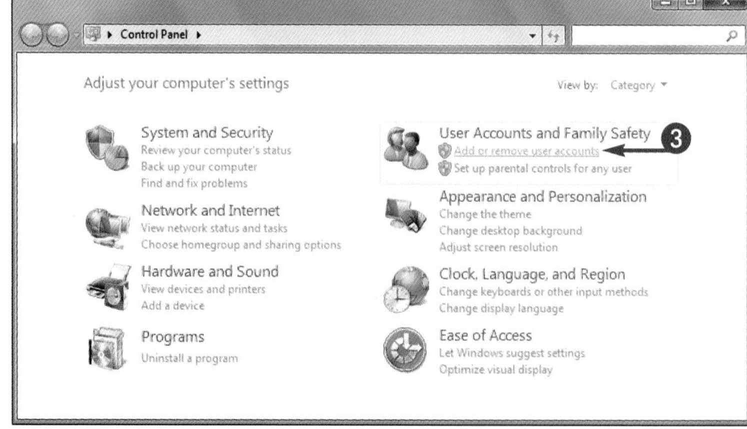

The Manage Accounts window appears.

- An administrator account is created when you install Windows 7. When you start Windows 7, you log on with this account.
- The Guest account is also created when you install Windows 7, but is turned off by default. The Guest account is a limited permission account that enables a person who does not have an account to use the computer. To turn on the Guest account, click **Guest**, and then click **Turn On**.

4 When you have finished working with user accounts, click the **Close** button (X) to close the Manage Accounts window.

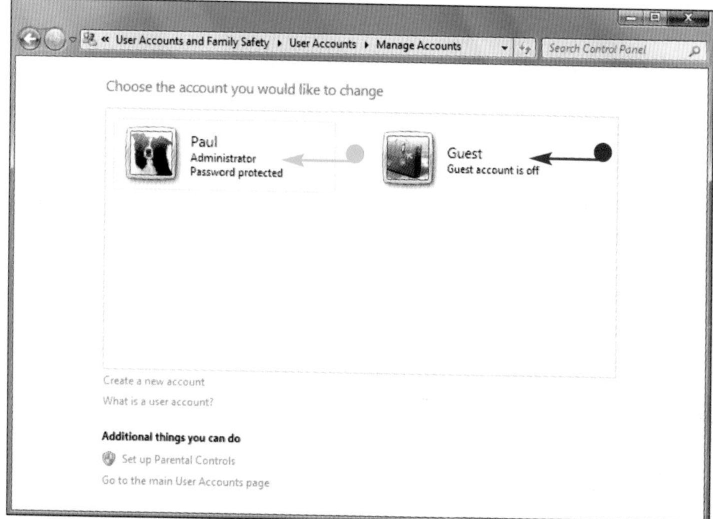


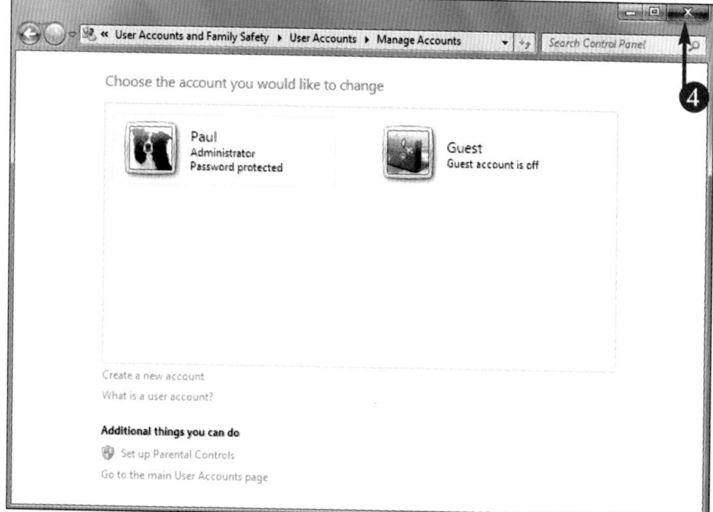

**How do user accounts help me share my computer with other people?**

Without user accounts, anyone who uses your computer can view and even change your documents, Windows 7 settings, e-mail accounts and messages, Internet Explorer favorites, and more.

With user accounts, users get their own libraries (Documents, Pictures, Music, and so on), personalized Windows 7 settings, e-mail accounts, and favorites. In short, users get their own versions of Windows 7 to personalize without interfering with anyone else's.

Also, user accounts enable you to safely share documents and folders with people who use your computer and with people on your network.

# Create a User Account

If you want to share your computer with another person, you need to create a user account for that individual. You should also safeguard each account with a password.

**Note that you must be logged on to Windows 7 with an administrator account or know an administrator's password to create a user account.**

## Create a User Account

### CREATE A USER ACCOUNT

1. Display the Manage Accounts window.

*Note: See "Display User Accounts," earlier in this chapter to learn how to display the Manage Accounts window.*

2. Click **Create a new account**.

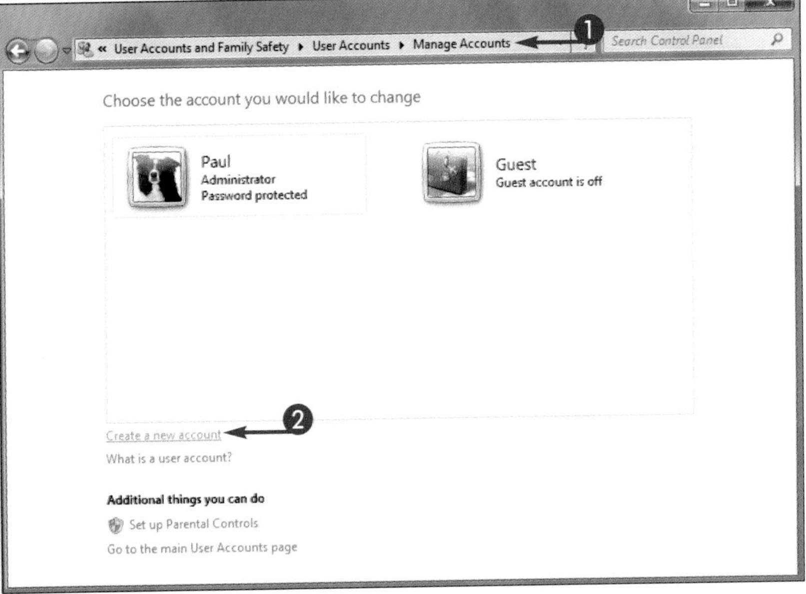

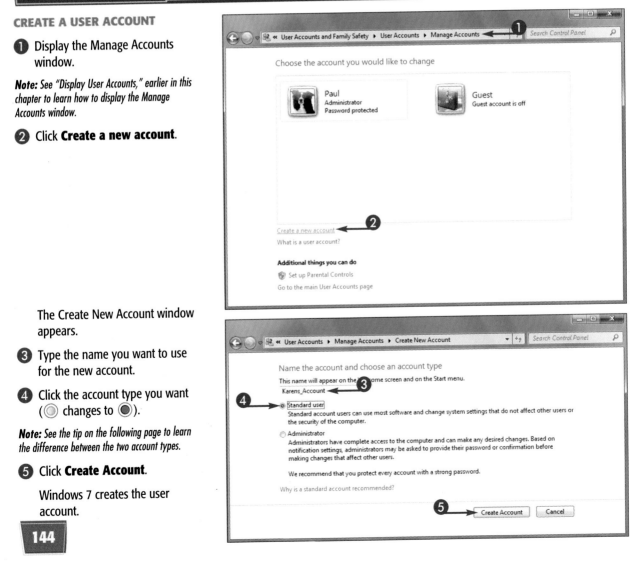

The Create New Account window appears.

3. Type the name you want to use for the new account.
4. Click the account type you want (◎ changes to ◉).

*Note: See the tip on the following page to learn the difference between the two account types.*

5. Click **Create Account**.

Windows 7 creates the user account.

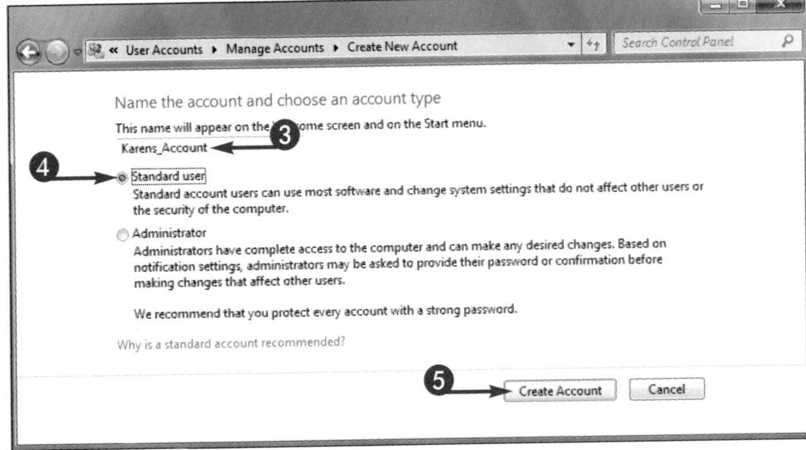

## CREATE A PASSWORD FOR THE USER ACCOUNT

1. Click the user account.

   The Change an Account window appears.

2. Click **Create a password**.

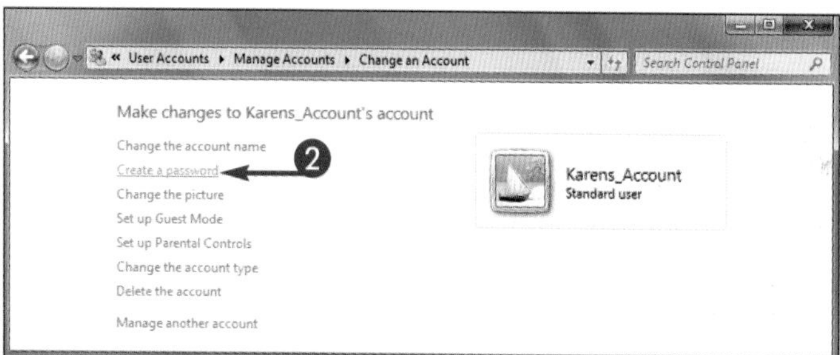


   The Create Password window appears.

3. Type the password.

   - The password characters appear as dots for security reasons.

4. Type the password again.
5. Type a hint that will help you or the user remember the password.
6. Click **Create password**.

   Windows 7 adds the password to the account.

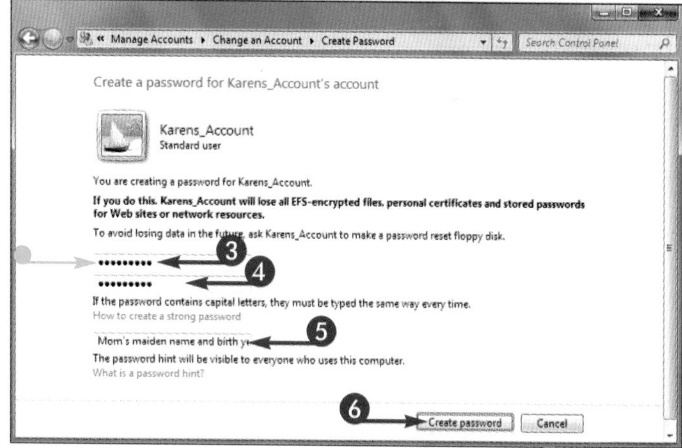

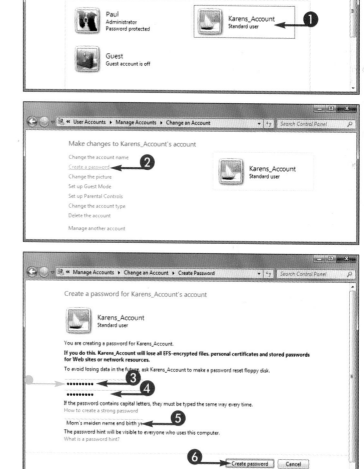


### How do I decide what type of account to give each user?

The two different account types — administrator and standard — affect the extent to which the user can interact with the computer:

- An administrator has complete access to the computer, including access to all users' documents. Administrators can also install programs and devices and add, change, and delete user accounts.
- Standard users have partial access to the computer. They can access only their own documents, as well as any documents that other users have designated to share. Standard users can modify only their own settings, and can change some aspects of their user accounts, including their passwords and pictures.

# Switch Between Accounts

After you have created more than one account on your computer, you can switch between accounts. This is useful when one person is already working in Windows 7 and another person needs to use the computer.

**Windows 7 leaves the original user's programs and windows running so that after the second person is finished, the original user can log on again and continue working as before.**

## Switch Between Accounts

1. Click **Start**.
   - The current user's name and picture appear on the Start menu.
2. Click the power button arrow (▶) to display the menu.
3. Click **Switch user**.

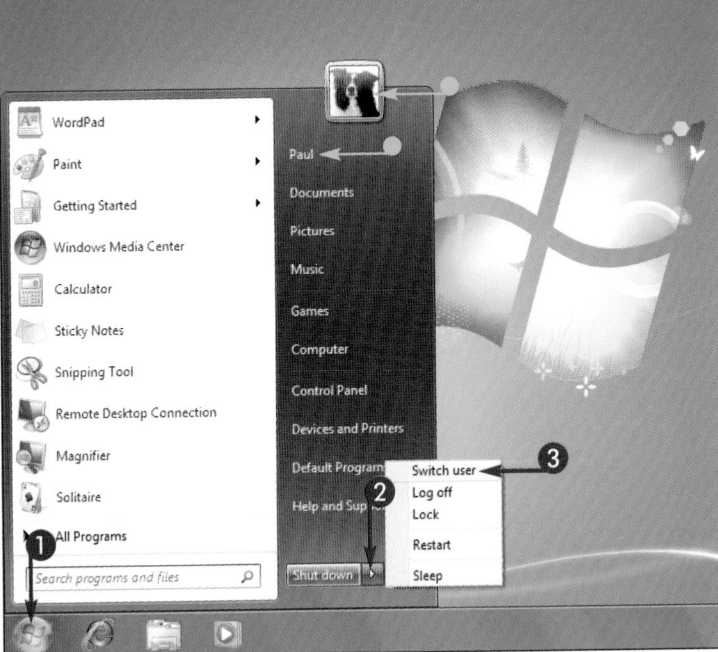


The Welcome screen appears.

4. Click the user account you want to switch to.

- If the account is protected by a password, the password box appears.

***Note:*** *See "Protect an Account with a Password" in Chapter 12 for details on protecting an account with a password.*

5. Type the password.
6. Click the **Go** button ( ).

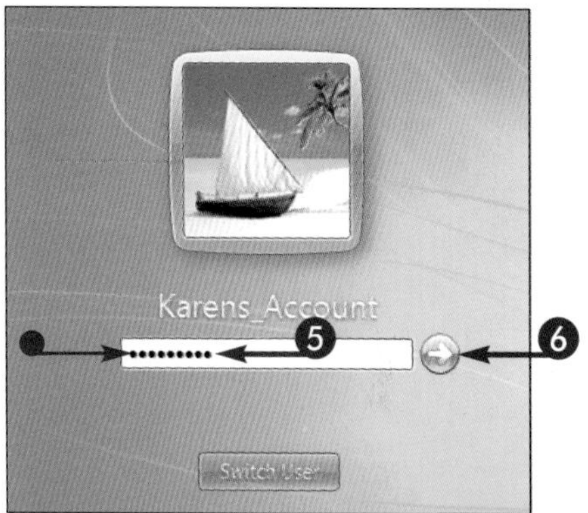


7. Click **Start**.

- The user's name and picture now appear in the Start menu.

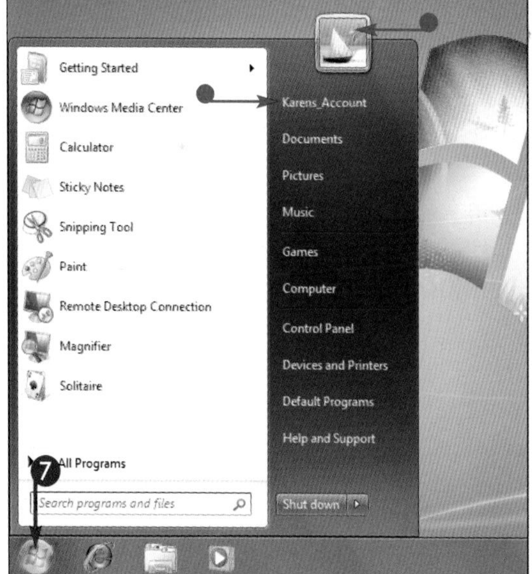

### What happens if I forget my password?

When you set up your password as described in the previous section, Windows 7 asks you to supply a hint to help you remember the password. If you cannot remember your password, follow these steps:

1. Type anything into the password box.
2. Click the **Go** button ( ).

   Windows 7 tells you the password is incorrect.

3. Click **OK** to return to the Welcome screen.

- Windows 7 displays the password hint.

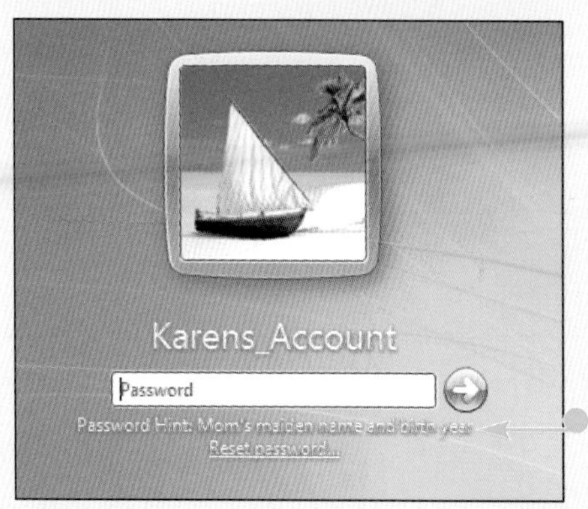

# Change a User's Name

If the user name you are using now is not suitable for some reason, you can change it to a different name.

**When you change the user's name, you are changing the name that appears on the Start menu, in the Manage Accounts window, and the Windows 7 Welcome screen.**

## Change a User's Name

1. Display the Manage Accounts window.

*Note: See "Display User Accounts," earlier in this chapter, to learn how to display the Manage Accounts window.*

2. Click the user account you want to work with.

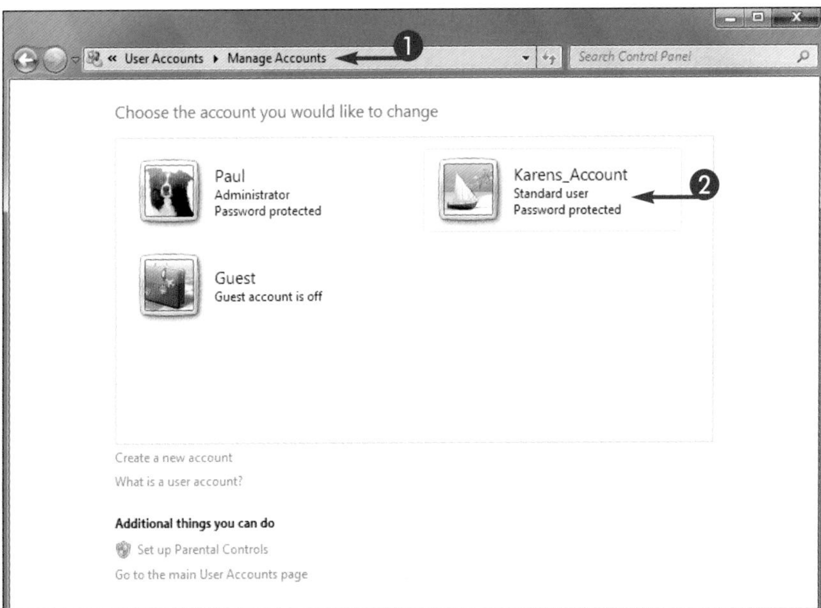


The Change an Account window appears.

3. Click **Change the account name**.

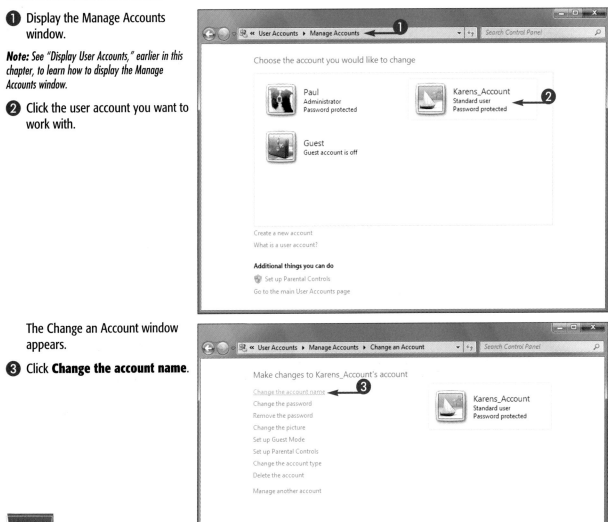

4. Type the new name.
5. Click **Change Name**.

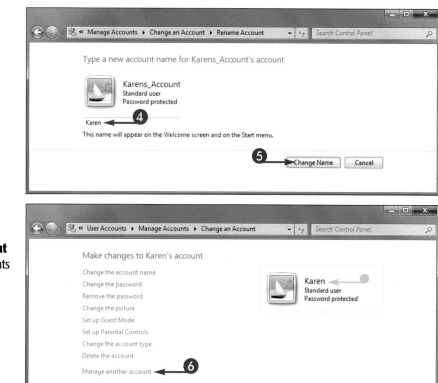

- The new name appears in the user's window.

6. Click **Manage another account** to return to the Manage Accounts window.

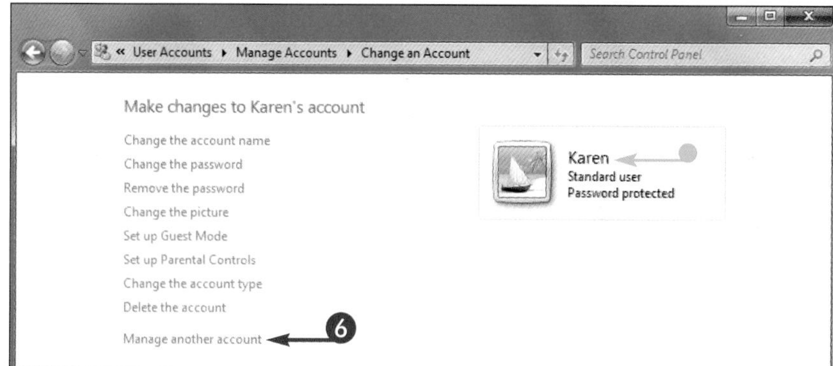


## TIP

### Are there any restrictions in the names I can use?

Yes, you have to watch out for the following:

- The name cannot be any longer than 20 characters.
- The name cannot include any of the following characters: , < > / ? ; : " [ ] \ | = + *
- The name cannot be the same as the computer's name. To check the computer name, click **Start**, click **Control Panel**, click **System and Security**, and then click **See the name of this computer**. In the System window, look for the Computer Name setting.

# Change a User's Picture

Windows 7 assigns a random picture to each new user account, and this picture appears in the Manage Accounts window, the Welcome screen, and the Start menu. If you do not like your picture, or if you have a more suitable picture that you would prefer to use, you can change your picture.

## Change a User's Picture

1. Display the Manage Accounts window.

***Note:*** *See "Display User Accounts," earlier in this chapter, to learn how to display the Manage Accounts window.*

2. Click the user account you want to work with.

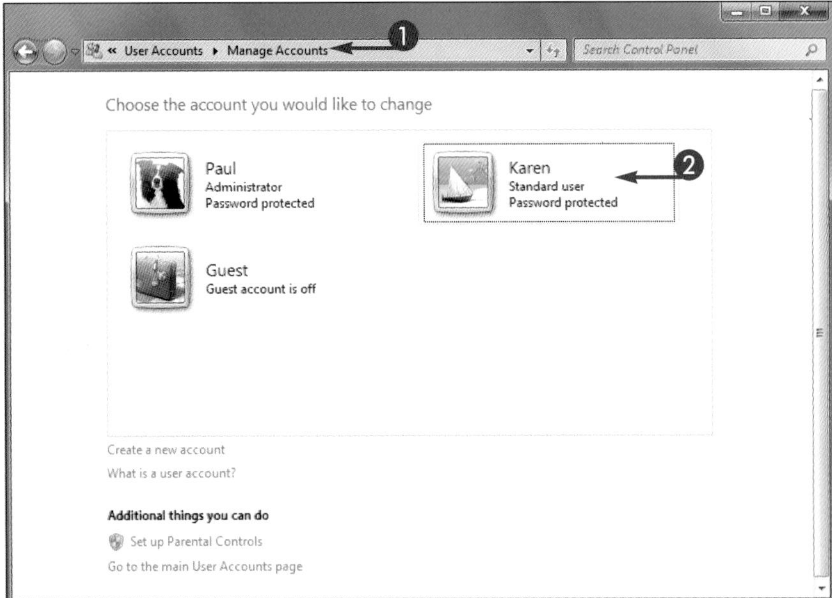


The Change an Account window appears.

3. Click **Change the picture**.

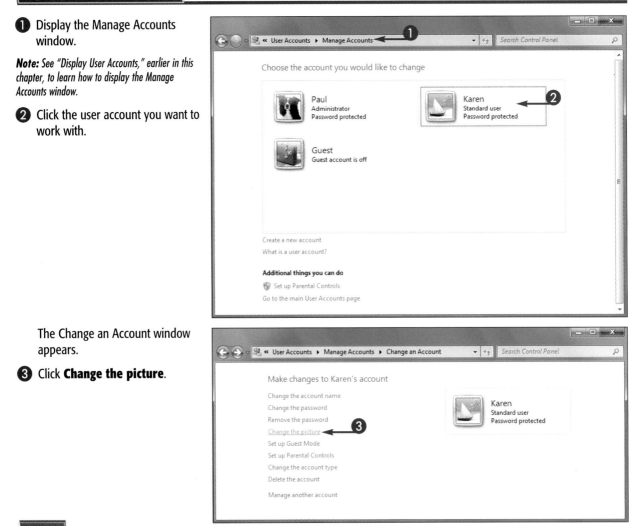

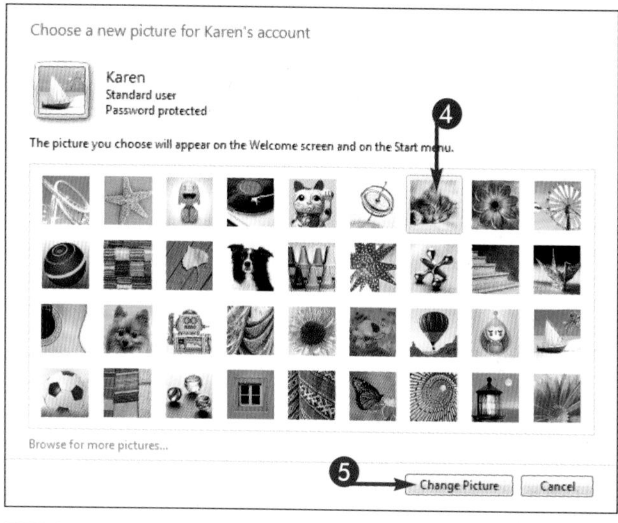


The Choose Picture window appears.

4. Click the picture you want to use.
5. Click **Change Picture**.

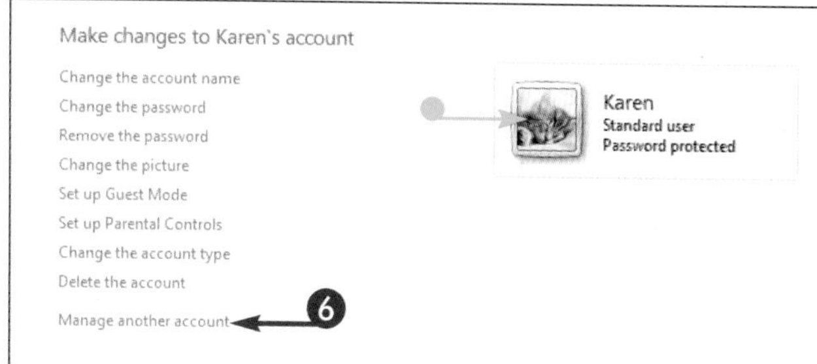


- The user's window appears and displays the new picture.

6. Click **Manage another account** to return to the Manage Accounts window.

## How do I use one of my own pictures?

Follow these steps:

1. Follow Steps **1** to **3**.
2. Click **Browse for more pictures**.

   The Open dialog box appears.
3. Open the folder containing the picture you want to use.
4. Click the picture.
5. Click **Open**.

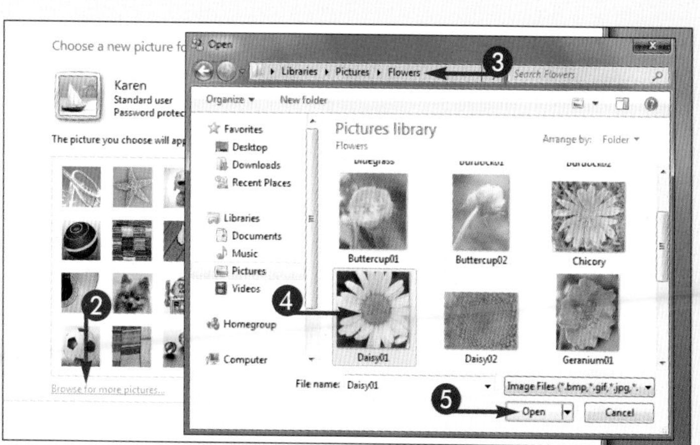

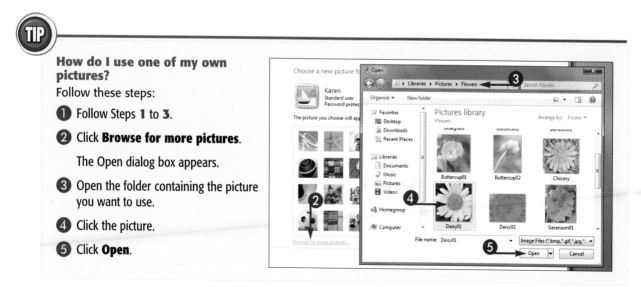

# Delete an Account

You can delete a user's account when it is no longer needed. This reduces the number of users in the Manage Accounts windows and on the Welcome screens, and can also free up some disk space.

## Delete an Account

1. Display the Manage Accounts window.

*Note:* *See "Display User Accounts," earlier in this chapter, to learn how to display the Manage Accounts window.*

2. Click the user account you want to delete.

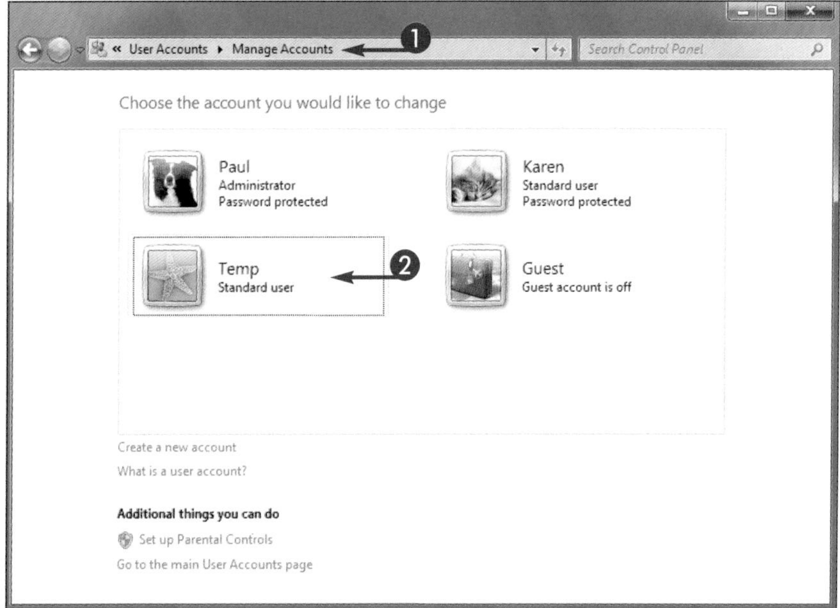

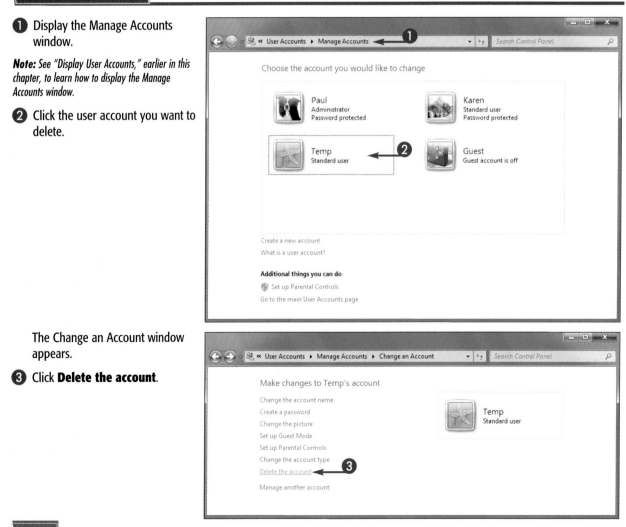

The Change an Account window appears.

3. Click **Delete the account**.

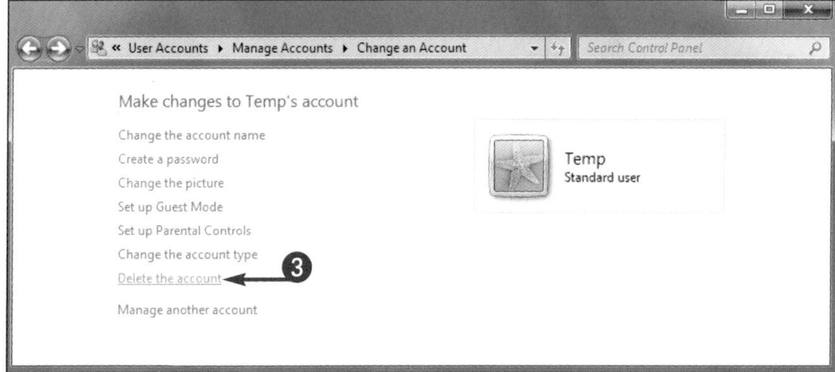

The Delete Account window appears.

4. Click to specify whether you want to keep or delete the user's personal files.

***Note:*** *See the tip, below, to learn the difference between these two options.*

User Accounts ▸ Manage Accounts ▸ Delete Account

Do you want to keep Temp's files?

Before you delete Temp's account, Windows can automatically save the contents of Temp's desktop and Documents, Favorites, Music, Pictures and Videos folders to a new folder called 'Temp' on your desktop. However, Windows cannot save Temp's e-mail messages and other settings.

4 Delete Files | Keep Files | Cancel

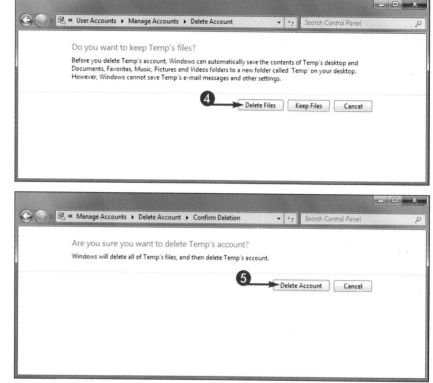

The Confirm Deletion window appears.

5. Click **Delete Account**.

Windows 7 deletes the account.

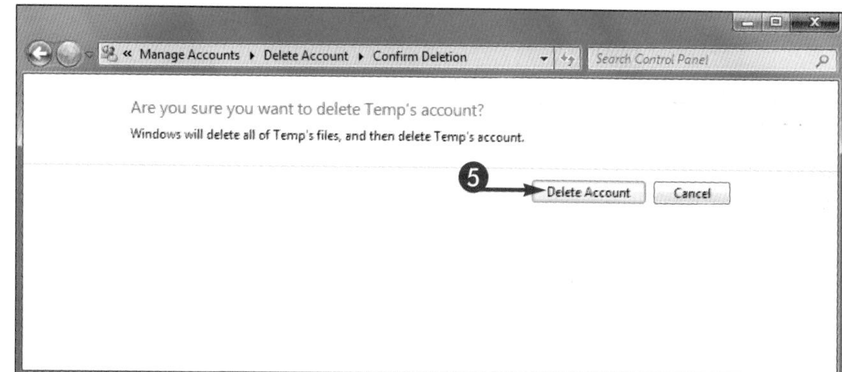

**My user account does not offer the Delete the Account task. Why not?**

If yours is the only computer administrator account left on the computer, Windows 7 does not allow you to delete it. Windows 7 requires that there always be at least one computer administrator account on the computer.

**What is the difference between the Keep Files and Delete Files options?**

The options enable you to handle user files two ways:

- Click **Keep Files** to retain the user's personal files — the contents of his or her Documents folder and desktop. These files are saved on your desktop in a folder named after the user. All other personal items — settings, e-mail accounts and messages, and Internet Explorer favorites — are deleted.
- Click **Delete Files** to delete all of the user's personal files, settings, messages, and favorites.

# Create a Homegroup

You can share documents and media easily with other Windows 7 computers by creating a homegroup on your network. A homegroup simplifies network sharing by making it easy to create a homegroup and share documents.

**You use one Windows 7 computer to create the homegroup, and then you use the homegroup password to join your other Windows 7 computers. See "Join a Homegroup," later in this chapter.**

## Create a Homegroup

1. Click **Start**.
2. Click **Documents**.

The Documents library appears.

3. Click **Homegroup**.
4. Click **Create a homegroup**.

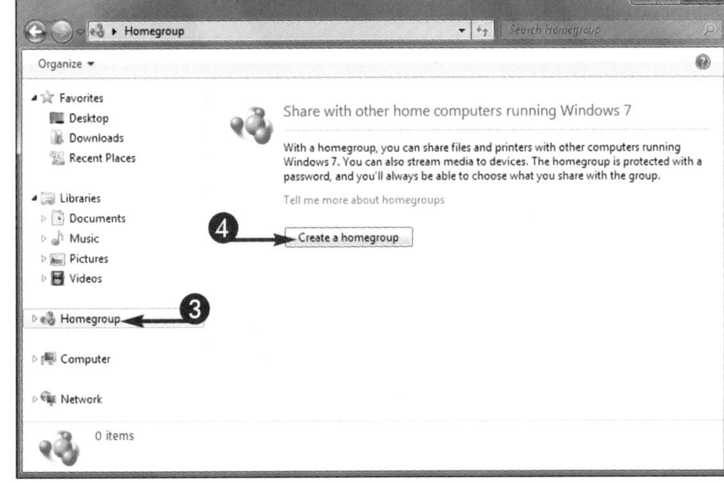

The Create a Homegroup wizard appears.

5. Click the check box for each type of file you want to share with the homegroup (☐ changes to ☑).
6. Click **Next**.

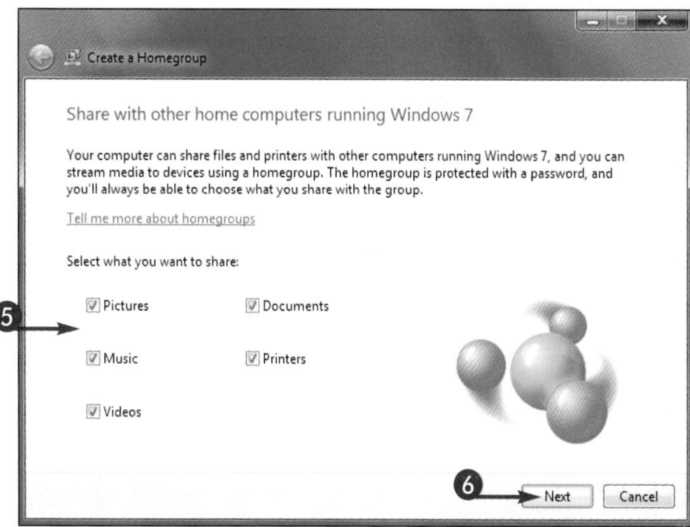


Windows 7 creates the homegroup.

- The Create a Homegroup wizard displays the homegroup password.

7. Write down the homegroup password.

- Alternatively, you can click this link to print the password.

8. Click **Finish**.

You can now join your other Windows 7 computers to the homegroup, as described in the next section.

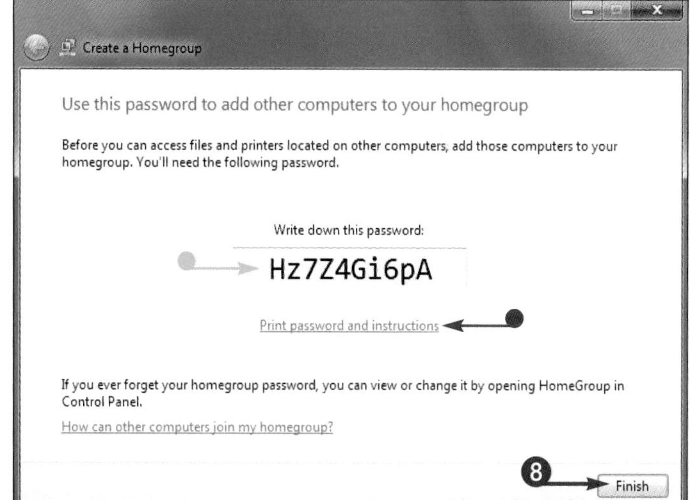

### I have lost my homegroup password. How do I view it again?

Click **Start**, and then click **Control Panel** to open the Control Panel window. Under the Network and Internet heading, click **Choose homegroup and sharing options** to open the Homegroup window. Click the **View or print homegroup password** link to see your password. To print the password, click **Print this page**.

### Is it possible to change the homegroup password?

Yes. Click **Start**, and then click **Control Panel** to open the Control Panel window. Under the Network and Internet heading, click **Choose homegroup and sharing options** to open the Homegroup window. Click the **Change the password** link and then click **Change the password** to generate a new homegroup password. If one or more computers have already joined the homegroup, you need to provide them with the new password.

# Join a Homegroup

If there is a homegroup on your network, you can join your Windows 7 computer to that homegroup. This enables you to access shared resources on other homegroup computers, and to share your own resources with the homegroup.

**This section assumes you have already set up a homegroup as described in the "Create a Homegroup" section and that you have the homegroup password.**

## Join a Homegroup

1. Click **Start**.
2. Click **Documents**.

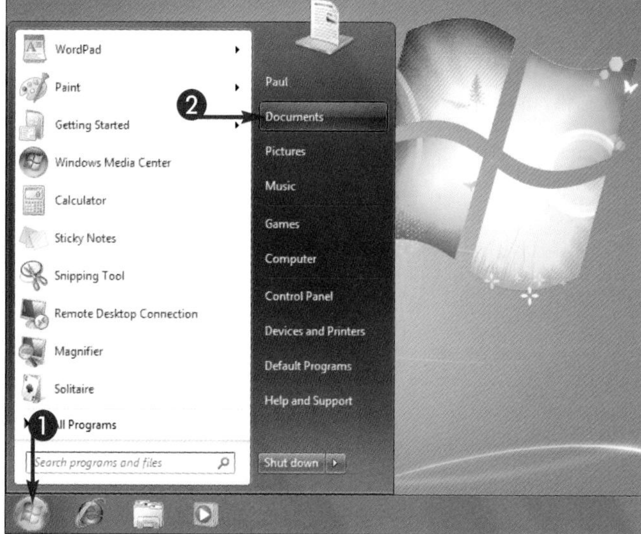


The Documents library appears.

3. Click **Homegroup**.
4. Click **Join now**.

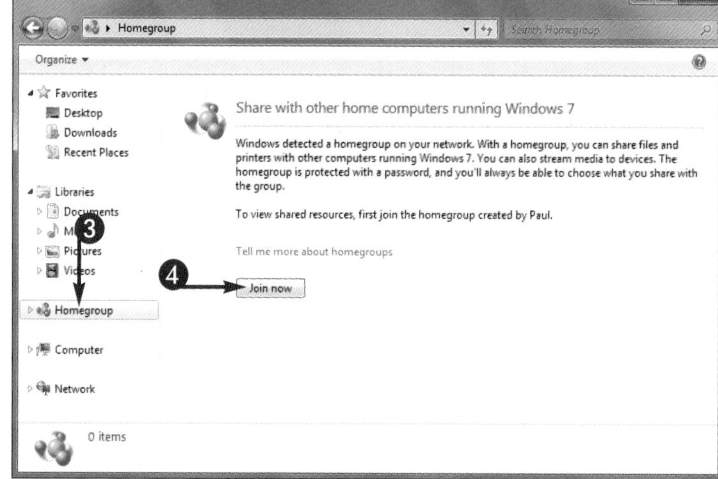

The Join a Homegroup wizard appears.

5 Click the check box for each type of file you want to share with the homegroup ( changes to ).

6 Click **Next**.

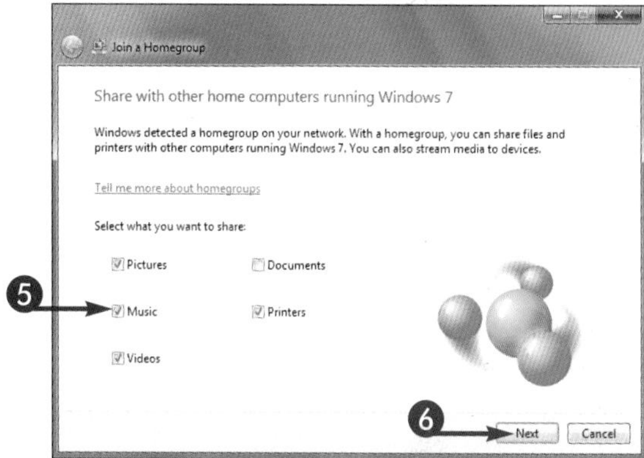


The Join a Homegroup wizard prompts you for the homegroup password.

7 Type the homegroup password.

8 Click **Next** (not shown).

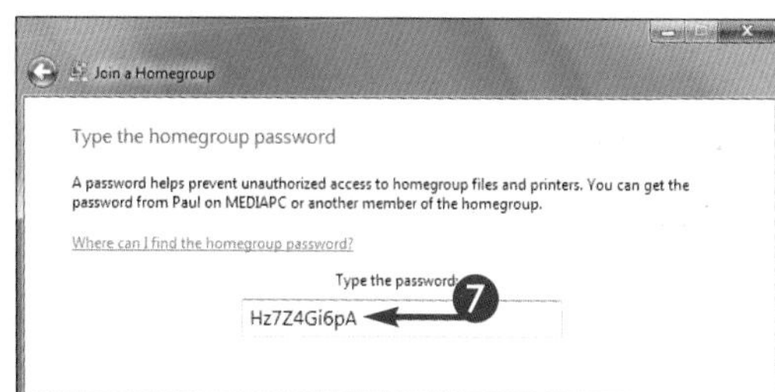


Windows 7 joins the computer to the homegroup.

9 Click **Finish** (not shown).

You can now access other homegroup computers and share your files with the homegroup.

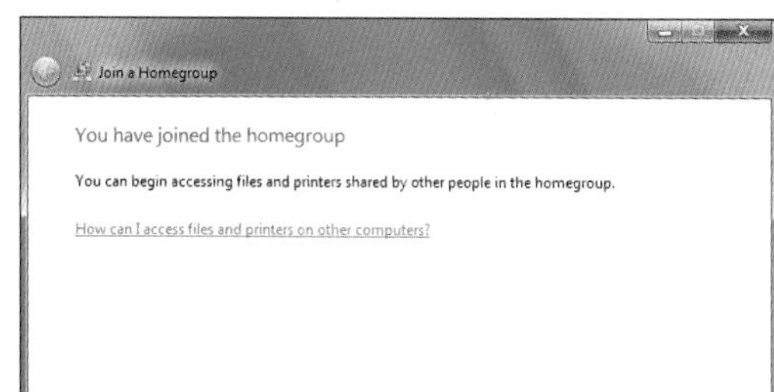

**Can I use my homegroup to stream media to other computers and devices on my network?**

Yes. To enable media streaming, click **Start**, and then click **Control Panel** to open the Control Panel window. Under the Network and Internet heading, click **Choose homegroup and sharing options** to open the Homegroup window. Click the **Stream my pictures, music, and videos to all devices on my home network** check box ( changes to ). Click **Save changes**.

**Can I leave a homegroup if I no longer need it?**

Yes. Click **Start**, and then click **Control Panel** to open the Control Panel window. Under the Network and Internet heading, click **Choose homegroup and sharing options** to open the Homegroup window. Click the **Leave the homegroup** link and then click **Leave the homegroup**. Windows 7 removes your computer from the homegroup. Click **Finish**.

# Share a Document or Folder

You can share documents and folders of your choice with your homegroup, if your network has one. You can also share a document or folder with other users set up on your computer.

**You can set up each document or folder with Read or Read/Write permissions. Read means that users cannot make changes to the document or file; Read/Write means that users can make changes.**

## Share a Document or Folder

### SHARE WITH THE HOMEGROUP

1. Open the folder containing the document or subfolder you want to share.
2. Click the document or subfolder.

***Note:*** *If you want to share more than one object, select all the objects you want to share.*

3. Click **Share with**.
4. Click **Homegroup (Read)**.

- If you want homegroup users to make changes to the item, click **Homegroup (Read/Write)**, instead.

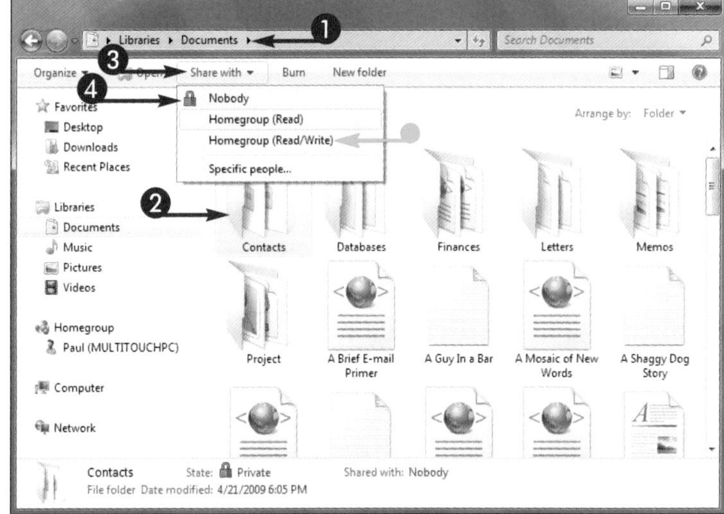


- The State property changes to Shared.
- The Shared with property changes to Homegroup.

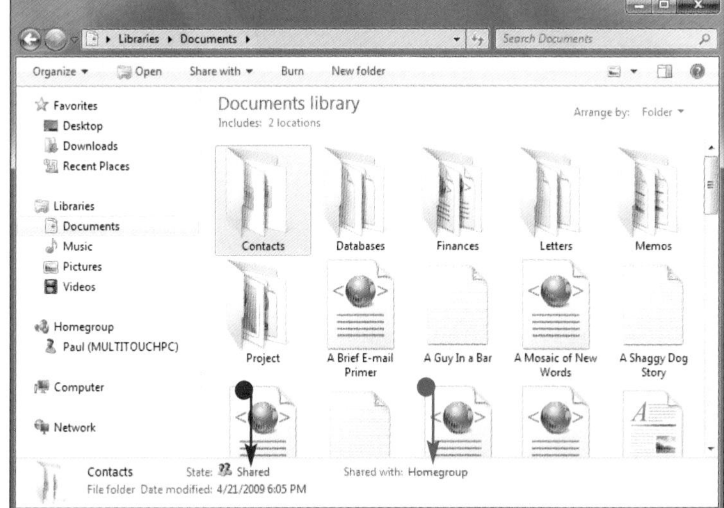

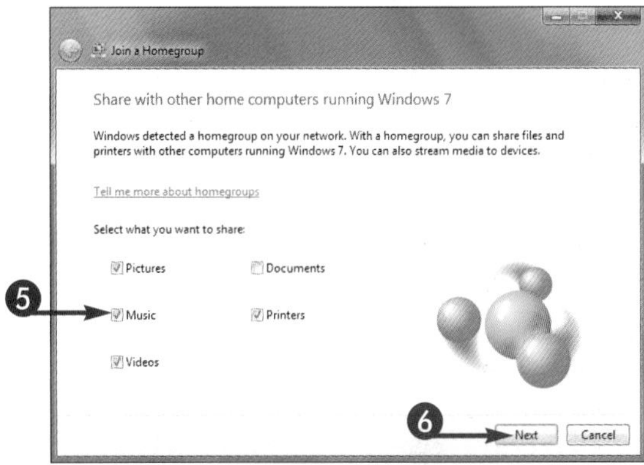


The Join a Homegroup wizard appears.

5 Click the check box for each type of file you want to share with the homegroup (☐ changes to ☑).

6 Click **Next**.

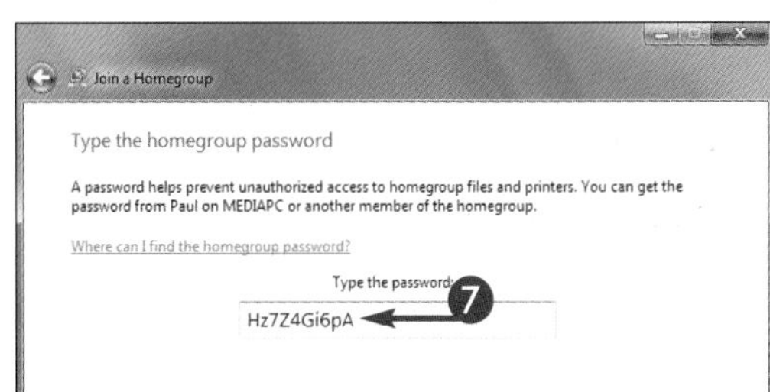


The Join a Homegroup wizard prompts you for the homegroup password.

7 Type the homegroup password.

8 Click **Next** (not shown).

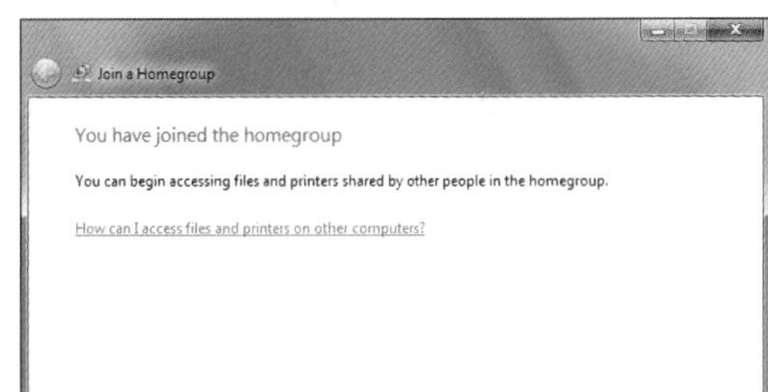


Windows 7 joins the computer to the homegroup.

9 Click **Finish** (not shown).

You can now access other homegroup computers and share your files with the homegroup.

### Can I use my homegroup to stream media to other computers and devices on my network?

Yes. To enable media streaming, click **Start**, and then click **Control Panel** to open the Control Panel window. Under the Network and Internet heading, click **Choose homegroup and sharing options** to open the Homegroup window. Click the **Stream my pictures, music, and videos to all devices on my home network** check box (☐ changes to ☑). Click **Save changes**.

### Can I leave a homegroup if I no longer need it?

Yes. Click **Start**, and then click **Control Panel** to open the Control Panel window. Under the Network and Internet heading, click **Choose homegroup and sharing options** to open the Homegroup window. Click the **Leave the homegroup** link and then click **Leave the homegroup**. Windows 7 removes your computer from the homegroup. Click **Finish**.

# Share a Document or Folder

You can share documents and folders of your choice with your homegroup, if your network has one. You can also share a document or folder with other users set up on your computer.

**You can set up each document or folder with Read or Read/Write permissions. Read means that users cannot make changes to the document or file; Read/Write means that users can make changes.**

## Share a Document or Folder

### SHARE WITH THE HOMEGROUP

1. Open the folder containing the document or subfolder you want to share.
2. Click the document or subfolder.

***Note:** If you want to share more than one object, select all the objects you want to share.*

3. Click **Share with**.
4. Click **Homegroup (Read)**.

- If you want homegroup users to make changes to the item, click **Homegroup (Read/Write)**, instead.

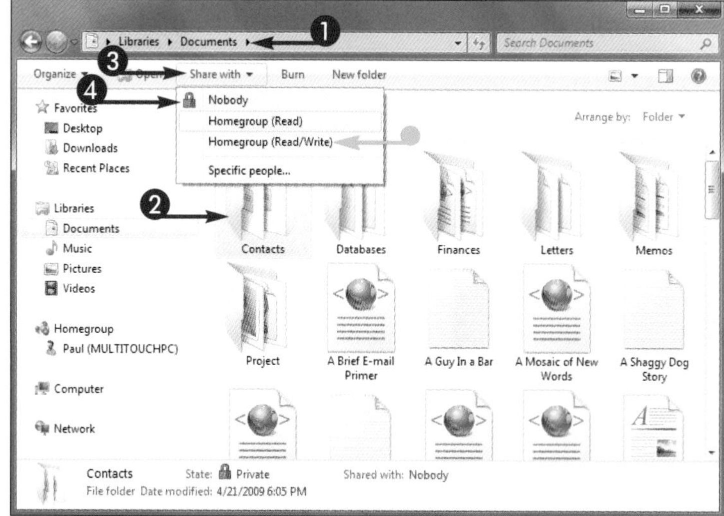


- The State property changes to Shared.
- The Shared with property changes to Homegroup.

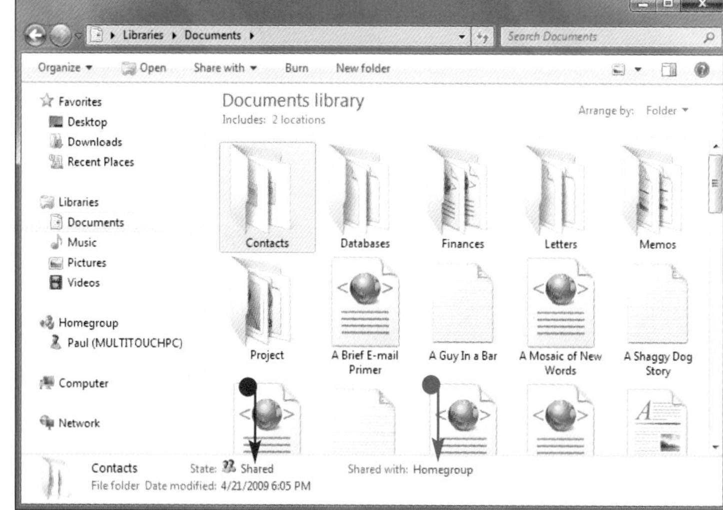

## SHARE WITH A SPECIFIC USER

1. Open the folder containing the document or subfolder you want to share.
2. Click the document or subfolder.
3. Click **Share with**.
4. Click **Specific people**.

   The File Sharing dialog box appears.

5. Click ▾ and then click the name of the user.
6. Click **Add**.
7. Click ▾ and then click the permission level.
8. Click **Share**.

   Windows 7 shares the document or folder.

- Be sure to give the user the address that appears here.

9. Click **Done**.

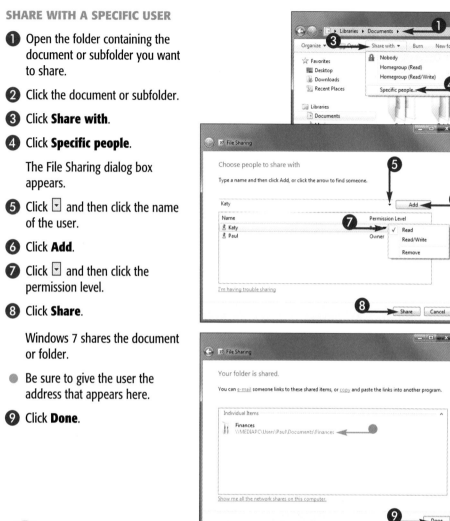

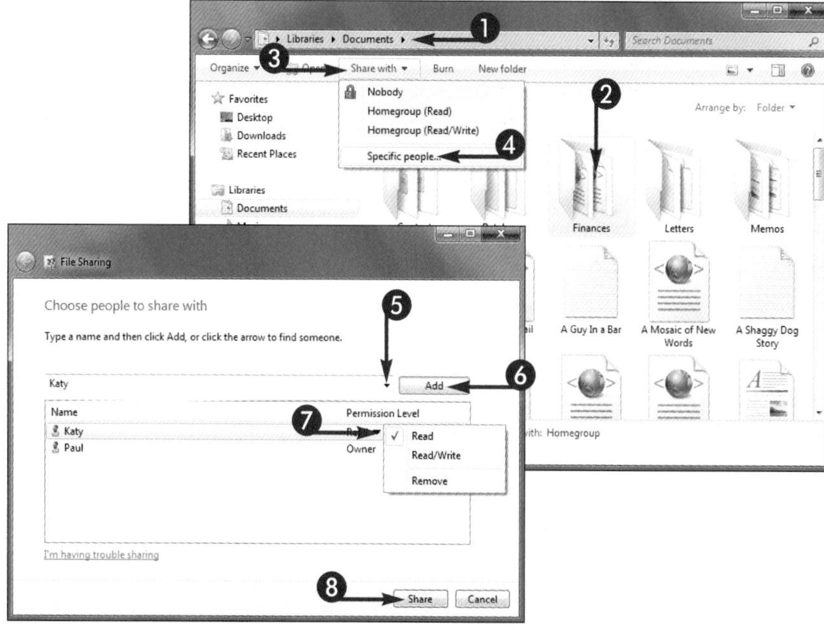


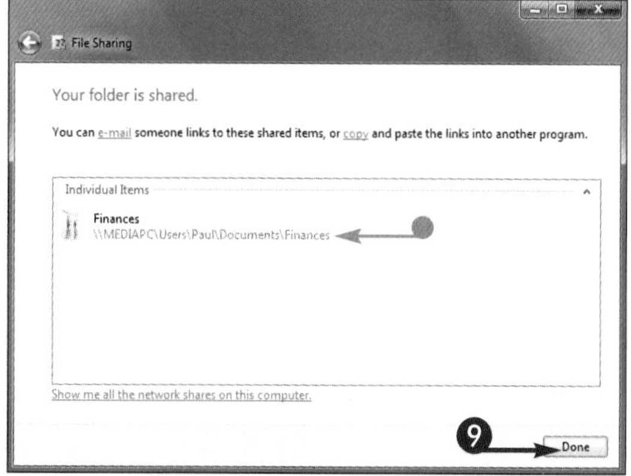

### How do the other users access the shared document or folder?

You need to send them the address that appears in the final File Sharing dialog box. You have two choices: Click **e-mail** to send the address via e-mail or click **copy** to copy the address to memory. You can then open a program such as WordPad, click **Edit**, and then click **Paste** to paste the address.

### Can I see all the documents and folders that I am sharing with other users?

Yes, you can do this in two ways. In the final File Sharing dialog box, click **Show me all the network shares on this computer**. Alternatively, in any folder window, click **Network** and then double-click your computer.

# Connect to a Wireless Network

If you have a wireless access point in your home or office, you can connect to it to access your network. If your wireless access point is connected to the Internet, then connecting to the wireless network gives your computer Internet access, as well.

**Most wireless networks are protected with a security key, which is a kind of password. Be sure you know the key before attempting to connect.**

## Connect to a Wireless Network

1. Click the **Network** icon ( ) in the taskbar's notification area.

- Windows 7 displays a list of wireless networks in your area.
- Windows 7 displays the Unsecured icon ( ) for networks not protected by a security key.

2. Click your network.

3. To have Windows 7 connect to your network automatically in the future, click to activate the **Connect automatically** check box ( changes to ).
4. Click **Connect**.

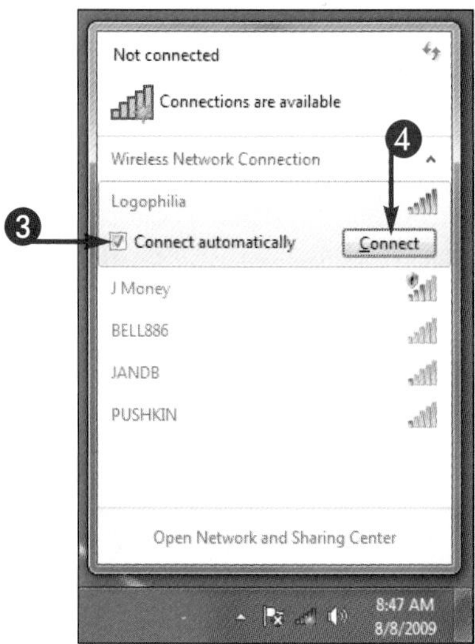

If the network is protected by a security key, Windows 7 asks you to enter it.

5 Type the security key.

- If you are worried that someone nearby might see the security key, you can click **Hide characters** (☐ changes to ☑) to display the characters you type as dots.

6 Click **OK**.

Windows 7 connects to the network.

- The network icon changes from [icon] to [icon] to indicate that you now have a wireless network connection.

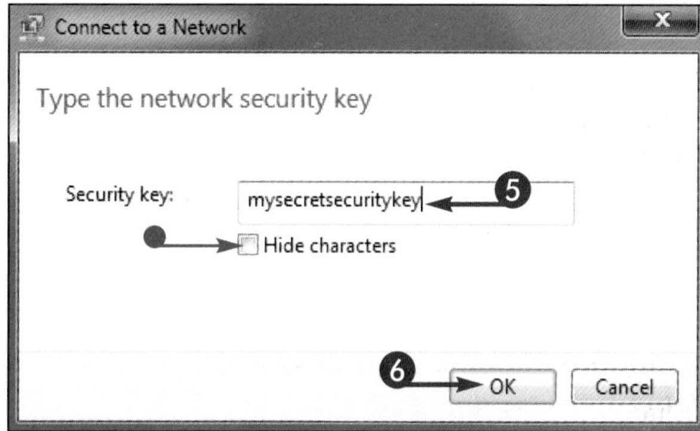


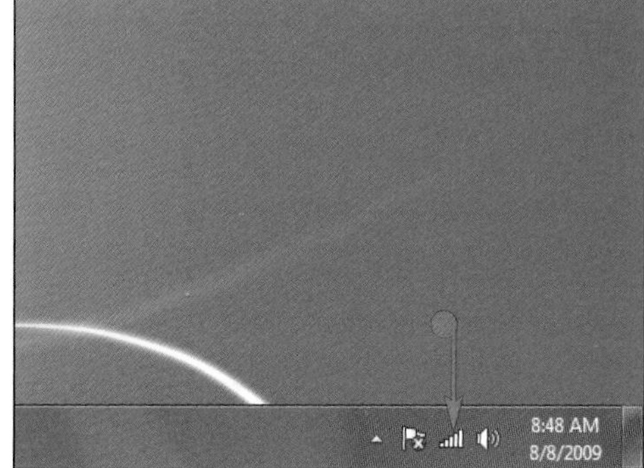


TIP

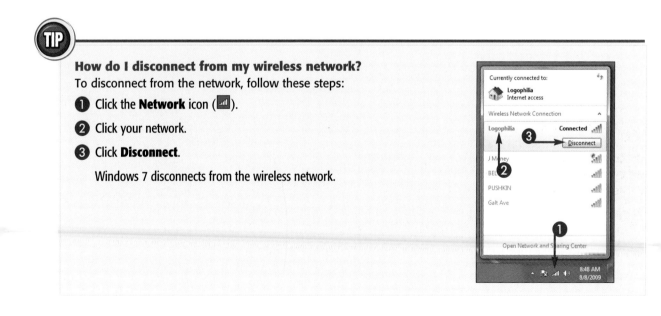

**How do I disconnect from my wireless network?**

To disconnect from the network, follow these steps:

1 Click the **Network** icon ([icon]).

2 Click your network.

3 Click **Disconnect**.

Windows 7 disconnects from the wireless network.

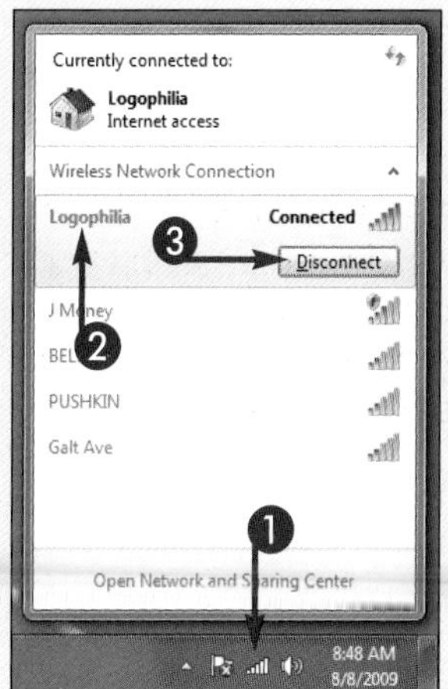

# View Network Resources

To see what other network users have shared on your homegroup, you can use the Homegroup folder to view the other computers and see their shared resources. If your network does not have a homegroup, you can use the Network folder, instead.

**A network resource can be a folder, hard drive, CD or DVD drive, removable disk drive, printer, scanner, or other shared device.**

## View Network Resources

### VIEW HOMEGROUP RESOURCES

1. Click **Start**.
2. Click **Documents**.

***Note:*** *You can access the Homegroup folder from any folder window.*

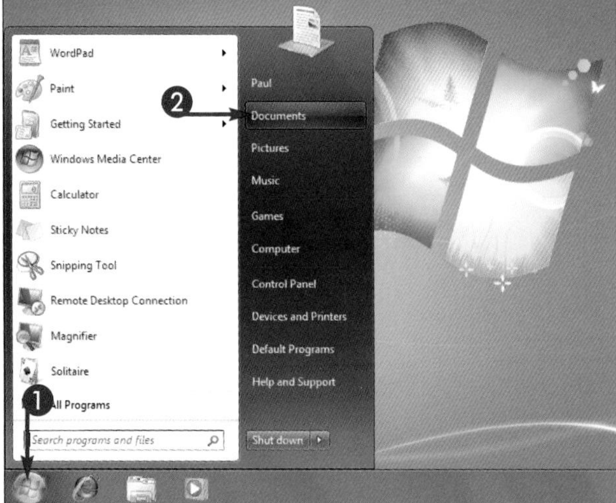


The Documents library appears.

3. Double-click the **Homegroup** folder.
4. Click the computer you want to access.

- The resources shared by the computer appear here.

5. Double-click an icon to access the resource.

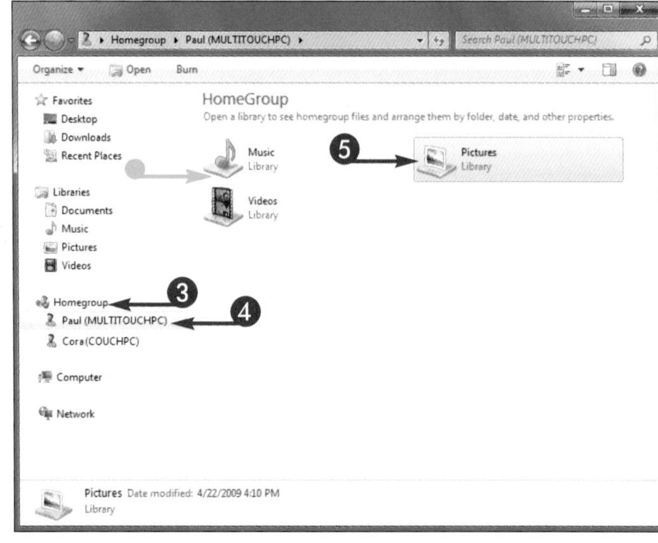

### VIEW NETWORK RESOURCES

1. Click **Start**.
2. Click **Documents**.

***Note:*** *You can access the Network folder from any folder window.*

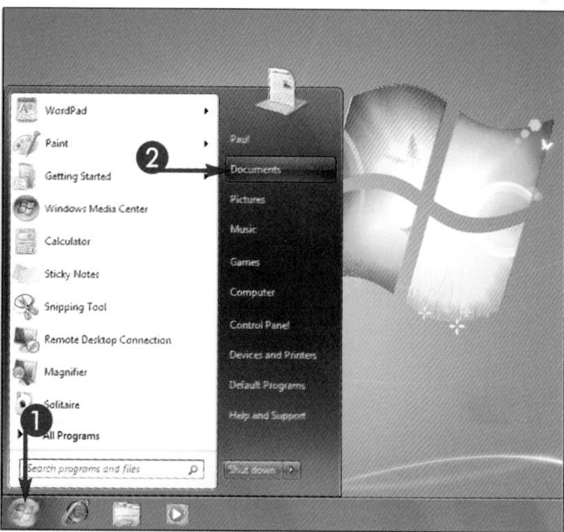

The Documents library appears.

3. Double-click the **Network** folder.
4. Click the computer you want to access.

- The resources shared by the computer appear here.

5. Double-click an icon to access the resource.

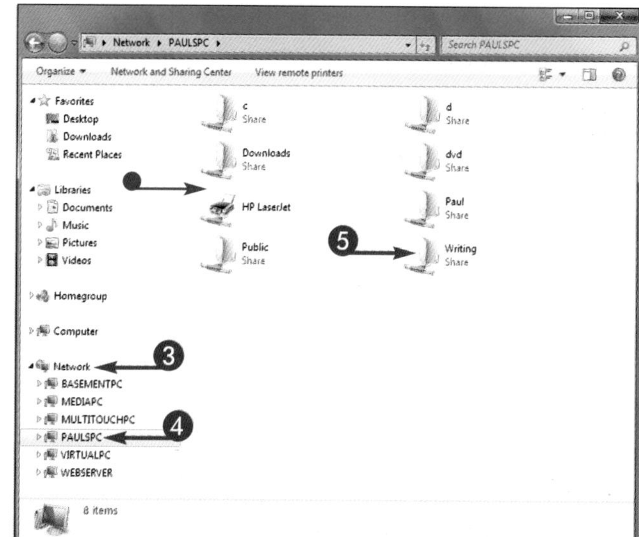

## My network is not working. Is there a way to fix the problem?

Yes. Windows 7 comes with a network repair tool called Windows Network Diagnostics that can solve most network problems. Right-click the network icon in the taskbar's notification area, and then click **Troubleshoot problems** to start the Windows Network Diagnostics. Follow whatever repair techniques Windows 7 suggests.

## How do I change the network name of my computer?

Click **Start**, right-click **Computer**, and then click **Properties** to open the System window. Click the **Change settings** link to open the System Properties dialog box with the Computer Name tab displayed, and then click **Change**. Use the Computer Name text box to type the new name, and then click **OK**.

# Using Windows 7's Notebook Features

Windows 7 comes with many features designed specifically for notebook computers. In this chapter, you learn how to use the new Mobility Center, monitor battery life, specify a scheme for saving power, use a pen to input text, synchronize files between a notebook and a desktop PC, and more.

# Display Mobility Settings

You can quickly see and change certain notebook settings by displaying Windows 7's Mobility Center feature. The Mobility Center enables you to monitor battery power and your wireless network connection, adjust the volume, rotate the screen of a Tablet PC, and more.

## Display Mobility Settings

1. Click **Start**.
2. Click **Control Panel**.

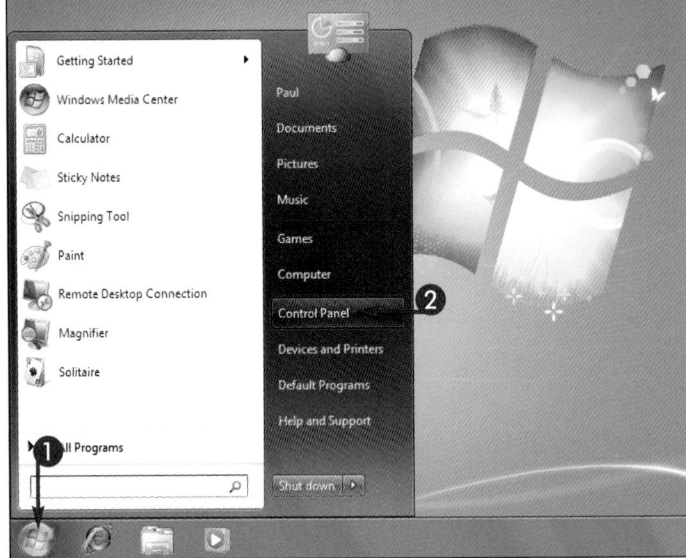


The Control Panel window appears.

3. Click **Adjust commonly used mobility settings**.

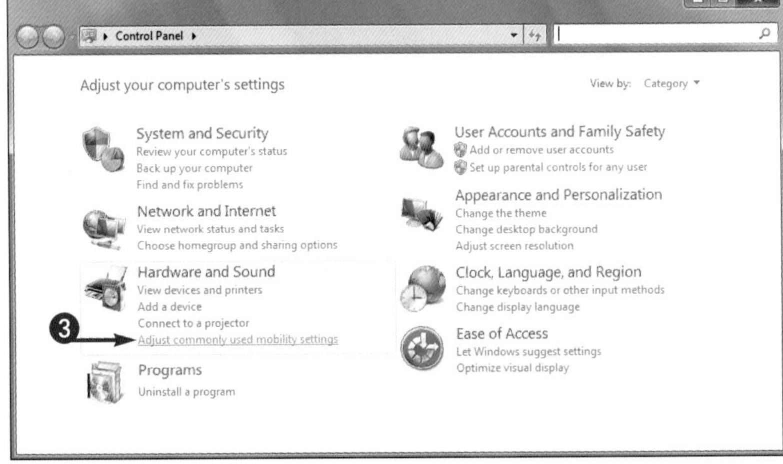

The Windows Mobility Center window appears.

- The top part of each section tells you the current status of the setting.
- The middle part of each section offers a control that you can use to change the setting.
- The bottom part of each section tells you the name of the setting.

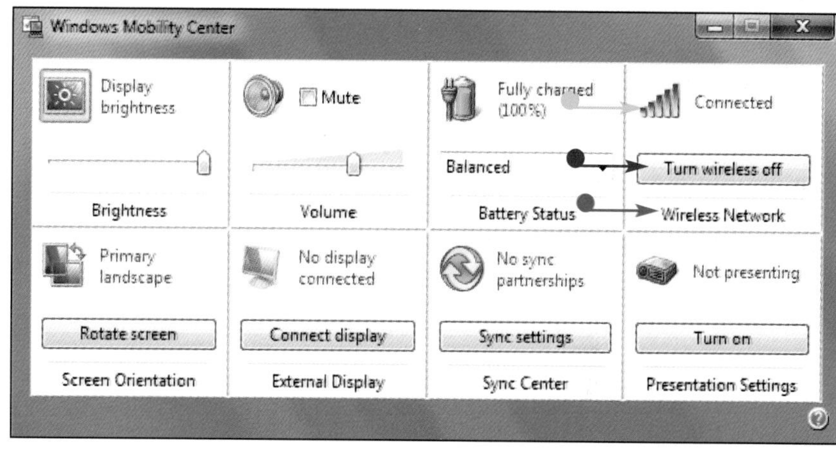


4. When you are done, click the **Close** button (![Close]) to shut down the Mobility Center.

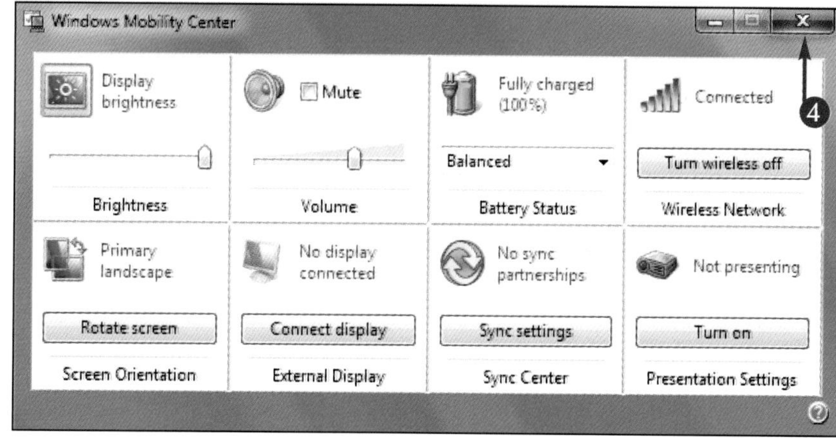


TIPS

### Why can I not change some of the settings in the Mobility Center?

All notebook PCs do not support the eight settings in the default Mobility Center. For example, only Tablet PCs support the Screen Orientation setting. Similarly, you can only use the External Display settings if you have an external monitor attached to your notebook PC.

### Is there a quicker way to open the Mobility Center?

Yes. Follow these steps:

1. Right-click the **Power** icon (![Power]) in the taskbar's notification area.
2. Click **Windows Mobility Center**.

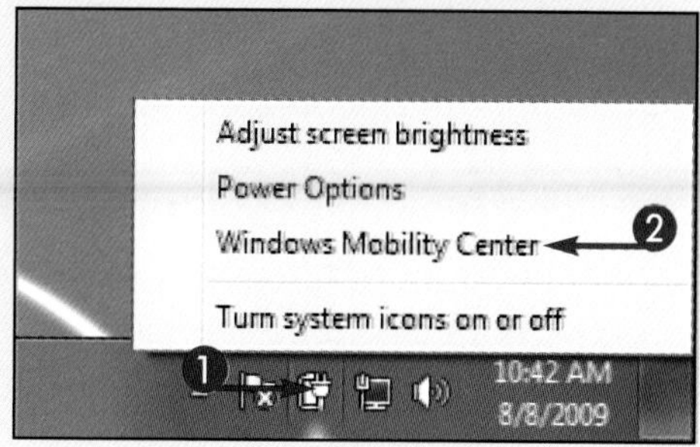

# Display Power Options

You can get the most out of your notebook battery by shutting down components when you are not using them. The Power Options window enables you to choose a power plan that configures Windows 7 to shut down notebook components for you automatically.

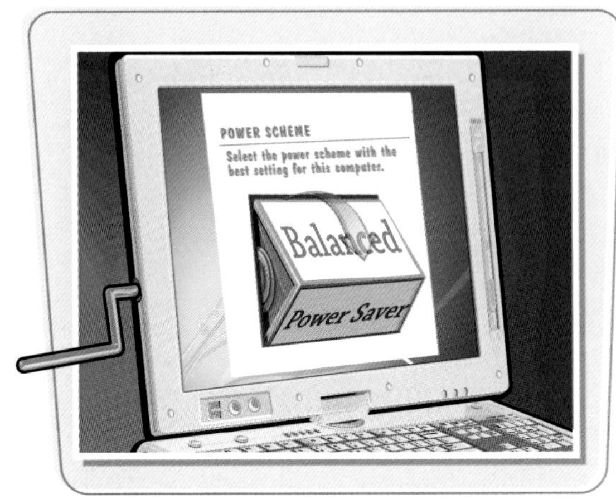


## Display Power Options

### OPEN THE POWER OPTIONS WINDOW

1. Click **Start**.
2. Click **Control Panel**.

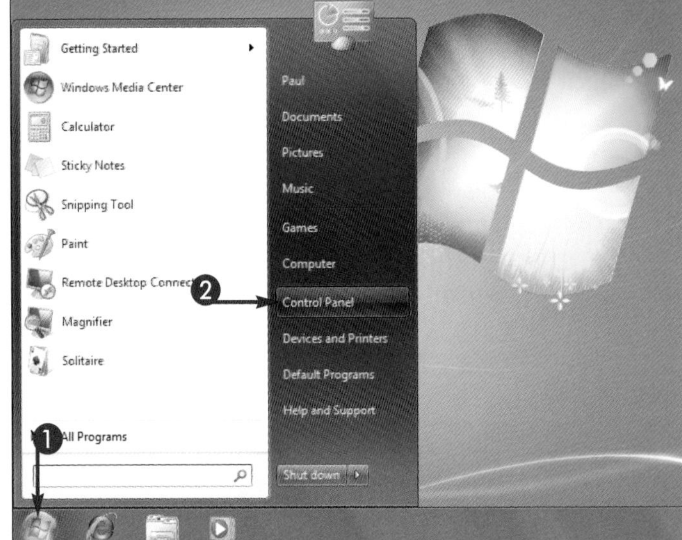


The Control Panel window appears.

3. Click **Hardware and Sound**.

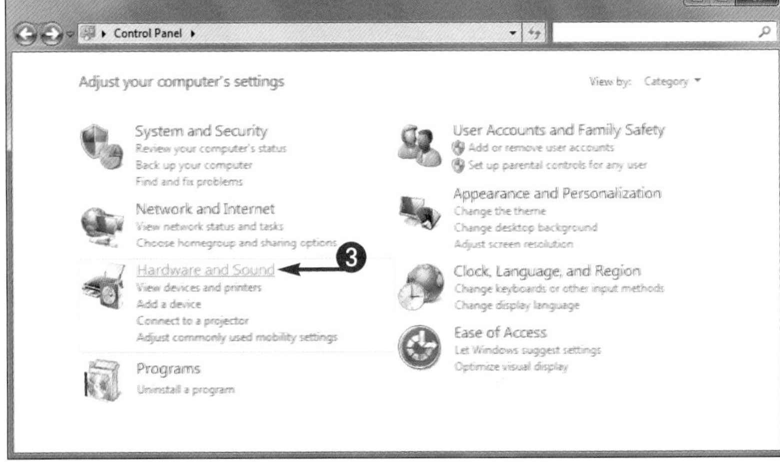

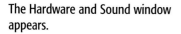

The Hardware and Sound window appears.

4 Click **Power Options**.

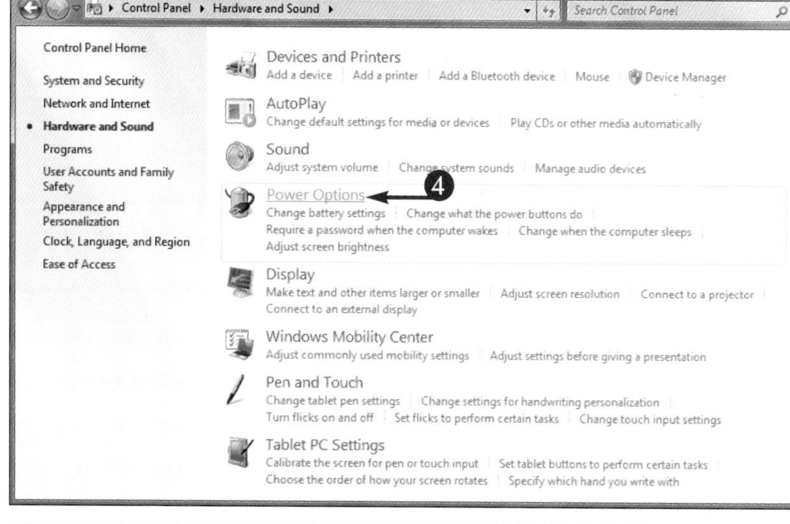


The Power Options window appears.

## CHOOSE A POWER PLAN

- Click here to display more power plans.

1 Click the power plan you want to use (◯ changes to ◉).

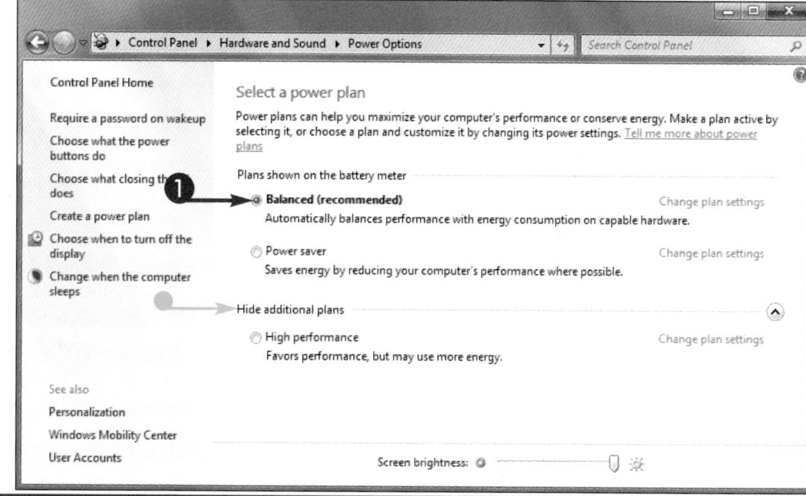

### Is there a quicker way to open the Power Options window or choose a power plan?

Yes. Follow these steps:

1 Click the **Power** icon ( ).

2 Click the power plan you want (◯ changes to ◉).

- To open Power Options, click **More power options**.

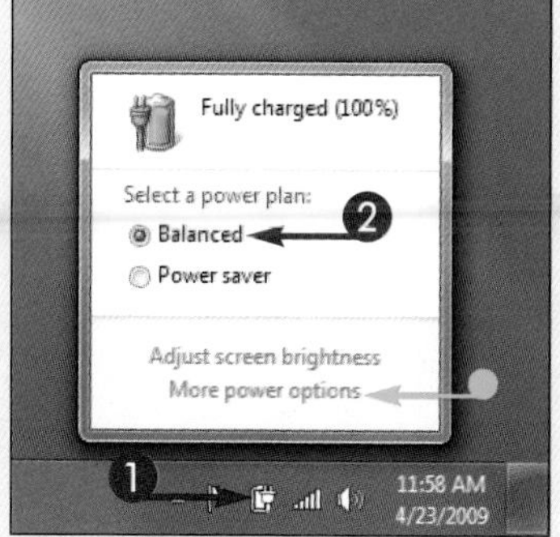


### Which power plan should I use?

The power plan you choose depends on how you are using your notebook computer. If you are on battery power, choose the Power Saver plan to maximize battery life. If you are running on AC power, choose the High Performance plan to reduce the frequency with which Windows 7 shuts down the computer components. If you do not want to bother switching plans, choose the Balanced plan.

# Customize a Power Plan

You can preserve battery power by setting up a custom *power plan* that turns off the monitor or the entire computer after you have not used the machine for a while.

**A power plan is useful because even when your notebook is sitting idle, it is still using the battery to power the monitor and the constantly spinning hard drive.**

## Customize a Power Plan

1. Display the Power Options window.

***Note:*** *See the previous section, "Display Power Options," to display the Power Options window.*

2. Under the power plan you want to customize, click **Change plan settings**.

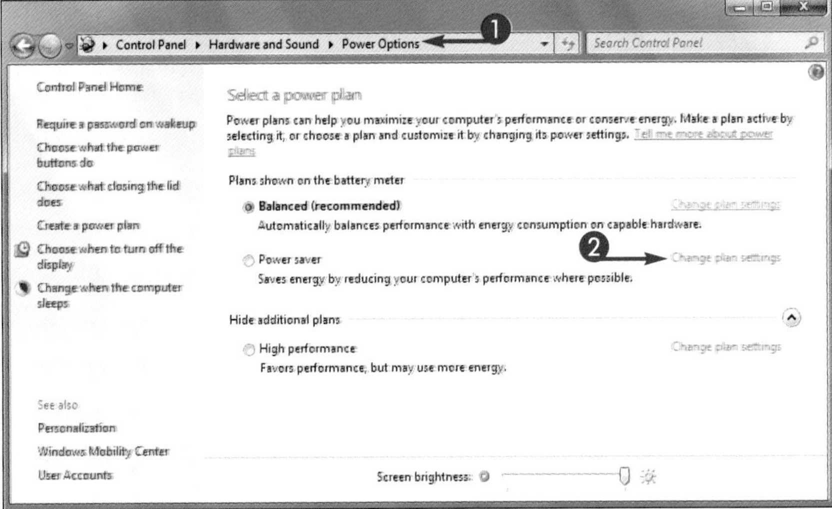


The Edit Plan Settings window appears.

3. Click ▾ to specify the amount of idle time after which the monitor dims.
4. Click ▾ to specify the amount of idle time after which the monitor turns off.
5. Click ▾ to specify the amount of idle time after which the computer goes to sleep.
6. Click **Save changes**.

Windows 7 puts the new power plan settings into effect.

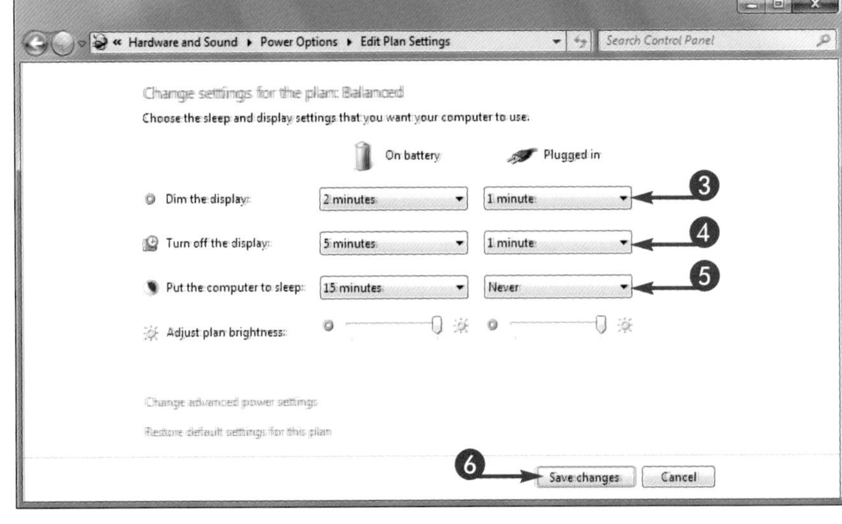

# Configure Power Buttons

You can configure your notebook's power buttons to perform actions, such as going into sleep mode or hibernating. This gives you a quick way to initiate these actions.

**There are three power "buttons" on most notebooks: The on/off (power) button, the sleep button, and closing the lid. If your notebook does not have a sleep button, you can usually simulate one by tapping the on/off button quickly.**

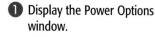

## Configure Power Buttons

1. Display the Power Options window.

*Note:* *See the section "Display Power Options" to display the Power Options window.*

2. Click **Choose what the power buttons do**.

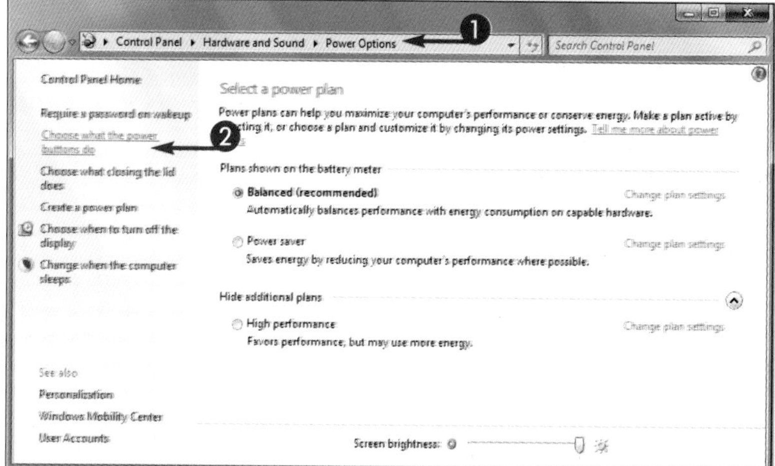


The System Settings window appears.

3. Click ▾ and click the action to perform when you press the notebook's power button.

4. Click ▾ and click the action to perform when you press the notebook's sleep button.

5. Click ▾ and click the action to perform when you close the notebook's lid.

6. Click **Save changes**.

Windows 7 puts the new settings into effect.

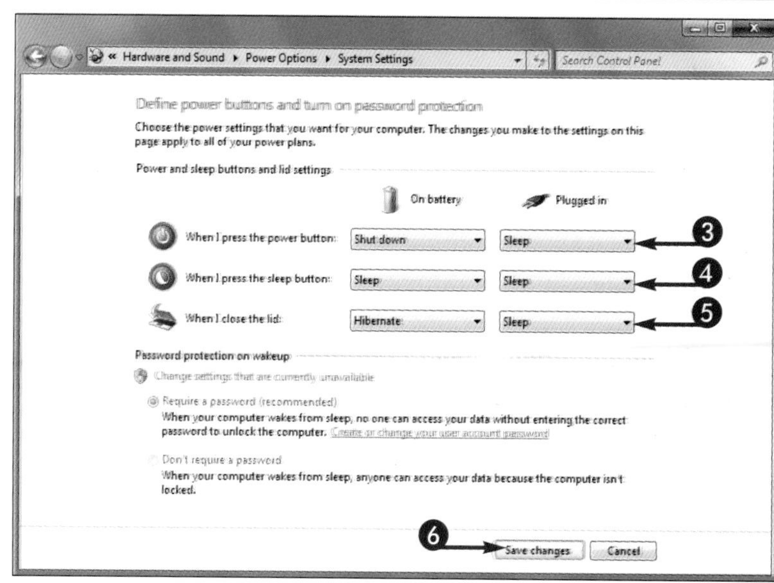

# Adjust Screen Brightness

You can extend the battery life of your notebook computer by turning down the screen brightness. Your notebook screen uses a lot of power, so turning down the brightness reduces battery drain.

**If you have trouble seeing the data on your notebook screen, you can often fix the problem by increasing the screen brightness.**

## Adjust Screen Brightness

1. Display the Power Options window.

***Note:** See the previous section, "Display Power Options," to display the Power Options window.*

- You can click and drag this slider to set the screen brightness for all power plans.

2. Under the power plan you want to customize, click **Change plan settings**.

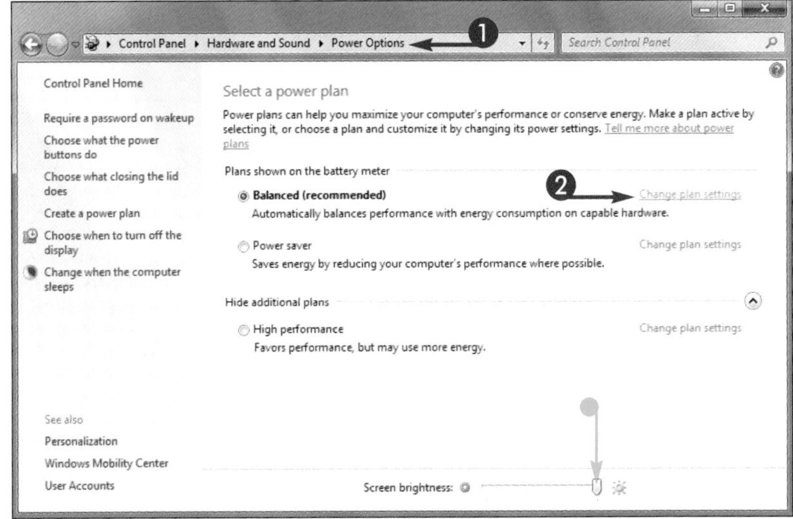


The Edit Plan Settings window appears.

3. Click and drag this slider to set the screen brightness while on battery power.
4. Click and drag this slider to set the screen brightness while your notebook is plugged in.
5. Click **Save changes**.

Windows 7 puts the new power plan settings into effect.

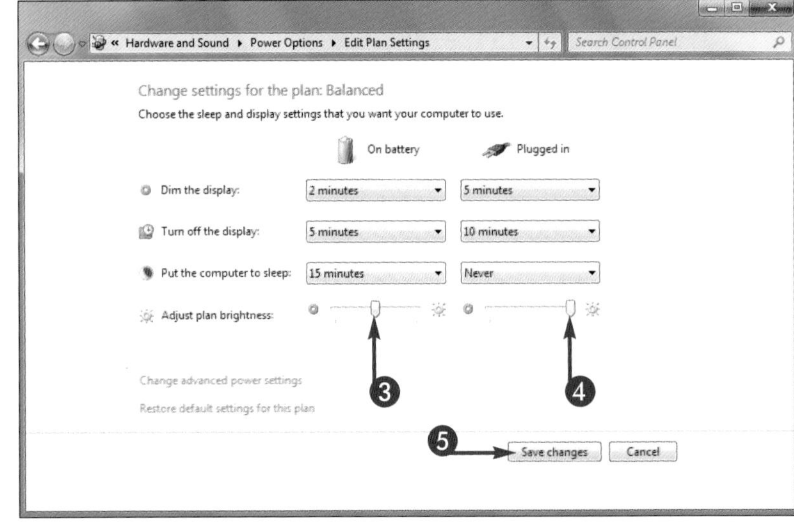

# Monitor Battery Power

You can use the Power icon in the taskbar's notification area to monitor your notebook's remaining battery power. When the battery is at maximum charge, the icon shows as all white. As the battery charge falls, the amount of white in the icon also falls.

**You can also position your mouse over the icon or click the icon to see a banner that shows you the current battery level.**

## Monitor Battery Power

### DISPLAY THE BATTERY LEVEL BANNER

1. Remove the power cord from your notebook to switch to battery power.

   The Power icon changes from changes to .

2. Position the mouse over the Power icon.

- Windows 7 displays a banner showing you how much battery power is left.

### DISPLAY THE BATTERY LEVEL FLY-OUT

1. Click the Power icon.

- Windows 7 displays a fly-out that shows the current battery level.

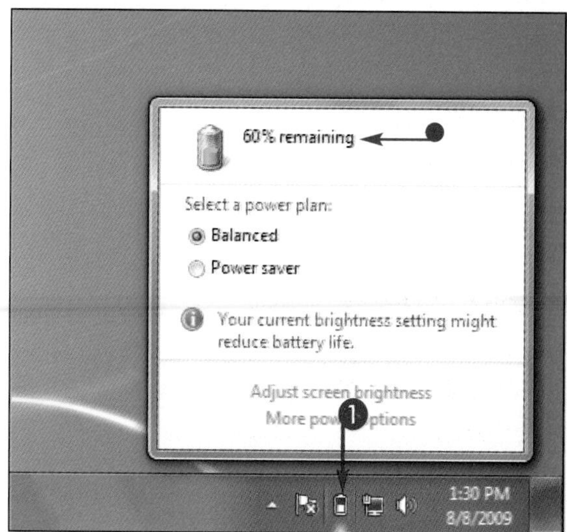

# Input Text with a Pen

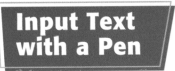

A Tablet PC comes with a touch-sensitive screen and a digital pen. By pressing lightly on the screen with the digital pen, you can insert text by hand and handwrite notes.

**When you use a digital pen, tapping the screen is the same as clicking the mouse. If you have a touch-sensitive screen, tapping the screen with your finger is the same as clicking the mouse.**

## Input Text with a Pen

### DISPLAY THE INPUT PANEL

1. Position your digital pen within range of the screen to display the Input Panel tab.
2. Position the pen over the Input Panel tab.
   - The Input Panel tab expands.
3. Tap the **Input Panel** tab.

- The Input Panel appears.

4. Tap the **Close** button (✕) when you are finished working with the Input Panel.

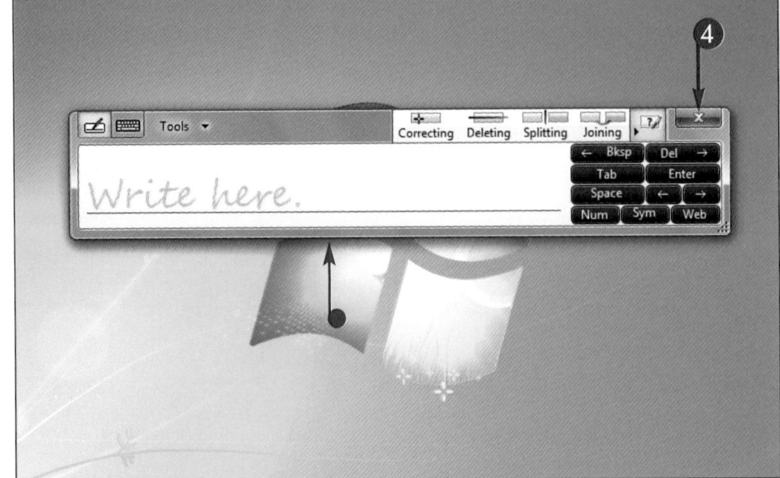

## INPUT TEXT WITH THE WRITING PAD

1. Open the program into which you want to insert the text.
2. Tap the text box or other area where you want the text inserted.
3. In the Input Panel, click the **Writing Pad** button.
4. Use the digital pen to handwrite the text in the Writing Pad.
5. Tap **Insert**.

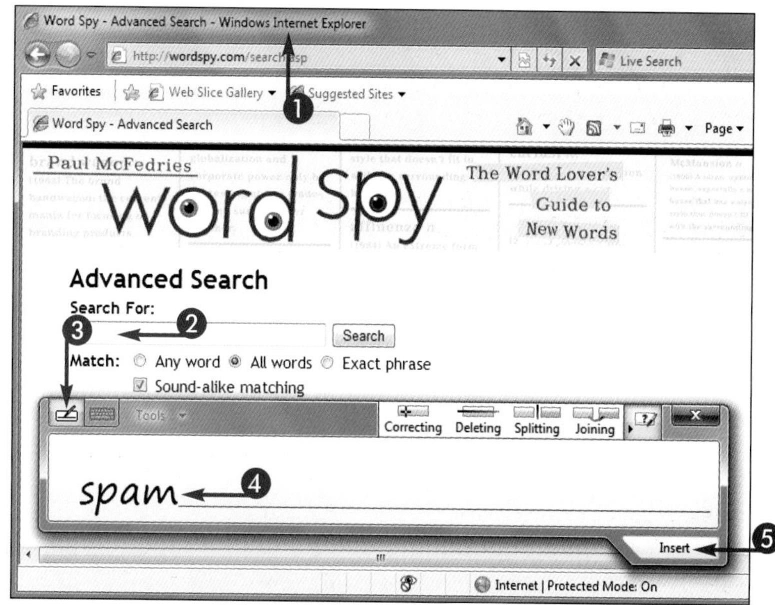


- Windows 7 inserts the text.
- Windows 7 clears the Writing Pad so you can enter more text.

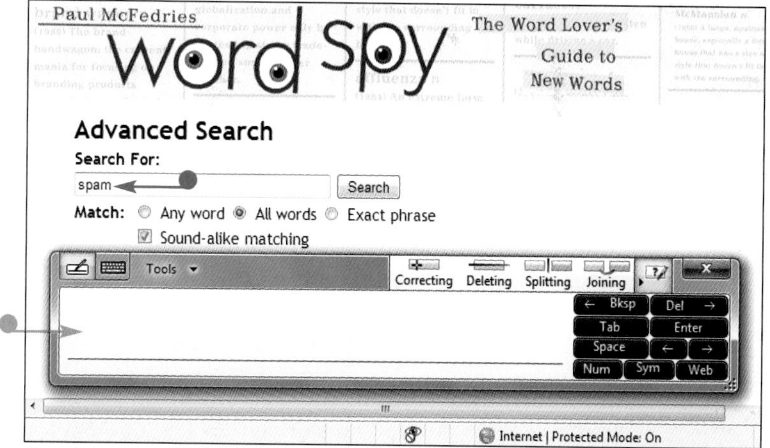

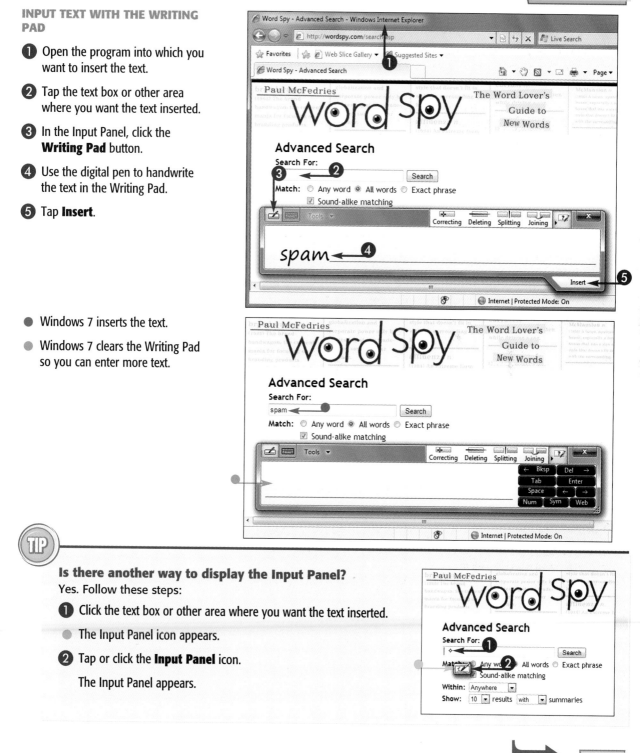

**TIP**

**Is there another way to display the Input Panel?**

Yes. Follow these steps:

1. Click the text box or other area where you want the text inserted.
   - The Input Panel icon appears.
2. Tap or click the **Input Panel** icon.

   The Input Panel appears.

continued

# Input Text with a Pen *(continued)*

If you have just a few characters to input, or if you are using your finger on a multi-touch screen, use the Input Panel's Touch Keyboard, which gives you more control over each character. For longer handwritten notes, use the Windows Journal program.

## Input Text with a Pen *(continued)*

### INPUT TEXT WITH THE TOUCH KEYBOARD

1. Open the program into which you want to insert the text.
2. Tap the text box or other area where you want the text inserted.
3. In the Input Panel, tap the **Touch Keyboard** button.

- Windows 7 displays the Touch Keyboard.

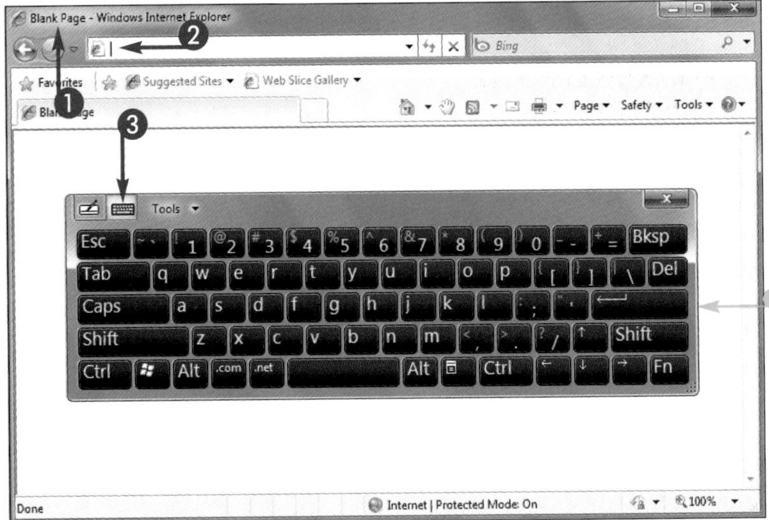


4. Use the keys to tap the characters you want to input.

- Windows 7 inserts the text.
- To tap an uppercase letter, tap **Shift** and then tap the letter.

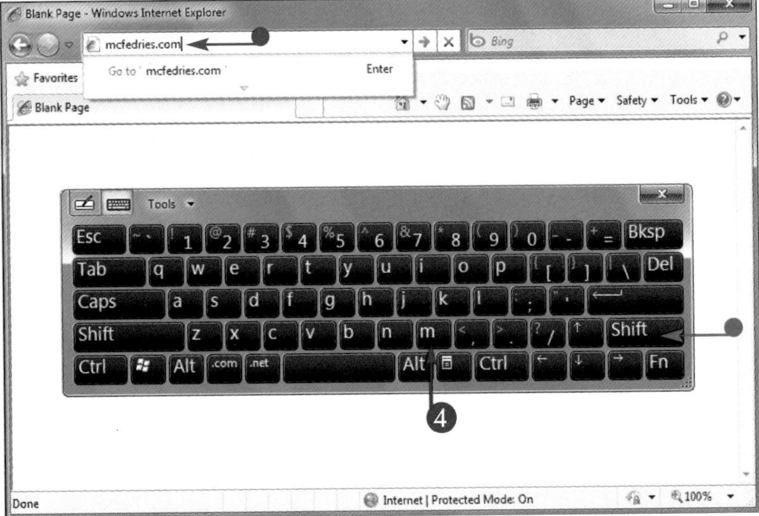

## HANDWRITE TEXT WITH WINDOWS JOURNAL

1. Tap **Start**.
2. Tap **journal**.
3. Tap **Windows Journal**.

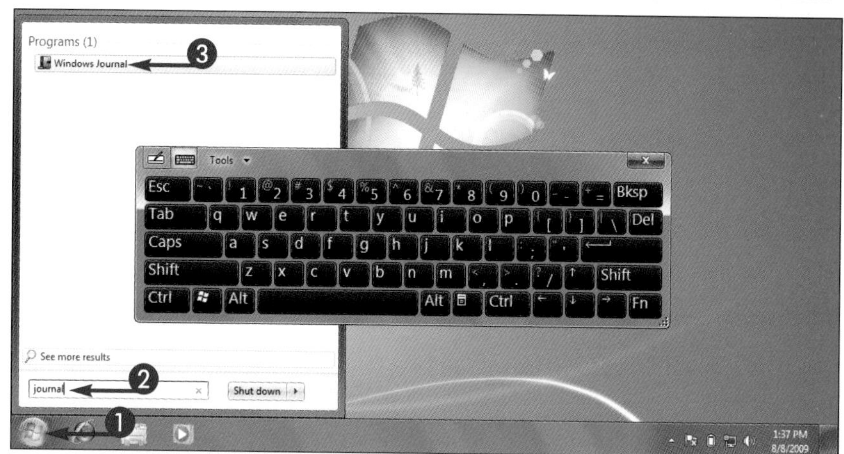

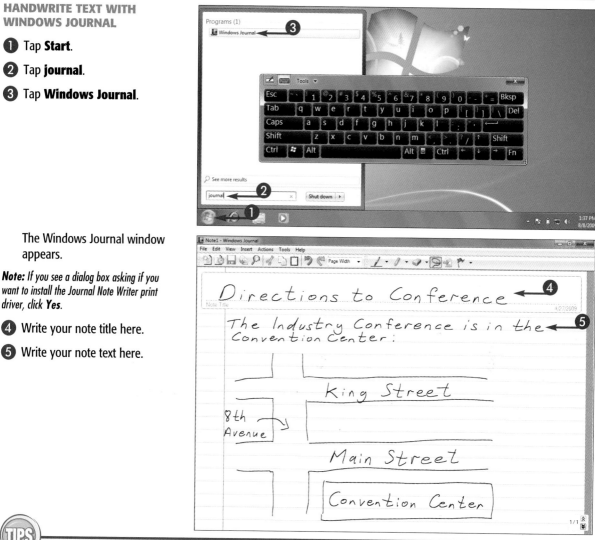

The Windows Journal window appears.

***Note:*** *If you see a dialog box asking if you want to install the Journal Note Writer print driver, click* ***Yes****.*

4. Write your note title here.
5. Write your note text here.

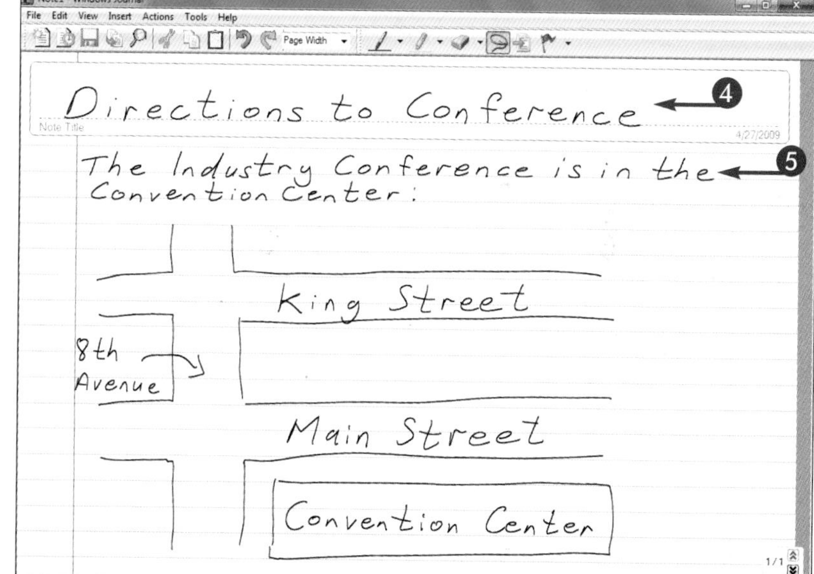

### How do I delete handwritten text?

Windows 7 offers five "scratch-out" gestures you can use to delete text:

- **Strikethrough**: A horizontal line (straight or wavy) through the text.
- **Vertical**: An M- or W-shaped gesture through the text.
- **Z**: A Z-shaped gesture through the text.
- **Circular**: A circle or an oval around the text.
- **Angled**: An angled line (straight or wavy) through the text. The angle can be from top left to bottom right, or from bottom left to top right.

### Can I convert handwriting to text?

Yes. In Windows Journal, click **Edit**, click **Selection Tool**, and then click and drag the mouse or pen around the handwriting that you want to convert. Click **Actions**, and then click **Convert Handwriting to Text**. Use the Text Correction dialog box to correct any errors and to choose what you want to do with the converted text.

# Synchronize Files Between Computers

If you use both a notebook computer and a desktop computer, you may often have to use the same files on both computers. To avoid having multiple versions of a file or losing work by accidentally copying over a file, Windows 7 enables you to synchronize files between the two computers.

**The synchronization between two computers is called a *sync partnership*. The file synchronization is handled automatically when you use Windows 7's new Sync Center feature.**

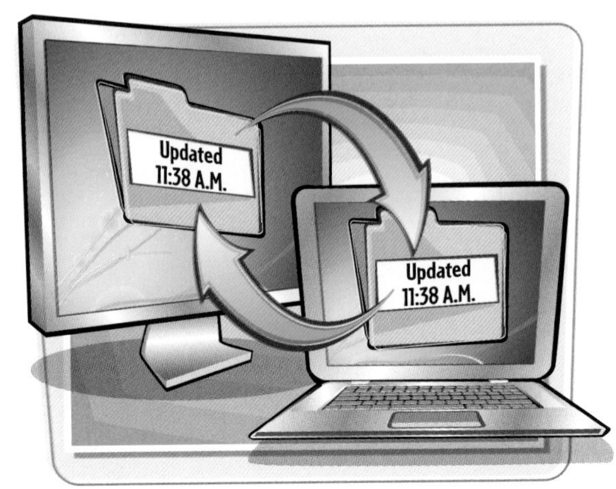


## Synchronize Files Between Computers

### SET UP A SYNC PARTNERSHIP

1 Click **Windows Explorer** ( ).

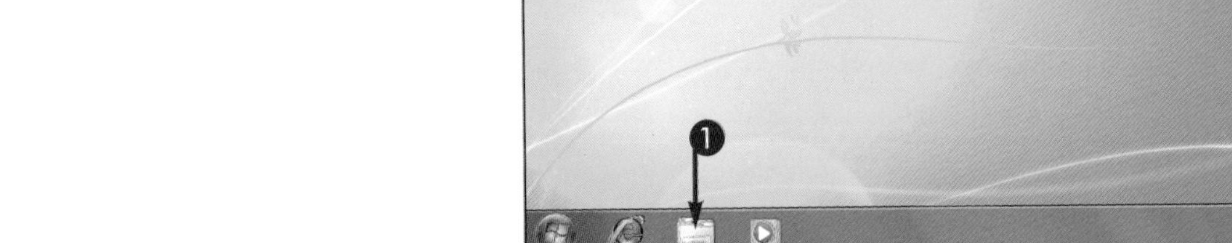

The Libraries window appears.

2 Click **Network**.

- If you have a homegroup on your network, click **Homegroup**, instead.

3 Double-click the computer that has the folder you want to synchronize.

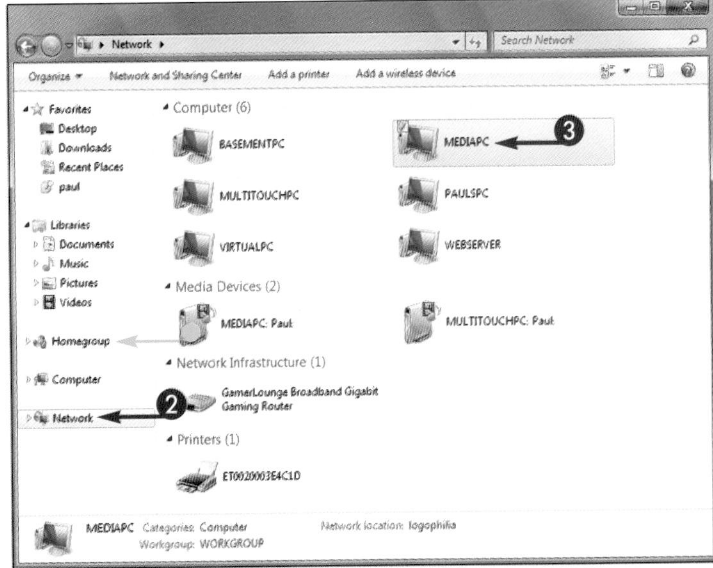

The folders shared by the computer appear.

4. Right-click the folder you want to synchronize.
5. Click **Always available offline**.

Windows 7 establishes a sync partnership with the other computer and prepares the folder to be used offline.

***Note:** "Offline" means when your computer is no longer connected to the network.*

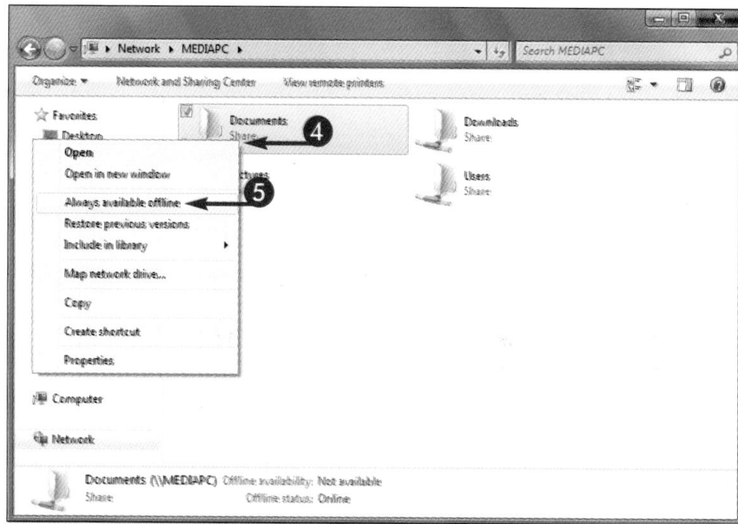

- The Sync icon appears, letting you know the folder is available offline.
- The Offline availability property now shows Always Available.

6. Click **Close**.

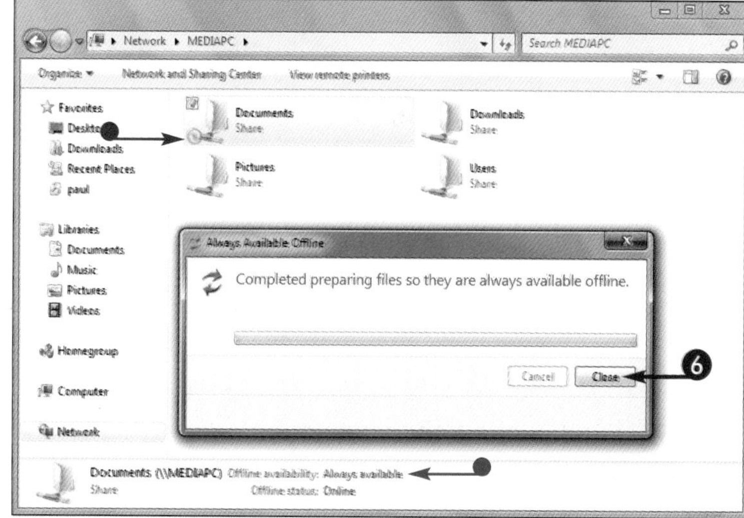

TIPS

### Do I have to have an account on the other computer?

Yes, in most cases. Windows 7's sync partnerships work best if you have the same user name and password on both computers. If you do not have an account under your user name on the other computer, you need to create one. See the "Create an Account" section in Chapter 7.

### Can I sync without being on a network?

No. Sync partnerships work only with computers that are part of a network. If you want to sync with a computer that is not on a network, use a Briefcase folder, as described in *Teach Yourself VISUALLY Windows XP,* 2nd Edition (Wiley, 2005).

continued

# Synchronize Files Between Computers *(continued)*

When you first set up a sync partnership, Windows 7 performs an initial synchronization between the two computers. If any of the files change, either on your computer or on the other computer, you need to perform a synchronization.

**It is a good idea to run a synchronization each time you log on and log off the network. You can sync using either the Mobility Center or the Sync Center.**

## Synchronize Files Between Computers *(continued)*

### SYCHRONIZE USING MOBILITY CENTER

1. Open the Mobility Center.

***Note:*** *See "Display Mobility Settings," earlier in this chapter.*

2. Click **Sync settings**.

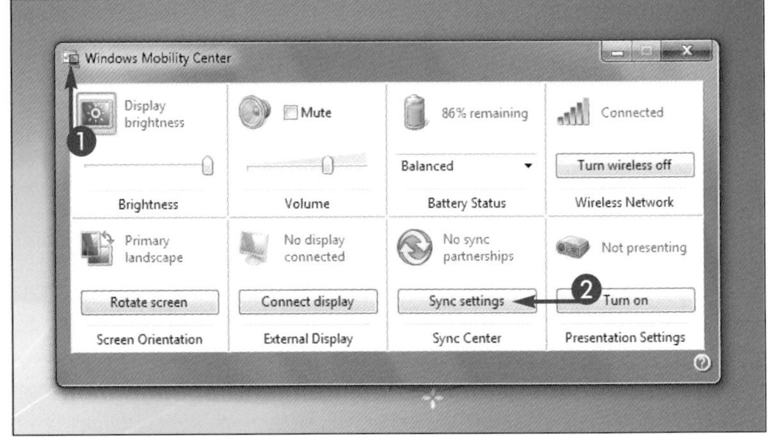


### SYCHRONIZE USING SYNC CENTER

1. Click **Start**.
2. Type **sync**.
3. Click **Sync Center**.

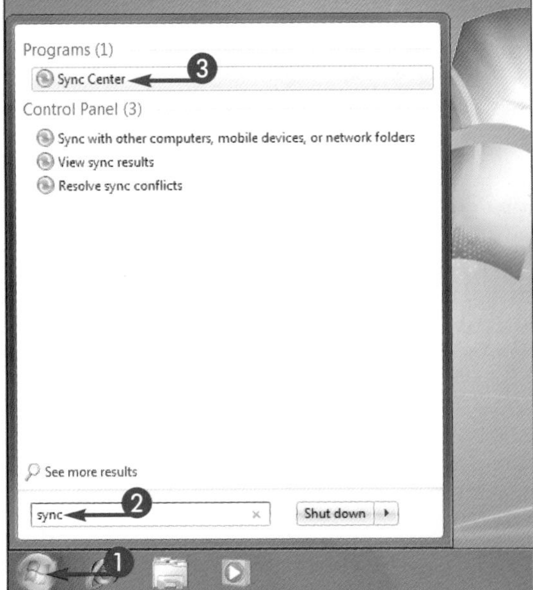

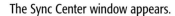

The Sync Center window appears.

4. Click **View sync partnerships**.
5. Click **Offline Files**.

   The Network and Internet window appears.

6. Click **Sync**.

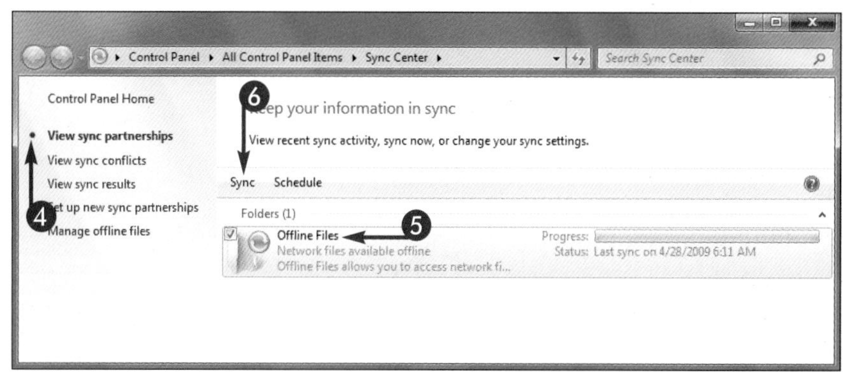


Windows 7 syncs the files with the other computer.

- The sync progress and results appear here.

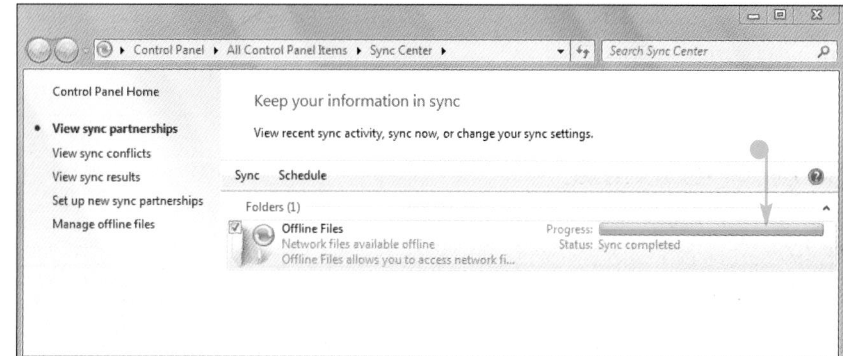


## TIPS

### If I have multiple folders to sync, can I synchronize just one of them?

Yes. In the Sync Center window, double-click the **Offline Files** icon to open the Offline Files window. This window displays a list of your offline folders. Click the folder you want to synchronize and then click **Sync**.

### Can I configure Windows 7 to sync with the other computer automatically?

Yes. In the Sync Center, click **View sync partnerships**, click **Offline Files**, and then click **Schedule**. Click **Next** in the first dialog box. If you want the sync to occur at a particular time, click **At a scheduled time** and then set up the schedule. If you prefer to sync when you log on or when your computer is idle, click **When an event occurs**, instead.

# Configure Presentation Settings

If you use your notebook to make presentations, you can tell Windows 7 when you are about to start a presentation and it turns off system notifications (such as e-mail alerts) and prevents the computer from going to sleep.

**You can also turn off the screen saver, set the volume level, and specify a desktop background suitable for your presentation.**

## Configure Presentation Settings

### CONFIGURE PRESENTATION SETTINGS

1. Open the Mobility Center.

*Note: See "Display Mobility Settings," earlier in this chapter.*

2. Click the **Change presentation settings** icon.

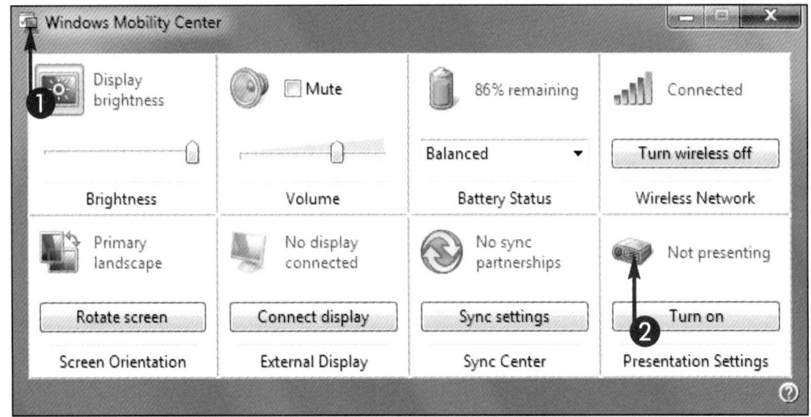


The Presentation Settings dialog box appears.

3. To make sure the screen saver does not activate during your presentation, click **Turn off the screen saver** (☐ changes to ☑).

4. Click **Set the volume to** ((☐ changes to ☑) and then click and drag the slider to set the presentation volume level.

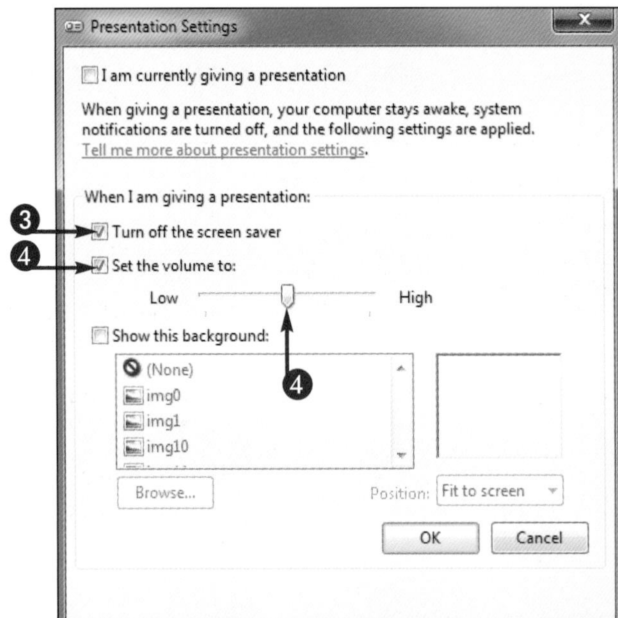

5. Click **Show this background** (☐ changes to ☑).
6. Click the background image you want to use.
7. In the Position list, click **Center**, **Tile**, or **Fit to screen**.
8. Click **OK**.

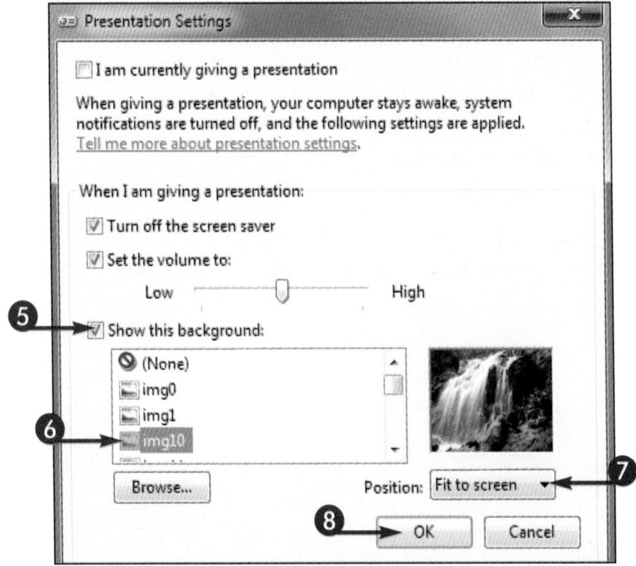

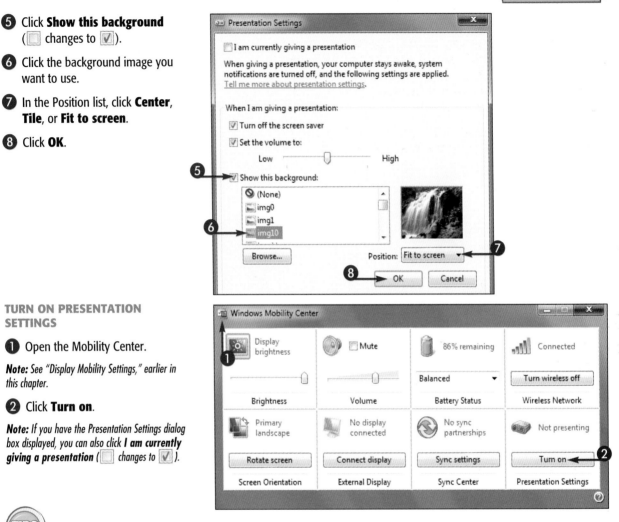

### TURN ON PRESENTATION SETTINGS

1. Open the Mobility Center.

***Note:*** *See "Display Mobility Settings," earlier in this chapter.*

2. Click **Turn on**.

***Note:*** *If you have the Presentation Settings dialog box displayed, you can also click **I am currently giving a presentation** (☐ changes to ☑).*

## TIPS

### Why should I use presentation settings?

When you are giving a presentation, your goal should always be to keep your audience focused on your message. If your notebook goes to sleep, your screen saver kicks in, or an e-mail alert appears, it takes your audience's attention away from your presentation.

### I have a special desktop background for presentations. How do I use it?

If you have a company logo or other background that you prefer to display during presentations, click **Show this background** (☐ changes to ☑) and then click **Browse** to open the Browse dialog box. Click the image file you want to use, and then click **Open**.

# Getting Connected to the Internet

The Internet is a global network that enables you to read World Wide Web pages, send e-mail messages, and have a vast world of information at your fingertips. This chapter shows you how to get your computer connected to the Internet.

# Understanding Internet Connections

Before you connect to the Internet, you need to know how to set up your dial-up modem and how to choose an Internet service provider.

**If you want to set up a wireless or high-speed Internet connection, you can skip the dial-up modem configuration.**

### Serial Cable

Run this cable from the modem to the serial port in the back of your computer. You do not need to do this if your modem resides inside your computer's case.

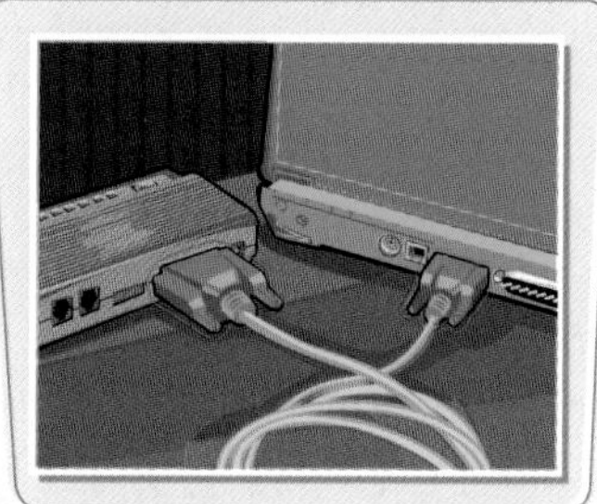

### Phone Line

Run one phone cable from the wall jack to the jack labeled *Line* on the back of the modem. This jack may also be labeled *Telco* or it may just show a picture of a wall jack.

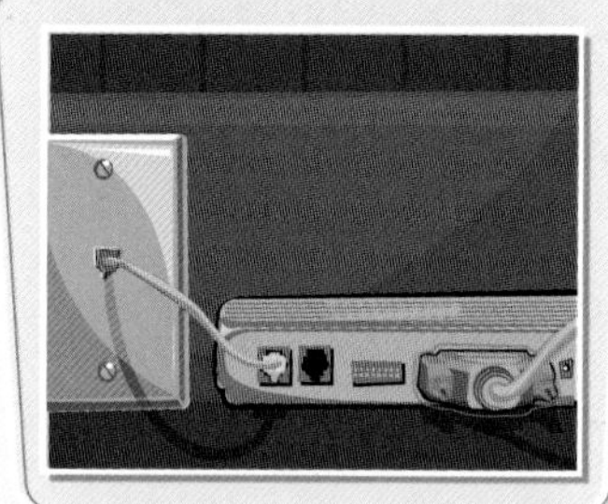

### Telephone Connection

Run a second phone cable from the telephone to the jack labeled *Phone* in the back of the modem. This jack may also just show a picture of a telephone.

### Internet Service Provider

An *Internet service provider* (ISP) supplies you with an account that enables you to access the Internet. You dial up the ISP using your computer's modem, and then the ISP connects your computer to the Internet.

### Connection Charges

The ISP charges you a monthly fee, which can range from a few dollars a month to $40 or $50 dollars a month, depending on the connection speed and how many minutes of connection time you are allowed each month. Note that although most ISPs offer a flat rate, some charge an extra fee per hour if you exceed your allotted time.

### Connection Speed

Internet connections have different speeds, and this speed determines how fast the Internet data is sent to your computer. If you connect to your ISP using a dial-up modem, the connection speed may be up to 56 kilobits per second, although connection quality may slow transmission speeds. High-speed — or *broadband* — connections such as cable, satellite, and DSL/ADSL offer speeds typically ranging from 1 megabit per second to 30 megabits per second.

# Get an Internet Connection Started

You can get on the Internet using Windows 7's Connect to the Internet feature, which takes you step-by-step through the process. This is much easier than trying to set up the connection on your own.

**The Connect to the Internet feature enables you to set up three types of connections: wireless, broadband, and dial-up. This section shows you how to get the connection started, and the next three sections show you how to set up each connection type.**

## Get an Internet Connection Started

1. Click the **Network** icon ( ).
2. Click **Open Network and Sharing Center**.

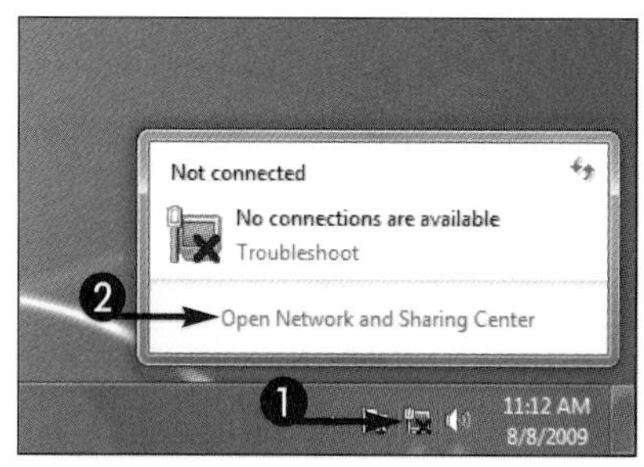


The Network and Sharing Center window appears.

3. Click **Set up a new connection or network**.

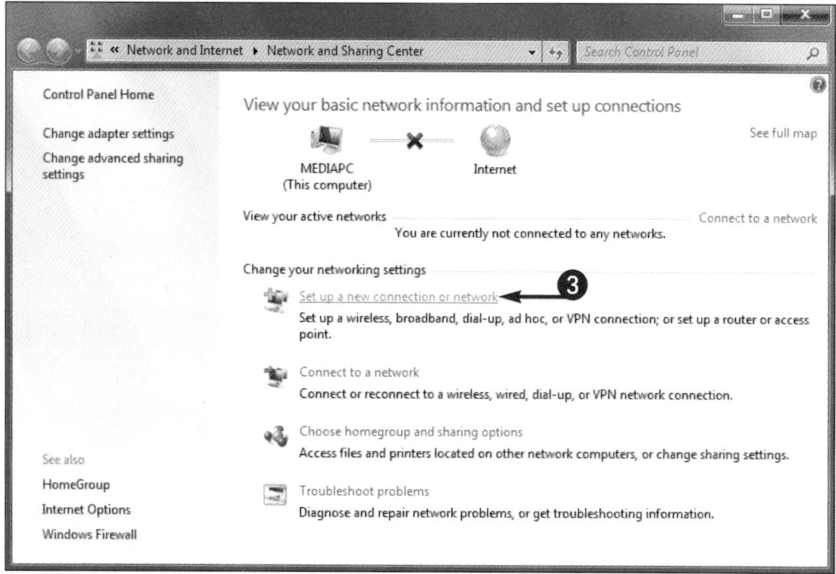

The Choose a Connection Option dialog box appears.

4. Click **Connect to the Internet**.
5. Click **Next**.

Windows 7 launches the Connect to the Internet feature and displays the How Do You Want to Connect dialog box.

***Note:*** *The next three sections take you through the specifics of the three connection types.*

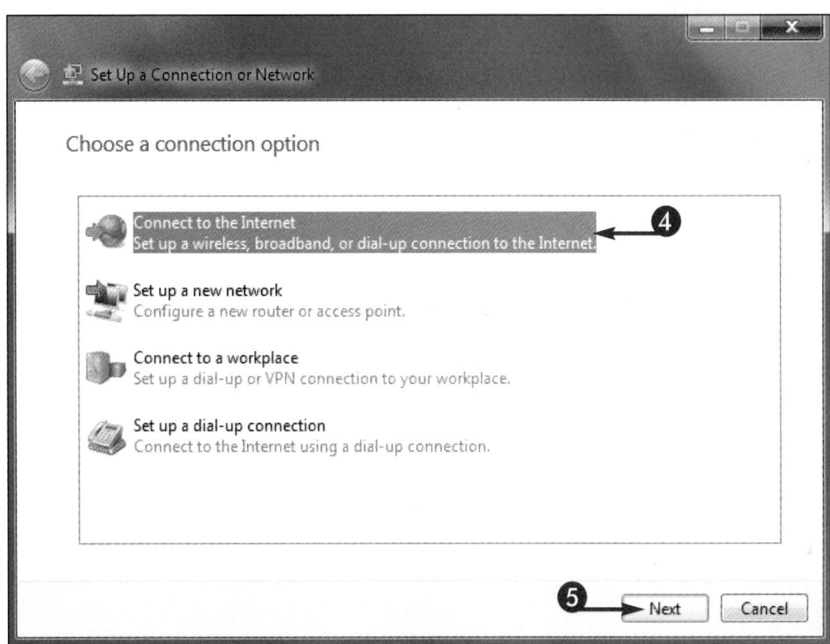

### How do I know which Internet connection type to choose?

The Internet connection you set up depends on the type of Internet account you have, the equipment attached to your computer, and whether you are connected to a network. For dial-up, you need a dial-up modem attached to your computer and a dial-up ISP account; for broadband, you need a broadband modem and a broadband account; for wireless, you need a wireless network adapter attached to your computer and a wireless router or router attached to a broadband modem.

### When I click Set Up a New Connection or Network, Windows 7 tells me I am already connected to the Internet. Why?

If your computer is part of a network that has Internet access, then Windows 7 automatically detects the network and sets up the Internet connection for you. To check this, click the **Network** icon ( ). In the window that pops up, look for the Internet Access message ( ).

# Create a Wireless Connection

If you have a wireless router in your home or office, and that router is connected to the Internet, you can get wireless Internet access for your computer by connecting to that router.

**Many wireless networks are protected with a security key or password, so be sure you know the key or password before attempting to connect.**

## Create a Wireless Connection

1. In the How Do You Want to Connect dialog box, click **Wireless**.

***Note:*** *See the previous section, "Get an Internet Connection Started," to access this dialog box.*

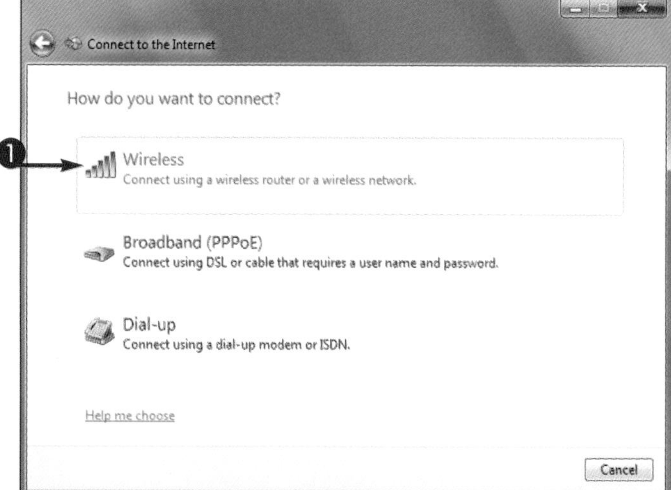


Windows 7 displays a list of wireless networks in your area.

2. Click your network.
3. Click **Connect**.

If the network is protected by a security key or password, Windows 7 asks you to enter it.

4. Type the security key or password.

- If you are concerned that someone in the vicinity might attempt to read the security key as you type it, click **Hide characters** ( changes to ) to display the characters as dots.

5. Click **OK**.

Windows 7 connects to the network and to the Internet.

6. To confirm Internet access, click the **Network** icon ( ).

- Windows 7 displays Internet Access here.

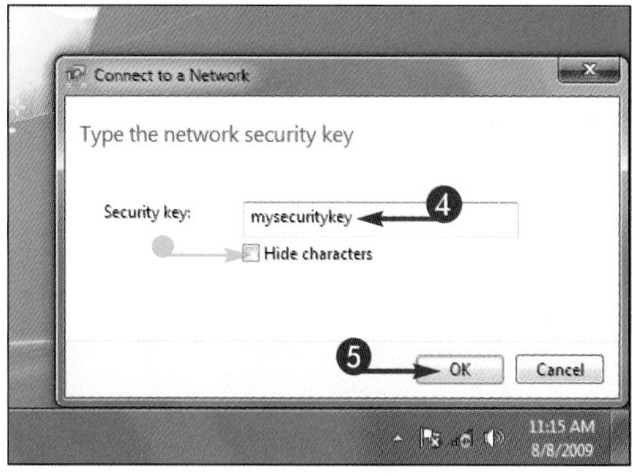

### How do I connect my wireless router to my broadband modem?

You should first turn off the router and the broadband modem, and then run a network cable from the modem to the WAN port on the back of the router. To configure the router, run another network cable from one of your computers to any LAN port on the back of the router, and then turn on the router and modem.

### How do I configure my router to connect to the Internet?

On the computer connected to the router, start your Web browser, type the router address (usually either **http://192.168.1.1** or **http://192.168.0.1**), and press Enter. If required, type the default user name and password (supplied by the router manufacturer). The router's setup page appears. Choose either the **DHCP** or **PPPoE** option, depending on your ISP; for the latter, type your ISP user name and password.

# Create a Broadband Connection

If you have a broadband account with your Internet service provider, you can configure Windows 7 to use a broadband Internet connection.

**Your Internet service provider should have given you a broadband modem for the connection, and it should have told you your user name and password.**

## Create a Broadband Connection

1. In the How Do You Want to Connect dialog box, click **Broadband (PPPoE)**.

*Note: See the "Get an Internet Connection Started" section to access this dialog box.*

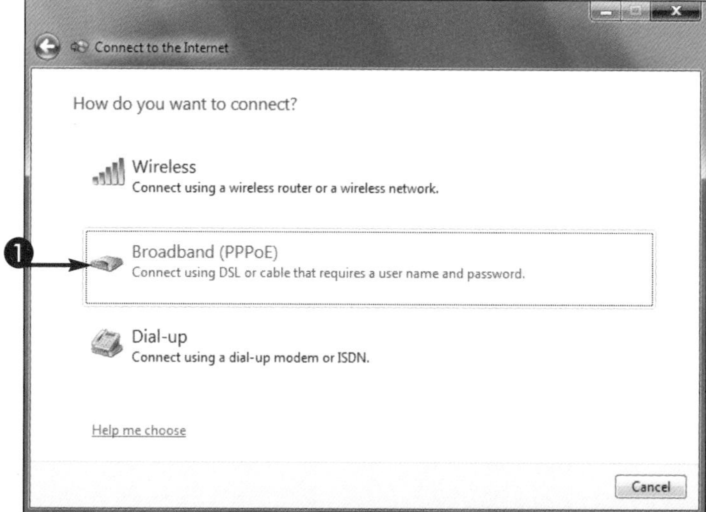


The Type the Information from Your Internet Service Provider (ISP) dialog box appears.

2. Type your user name.
3. Type your password.
4. To avoid having to type the name when you connect in the future, click **Remember this password** (☐ changes to ☑).
5. Edit the connection name, if desired.

*Note: The connection name is for your own use, so create a name that will help you remember what the connection is.*

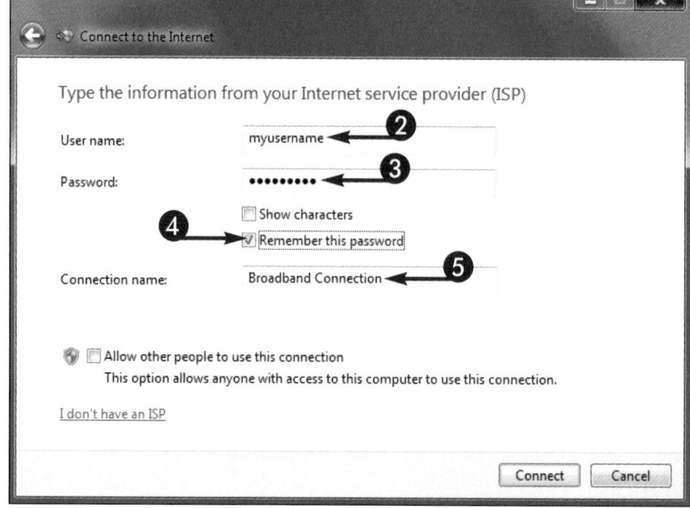

6 Click **Connect**.

Windows 7 sets up the connection and then connects to your ISP through the broadband modem.

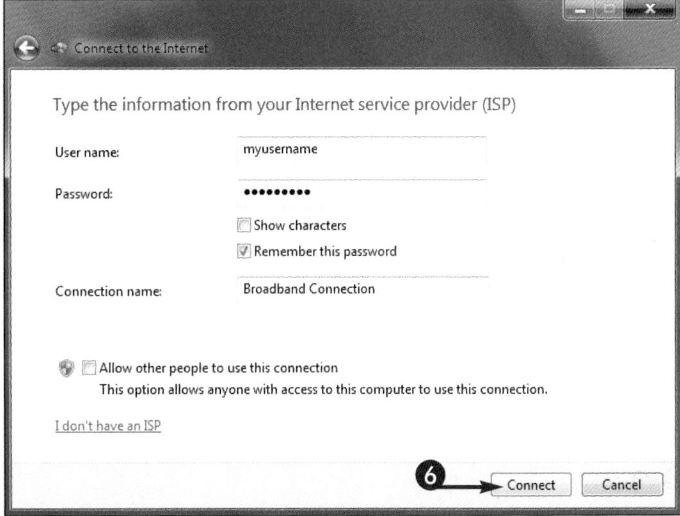


When the connection is complete, Windows 7 displays the The Connection to the Internet Is Ready to Use dialog box.

7 Click **Close**.

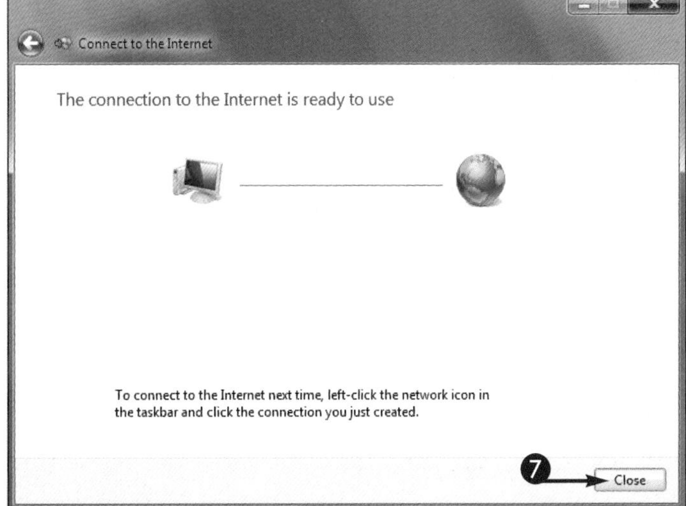


## TIPS

**How do I connect my broadband modem to my computer?**

You should first turn off the broadband modem. Run a phone cable from the wall jack to the phone jack in the back of the modem, run a network cable from the modem to the port on your network adapter in the back of the router, and then turn on the modem.

**I have other user accounts on my computer. Can they use the same connection?**

If you have other user accounts on your computer, you can save them time by making the Internet connection available when they log on. In the Type the Information from Your Internet Service Provider (ISP) dialog box, click **Allow other people to use this connection** (☐ changes to ☑).

# Create a Dial-Up Connection

If you have a dial-up account with your Internet service provider, you can configure Windows 7 to use a dial-up Internet connection.

**If you have an external modem, be sure to turn the modem on before starting this section.**

## Create a Dial-Up Connection

1. In the How Do You Want to Connect dialog box, click **Dial-up**.

***Note:*** *See the "Get an Internet Connection Started" section to access this dialog box.*

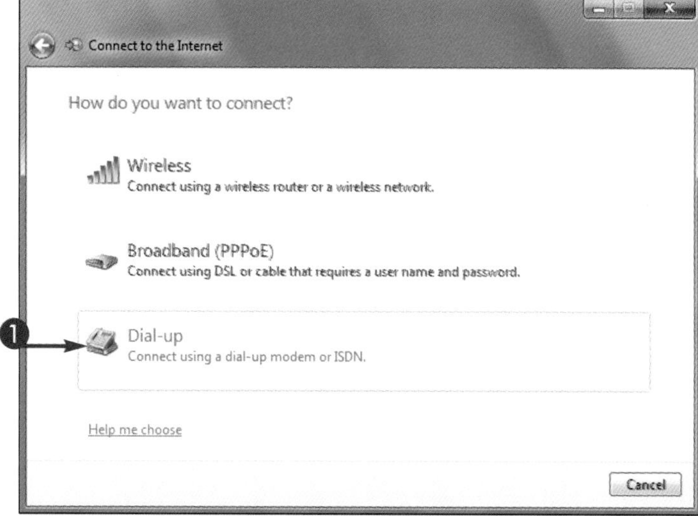


The Type the Information from Your Internet Service Provider (ISP) dialog box appears.

2. Type the dial-up phone number.
3. Type your user name.
4. Type your password.
5. To avoid having to type the name when you connect in the future, click **Remember this password** (☐ changes to ☑).
6. Edit the connection name, if desired.

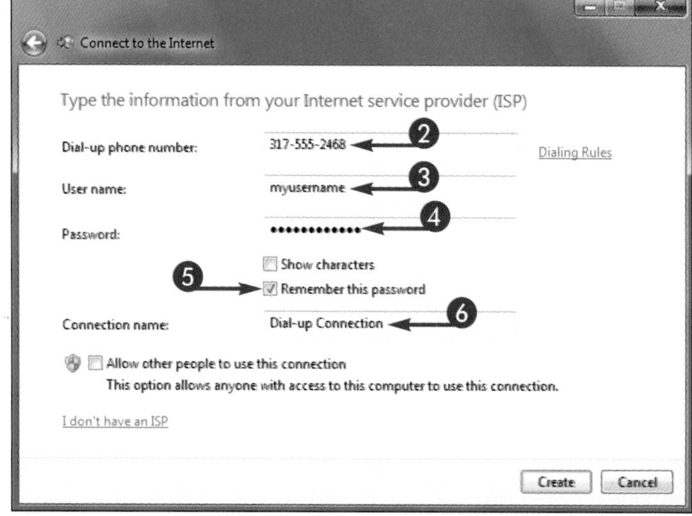

7 Click **Create**.

Windows 7 sets up the connection and then dials your modem.

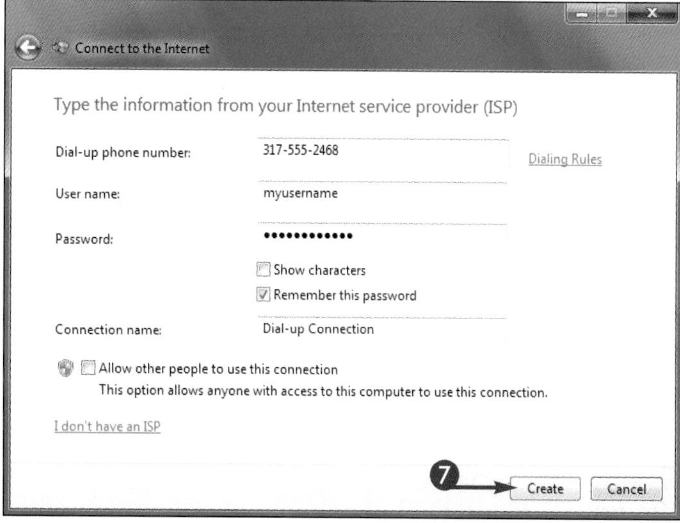


When the connection is complete, Windows 7 displays the The Connection to the Internet is Ready to Use dialog box.

8 Click **Close**.

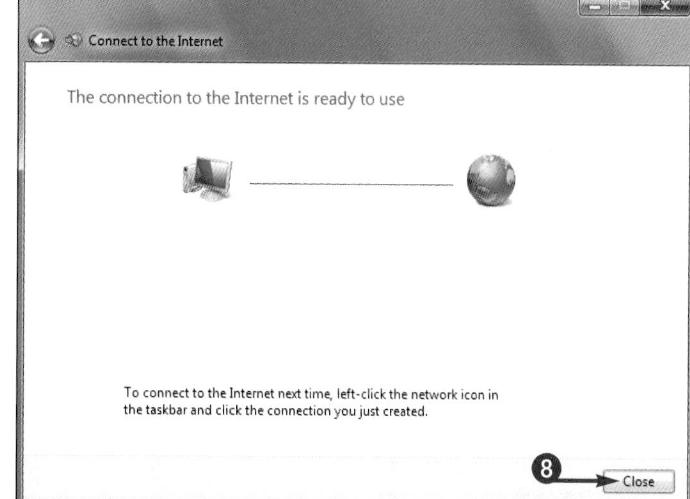


## TIPS

### What information do I need to configure my dial-up account?

When you signed up for your account, the ISP you chose will have sent you the details you require to set up the account manually. There are three items you must have: Your user name, your password, and the phone number your modem must dial to connect to the ISP.

### My area requires 10-digit dialing. How do I handle this?

When you fill in the ISP's phone number, add the area code in front of the phone number. For example, if the area code is 317 and the phone number is 555-1212, type **317-555-1212**.

# Connect to the Internet

**Once you have your Internet account configured, you can use it to connect to the Internet.**

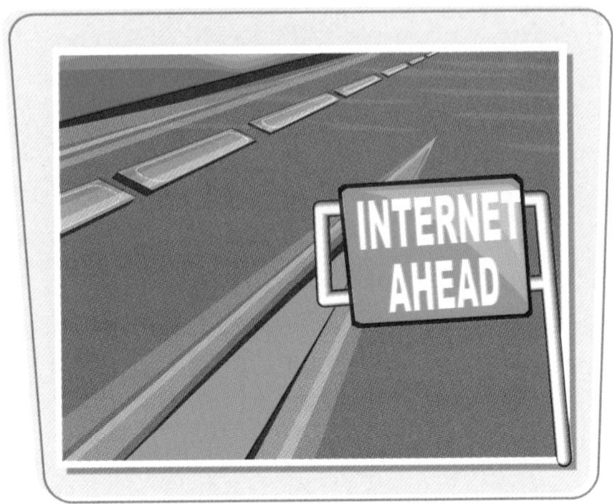


## Connect to the Internet

1. Click the **Network** icon (▣).
2. Click your Internet connection.
3. Click **Connect**.

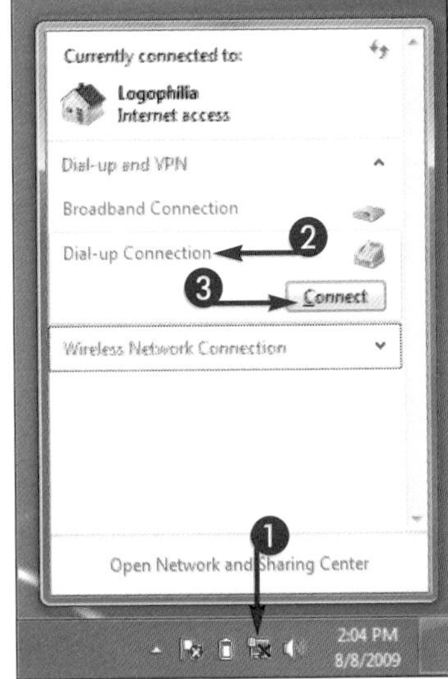


If you chose a dial-up connection, the Connect *Connection* dialog box appears (where *Connection* is the name you gave to the connection).

4. Click **Dial**.

Windows 7 connects to the Internet.

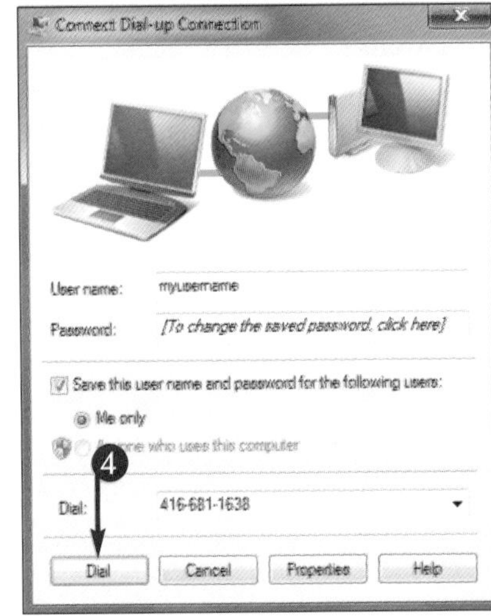

# Disconnect from the Internet

After you have completed your dial-up Internet session, you should disconnect to avoid running up your connection time unnecessarily.

**If your dial-up or broadband ISP limits your connection time per month, or charges you on a time-used basis, you should disconnect when you are done to avoid running up your connection charges.**

## Disconnect from the Internet

1. Click the **Network** icon ().
2. Click your Internet connection.

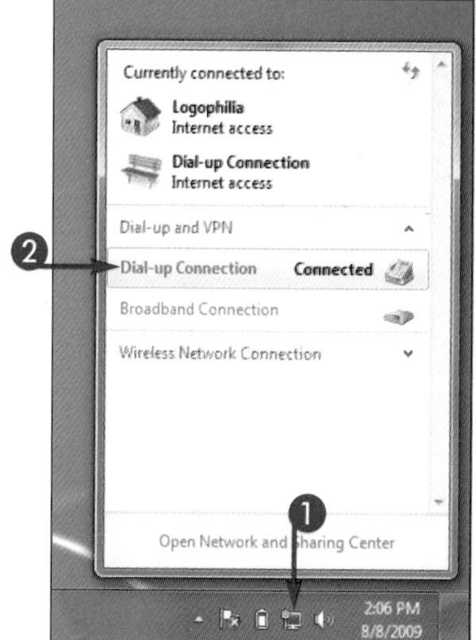


3. Click **Disconnect**.

   Windows 7 disconnects from the Internet.

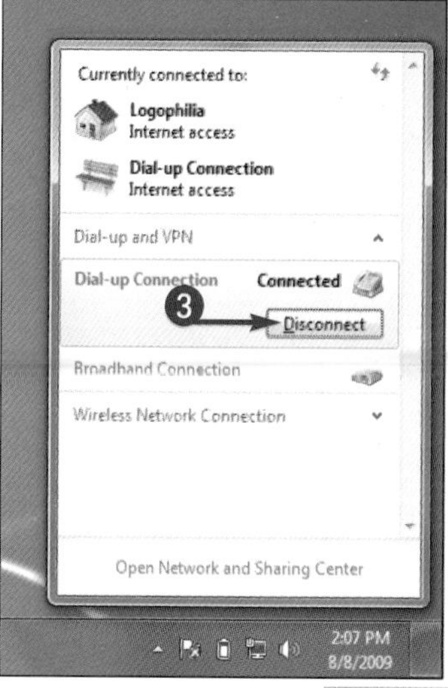

CHAPTER 10

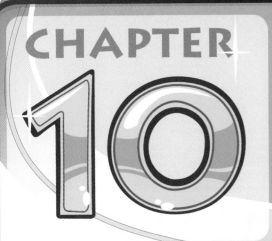

# Surfing the World Wide Web

After you have your Internet connection up and running, you can use Windows 7's Internet Explorer program to navigate — or *surf* — the sites of the World Wide Web. This chapter explains the Web and shows you how to navigate from site to site.

# Understanding the World Wide Web

**The World Wide Web — the Web, for short — is a massive storehouse of information that resides on computers, called *Web servers*, located all over the world.**

## Web Page

World Wide Web information is presented on Web pages, which you download to your computer using a Web browser program, such as Windows 7's Internet Explorer. Each Web page can combine text with images, sounds, music, and even video to present you with information on a particular subject. The Web consists of billions of pages covering almost every imaginable topic.

## Web Site

A Web site is a collection of Web pages associated with a particular person, business, government, school, or organization. Web sites are stored on a Web server, a special computer that makes Web pages available for people to browse.

## Web Address

Every Web page has its own Web address that uniquely identifies the page. This address is sometimes called a *URL* (pronounced *yoo-ar-ell* or *erl*), which is short for Uniform Resource Locator. If you know the address of a page, you can plug that address into your Web browser to view the page.

## Links

A *link* (also called a hyperlink) is a kind of "cross-reference" to another Web page. Each link is a bit of text (usually shown underlined and in a different color) or an image that, when you click it, loads the other page into your Web browser automatically. The other page is often from the same site, but it is common to come across links that take you to pages anywhere on the Web.

# Start Internet Explorer

You can use Internet Explorer, Windows 7's built-in Web browser program, to surf the Web. To do this, you must first start Internet Explorer.

**Some versions of Windows 7, particularly those sold in the European Union, do not include the Internet Explorer Web browser. To obtain Internet Explorer, contact your computer manufacturer or Microsoft.**

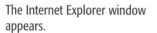

## Start Internet Explorer

1. Connect to the Internet.
2. Click **Internet Explorer**.

*Note: If you do not see the Internet Explorer icon in the taskbar, click **Start**, click **All Programs**, and then click **Internet Explorer**.*

The Internet Explorer window appears.

*Note: If you see the Welcome to Internet Explorer 8 dialog box, click **Next**, click **Use express settings** (◯ changes to ◉), and then click **Finish**.*

3. When you are finished with the Web, click the **Close** button (☒) to shut down Internet Explorer.

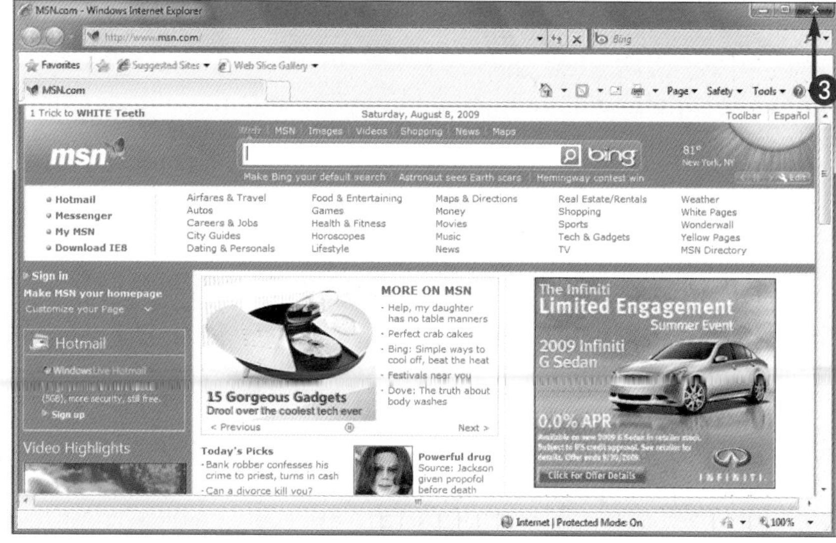

# Navigate Internet Explorer

You can easily surf the Web if you know your way around the Internet Explorer Web browser.

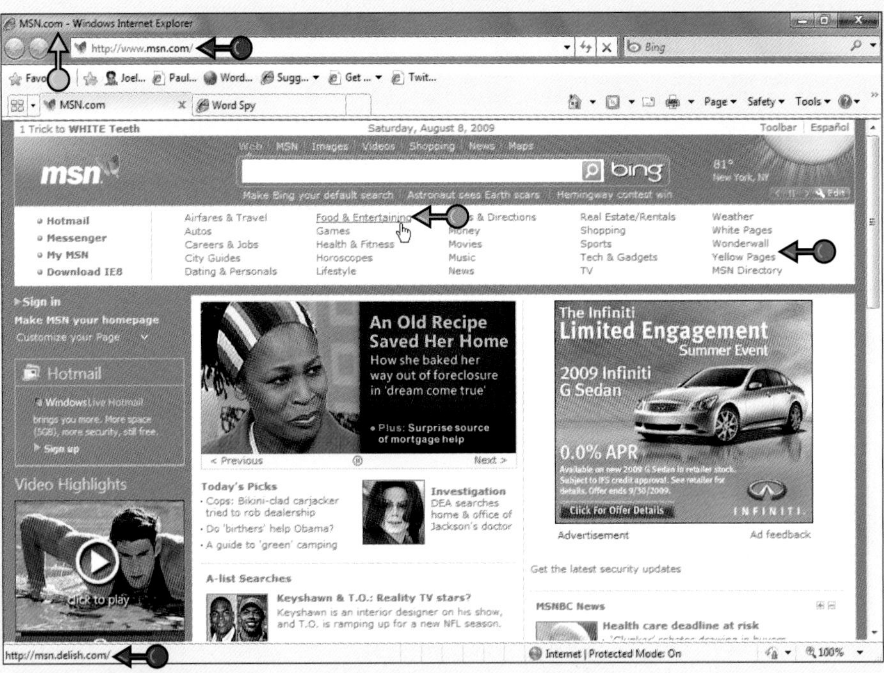


**Web Page Title**

This part of the Internet Explorer title bar displays the title of the displayed Web page.

**Address Bar**

This text box displays the address of the displayed Web page. You can also use the address bar to type the address of a Web page that you want to visit.

**Links**

Links appear either as text or as images. On most pages (although not the page shown here), text links appear underlined and in a different color (usually blue) than the regular page text.

**Current Link**

This is the link that you are currently pointing at with your mouse. The mouse pointer changes from ⇖ to ☝. On some pages, the link text also becomes underlined (as shown here) and changes color.

**Status Bar**

This area displays the current status of Internet Explorer. For example, it displays "Opening page" when you are downloading a Web page, and "Done" when the page is fully loaded. When you point at a link, the status bar displays the address of the page associated with the link.

# Select a Link

Almost all Web pages include links to other pages that contain information related to something in the current page, and you can use these links to navigate to other Web pages. When you select a link, your Web browser loads the other page.

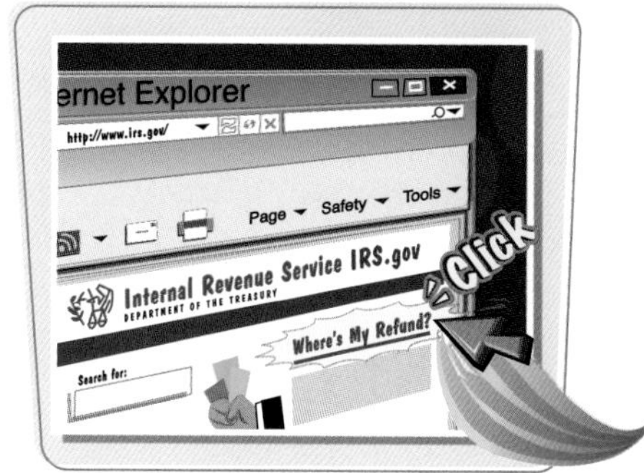


**Knowing what words, phrases, or images are links is not always obvious. The only way to tell for sure in many cases is to position the pointer over the text or image; if the pointer changes to a hand, you know you are dealing with a link.**

## Select a Link

1. Position the pointer over the link (pointer changes to hand).
2. Click the text or image.
   - The status bar shows the current download status.

***Note:*** *The address shown in the status bar when you point at a link may be different from the one shown when the page is downloading. This happens when the Web site "redirects" the link, which happens frequently.*

The linked Web page appears.

- The Web page title and address change after the linked page is loaded.
- The status bar shows Done when the page is completely loaded.

# Enter a Web Page Address

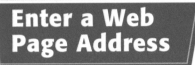

If you know the address of a specific Web page, you can type that address into the Web browser and the program will display the page.

### TYPE A WEB PAGE ADDRESS

1. Click in the address bar.
2. Type the address of the Web page.

3. Click the **Go** button (→) or press Enter.

The Web page appears.

- The Web page title changes after the page is loaded.

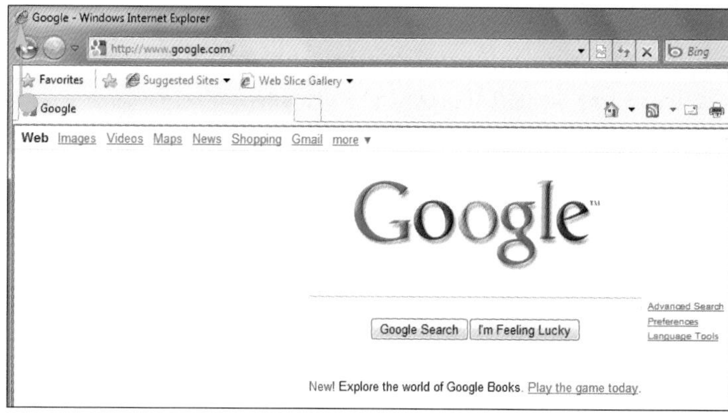

## REDISPLAY A WEB PAGE

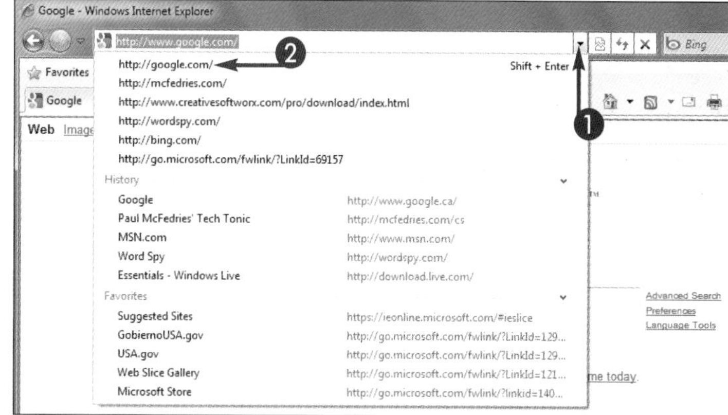

1. Click ▾ in the address bar.

   A list of the addresses you have typed appears.

2. Click the address you want to display.

   The Web page appears.

***Note:*** *If you type the first few letters of the address (such as* ***goog****), the address bar displays a list of addresses that match what you have typed. If you see the address you want, click it to load the page.*

### Are there any shortcuts I can use to enter Web page addresses?

Here are some useful keyboard techniques:

- After you finish typing the address, press Enter instead of clicking →.
- Most Web addresses begin with *http://*. You can leave off these characters when you type your address; Internet Explorer adds them automatically.
- If the address uses the form http://www.something.com, type just the "something" part and press Ctrl + Enter. Internet Explorer automatically adds *http://www.* at the beginning and *.com* at the end.

### When I try to load a page, why does Internet Explorer tell me "The page cannot be displayed"?

This message means that Internet Explorer is unable to contact a Web server at the address you typed. This is often a temporary glitch, so click **Refresh** (↻) to try loading the page again. If the trouble persists, double-check your address to ensure that you typed it correctly. If you did, the site may be unavailable for some reason. Try again in a few hours.

# Open a Web Page in a Tab

You can make it easier to work with multiple Web pages simultaneously by opening each page in its own tab.

**You can open as many pages as you want in their own tabs. This is convenient because all the pages appear within a single Internet Explorer window.**

## Open a Web Page in a Tab

### OPEN A WEB PAGE IN A TAB

1. Right-click the link you want to open.
2. Click **Open in New Tab**.

- A new tab appears with the page title.

3. Click the tab to display the page.

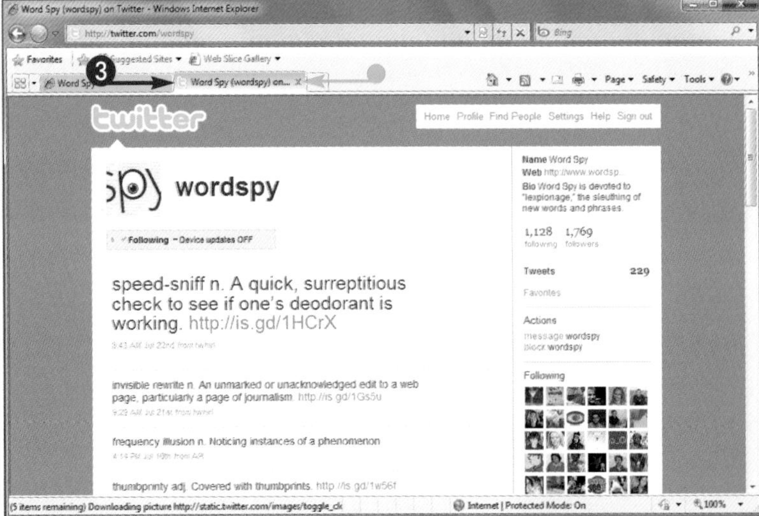

## NAVIGATE TABS

1. Click the **Tab Left** button («) or the **Tab Right** button (») to display the tab you want.

*Note: You see the Tab Left and Tab Right buttons only if Internet Explorer does not have enough room to display all the tabs.*

2. Click the tab.

- The Web page loaded in the tab appears.

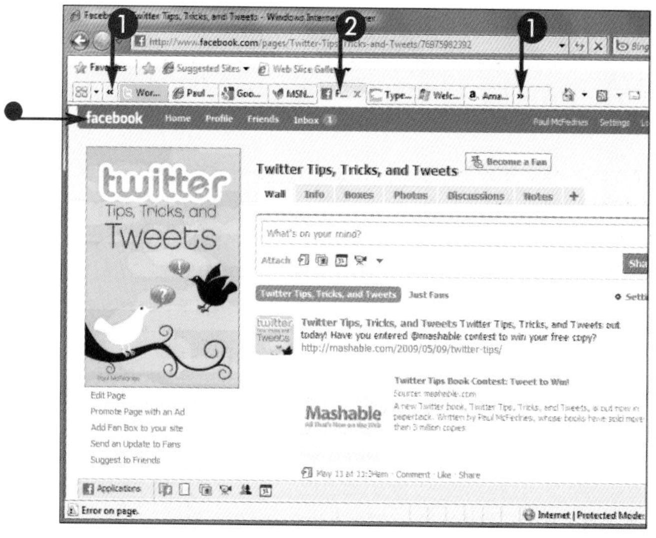

## DISPLAY QUICK TABS

1. Click the **Quick Tabs** button (⊞).

- Internet Explorer displays thumbnail images of the Web pages open in each tab.

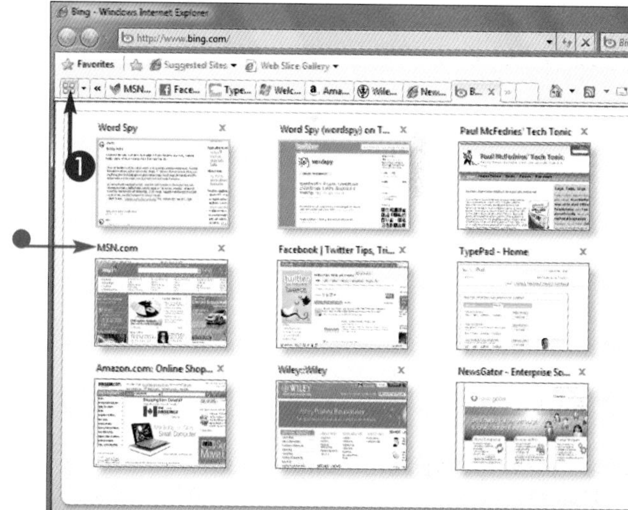

**Are there any shortcuts I can use to open Web pages in tabs?**

- Press and hold Ctrl and click a link to open the page in a tab.
- Press and hold Ctrl + Shift and click a link to open the page in a tab and display the tab.
- Type an address and then press Alt + Enter to open the page in a new tab.
- Press Ctrl + Q to display the Quick Tabs.
- Press Ctrl + Tab or Ctrl + Shift + Tab to cycle through the tabs.
- Press Ctrl + W to close the current tab.
- Press Ctrl + Alt + F4 to close every tab but the current one.

# Navigate Web Pages

After you have visited several pages, you can return to a page you visited earlier. Instead of making you retype the address or look for the link, Internet Explorer gives you some easier methods.

**When you navigate Web pages, you can go back to a page you have visited in the current browser session. After you have done that, you can also reverse course and go forward through the pages again.**

## Navigate Web Pages

### GO BACK ONE PAGE

1. Click the **Back** button (⬅).

   The previous page you visited appears.

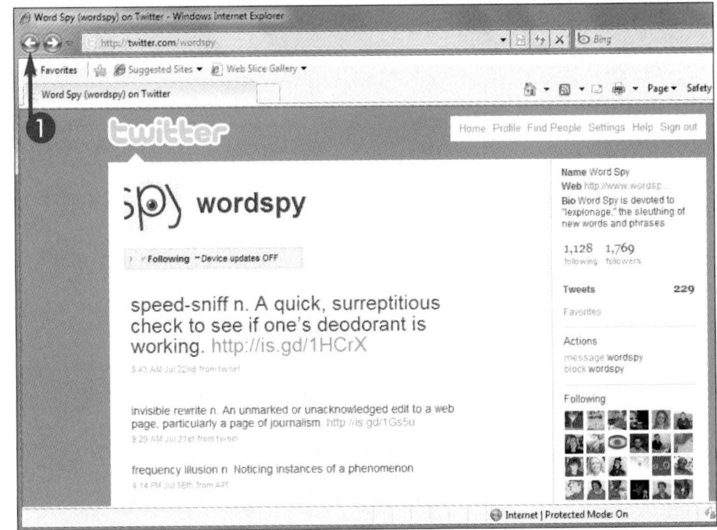


### GO BACK SEVERAL PAGES

1. Click the **Recent Pages** ▾.

   A list of the sites you have visited appears.

- The current site appears with a check mark (☑) beside it.
- Items listed below the current site are ones you visited prior to the current site. When you position the mouse ⇖ over a previous site, Internet Explorer displays the **Go Back** arrow (⬅).

2. Click the page you want to display.

   The page appears.

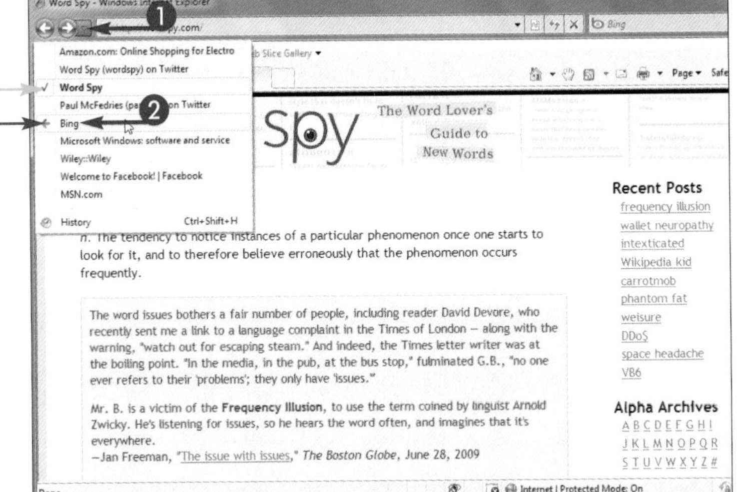

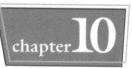

### GO FORWARD ONE PAGE

1. Click the **Forward** button (➡).

   The next page you visited appears.

***Note:** If you are at the last page viewed up to that point, the Forward button (➡) is not active.*

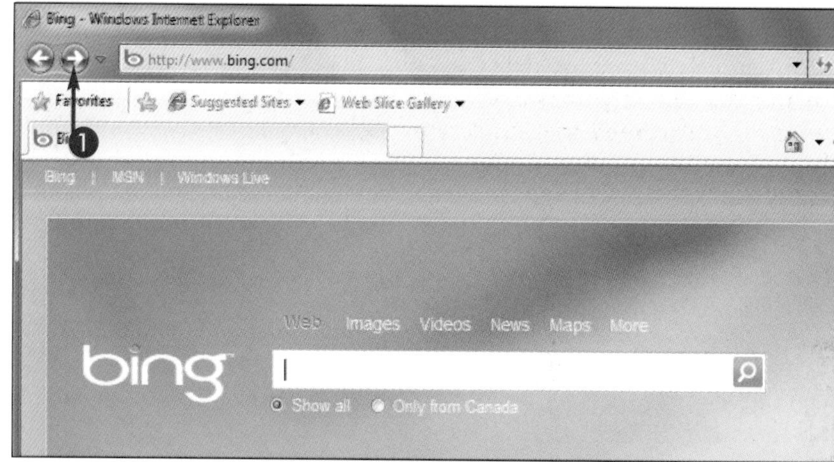

### GO FORWARD SEVERAL PAGES

1. Click the **Recent Pages** ▾.

   A list of the sites you have visited appears.

- Items listed above the current site are ones you visited after the current site. When you position the mouse ↖ over a previous site, Internet Explorer displays the Go Forward arrow (➔).

2. Click the page you want to display.

   The page appears.

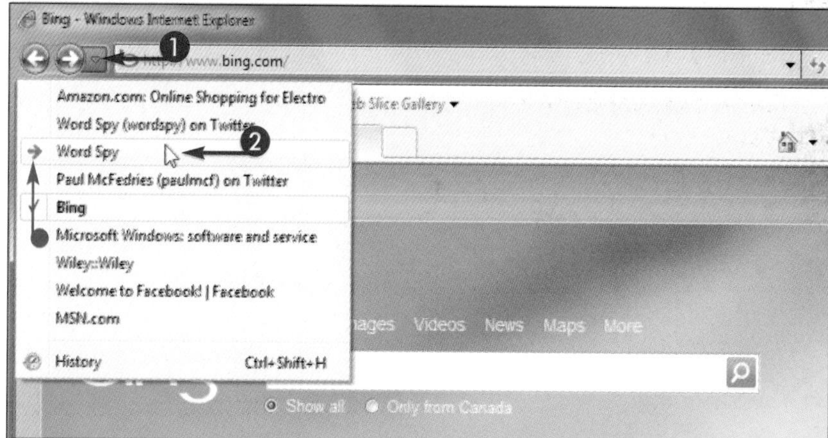

**How do I go back or forward to a page, but also keep the current page on-screen?**

You can do this by opening a second Internet Explorer window. Keep the current page in the original window and then use the second window to go back or forward. Here are the steps to follow:

1. Press Ctrl + N.

- A new Internet Explorer window appears.

2. Use the techniques described in this section to navigate to the page you want.

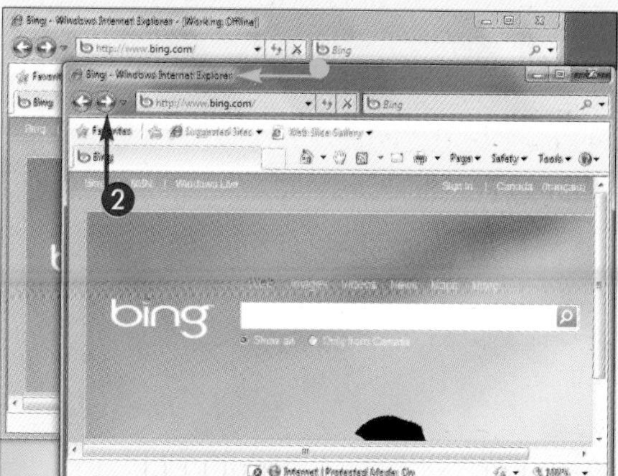

# Navigate with the History List

The Back and Forward buttons (⬅ and ➡) enable you to navigate pages only in the current browser session. To redisplay sites that you have visited in the past few days or weeks, you need to use the History list.

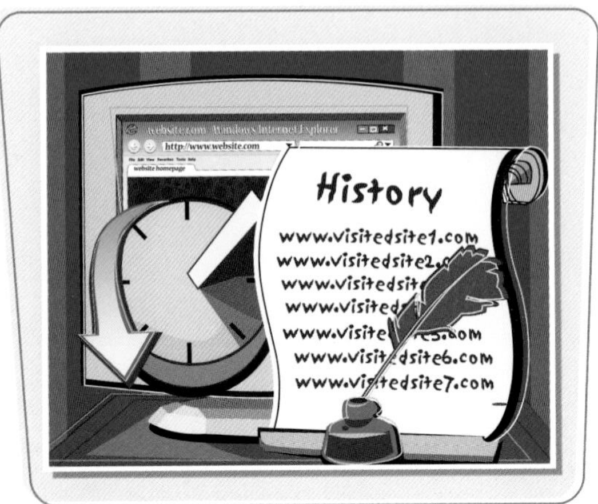


## Navigate with the History List

1. Click the **Favorites Center** button (☆).
2. Click **History**.

- The History list appears.

3. Click the day or week that you visited the site.

A list of sites that you visited during that day or week appears.

4 Click the site that contains the page you want to display.

A list of pages you visited in the site appears.

5 Click the page you want to display.

- The page appears.

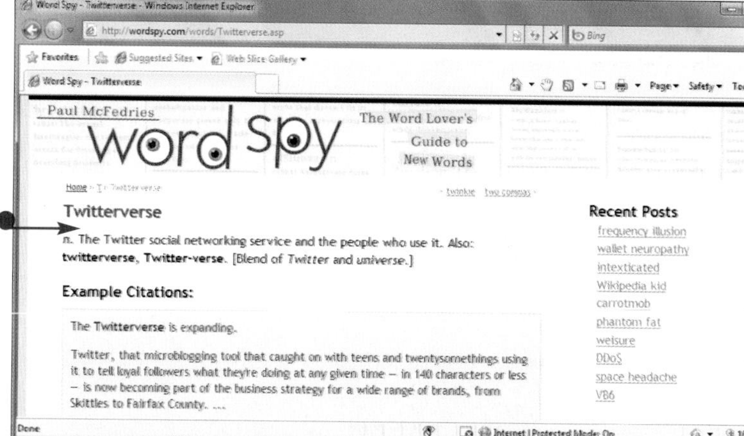

TIP

**Can I clear my History list?**

Yes, by following these steps:

1 Click **Safety** and then **Delete Browsing History**.

2 Click **History** (☐ changes to ☑).

3 Click to deactivate the other check boxes (☑ changes to ☐).

4 Click **Delete**.

Internet Explorer deletes the History list and then closes the dialog box.

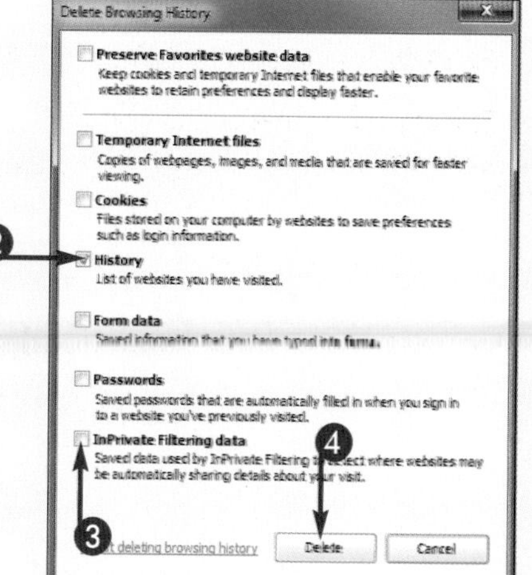

# Change Your Home Page

Your home page is the Web page that appears when you first start Internet Explorer. The default home page is usually the MSN.com site, but you can change that to any other page you want.

**In the Windows 7 version of Internet Explorer, you can have a single home page or you can have multiple home pages that load in separate tabs each time you start the program.**

## Change Your Home Page

### CHANGE A SINGLE HOME PAGE

1. Display the Web page that you want to use as your home page.
2. Click the **Home** button (▾).
3. Click **Add or Change Home Page**.

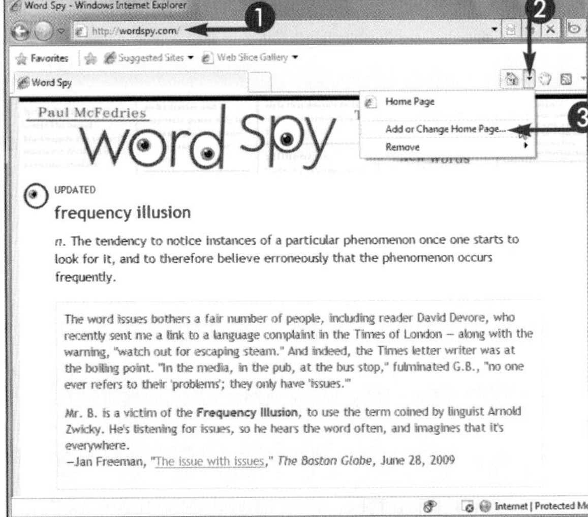


The Add or Change Home Page dialog box appears.

4. Click **Use this webpage as your only home page** (◯ changes to ◉).
5. Click **Yes**.

Internet Explorer changes your home page.

- You can click the **Home** button (🏠) to display the home page at any time.

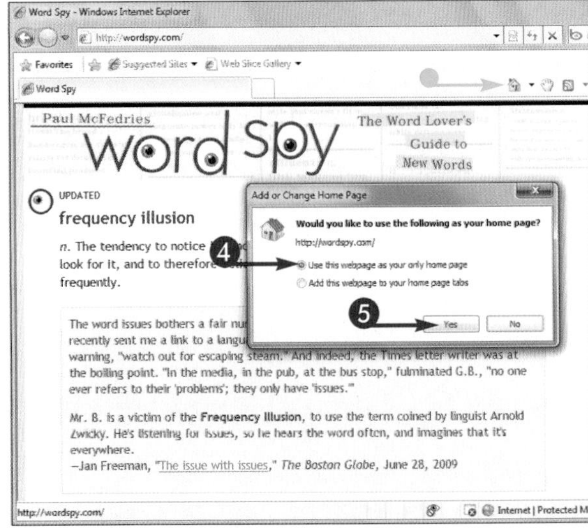

## ADD A PAGE TO YOUR HOME PAGE TABS

1. Display the Web page that you want to add to your home page tabs.
2. Click the **Home** button ▾.
3. Click **Add or Change Home Page**.

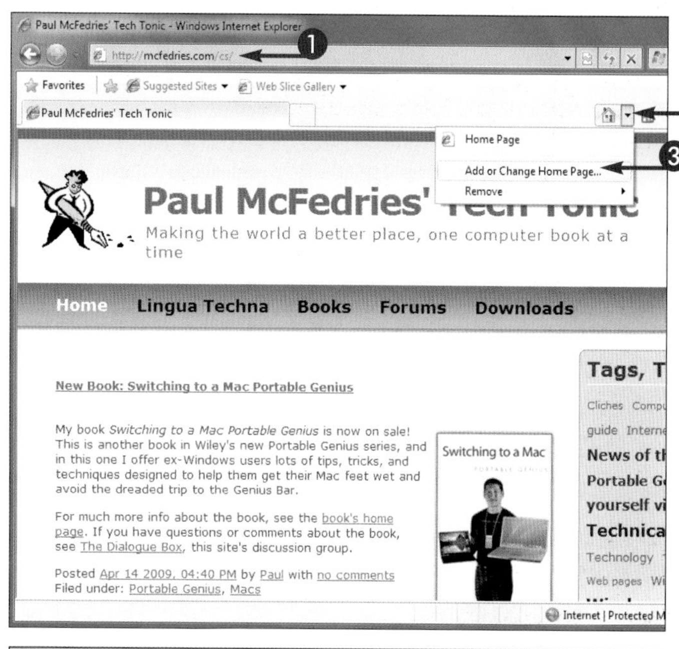

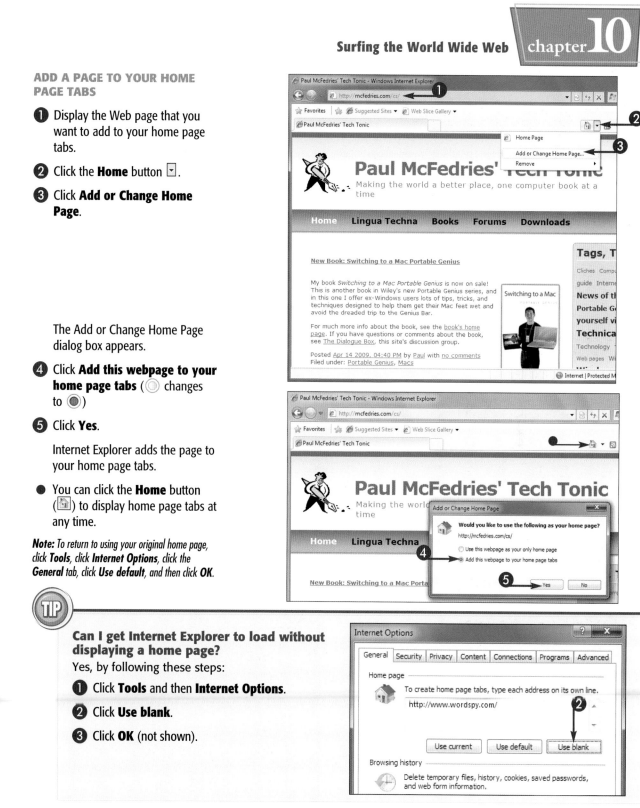

The Add or Change Home Page dialog box appears.

4. Click **Add this webpage to your home page tabs** (◯ changes to ◉)
5. Click **Yes**.

Internet Explorer adds the page to your home page tabs.

- You can click the **Home** button (🏠) to display home page tabs at any time.

***Note:** To return to using your original home page, click **Tools**, click **Internet Options**, click the **General** tab, click **Use default**, and then click **OK**.*

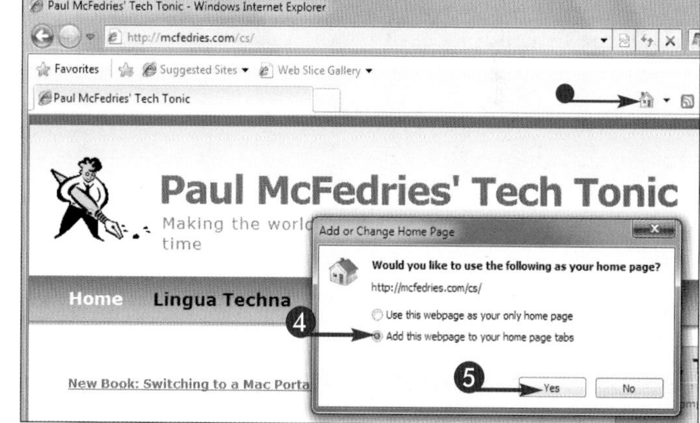

### Can I get Internet Explorer to load without displaying a home page?

Yes, by following these steps:

1. Click **Tools** and then **Internet Options**.
2. Click **Use blank**.
3. Click **OK** (not shown).

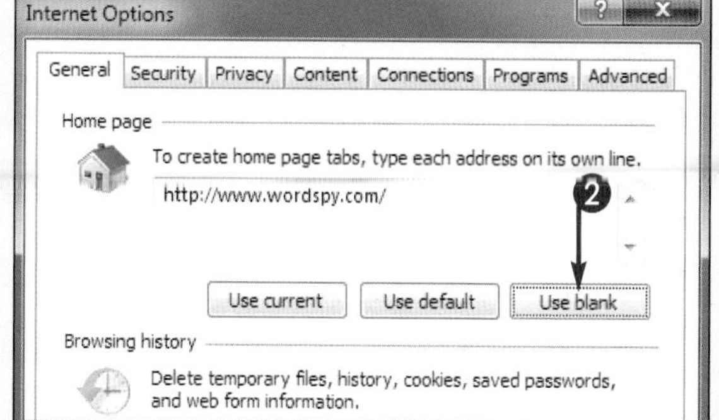

# Save Favorite Web Pages

If you have Web pages that you visit frequently, you can save yourself time by saving those pages as favorites within Internet Explorer. This enables you to display the pages with just a couple of mouse clicks.

**The Favorites feature is a list of Web pages that you have saved. Instead of typing an address or searching for one of these pages, you can display the Web page by selecting its address from the Favorites list.**

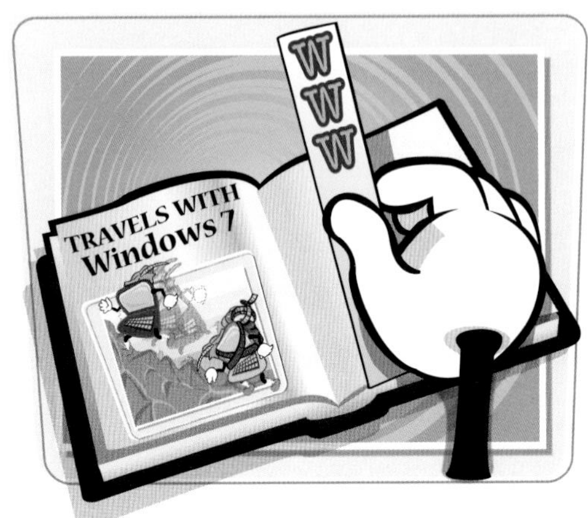


## Save Favorite Web Pages

### SAVE A FAVORITE WEB PAGE

1. Display the Web page you want to save as a favorite.
2. Click the **Favorites Center** button (☆).
3. Click **Add to Favorites** (☆).

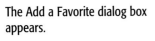

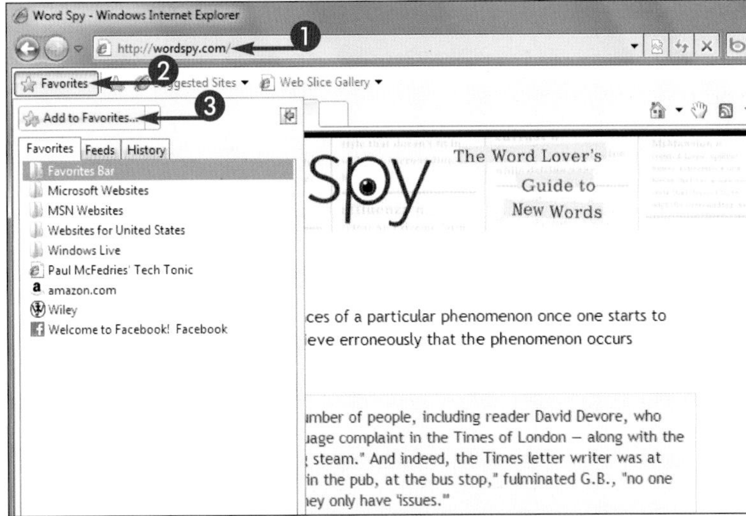


The Add a Favorite dialog box appears.

***Note:** You can also display the Add a Favorite dialog box by pressing* Ctrl + D.

4. Edit the page name, as necessary.
5. Click **Add**.

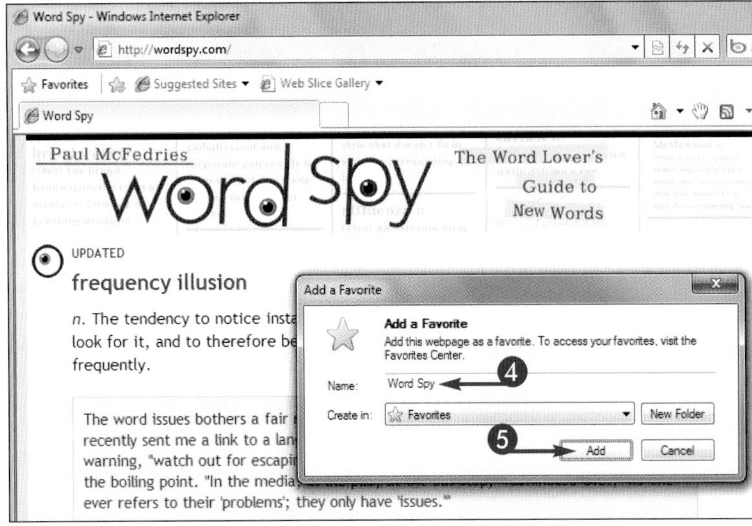

### DISPLAY A FAVORITE WEB PAGE

1. Click the **Favorites Center** button (☆).
2. Click **Favorites**.

   The Favorites list appears.
3. Click the Web page you want to display.

The Web page appears.

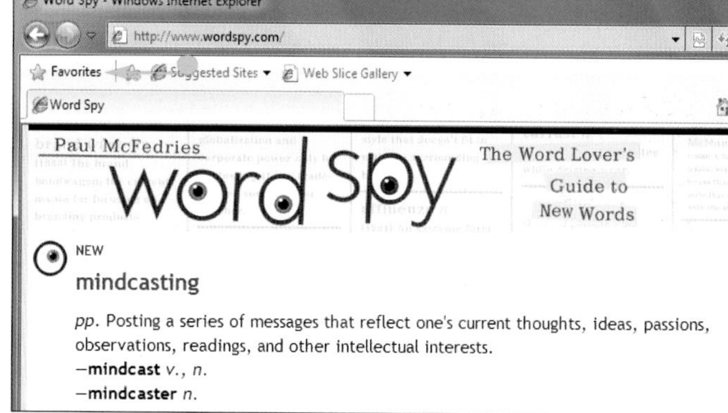


- If you use your Favorites list a lot, you can make it easier to display the pages by keeping the Favorites Center visible. Click the **Favorites Center** button (☆) and then click the **Pin the Favorites Center** button (⇦). Internet Explorer pins the Favorites Center to the left side of the window.

### How do I delete a favorite?

1. Click the **Favorites Center** button (☆).
2. Click **Favorites**.
3. Right-click the favorite you want to delete.
4. Click **Delete**.

   Internet Explorer asks if you are sure you want to delete the favorite.
5. Click **Yes**.

# Search for Sites

If you need information on a specific topic, Internet Explorer has a built-in feature that enables you to quickly search the Web for sites that have the information you require.

**The Web has a number of sites called *search engines* that enable you to find what you are looking for. By default, Internet Explorer uses Microsoft's Bing search engine, but you can use other sites.**

## Search for Sites

1. Click in the search box.

2. Type a word, phrase, or question that represents the information you want to find.

3. Click the **Search** button (🔍) or press Enter.

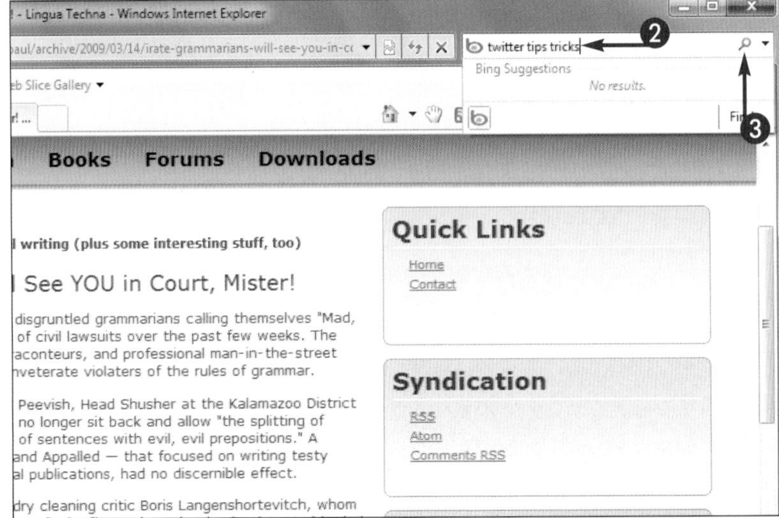

- A list of pages that match your search text appears.

4 Click a Web page.

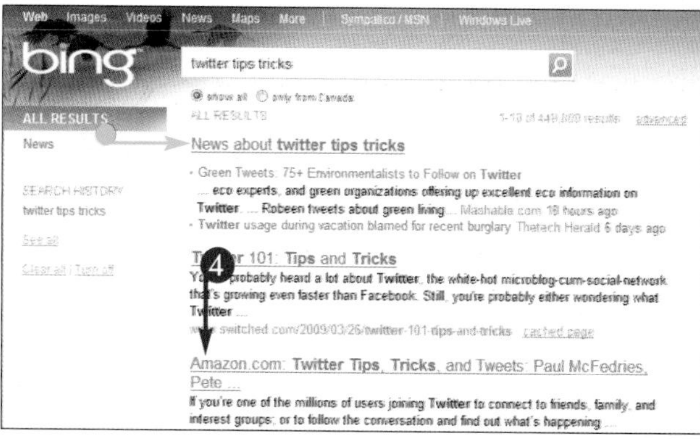

The page appears.

## TIP

**Can I use other search engines?**

Yes. To add another search engine, follow these steps:

1 Click the search box ▾.

2 Click **Find More Providers**.

3 Under the search engine you want to use, click **Add to Internet Explorer**.

4 Click **Add**.

To use the search engine, click the search box ▾ and then click the search engine name.

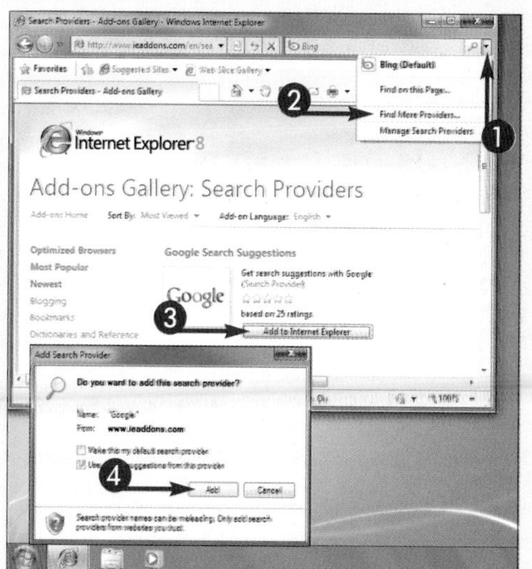

CHAPTER 11

# Working with E-mail, Contacts, and Events

You can install the Windows Live Mail program to send e-mail to and read e-mail from friends, family, colleagues, and even total strangers almost anywhere in the world. You can also use Windows Live Mail to enter contact data and track your events.

# Install Windows Live Essentials Programs

Windows Live Mail is not installed on Windows 7 by default. To use the program, you must access the Windows Live Essentials Web site and then install the program from there.

**You can also use the Windows Live Essentials site to install other programs, such as Windows Live Photo Gallery and Windows Live Movie Maker.**

## Install Windows Live Essentials Programs

1. Click **Start**.
2. Click the **Getting Started** arrow (▸).
3. Click **Get Windows Live Essentials**.

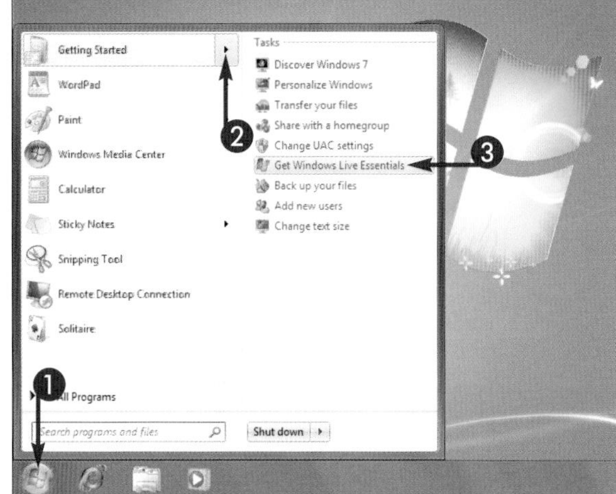


The Windows Live Essentials Web page appears.

4. Click **Download**.

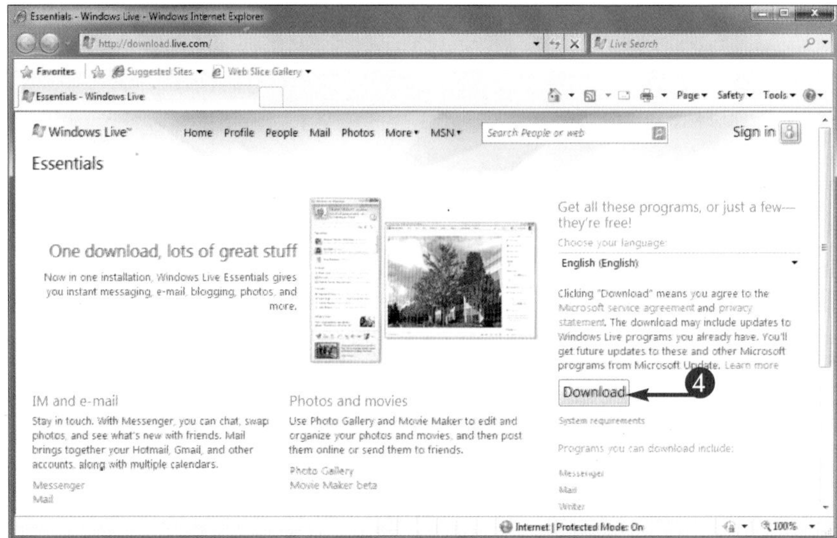

The File Download - Security Warning dialog box appears.

5. Click **Run**.

***Note:*** *If you see the User Account Control dialog box at this point, provide an administrator password, if asked for one, and click* ***Yes****.*

6. Click **Close** (X).

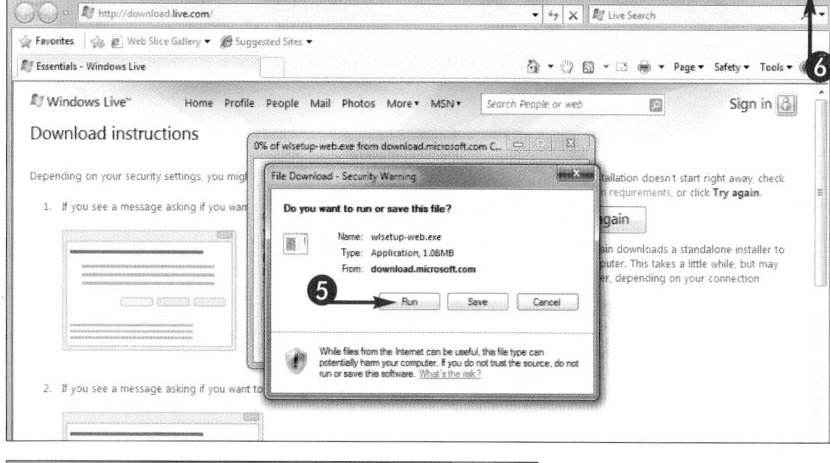


The Choose the Programs You Want to Install dialog box appears.

7. Click the check box beside each program you want to install (☐ changes to ☑).

8. Click **Install**.

Windows 7 installs your selected Windows Live Essentials programs.

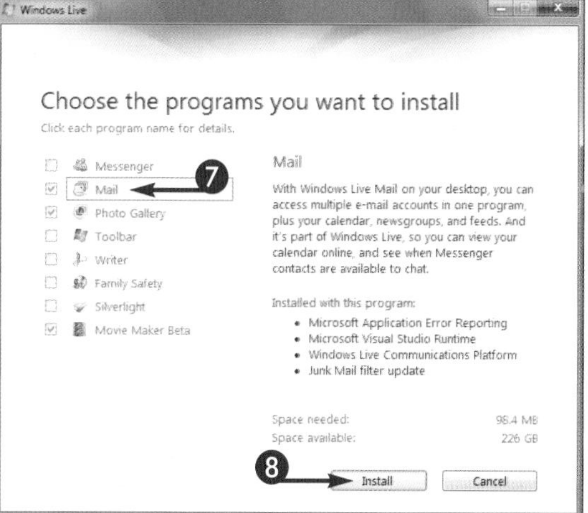

**Do I have to pay for any Windows Live Essential programs?**

No. All of the programs that are available on the Windows Live Essentials Web site, including Windows Live Mail, are free. Microsoft created the Windows Live Essentials programs as supplements to Windows 7, but did not include them in Windows 7 because many people prefer to use other programs, such as Microsoft Outlook for e-mail and contacts.

**How do I start a Windows Live Essentials program after it has been installed?**

The Windows Live Essentials installation program adds a new submenu named Windows Live to your Start menu. To launch any Windows Live Essential programs, click **Start**, click **All Programs**, and then click **Windows Live**. In the submenu that appears, click the name of the program you want to run, such as **Windows Live Mail**.

# Configure an E-mail Account

Before you can send an e-mail message, you must add your e-mail account to the Windows Live Mail application. This also enables you to use Windows Live Mail to retrieve the messages that others have sent to your account.

**Your e-mail account is usually a POP (Post Office Protocol) account supplied by your Internet service provider (ISP), which should have supplied you with the POP account details.**

## Configure an E-mail Account

1. Start Windows Live Mail.

   The first time you start the program, the Add an E-mail Account wizard appears.

*Note: If you are trying to configure a second e-mail account, click the* ***Add e-mail account*** *link in the Folder pane.*

2. Type your e-mail address.
3. Type your e-mail password.
4. Type your name.
5. Click **Next**.

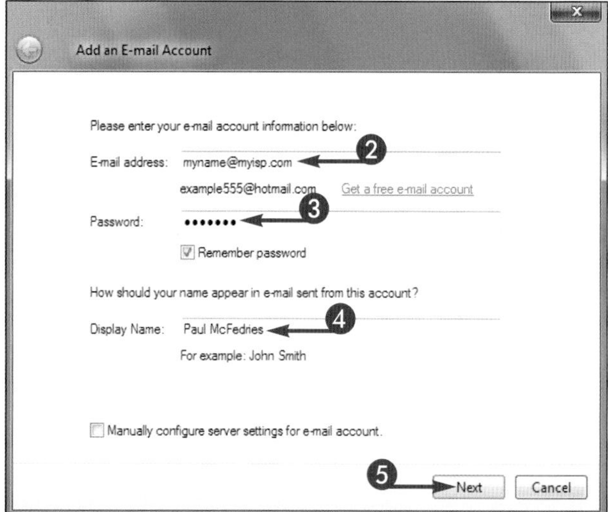


*Note: If Windows Live Mail tells you it has successfully set up your account, click* ***Finish*** *and skip the rest of these steps.*

Windows Live Mail prompts you for your e-mail account's server information.

6. Click ▾ and then click the type of e-mail account.
7. Type the name of your ISP's incoming mail server.
8. Type the e-mail account login user name.

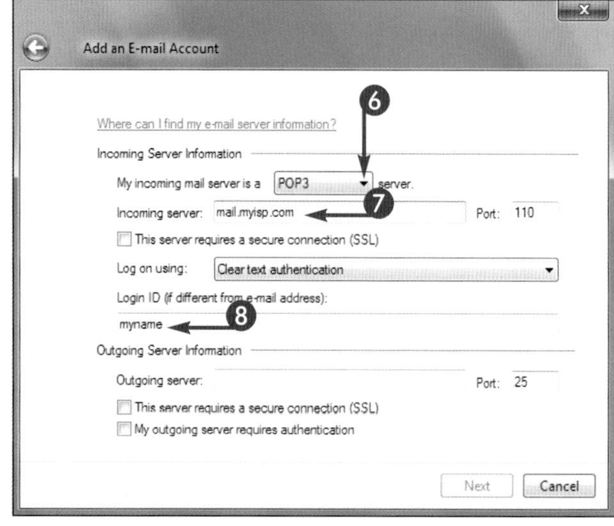

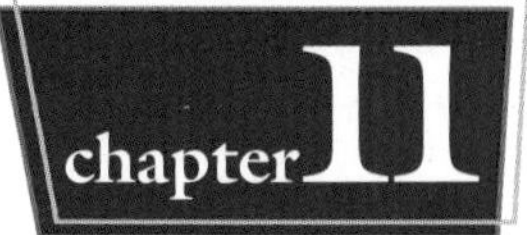


9. Type the name of your ISP's outgoing mail server.
10. If your ISP uses a different port for outgoing mail, type the port number.
11. Click this check box if your ISP's outgoing mail server requires authentication (☐ changes to ☑).
12. Click **Next**.

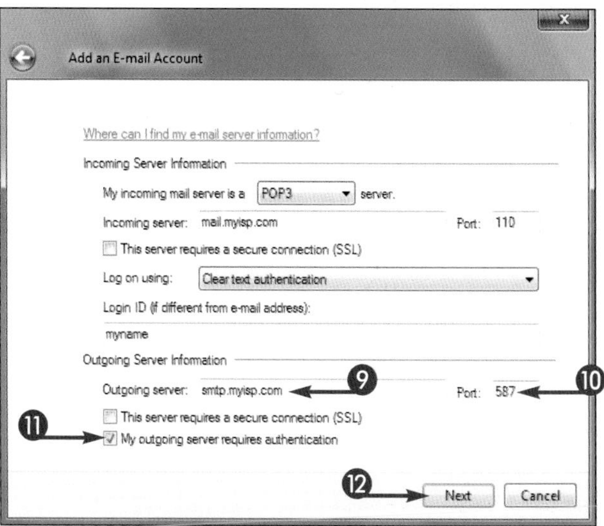

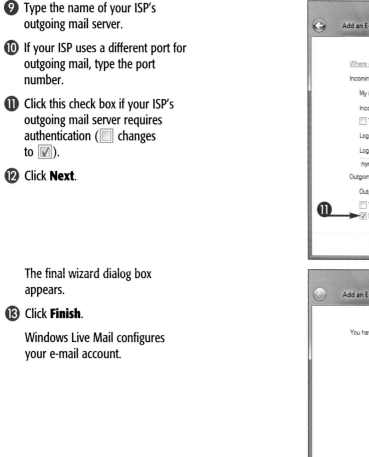

The final wizard dialog box appears.

13. Click **Finish**.

Windows Live Mail configures your e-mail account.

### How do I make changes to an e-mail account?

After you configure your e-mail account, Windows Live Mail adds the account to the Folder pane on the left side of the program window. To make changes to the account, right-click the account name and then click **Properties**. In the Properties dialog box that appears, use the tabs to make changes to your settings (●).

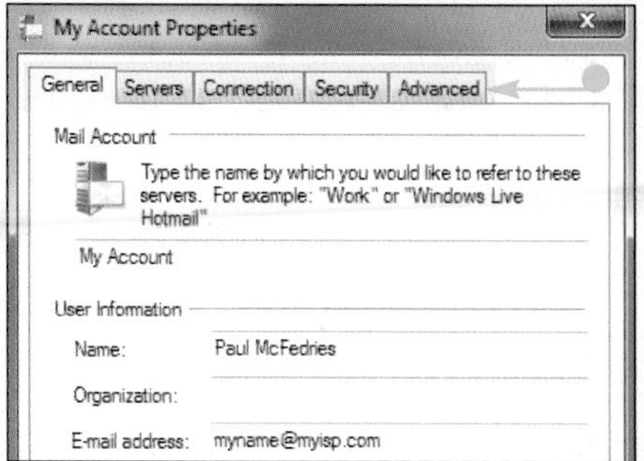

# Send an E-mail Message

If you know the e-mail address of a person or organization, you can send an e-mail message to that address. In most cases, the message is delivered within a few minutes.

**If you do not know any e-mail addresses, or, if at first, you prefer to just practice sending messages, you can send messages to your own e-mail address.**

## Send an E-mail Message

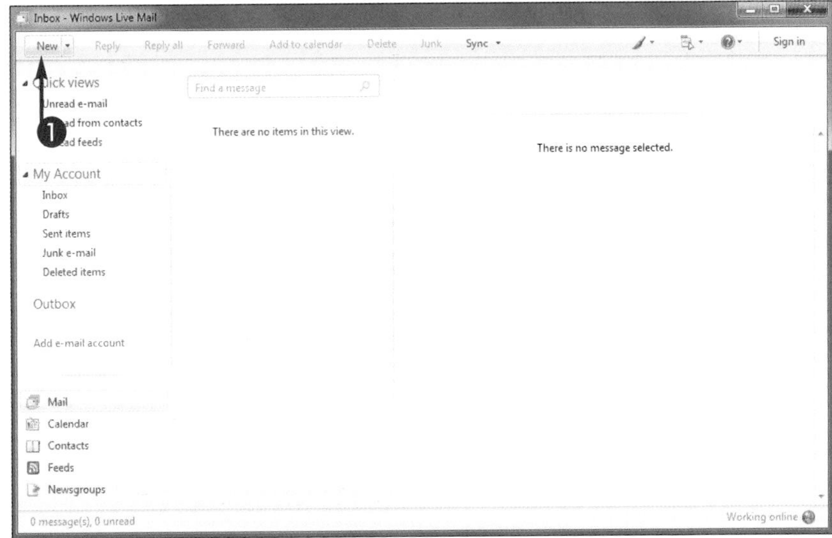

1. Click **New**.

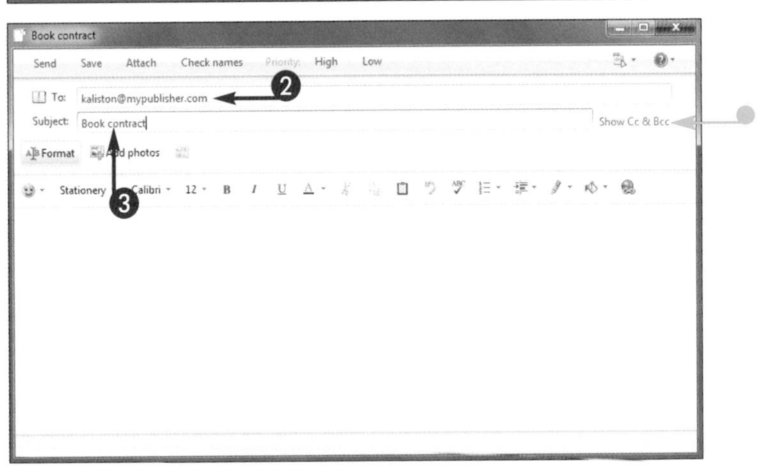

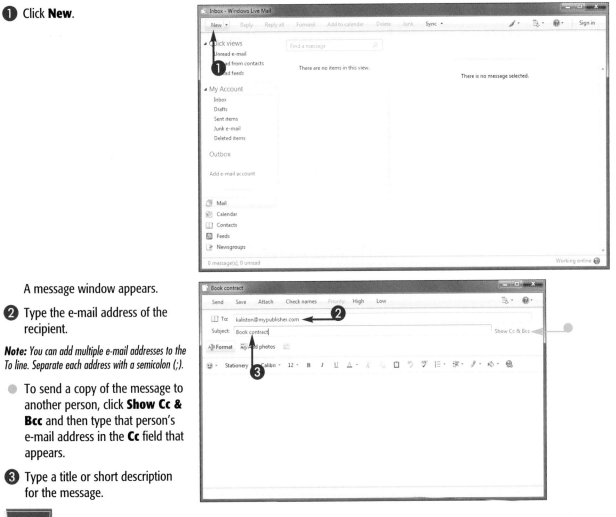

A message window appears.

2. Type the e-mail address of the recipient.

***Note:*** *You can add multiple e-mail addresses to the To line. Separate each address with a semicolon (;).*

- To send a copy of the message to another person, click **Show Cc & Bcc** and then type that person's e-mail address in the **Cc** field that appears.

3. Type a title or short description for the message.

4 Type the message.

5 Use the buttons in the Formatting bar to format the message text.

***Note:*** *Many people use e-mail programs that cannot process text formatting. Unless you are sure your recipient's program supports formatting, it is best to send plain text messages. To do this, press* Alt*, click **Format**, and then click **Plain text** (*  *appears beside the command).*

6 Click **Send**.

Windows Live Mail sends your message.

***Note:*** *Windows Live Mail stores a copy of your message in the Sent Items folder.*

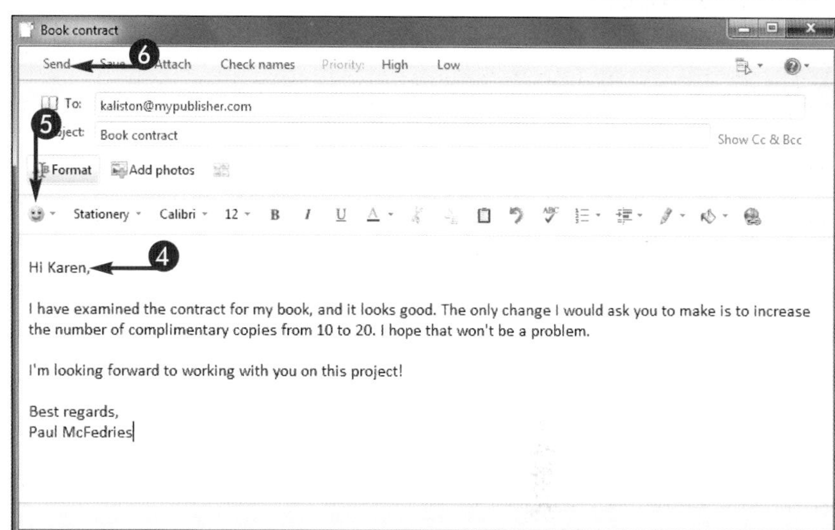

Book contract
Send
Save
Attach
Check names
Priority:
High
Low
To:
kaliston@mypublisher.com
Subject:
Book contract
Show Cc & Bcc
Format
Add photos
Stationery
Calibri
12
Hi Karen,
I have examined the contract for my book, and it looks good. The only change I would ask you to make is to increase the number of complimentary copies from 10 to 20. I hope that won't be a problem.
I'm looking forward to working with you on this project!
Best regards,
Paul McFedries
4
5
6


## TIP

**I have a large number of messages to compose. Do I have to be online to do this?**

No, composing all the messages while you are offline is possible. Follow these steps:

1 While disconnected from the Internet, start Windows Live Mail, and click **Cancel** if the program asks you to connect to the Internet.

- Windows Live Mail displays Working Offline in the status bar.

2 Compose and send the message. Each time you click **Send**, your messages are stored temporarily in the Outbox folder.

3 After you are done, connect to the Internet.

4 Click **Working Offline**.

Windows Live Mail changes the status bar text to Working Online.

5 Click the **Sync** ▾.

6 Click your e-mail account.

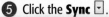

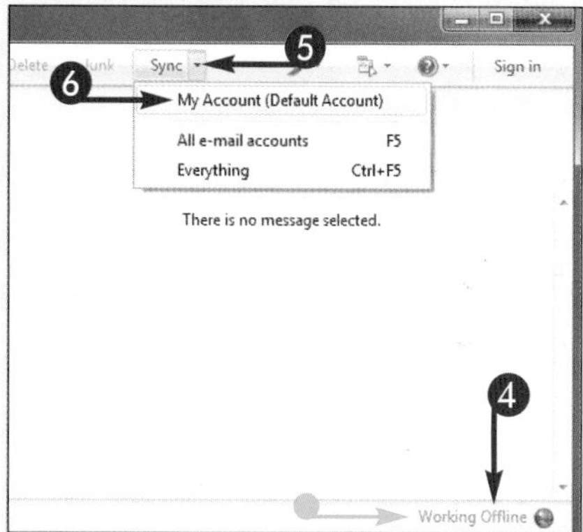

# Add Someone to Your Contacts

You can use the Windows Live Contacts to store the names and e-mail addresses of people with whom you frequently correspond.

**When you choose a name from Windows Live Contacts while composing a message, Windows Live Mail automatically adds the contact's e-mail address. This is faster and more accurate than typing the address by hand.**

## Add Someone to Your Contacts

1. Click **Contacts** (📖).

***Note:*** *You can also open Windows Live Contacts by pressing* Ctrl + Shift + C.

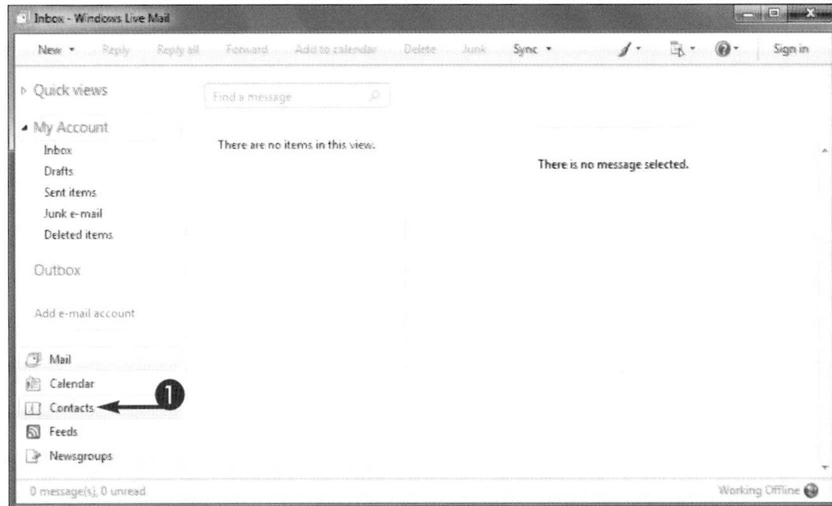

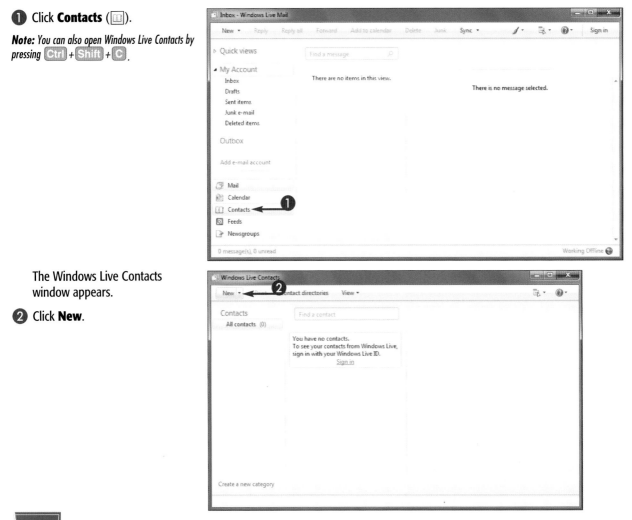

The Windows Live Contacts window appears.

2. Click **New**.

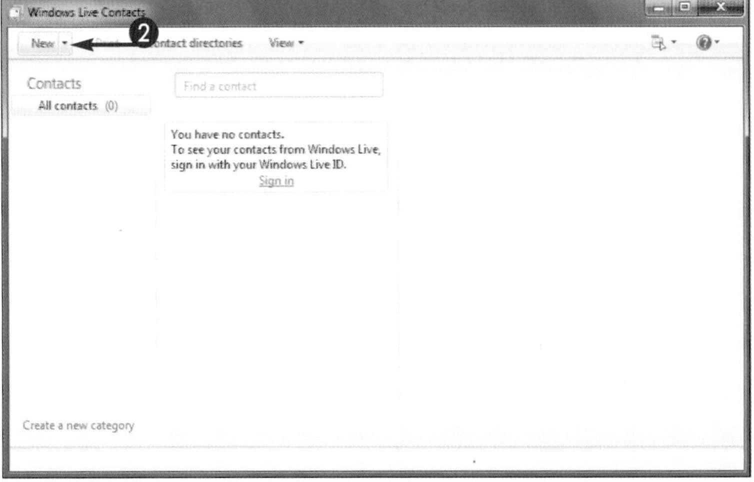

The Add a Contact dialog box appears.

3 Type the person's first name.

4 Type the person's last name.

5 Type the person's e-mail address.

***Note:** You can use the other tabs in the Add a Contact dialog box to store more information about the contact, including home and business addresses and phone numbers, spouse name, birthday, and more.*

6 Click **Add contact**.

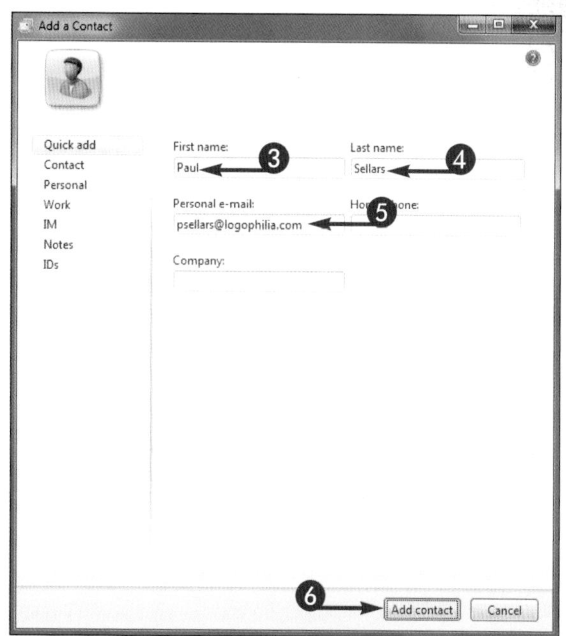


- Windows Live Contacts adds the person to the Contacts list.

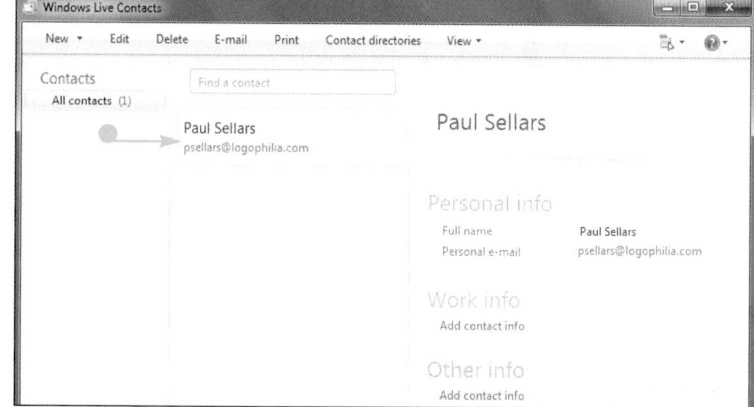

**How do I edit a person's contact data?**

In the Windows Live Contacts window, click the person you want to work with and then click **Edit** in the toolbar. (You can also double-click the person's name or click any of the **Add contact info** links that appear in the contact data section.) Use the Edit Contact dialog box to make your changes, and then click **Save**.

**How do I delete someone from my Contacts?**

In the Windows Live Contacts window, click the person you want to work with and then click **Delete** in the toolbar. When Windows Live Contacts asks you to confirm the deletion, click **OK**.

# Create a Contact Category

You can organize your contacts into one or more categories, which is useful if you want to view just a subset of your contacts. For example, you could create one category for your work colleagues, another for your family members, a third for people working on a current project, and so on.

## Create a Contact Category

1. Click the **New** ▾.
2. Click **Category**.
   - You can also click the **Create a new category** link.

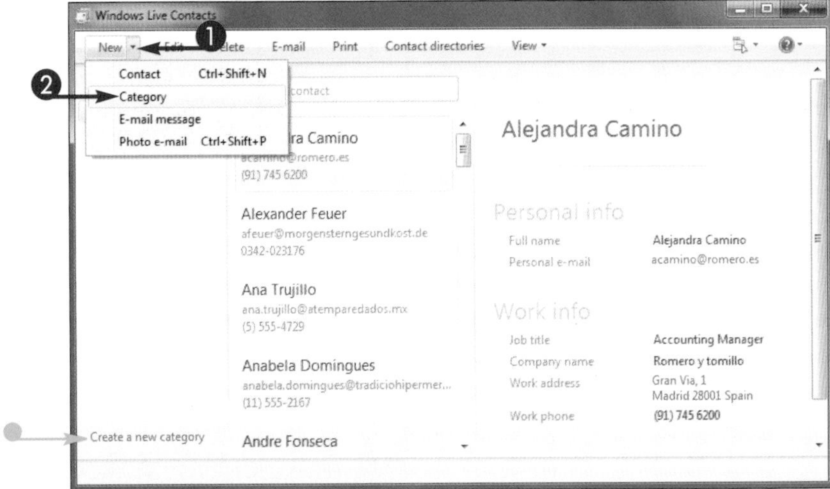

The Create a New Category dialog box appears.

3. Type a name for the category.
4. Click a contact that you want to include in the category.
   - Windows Live Contacts adds the contact to the category.

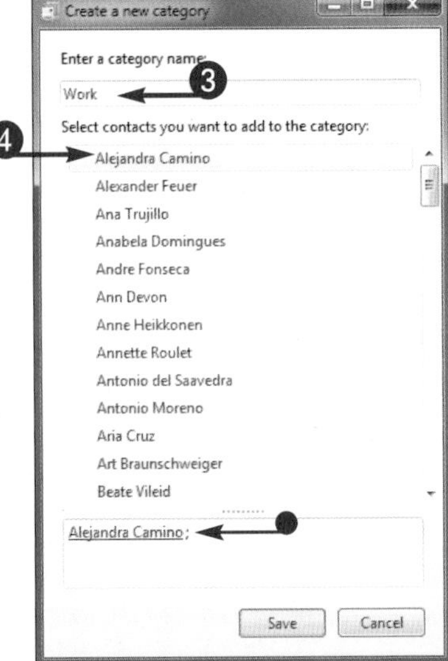

5. Repeat Step **4** for the other contacts you want to add to the category.

***Note:*** *If you add the wrong contact by accident, you can remove it by clicking the contact name again.*

6. Click **Save**.

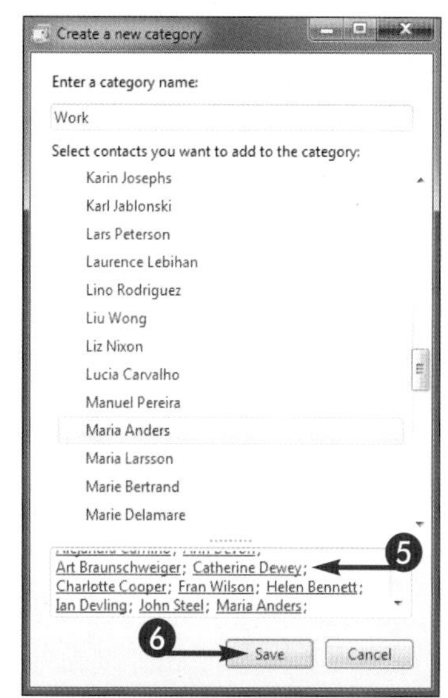

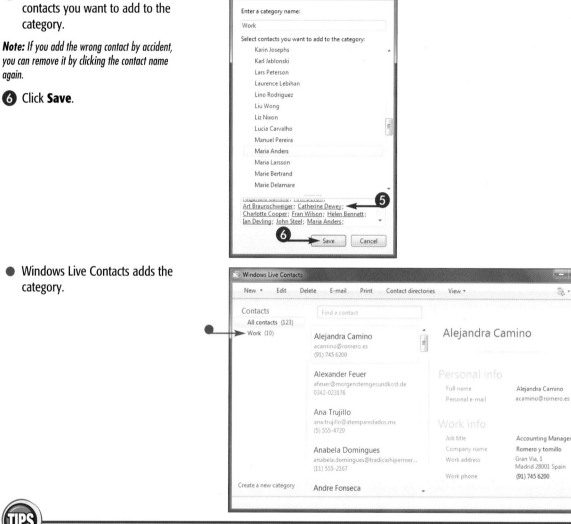

- Windows Live Contacts adds the category.

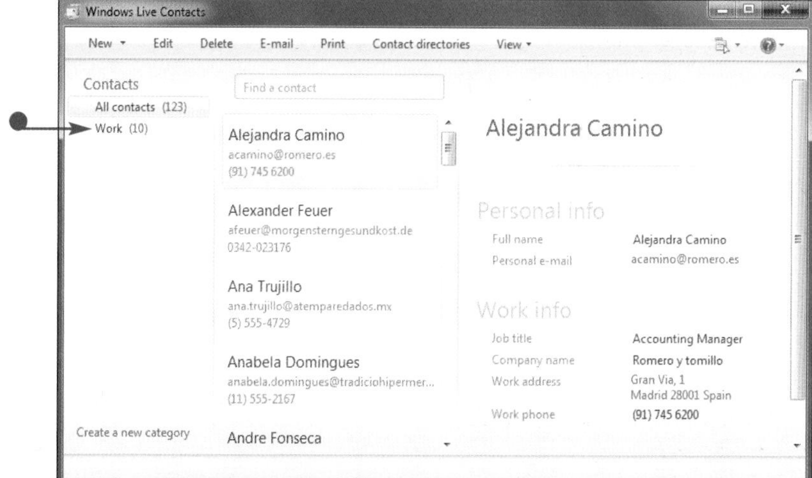

## TIPS

### Can I send an e-mail message to all the contacts in a category?

Yes, this is one of the best reasons to create a category. Normally, sending an e-mail message to multiple contacts involves typing or selecting multiple addresses. With a category, however, you send a single message to the category, and Windows Live Mail automatically sends a copy to each member. Right-click the category and then click **Send e-mail**.

### How do I edit or delete a category?

If you want to add new contacts to the category or delete existing contacts, right-click the category and then click **Edit Category** (or double-click the category). If you want to delete a category, right-click the category and then click **Delete Category**. When Windows Live Contacts asks you to confirm the deletion, click **OK**.

# Select a Contact Address

After you have some e-mail addresses and names in your Contacts list, when composing a message, you can select the address you want directly from Windows Live Contacts instead of typing the address.

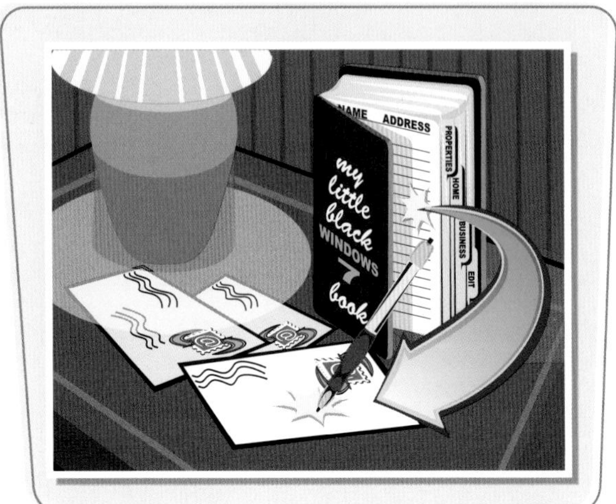


## Select a Contact Address

1. In Windows Live Mail, click **New** to start a new message.
2. Click **To**.

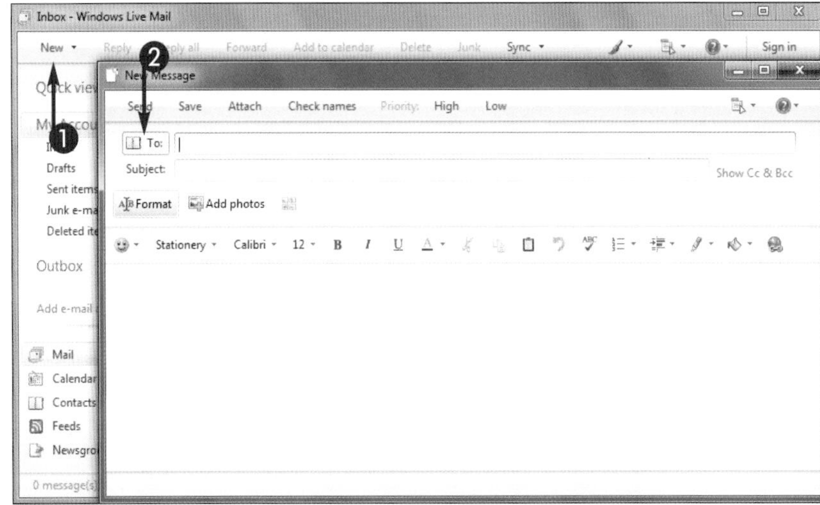

The Send an E-mail dialog box appears.

3. Click the person to whom you want to send the message.
4. Click **To**.

- The person's name appears in the To box.

5. Repeat Steps **3** and **4** to add other recipients to the To box.

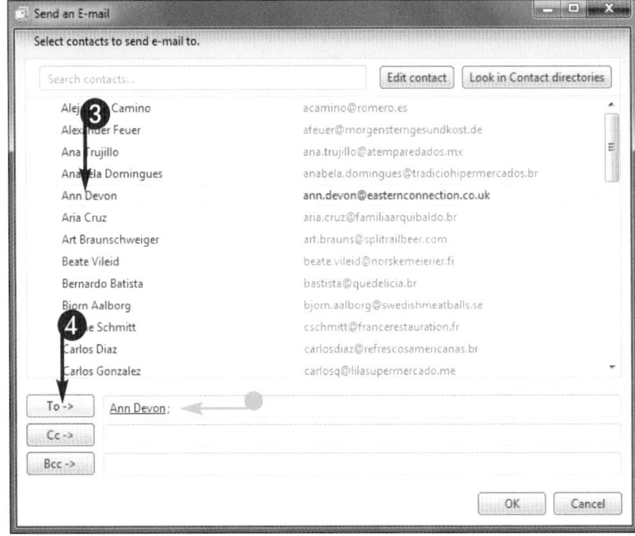

6 To send a copy of the message to a recipient, click the person's name.

7 Click **Cc**.

- The person's name appears in the message recipients box.

8 Repeat Steps **6** and **7** to add other recipients to the Cc line.

9 Click **OK**.

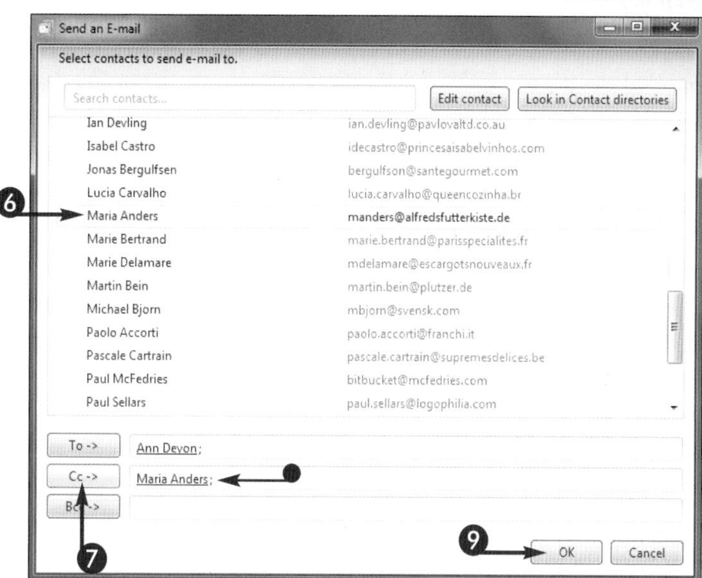


- Windows Live Mail adds the recipients to the To and Cc lines of the new message.

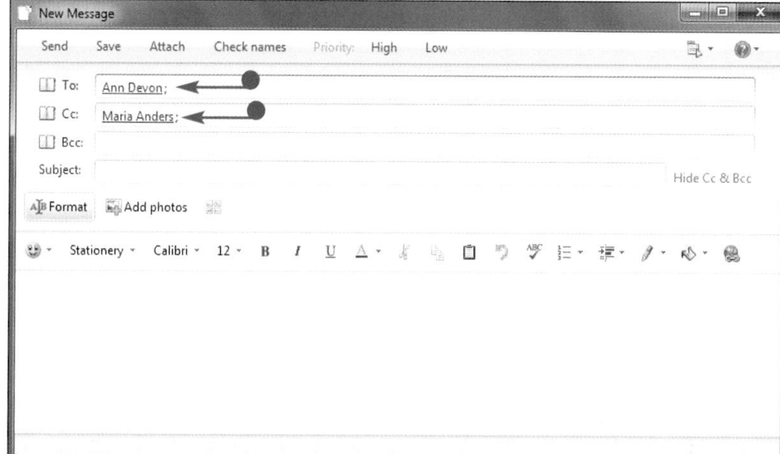

### Can I send a message from Windows Live Contacts?

Yes. In Windows Live Mail, click **Contacts** to open Windows Live Contacts. Click the name of the person you want to send a message to, and then click the **E-mail** button in the toolbar. Windows Live Contacts creates a new message and adds the contact's name to the To field automatically.

### In the Send an E-mail dialog box, what does the Bcc button do?

You click **Bcc** to add the current contact to the message's Bcc field. Bcc stands for *blind courtesy copy* and it means that any addresses in the Bcc field are not displayed to the other message recipients. If you do not want Windows Live Mail to display the Bcc field in the message window, click **Hide Cc & Bcc**.

# Add a File Attachment

If you have a memo, an image, or another document that you want to send to another person, you can attach the document to an e-mail message. The other person can then open the document after he or she receives your message.

## Add a File Attachment

### ADD AN ATTACHMENT FROM A DIALOG BOX

1. Click **New** to start a new message.
2. Click **Attach**.

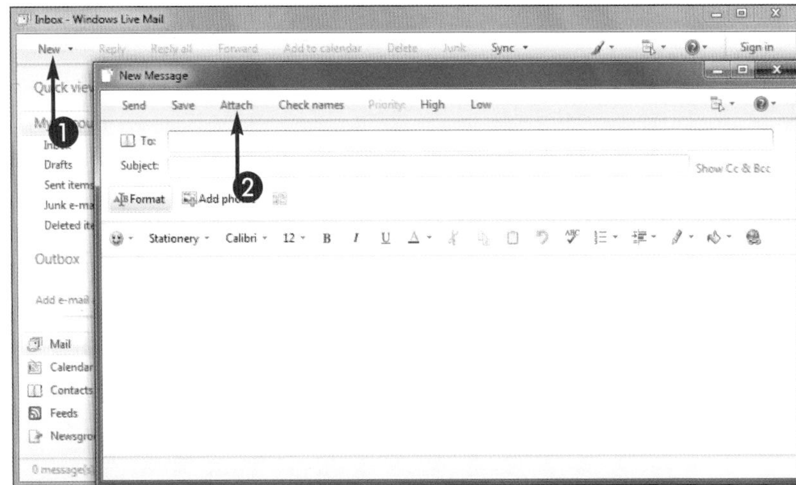

The Open dialog box appears.

3. Click the file you want to attach.
4. Click **Open**.

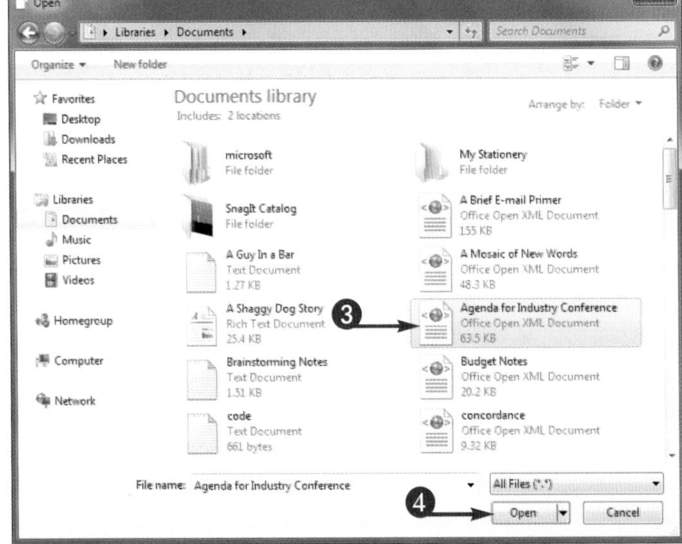

- Windows Live Mail attaches the file to the message.

5. Repeat Steps **2** to **4** to attach additional files to the message.

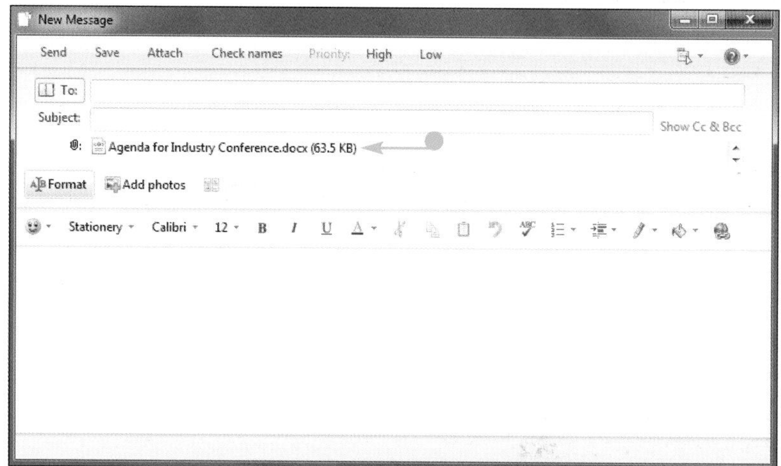


## ADD AN ATTACHMENT DIRECTLY

1. Open the folder that contains the file you want to send as an attachment.
2. Click the file.
3. Click **E-mail**.

   Windows Live Mail creates a new message and attaches the file.

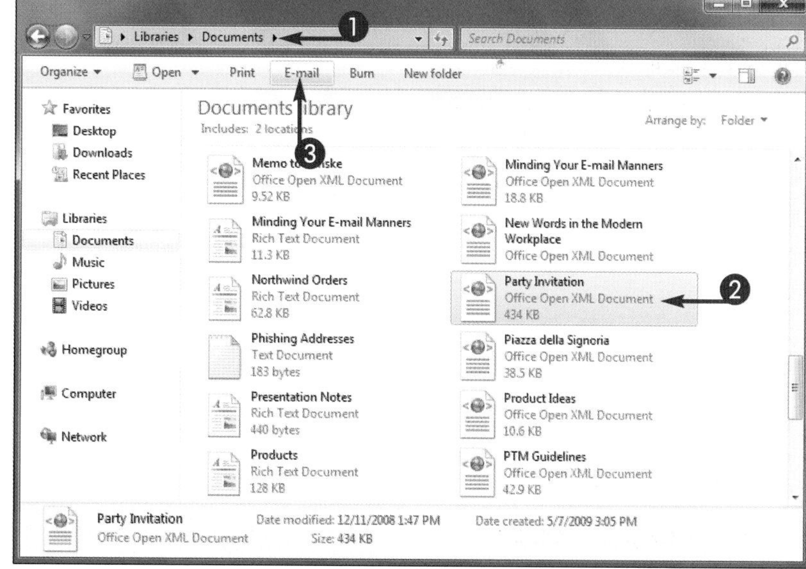

### Is there a limit to the number of files I can attach to a message?

There is no practical limit to the number of files you can attach to the message. However, you should be careful with the total *size* of the files you send. If you or the recipient has a slow Internet connection, sending or receiving the message can take an extremely long time. Also, many Internet service providers (ISPs) place a limit on the size of a message's attachments, which is usually between 2MB and 10MB. In general, use e-mail to send only a few small files at a time.

# Add a Signature

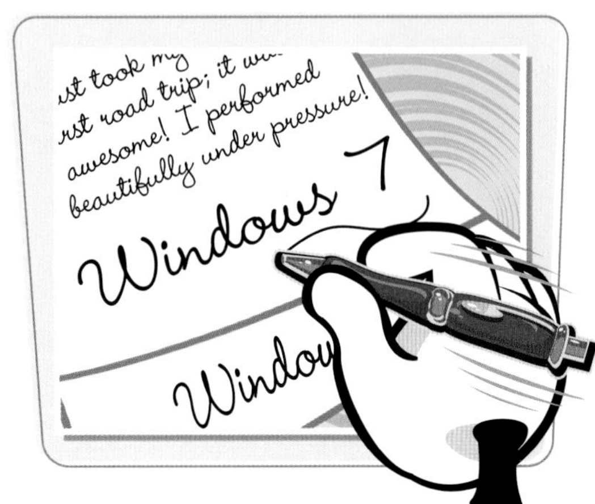


In an e-mail message, a *signature* is a small amount of text that appears at the bottom of the message. Instead of typing this information manually, you can create the signature once and then have Windows Live Mail add the signature automatically to any message you send.

**Signatures usually contain personal contact information, such as your phone numbers, business address, and e-mail and Web site addresses. Some people supplement their signatures with wise or witty quotations.**

## Add a Signature

### ADD A SIGNATURE

1. Click **Menus** (📄).
2. Click **Options**.

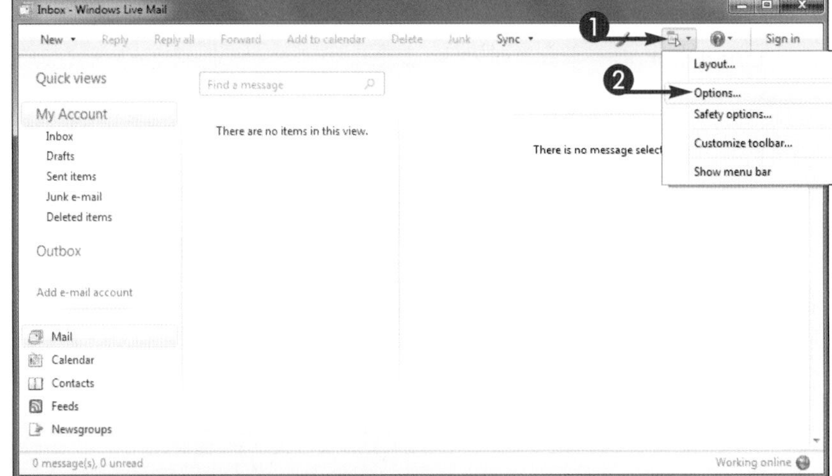


The Options dialog box appears.

3. Click the **Signatures** tab.
4. Click **New**.

- Windows Live Mail adds a new signature.

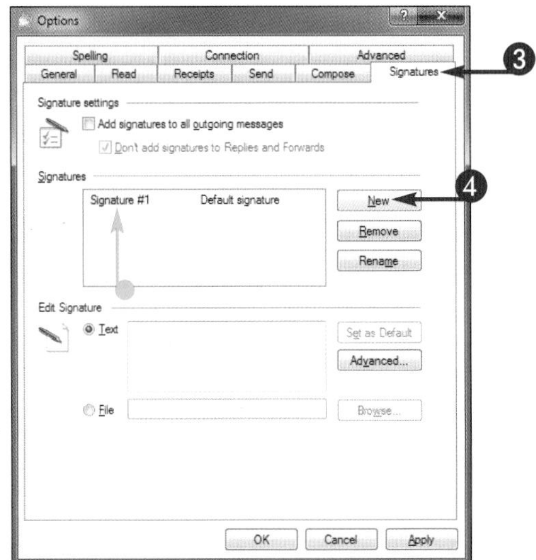

5. Type the signature text.
6. Click **Rename**.
7. Type a name for the signature.
8. Press Enter.
9. Click **OK**.

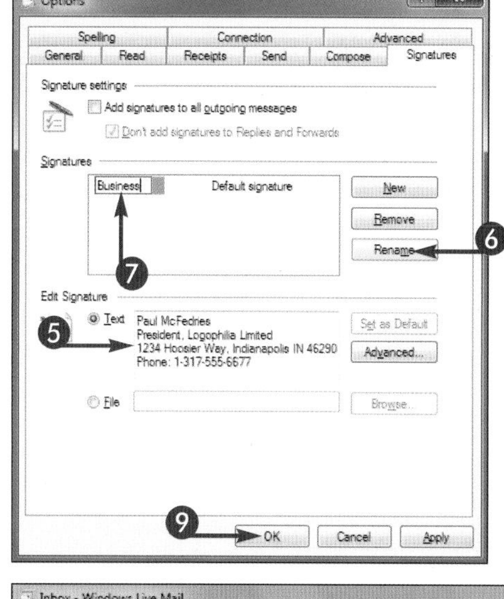

### INSERT THE SIGNATURE MANUALLY

1. Click **New** to start a new message.
2. In the message text area, move the insertion point to the location where you want the signature to appear.
3. Click **Menus** ( ).
4. Click **Insert signature**.

***Note:*** *If you have more than one signature, click the one you want to use from the menu that appears.*

- The signature appears in the message.

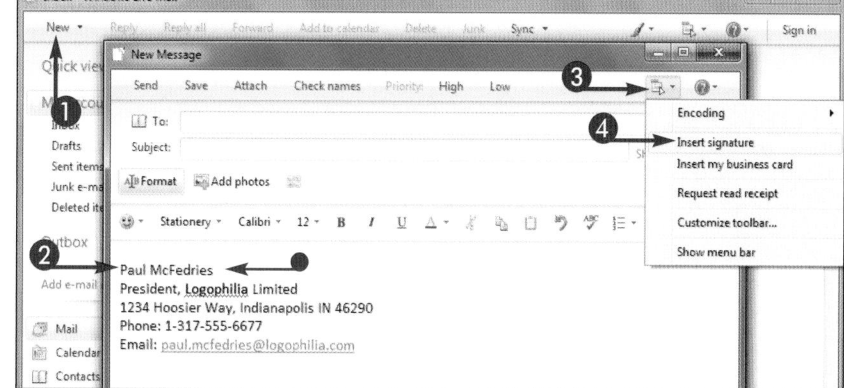

### Can I have more than one signature?

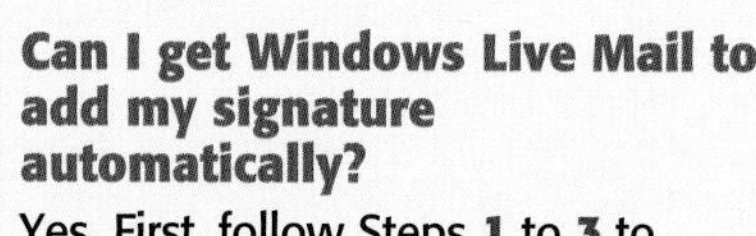


Yes, you can add as many signatures as you want. For example, you may want to have one signature for business use and another for personal use. To add multiple signatures, follow Steps **1** to **3** to display the Signatures tab, and then follow Steps **4** to **8** for each signature. Be sure to give each signature a descriptive name.

### Can I get Windows Live Mail to add my signature automatically?

Yes. First, follow Steps **1** to **3** to display the Signatures tab. Click **Add signatures to all outgoing messages** ( changes to ) to have Windows Live Mail add your signature to the bottom of every new message. Click **Don't add signatures to Replies and Forwards** ( changes to ) if you want Windows Live Mail to add your signature when you reply to and forward messages.

# Receive and Read E-mail Messages

A message sent to you by another person is stored on your ISP's e-mail server computer. You must connect to the ISP's computer to retrieve and read the message. As you see in this section, Windows Live Mail does most of the work for you automatically.

**Windows Live Mail checks for new messages automatically when you start the program, and then checks for more messages every 30 minutes while you are online.**

## Receive and Read E-mail Messages

### RECEIVE E-MAIL MESSAGES

1. Click **Inbox**.
2. Click **Sync**.

- If you have new messages, they appear in your Inbox folder in bold type.
- This symbol (📎) means that the message came with a file attached.
- This symbol (↓) means the message was sent as low priority.
- This symbol (!) means the message was sent as high priority.

## READ A MESSAGE

1. Click the message.
2. Read the message text in the preview pane.

***Note:*** *If you want to open the message in its own window, double-click the message.*

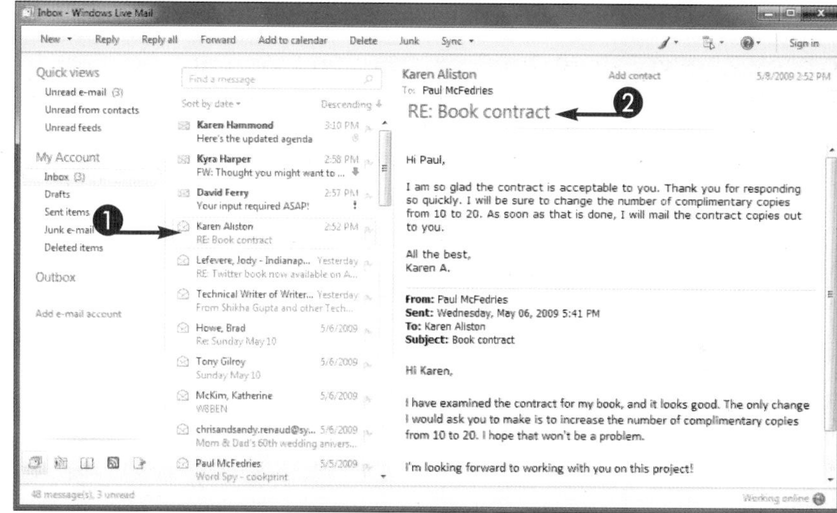

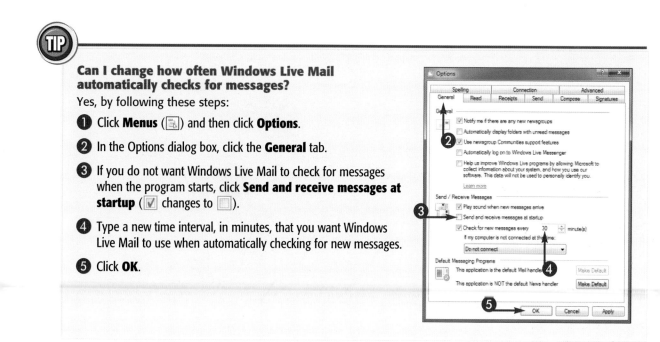

### Can I change how often Windows Live Mail automatically checks for messages?

Yes, by following these steps:

1. Click **Menus** (▣) and then click **Options**.
2. In the Options dialog box, click the **General** tab.
3. If you do not want Windows Live Mail to check for messages when the program starts, click **Send and receive messages at startup** (☑ changes to ☐).
4. Type a new time interval, in minutes, that you want Windows Live Mail to use when automatically checking for new messages.
5. Click **OK**.

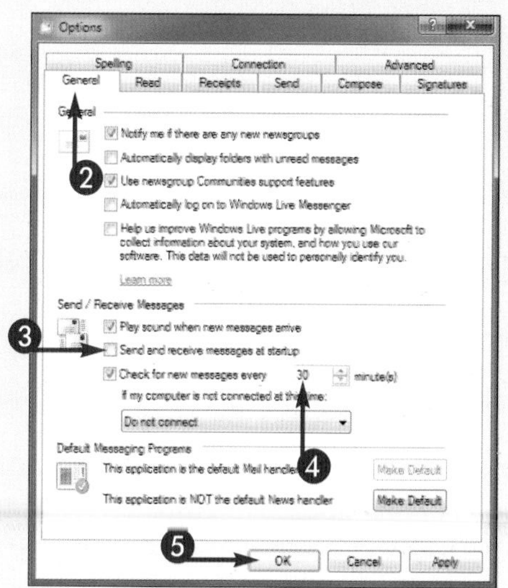

# Reply to a Message

When a message you receive requires some kind of response — whether it is answering a question, supplying information, or providing comments or criticisms — you can reply to any message you receive.

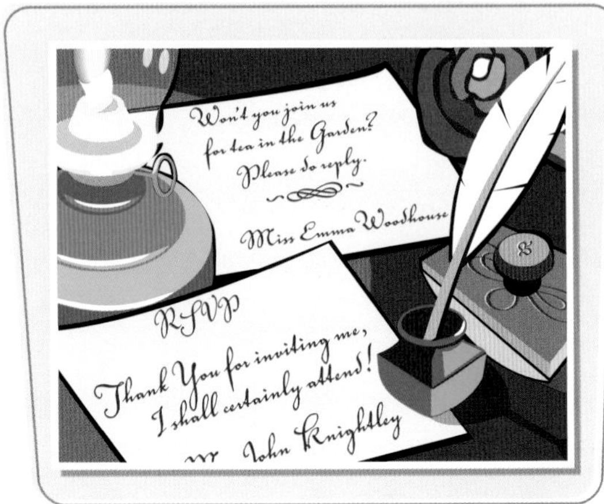


## Reply to a Message

1. Click the message to which you want to reply.
2. Click the reply type you want to use:

   Click **Reply** to respond only to the first address displayed on the From line.

   Click **Reply All** to respond to all the addresses in the From and Cc lines.

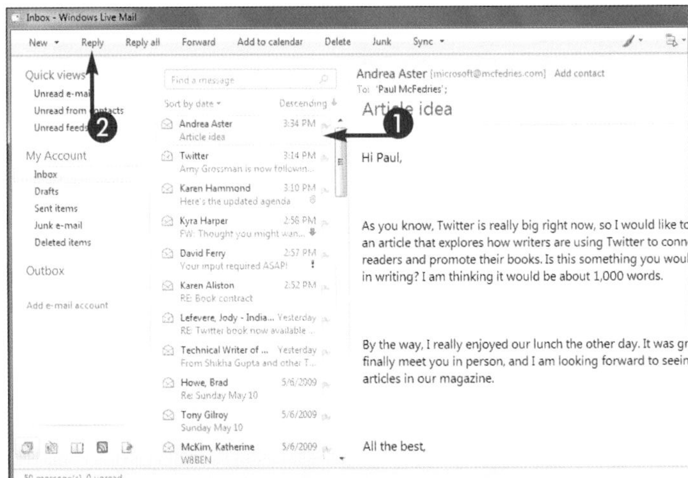


A message window appears.

- Windows Live Mail automatically inserts the recipient addresses.
- Windows Live Mail also inserts the subject line, preceded by Re.
- Windows Live Mail includes the original message's addresses (To and From), date, subject, and text at the bottom of the reply.

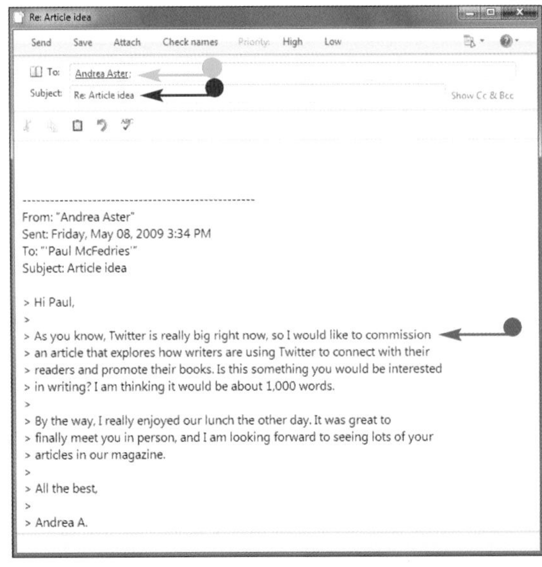

## READ A MESSAGE

1. Click the message.
2. Read the message text in the preview pane.

***Note:*** *If you want to open the message in its own window, double-click the message.*

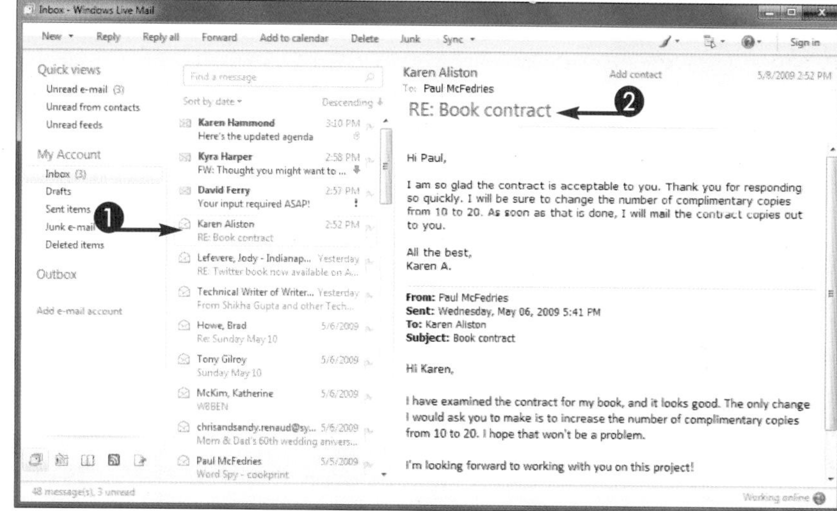

### Can I change how often Windows Live Mail automatically checks for messages?

Yes, by following these steps:

1. Click **Menus** (☐) and then click **Options**.
2. In the Options dialog box, click the **General** tab.
3. If you do not want Windows Live Mail to check for messages when the program starts, click **Send and receive messages at startup** (☑ changes to ☐).
4. Type a new time interval, in minutes, that you want Windows Live Mail to use when automatically checking for new messages.
5. Click **OK**.

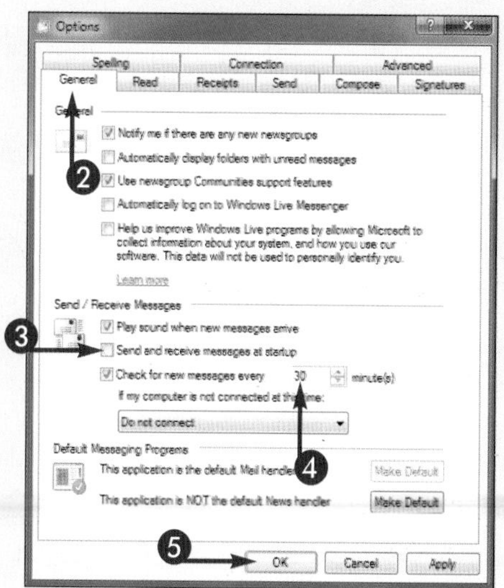

# Reply to a Message

When a message you receive requires some kind of response — whether it is answering a question, supplying information, or providing comments or criticisms — you can reply to any message you receive.

## Reply to a Message

1. Click the message to which you want to reply.
2. Click the reply type you want to use:

   Click **Reply** to respond only to the first address displayed on the From line.

   Click **Reply All** to respond to all the addresses in the From and Cc lines.

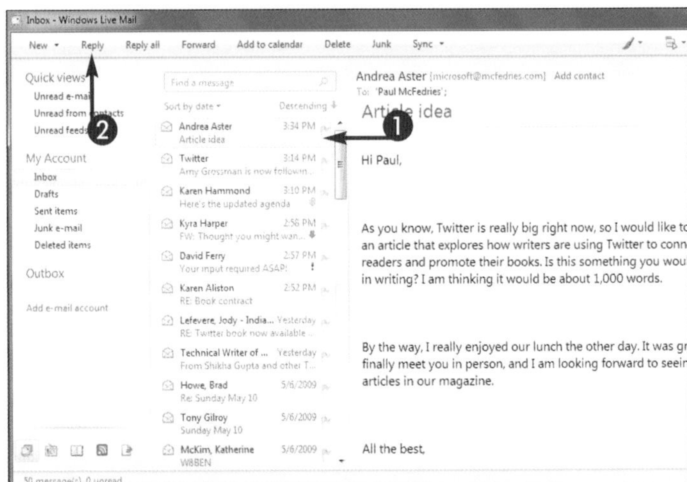


A message window appears.

- Windows Live Mail automatically inserts the recipient addresses.
- Windows Live Mail also inserts the subject line, preceded by Re.
- Windows Live Mail includes the original message's addresses (To and From), date, subject, and text at the bottom of the reply.

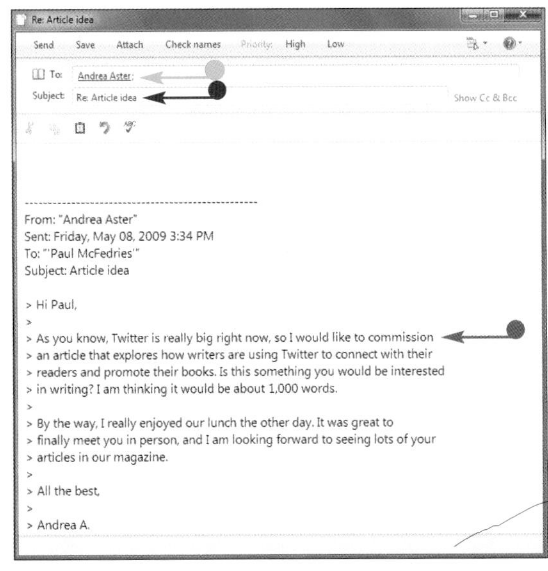

chapter 11

3. Edit the original message to include only the text relevant to your reply.

***Note:*** *If the original message is fairly short, you usually do not need to edit the text. However, if the original message is long, and your response deals only with part of that message, you will save the recipient time by deleting everything except the relevant portion of the text.*

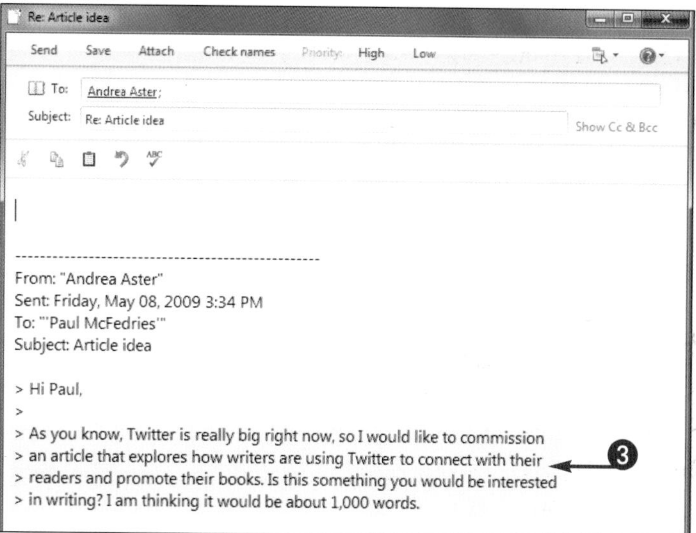

Re: Article idea
Send
Save
Attach
Check names
Priority: High
Low
To: Andrea Aster;
Subject: Re: Article idea
Show Cc & Bcc
From: "Andrea Aster"
Sent: Friday, May 08, 2009 3:34 PM
To: "'Paul McFedries'"
Subject: Article idea
> Hi Paul,
>
> As you know, Twitter is really big right now, so I would like to commission
> an article that explores how writers are using Twitter to connect with their
> readers and promote their books. Is this something you would be interested
> in writing? I am thinking it would be about 1,000 words.
3

4. Click the area above the original message text and type your reply.
5. Click **Send**.

   Windows Live Mail sends your reply.

***Note:*** *Windows Live Mail stores a copy of your reply in the Sent Items folder.*

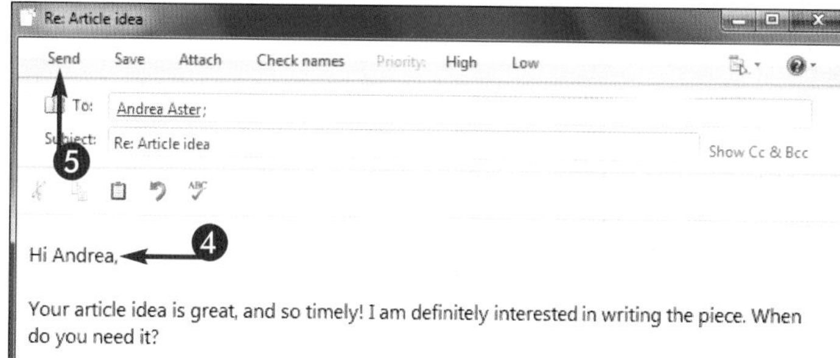

Re: Article idea
Send
Save
Attach
Check names
Priority: High
Low
To: Andrea Aster;
Subject: Re: Article idea
Show Cc & Bcc
5
Hi Andrea,
4
Your article idea is great, and so timely! I am definitely interested in writing the piece. When do you need it?

TIP

### After I reply to a message, Windows Live Mail sometimes adds the recipient to my Contacts list. How do I prevent this?

By default, Windows Live Mail adds a person to your Contacts list after the third time you send that person a reply. To turn this off, follow these steps:

1. Click **Menus** (icon) and click **Options**.
2. In the Options dialog box, click the **Send** tab.
3. Click **Automatically put people I reply to in my address book after the third reply** (☑ changes to ☐).
4. Click **OK** (not shown).

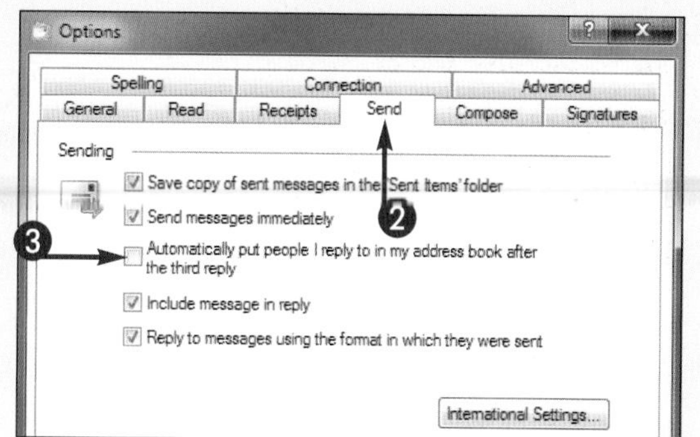

Options
Spelling
Connection
Advanced
General
Read
Receipts
Send
Compose
Signatures
Sending
Save copy of sent messages in the 'Sent Items' folder
Send messages immediately
Automatically put people I reply to in my address book after the third reply
Include message in reply
Reply to messages using the format in which they were sent
International Settings...
2
3

# Forward a Message

If a message has information that is relevant to or concerns another person, you can forward a copy of that message to the other recipient. You can also include your own comments in the forward.

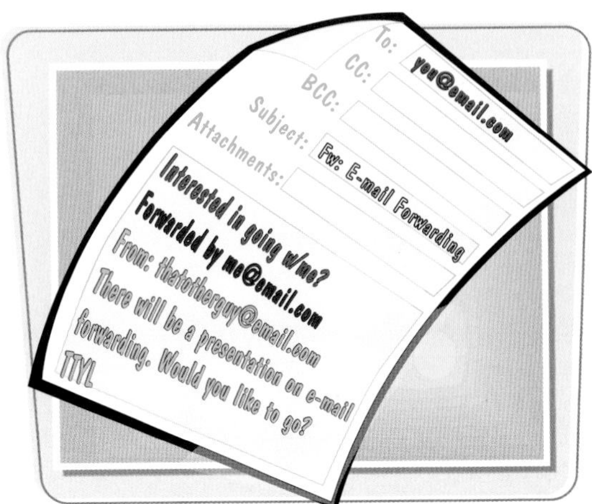


## Forward a Message

1. Click the message that you want to forward.
2. Click **Forward**.

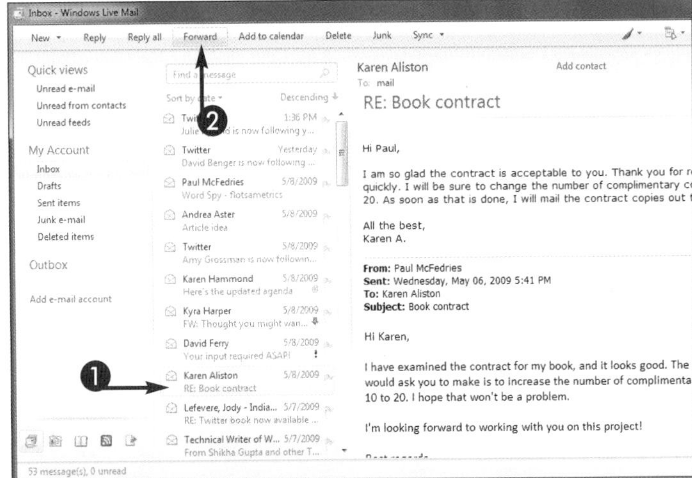

A message window appears.

- Windows Live Mail inserts the subject line, preceded by Fw.
- The original message's addresses (To and From), date, subject, and text are included at the bottom of the forward.

3. Type the e-mail address of the person to whom you are forwarding the message.

- To send a copy of the message to another person, click **Show Cc & Bcc** and then type that person's e-mail address in the **Cc** field that appears.

4. Edit the original message to include only the text relevant to your forward.
5. Click the area above the original message text.

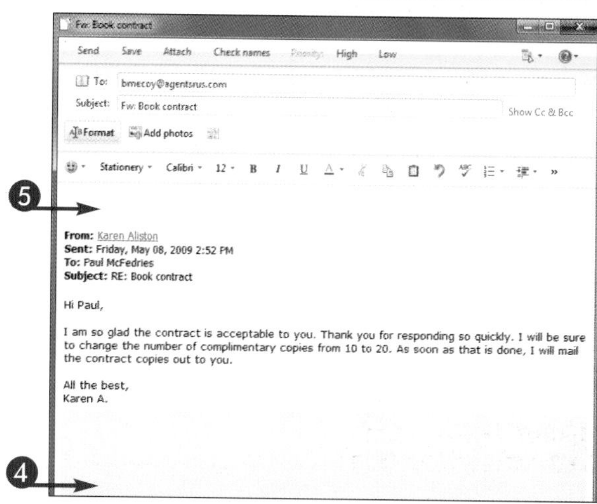

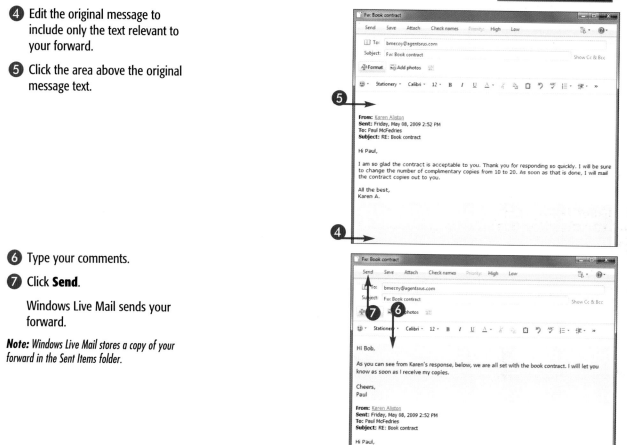

6. Type your comments.
7. Click **Send**.

   Windows Live Mail sends your forward.

***Note:*** *Windows Live Mail stores a copy of your forward in the Sent Items folder.*

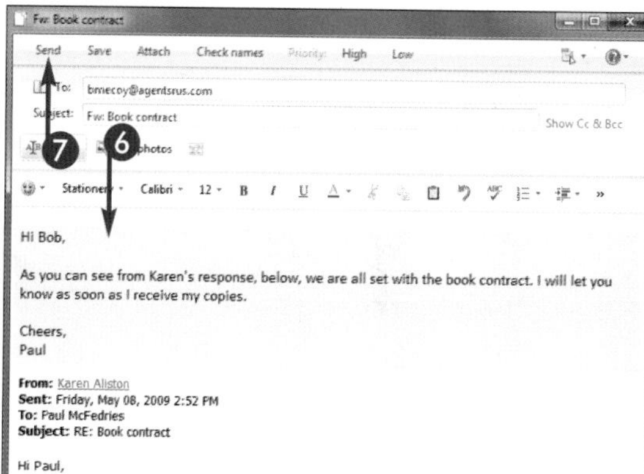

**How do I forward someone a copy of the actual message rather than just a copy of the message text?**

Click the message and then press Alt to display the Windows Live Mail menu bar. Click **Actions**, and then click **Forward as attachment**. Windows Live Mail creates a new message and includes the original message as an attachment.

**My replies and forwards do not always use the same format. How can I make Windows Live Mail use a single format?**

Click **Menus** ( ) and then click **Options** to open the Options dialog box. Click the **Send** tab and then click the **Reply to messages using the format in which they were sent** check box ( changes to ). In the Mail Sending Format area, click the format you want to use ( changes to ) and then click **OK**.

# Open and Save an Attachment

If you receive a message that has a file attached, you can open the attachment to view the contents of the file. You can also save the attachment as a file on your computer.

**Be careful when dealing with attached files. Computer viruses are often transmitted by e-mail attachments.**

## Open and Save an Attachment

### OPEN AN ATTACHMENT

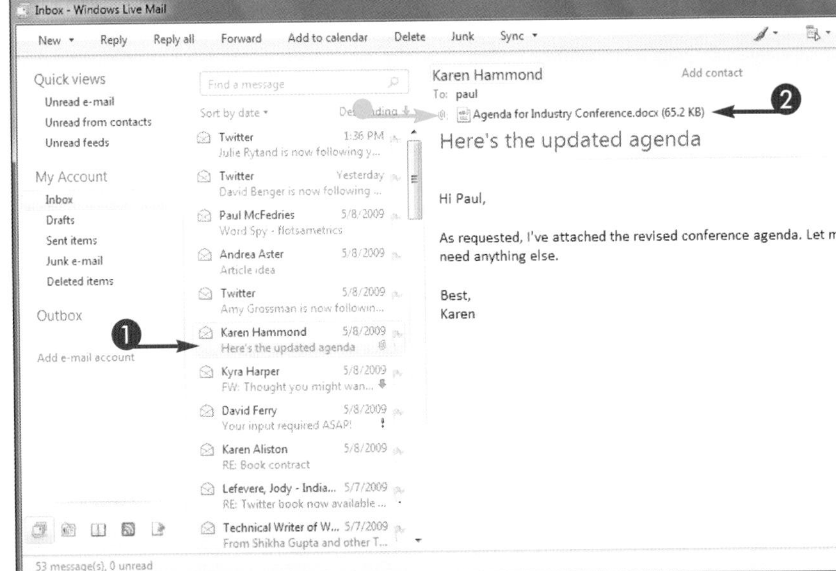


1. Click the message that has the attachment, as indicated by the **Attachment** symbol (📎).

- A list of the message attachments appears.

2. Double-click the attachment you want to open.

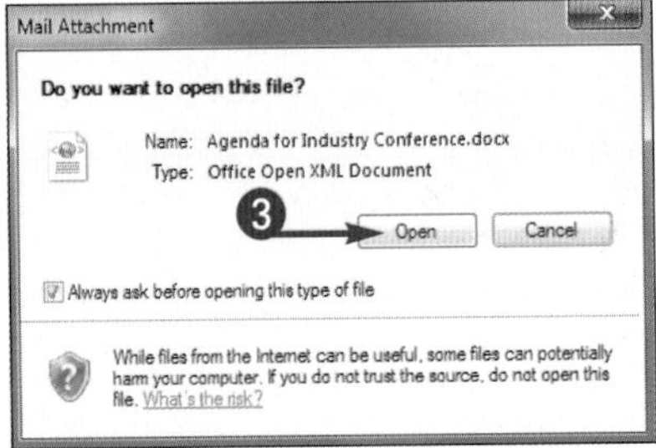


Windows Live Mail asks you to confirm that you want to open the file.

3. Click **Open**.

The file opens in the appropriate program.

***Note:*** *Instead of opening the file, Windows 7 may display a dialog box saying that the file "does not have a program associated with it." This means you need to install the appropriate program for the type of file. If you are not sure, ask the person who sent you the file what program you need.*

## SAVE AN ATTACHMENT

1. Click the message that has the attachment, as indicated by the **Attachment** symbol (📎).
   - A list of the message attachments appears.
2. Right-click the attachment you want to save.
3. Click **Save as**.

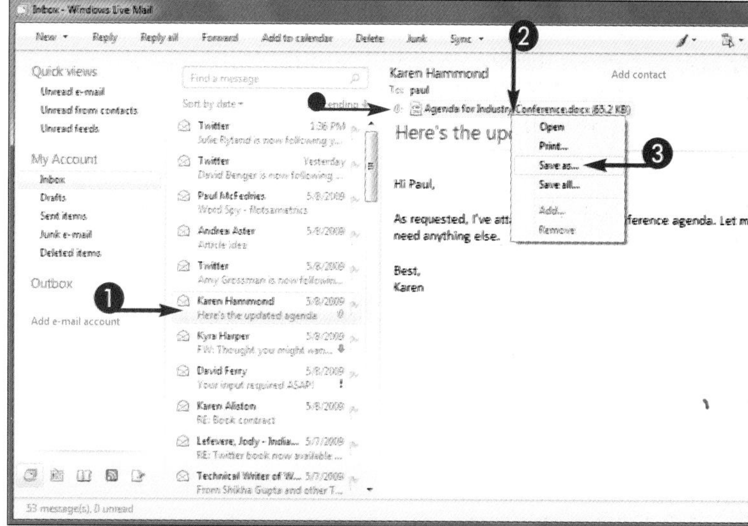

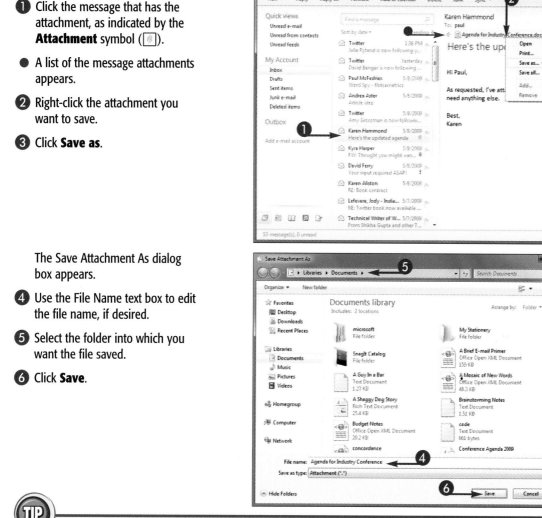

The Save Attachment As dialog box appears.

4. Use the File Name text box to edit the file name, if desired.
5. Select the folder into which you want the file saved.
6. Click **Save**.

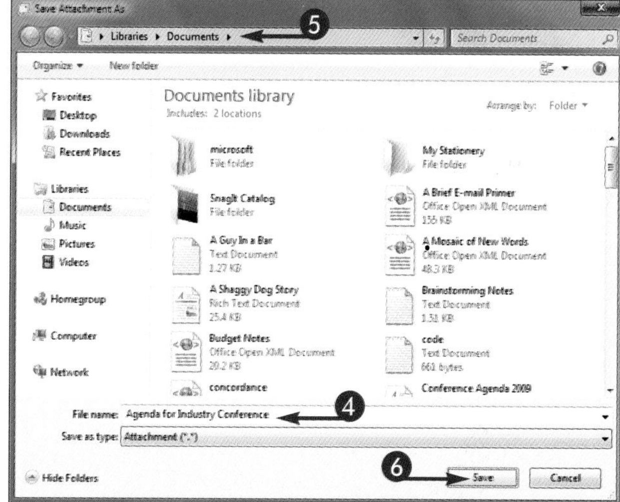

### When I right-click an attached file, why am I unable to click the Save As command?

Windows Live Mail has determined that the attached file may be unsafe, meaning that the file may harbor a virus or other malicious code. To confirm this, double-click the message to open it. Below the toolbar, you should see a message saying, "Windows Live Mail removed access to the following unsafe attachments in your mail." If you are certain the file is safe, turn off this feature by clicking **Menus** (▣), **Safety Options**, the **Security** tab, and then **Do not allow attachments to be saved or opened that could potentially be a virus** (☑ changes to ☐). Be sure to reactivate this feature after you have opened or saved the attachment.

# Create a Folder for Saving Messages

**After you have used Windows Live Mail for a while, you may find that you have many messages in your Inbox folder. To keep the Inbox uncluttered, you can create new folders and then move messages from the Inbox to the new folders.**

**You should use each folder you create to save related messages. For example, you could create separate folders for people you correspond with regularly, projects you are working on, different work departments, and so on.**

## Create a Folder for Saving Messages

### CREATE A FOLDER

1. Right-click the folder in which you want to create the new folder.
2. Click **New folder**.

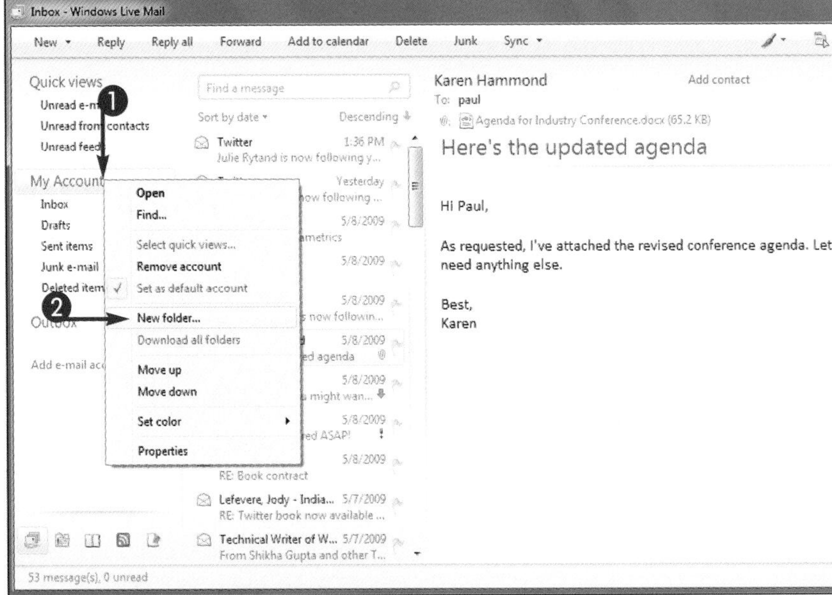


The Create Folder dialog box appears.

3. Type the name of the new subfolder.
4. Click **OK**.

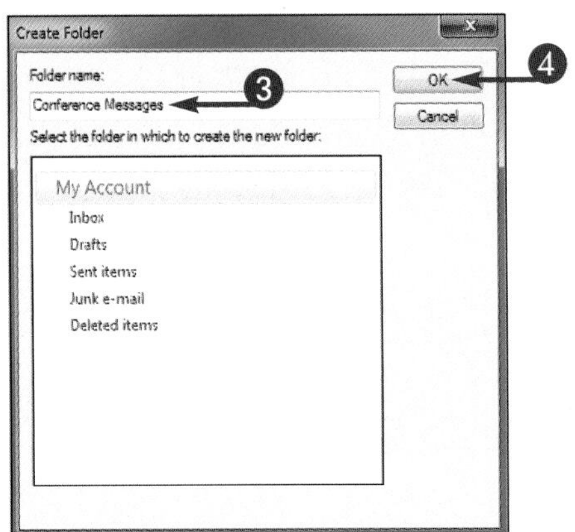

- The new subfolder appears in the Folders list.

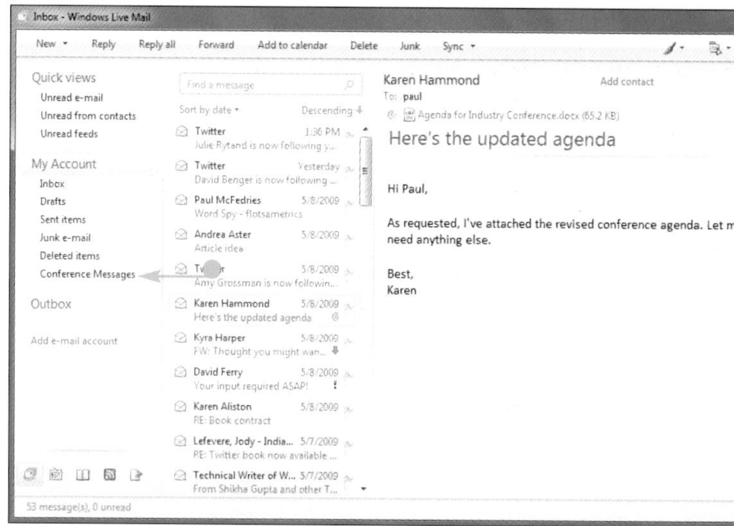

## MOVE A MESSAGE TO ANOTHER FOLDER

1. Click the folder that contains the message you want to move.
2. Position the mouse over the message you want to move.
3. Click and drag the message and drop it on the folder to which you want to move the message.

   Windows Live Mail moves the message.

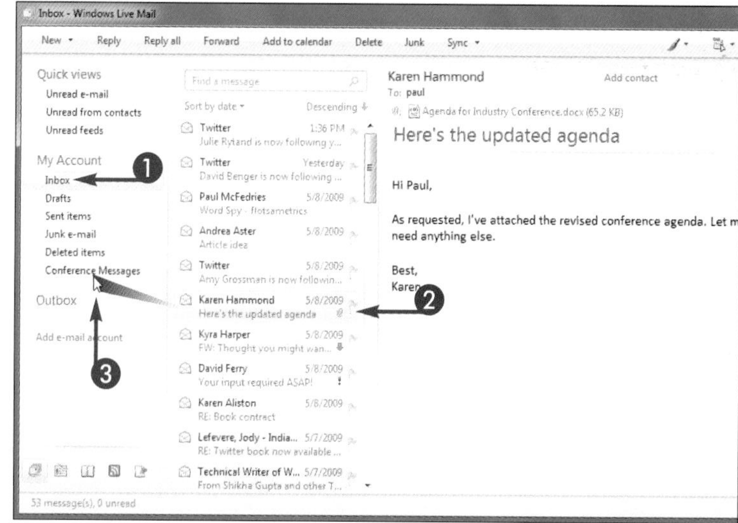

### How do I rename a folder?

Right-click the folder and then click **Rename**. Use the Rename Folder dialog box to type the new name and then click **OK**. Note that Windows Live Mail only allows you to rename those folders that you have created yourself.

### How do I delete a folder?

Right-click the folder and then click **Delete**. When Windows Live Mail asks you to confirm the deletion, click **Yes**. Note that Windows Live Mail only allows you to delete those folders that you have created yourself. Remember, too, that when you delete a folder, you also delete any messages stored in that folder.

# Create Rules to Filter Incoming Messages

You can make your e-mail chores faster and more efficient if you create *rules* that handle incoming messages automatically.

**A rule combines a condition and an action. The condition is one or more message criteria, such as the address of the sender or words in the subject line. The action is what happens to a message that satisfies the condition, such as moving the message to another folder or sending a reply.**

## Create Rules to Filter Incoming Messages

1. Press Alt.
   - The Windows Live Mail menu bar appears.
2. Click **Tools**.
3. Click **Message rules**.
4. Click **Mail**.

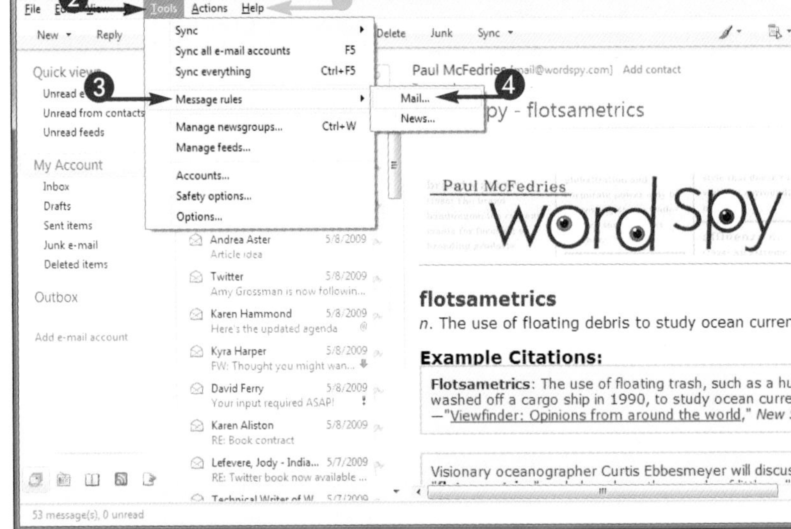

5. If you have already created at least one rule, the Rules dialog box appears. In that case, click **New**.

   The New Mail Rule dialog box appears.

6. In the Select One or More Conditions box, click the condition you want to use (☐ changes to ☑).
7. If the condition requires editing, click the underlined text.

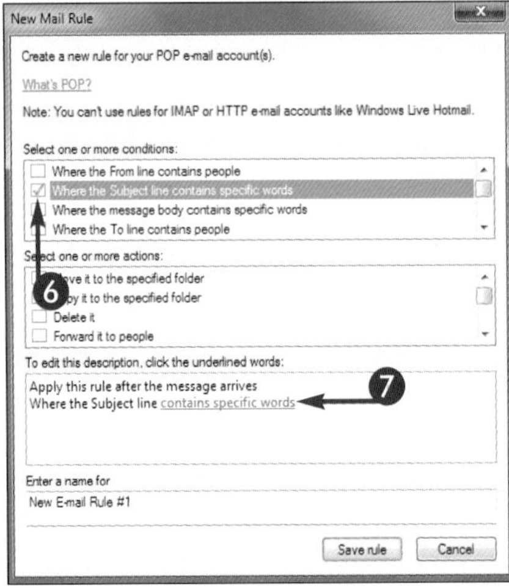

A dialog box appears, the layout of which depends on the condition.

8. Enter the text, address, or other required information.
9. Click **Add**.
10. Repeat Steps **6** and **7** to add other data to the rule.
11. Click **OK**.

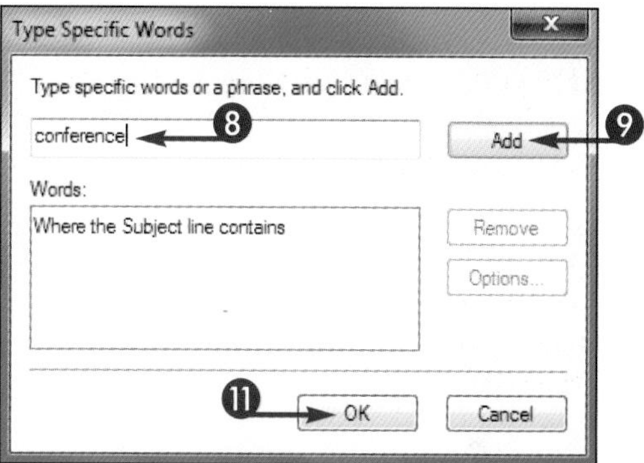


12. In the Select One or More Actions box, click the action you want to use (☐ changes to ☑).
13. If the action requires editing, follow Steps **7** to **9**.
14. Type a name for the rule.
15. Click **Save rule**.

Windows Live Mail adds the rule to the Rules dialog box.

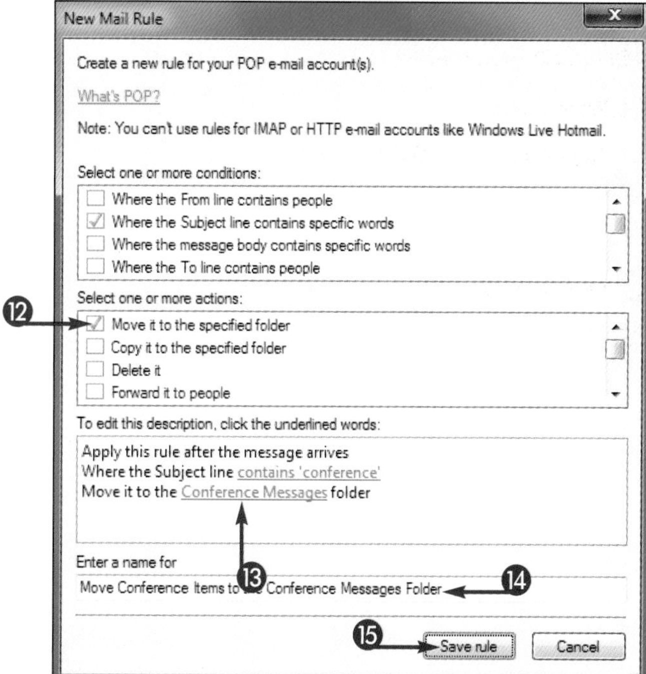

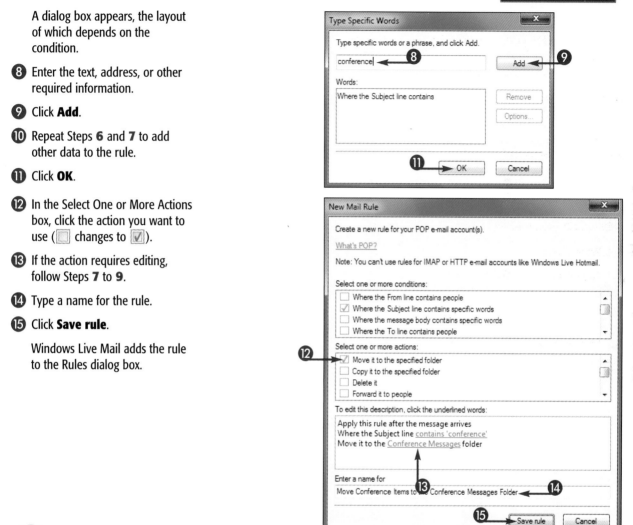

### I created my rule, but Windows Live Mail did not perform the action on my existing messages. Why?

By default, Windows Live Mail applies a new rule only on messages that you receive after you create the rule. If you want to apply the rule to existing messages, follow Steps **1** to **4** from this section to open the Rules dialog box. Click **Apply now** to open the Apply Mail Rules Now dialog box. Click the rule you want to apply, and then click **Apply Now**.

### How do I make changes to a rule?

Follow Steps **1** to **4** from this section to open the Rules dialog box. Click the rule you want to change and then click **Modify**. In the Edit Mail Rule dialog box that appears, follow Steps **6** to **15** to make your changes to the rule, and then click **OK**.

# Switch to Calendar

With Calendar, the scheduling program that comes with Windows Live Mail, you can record events and tasks, set reminders for when these items are due, and more. To get started, you must first switch to the Calendar feature.

## Switch to Calendar

1. Click **Calendar** ( ).

***Note:*** *You can also open the Calendar by pressing*

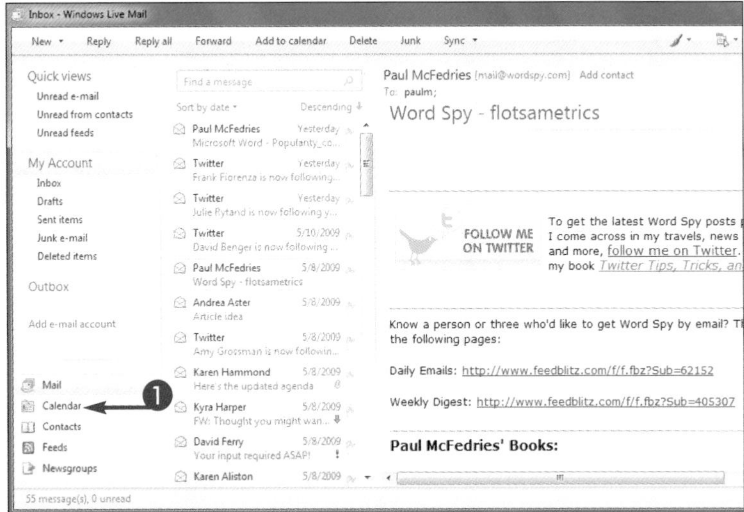


The Calendar window appears.

2. When you finish your scheduling chores, click the **Mail** button ( ), or press Ctrl + Shift + J , to return to the Mail feature.

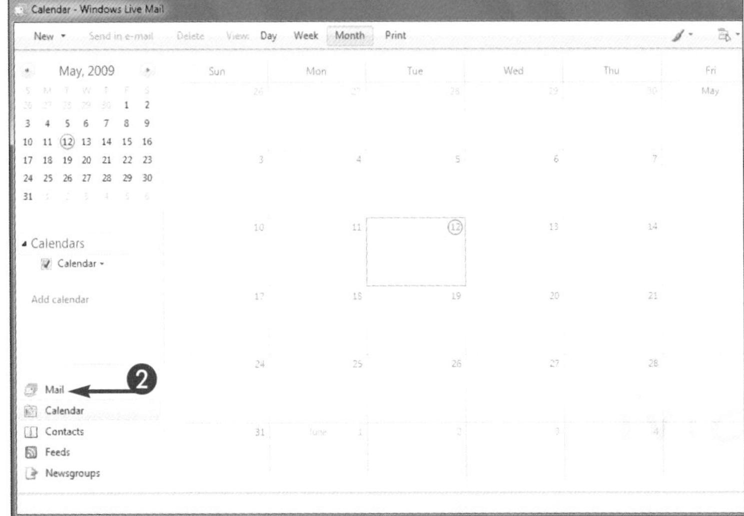

# Navigate the Calendar

Windows Live Mail's Calendar makes scheduling easy. However, you can make it even easier by taking some time now to learn the layout of the Calendar window.

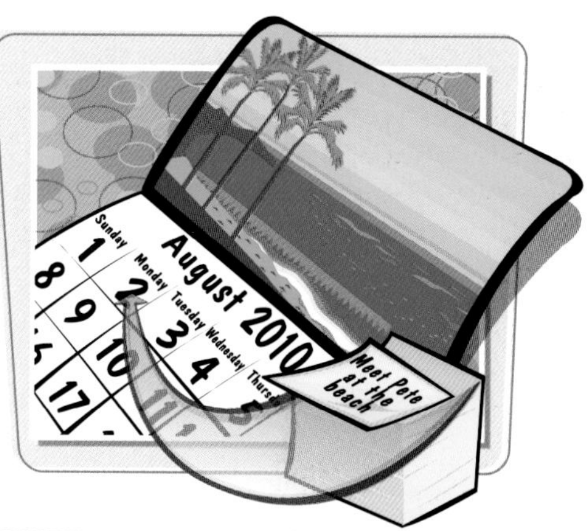


### Date Navigator

This area shows the current month, and you use the Date Navigator to select the date on which you want to schedule an event, all-day event, or task. See the "Display a Different Date" section, later in this chapter, to learn how to use the Date Navigator.

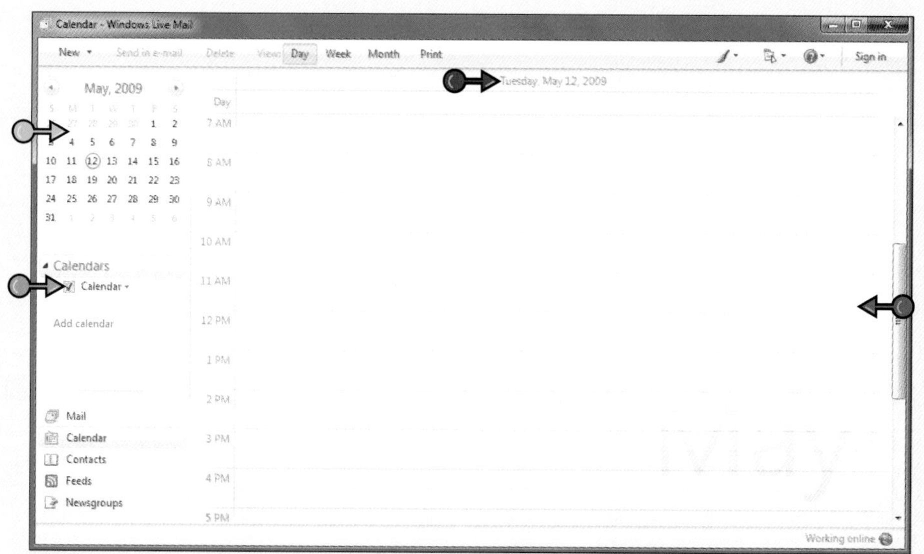


### Current Date

This area shows the date that is currently selected in the Date Navigator.

### Calendars

This area shows a list of your calendars. You get a single calendar to start with, but you can add more calendars as described in the "Add a Calendar" section, later in this chapter.

### Event List

This area shows the events that you have scheduled. In Day view, as shown here, the event list is divided into half-hour increments.

# Display a Different Date

Before you add an event to your calendar, you must first select the date when the event occurs. You use the Date Navigator to display a different date in Calendar, and you can navigate dates by month or by year.

## Display a Different Date

### NAVIGATE BY MONTH

1. In the Date Navigator, click the **Next Month** button (▶) until the month of your event appears.

- If you go too far, click the **Previous Month** button (◀) to move back to the month you want.

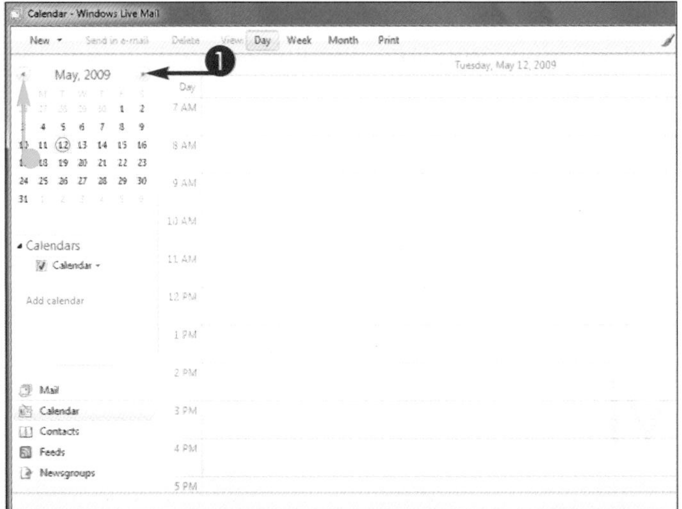


2. Click the date.

- The date appears in the events list.
- If you want to return to today's date, click **Go to today**.

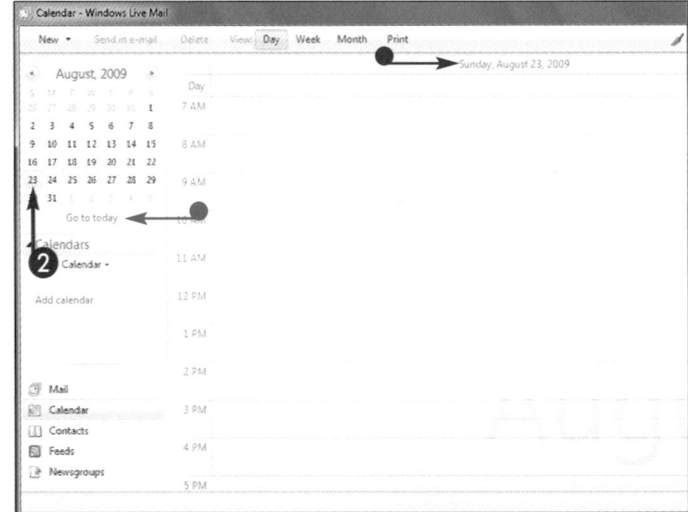

## NAVIGATE BY YEAR

1. In the Date Navigator, click the month.

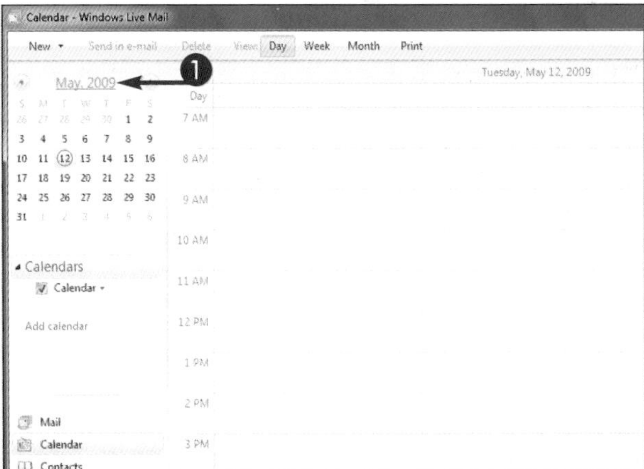

Calendar switches to Year view.

2. Click the **Next Year** button (▸) until the year of your event appears.

- If you go too far, click the **Previous Year** button (◂) to move back to the year you want.

3. Click the month when your event occurs.

Calendar switches back to Month view.

4. Use Steps **1** and **2** on the previous page to display and select the date when your event occurs.

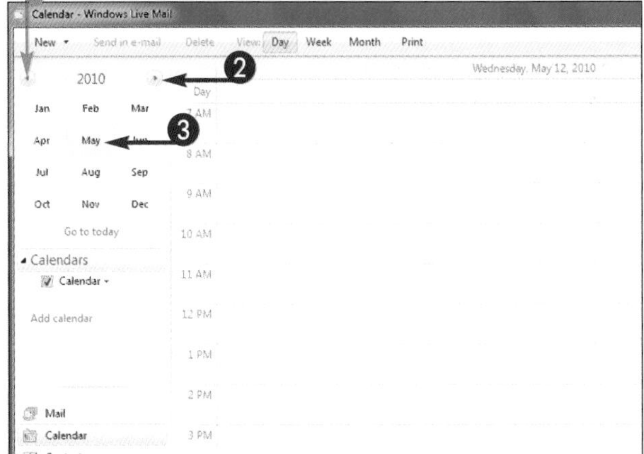

### Can I see more than one day at a time in the events list?

Yes. Use the following toolbar button to select the view you want to use:

- **Day**. Shows the date currently selected in the Date Navigator. (You can also press Ctrl + Alt + 1.)
- **Week**. Shows the full week that includes the date currently selected in the Date Navigator. (You can also press Ctrl + Alt + 2.)
- **Month**. Shows the month that includes the date currently selected in the Date Navigator. (You can also press Ctrl + Alt + 3.)

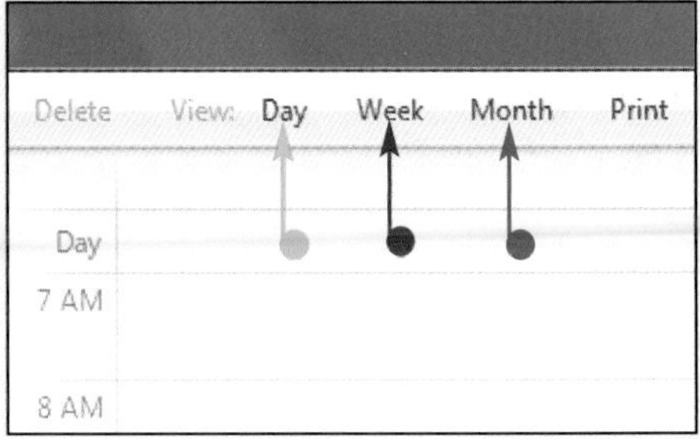

# Create an Event

You can help organize your life by using Windows Live Mail's Calendar to record your events on the date and time they occur.

**If the event has no set time — for example, a birthday, anniversary, or multiple-day event such as a sales meeting or vacation — you can create an all-day event.**

## Create an Event

1. Navigate to the date when the event occurs.
2. Click the time when the event starts.

***Note:*** *If the event is more than half an hour, you can also click and drag the mouse over the full event period.*

3. Click **New**.

***Note:*** *Another way to start a new event is to press* Ctrl + Shift + E.

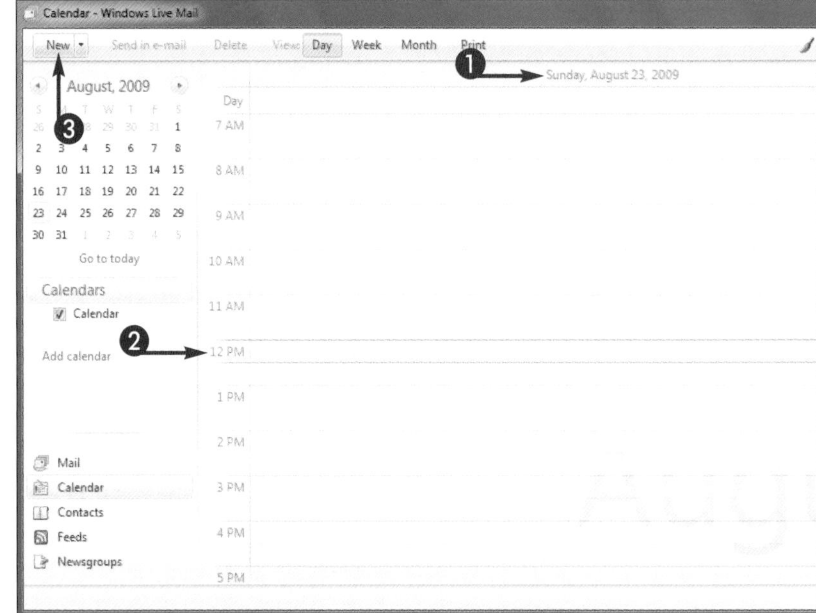

Calendar displays the New Event dialog box.

4. Type a name for the event.
5. Use the Location text box to type the event location.
6. If the event is an anniversary or other event that lasts all day, click **All day** (☐ changes to ☑).

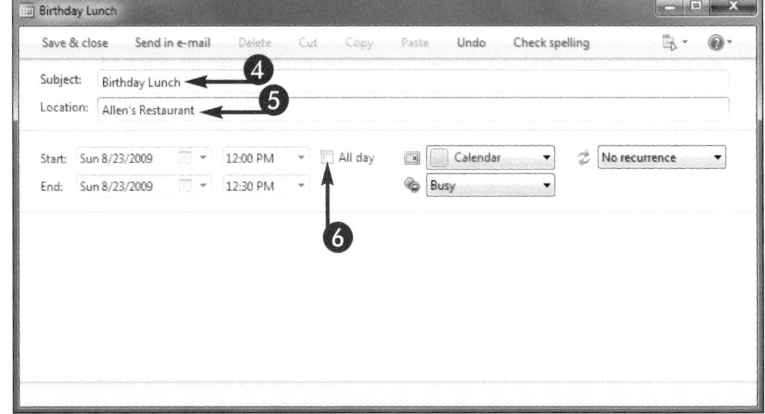

7. If the start time is incorrect, use the Start text box to type the correct time.
8. If the end time is incorrect, use the End text box to type the correct time.
9. Use the large text area to type notes related to the event.
10. Click **Save & close**.

- Calendar adds the event to the list.

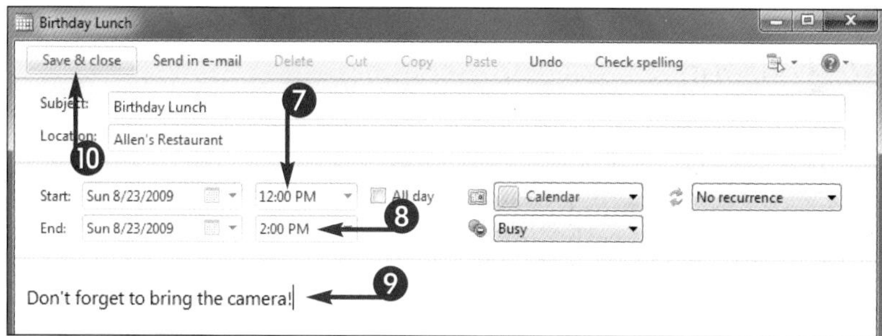


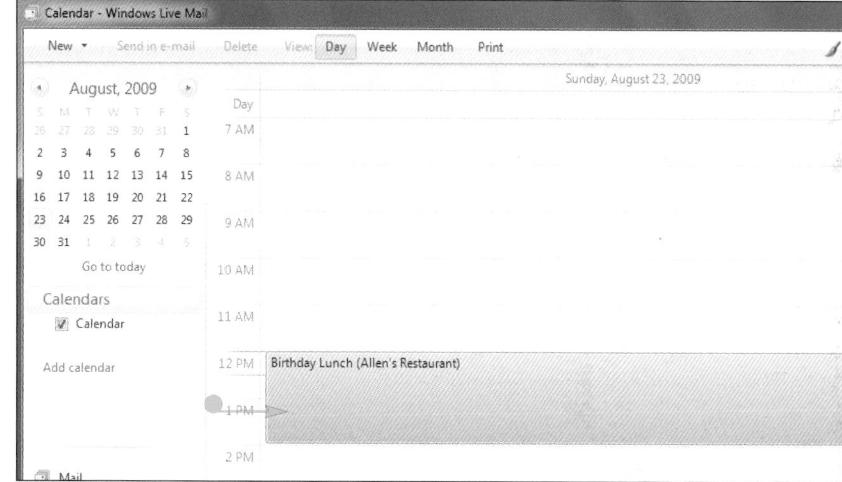

**Is there an easy way to schedule an event that occurs at a regular interval?**

Yes, you can set up a recurring event. Calendar can repeat an event at regular intervals such as daily, weekly, monthly, or yearly. You can also set up an advanced recurrence that uses a custom interval that you specify. Here are the steps to follow:

1. Follow Steps **1** to **9** to set up a regular event.
2. Click the **Set Recurrence** ▾.
3. Click the interval you want to use.

- If you want to set up your own recurrence, click **Custom** and use the Event Recurrence dialog box to specify your custom interval.

Windows Calendar repeats the event at the interval you specified.

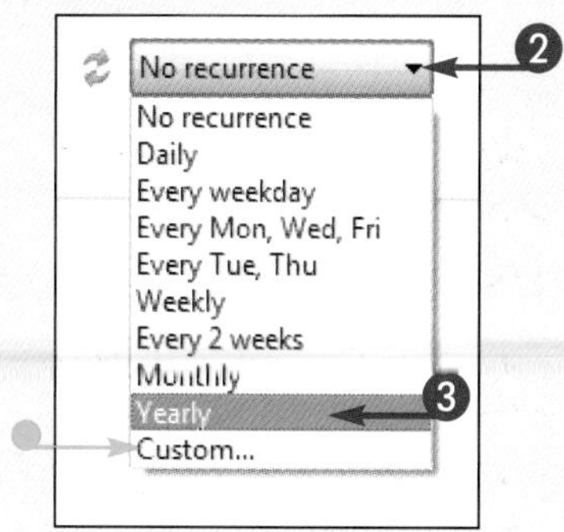

# Add a Calendar

If you have different schedules that you want to keep separate, you can add another calendar. For example, you might want to have one calendar for work events and a second calendar for personal events.

**You can assign different colors to each calendar, which helps you to see at a glance which event belongs to which calendar.**

## Add a Calendar

❶ Click **Add calendar**.

***Note:*** *Another way to start a new calendar is to press* Ctrl + Shift + D.

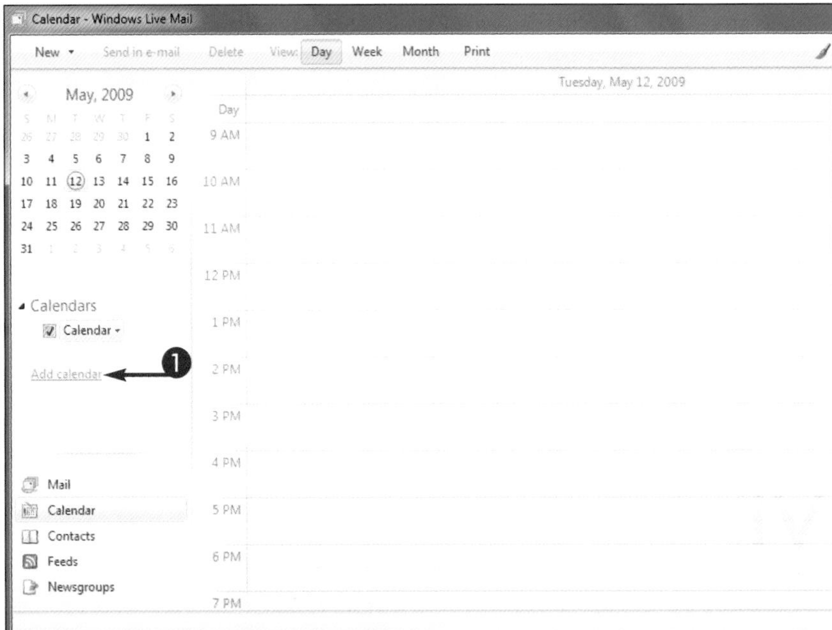


The Add a Calendar dialog box appears.

❷ Type a name for the calendar.

❸ Click the color you want to use for the calendar.

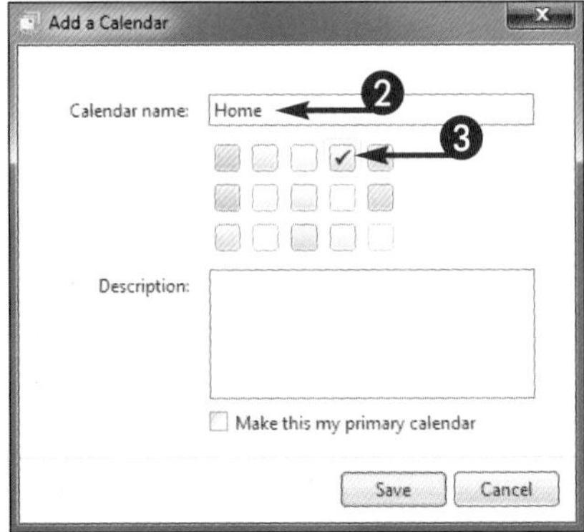

4. Type an optional description for the calendar.
5. If you want Windows Live Mail to use this calendar as the default for new events, click **Make this my primary calendar** (☐ changes to ☑).
6. Click **Save**.

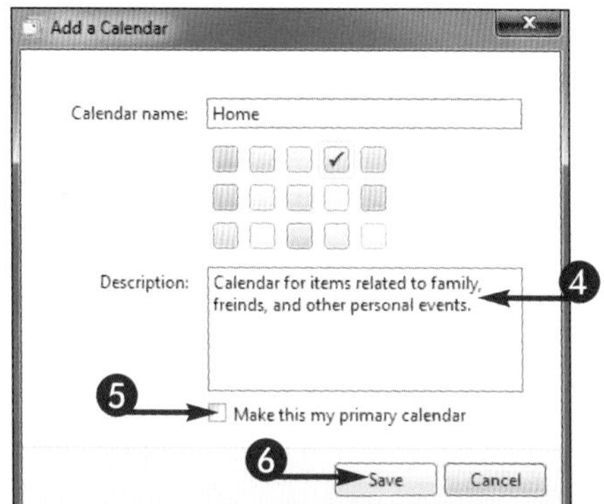

- The new calendar appears in the Calendars list.

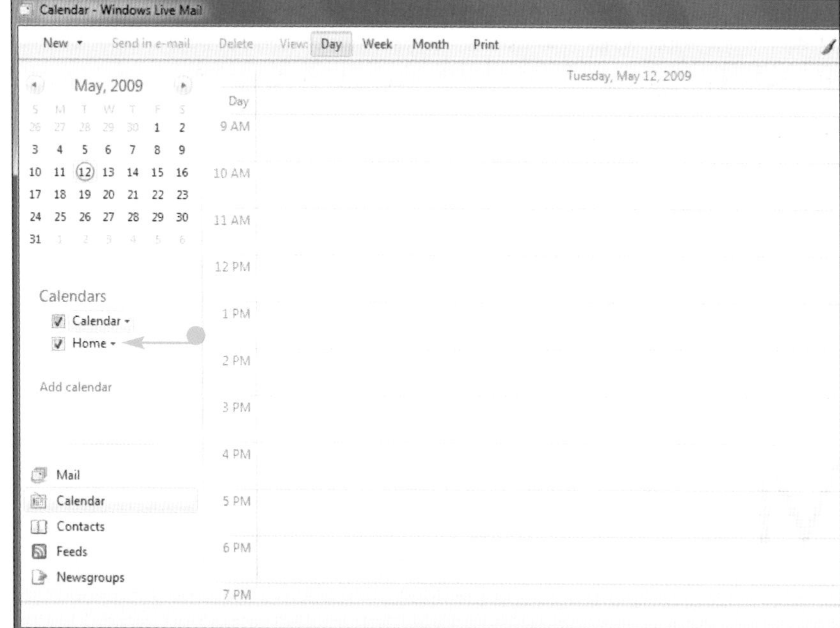

### How do I assign an event to a particular calendar?

For new events, click the calendar you want to use, and then click **New event** in the menu that appears. You can also click **New** to open the New Event window, click the **Calendar** ☐, and then click the calendar you want to use. For existing events, double-click the event, click the **Calendar** ☐, and then click the calendar.

### Can I rename the original calendar?

Yes. The default name of "Calendar" is not very descriptive, so it is a good idea to rename it to something more useful. In the Calendars list, click **Calendar** and then click **Properties** in the menu that appears. Use the **Calendar name** text box to type a new name, and then click **Save**.

CHAPTER

12

# Implementing Security in Windows 7

Threats to your computer-related security and privacy often come from the Internet in the form of system intruders, such as junk e-mail, viruses, and identity thieves. In addition, many security and privacy violations occur right at your computer by someone simply using your computer while you are not around. To protect yourself and your family, you need to understand these threats and know what you can do to thwart them.

# Understanding Windows 7 Security

Before getting to the details of securing your PC, it helps to take a step back and look at the security and privacy tools that Windows 7 makes available.

### User Account Password

Windows 7 security begins with assigning a password to each user account on the computer. This prevents unauthorized users from accessing the system, and it enables you to lock your computer. See "Protect an Account with a Password" and "Lock Your Computer," later in this chapter.

### User Account Control

User Account Control asks you to confirm certain actions that could conceivably harm your system. If you have an administrator account, you click **Yes** to continue; if you have a standard account, you must enter an administrator's user name and password to continue.

### Parental Controls

If one or more children use your computer, you can use Windows 7's Parental Controls to protect those children from inadvertently running certain programs, playing unsuitable games, and using the computer at inappropriate times. See "Set Up Parental Controls," later in this chapter.

## Windows Firewall

Because when your computer is connected to the Internet, it is possible for another person on the Internet to access your computer and infect it with a virus or cause other damage, Windows 7 comes with its Windows Firewall feature turned on. This prevents intruders from accessing your computer while you are online.

## Windows Defender

*Spyware* is a software program that installs on your computer without your knowledge or consent. This program surreptitiously gathers data from your computer, steals your passwords, displays advertisements, and hijacks your Web browser. To prevent spyware from installing on your computer, Windows 7 includes the Windows Defender program.

## Phishing

*Phishing* refers to e-mail messages or Web sites that appear to come from legitimate businesses and organizations, but actually come from a scam artist. The purpose of the message or site is to fool you into divulging personal or private data, such as passwords and credit card numbers. Internet Explorer and Windows Live Mail come with anti-phishing features to help prevent this.

## Junk E-mail

Junk e-mail — or *spam* — refers to unsolicited, commercial e-mail messages that advertise anything from baldness cures to cheap printer cartridges. Many spams advertise deals that are simply fraudulent, and others feature such unsavory practices as linking to adult-oriented sites, and sites that install spyware. Windows Live Mail comes with a junk e-mail filter; see "Set the Junk E-mail Protection Level," later in this chapter.

# Check Action Center for Security Problems

In Windows 7, the new Action Center displays messages about the current state of your PC. In particular, Action Center warns you if your computer has any current security problems.

**For example, the Action Center tells you if your PC does not have virus protection installed, or if the Windows Defender spyware database is out of date.**

## Check Action Center for Security Problems

1. Click **Start**.
2. Click **Control Panel**.

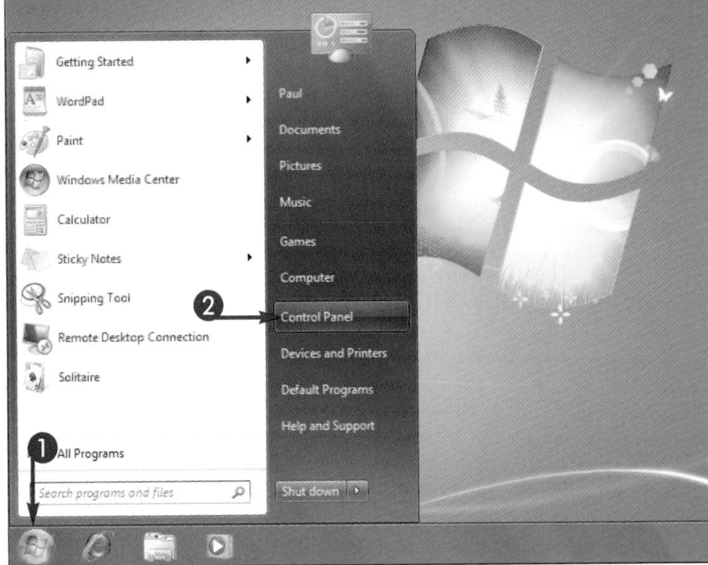


The Control Panel window appears.

3. Click **Review your computer's status**.

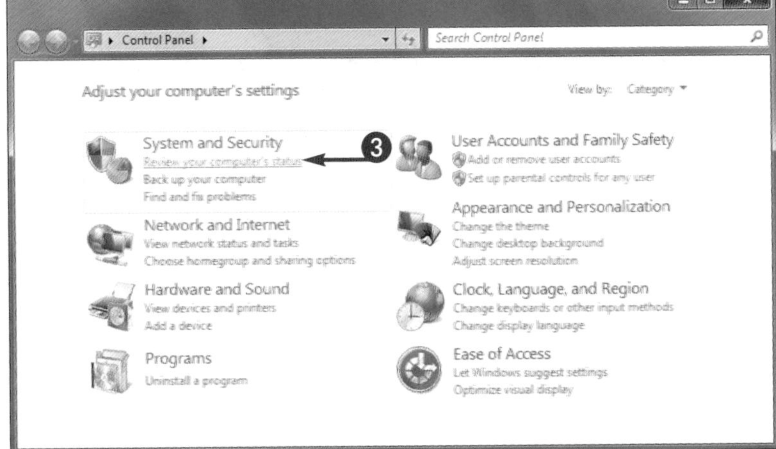

The Action Center window appears.

4. Review the messages in the Security section.
5. Click a message button to resolve the security issue, such as clicking **Update now** if Windows Defender is out of date.
6. Click **Security**.

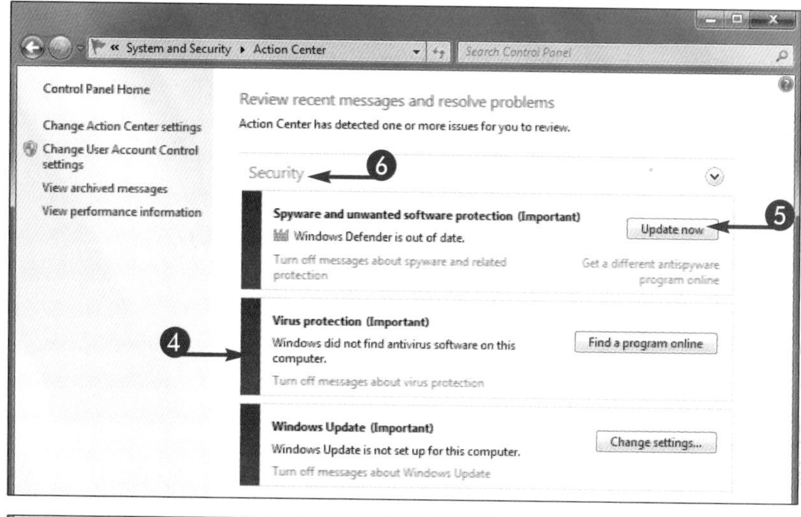


7. Scroll down the Action Center window.

- Action Center displays a summary of all your system's security settings.

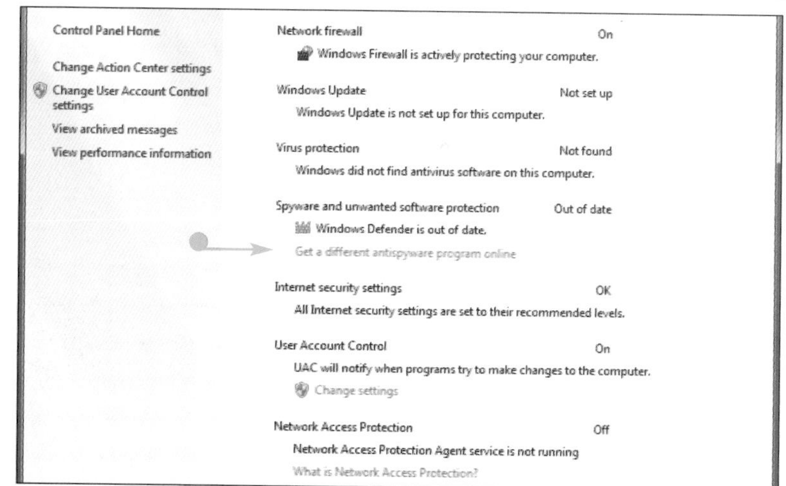

### Is there a quicker way to see Action Center messages?

Yes, you can view Action Center messages and open the Action Center more quickly by following these steps:

1. Click the **Action Center** icon (![]) in the taskbar's notification area.

- The current Action Center messages appear here.

2. To launch Action Center, click **Open Action Center**.

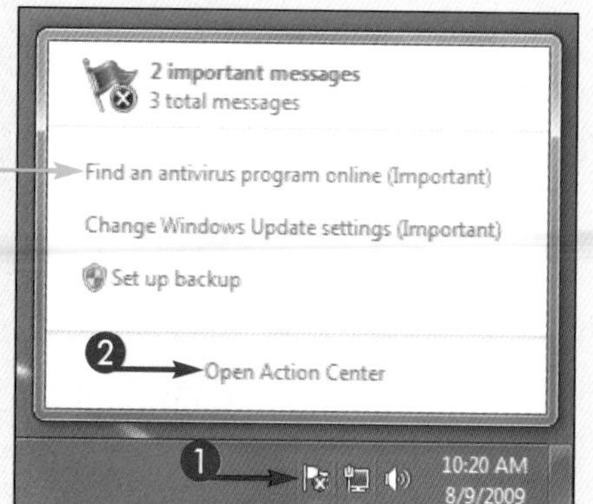

# Protect an Account with a Password

You can protect your Windows 7 user account with a password. This is a good idea because otherwise another user can log on to your account just by clicking your user name in the Welcome screen.

**For maximum security, make sure you create a strong password that cannot be easily guessed or hacked. See the tip on the next page.**

## Protect an Account with a Password

1. Click **Start**.
2. Click **Control Panel**.

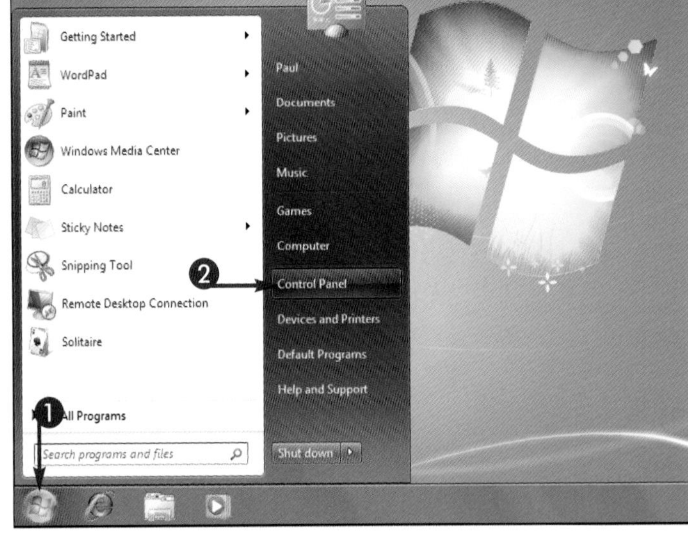


The Control Panel window appears.

3. Click **Add or remove user accounts**.

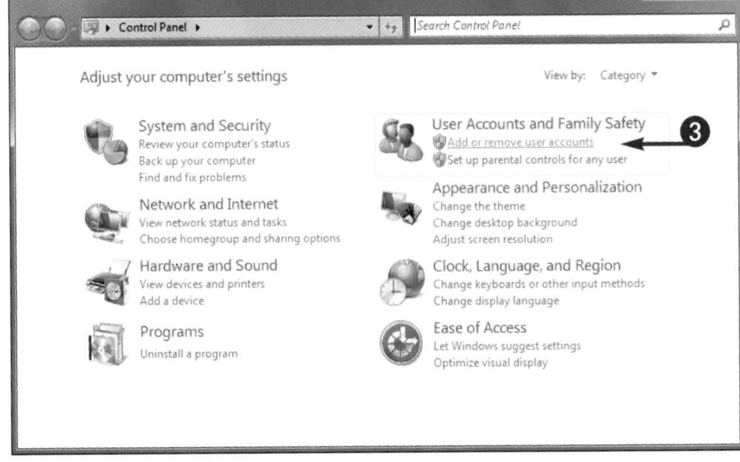

The Manage Accounts window appears.

4. Click the user account you want to work with.

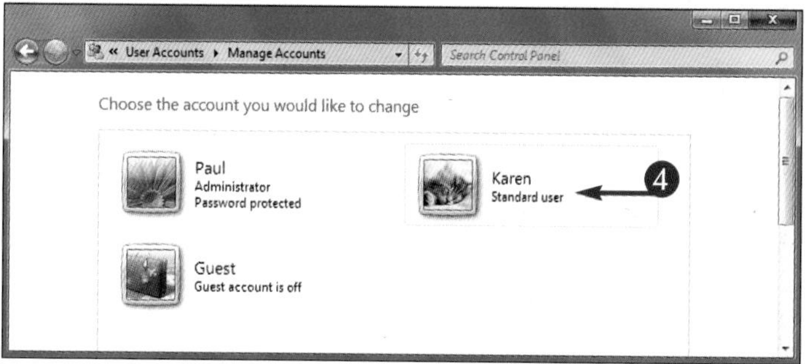


The Change an Account window appears.

5. Click **Create a password**.

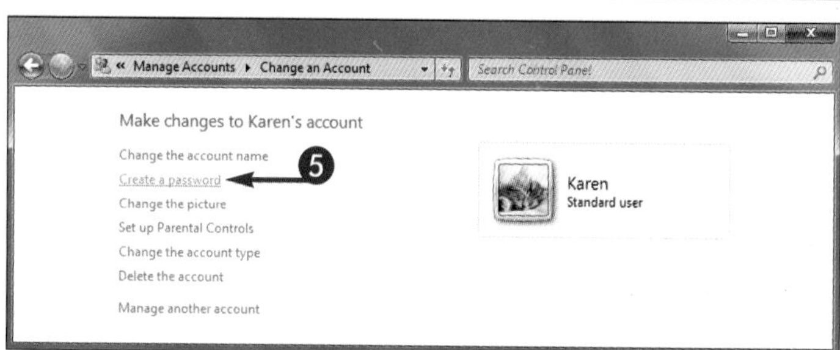


The Create Password window appears.

6. Type the password.
7. Type the password again.
8. Type a word or phrase to use as a password hint in case you forget the password.
9. Click **Create password**.

Windows 7 adds the password to the user account.

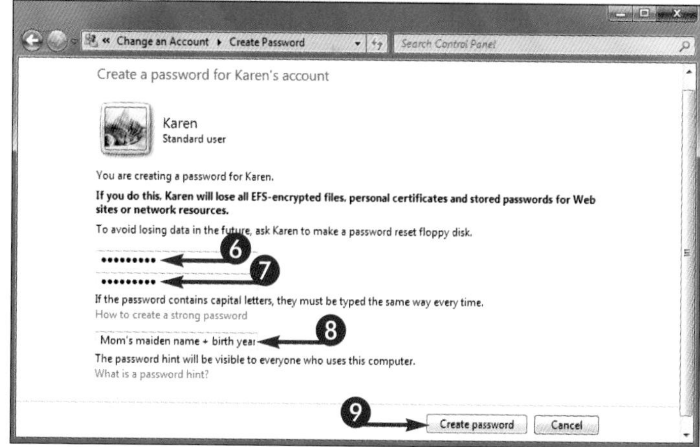

### What are the components of a strong password?

First, do not use obvious items such as your name or a word such as "password." Your password should be at least eight characters long, and it should include at least one character from each of the following three sets: lowercase letters, uppercase letters, and numbers. The strongest passwords also include at least one symbol such as % or &.

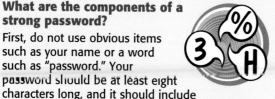

### How do I change the password?

Follow Steps **1** to **4** to open the Change an Account window. Click the **Change the password** link to open the Change Password dialog box. Type your existing password, follow Steps **6** to **8** to specify the new password and hint, and then click **Change password**.

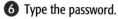

# Lock Your Computer

Protecting your account with a password prevents someone from logging on to your account, but what happens when you leave your desk? If you remain logged on to the system, any person who sits down at your computer can use it to view and change files. To prevent this, lock your computer.

**Once your computer is locked, anyone who tries to use your computer will first have to enter your password.**

## Lock Your Computer

### LOCK YOUR COMPUTER

1. Click **Start**.
2. Click the power button arrow (▷).
3. Click **Lock**.

Windows 7 locks your computer.

- The word "Locked" appears under your user name.

## UNLOCK YOUR COMPUTER

1. Click inside the password text box.

2. Type your password.
3. Click **Go** (➔).

   Windows 7 unlocks your computer and restores your desktop.

### TIP

**I use the Lock command frequently. Is there a way to make it easier to access?**

Yes, there are two faster methods you can use. The first method is to press ⊞ + L. The second method is to customize the Start menu's Power button to lock your computer instead of shutting it down:

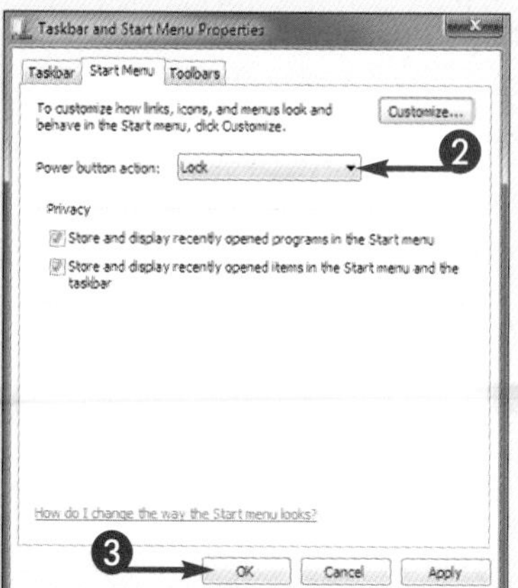


1. Right-click **Start** and then click **Properties**.
2. In the Taskbar and Start Menu Properties dialog box, click the **Power button action** ▾ and then click **Lock**.
3. Click **OK**.

# Set Up Parental Controls

If your children have computer access, you can protect them from malicious content by setting up parental controls for activities such as playing games and running programs.

**Before you can apply parental controls, you must set up a Windows 7 user account for each child. See "Create a User Account" in Chapter 7.**

## Set Up Parental Controls

### ACTIVATE PARENTAL CONTROLS

1. Click **Start**.
2. Click **Control Panel**.

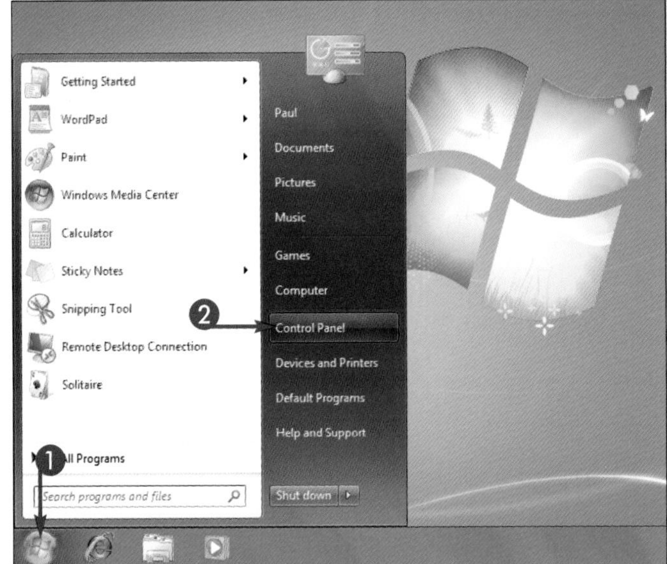


The Control Panel window appears.

3. Click **Set up parental controls for any user**.

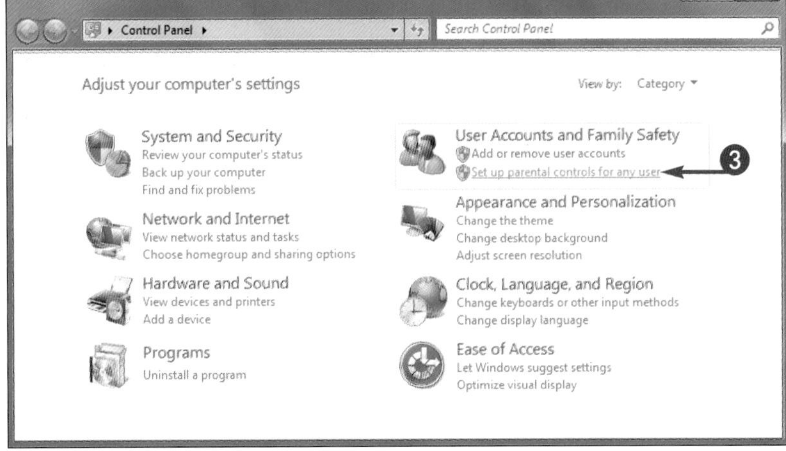

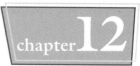

The Parental Controls window appears.

4 Click the user you want to work with.

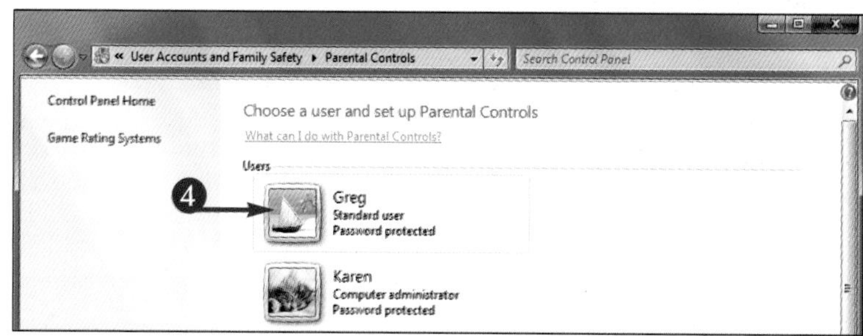


The User Controls window appears.

5 Click **On, enforce current settings** (◎ changes to ◉).

Windows 7 turns on parental controls for the user.

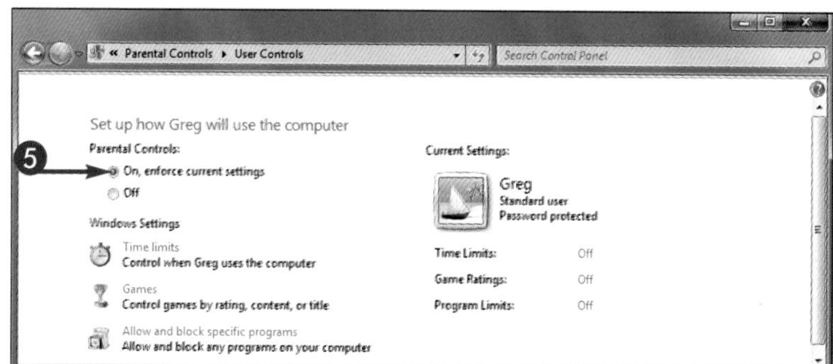


## SET COMPUTER TIME LIMITS

6 Click **Time limits**.

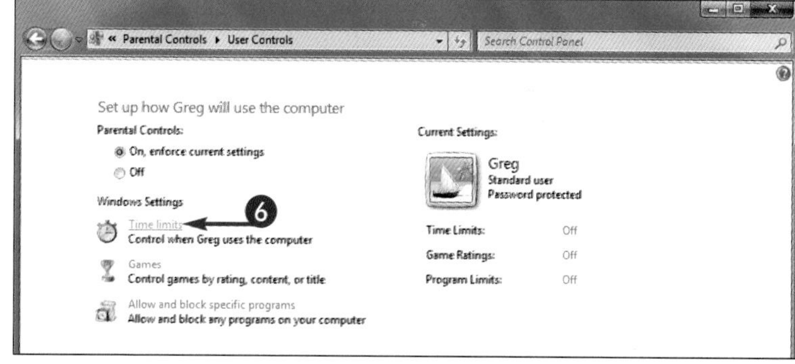

### Can I use Parental Controls to monitor my kids' computer activities or restrict what they see on the Web?

ACTIVITY REPORT • WEB SITES • FILE DOWNLOADS • LOGON TIMES • IMS & E-MAILS

No, activity reporting and Web filtering are not part of the default Parental Controls in Windows 7. However, these controls are available from third-party companies, and Microsoft provides links to them at http://windowshelp.microsoft.com. After you install a new control, it appears in the Parental Controls window in the Additional Controls section.

### Can I choose which game rating system Windows 7 uses?

PARENTAL CONTROLS click GAME RATING SYSTEMS

Yes, Windows 7 supports several game rating systems, including classifications from the Entertainment Software Rating Board (this is the default system), Computer Entertainment Rating Organization, and Game Rating Board. Return to the Parental Controls window, click **Game Rating Systems**, click the system you want to use (◎ changes to ◉), and then click **OK**.

continued

# Set Up Parental Controls *(continued)*

With parental controls activated, you can now set up specific restrictions. For example, you can set up times when children are not allowed to use the computer.

**Windows 7's parental controls also enable you to set the maximum game rating that kids can play and block specific programs.**

## Set Up Parental Controls *(continued)*

The Time Restrictions window appears.

7. Click each hour that you want to block access to the computer.

- Blocked hours appear in blue.
- Allowed hours appear in white.

***Note:** To block out a number of hours over a number of days, click and drag the mouse over the hours.*

8. Click **OK**.

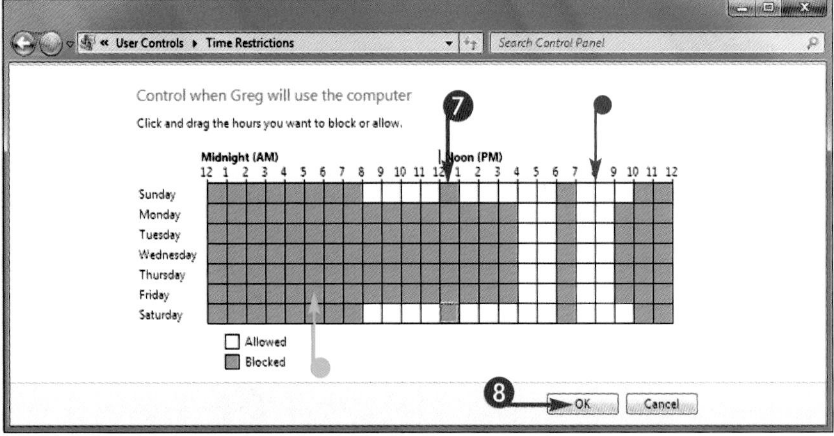


### RESTRICT GAME USAGE

9. Click **Games**.

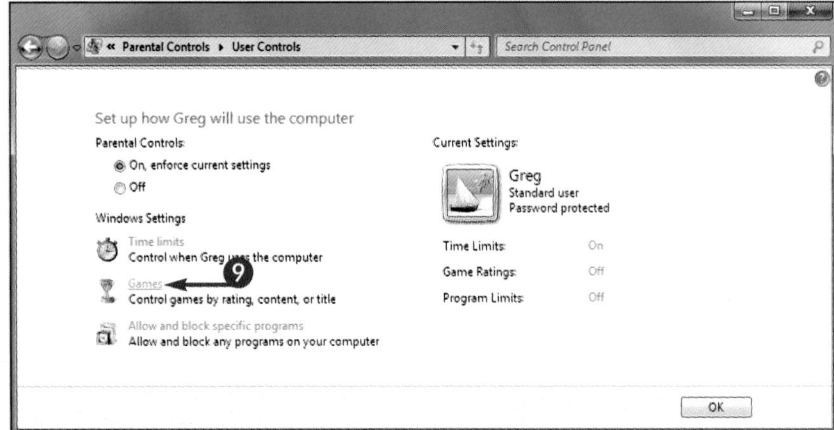

The Game Controls window appears.

⑩ Click **Yes** (◎ changes to ◉).

- If you do not want the user to play any games, click **No**, instead.

⑪ Click **Set game ratings**.

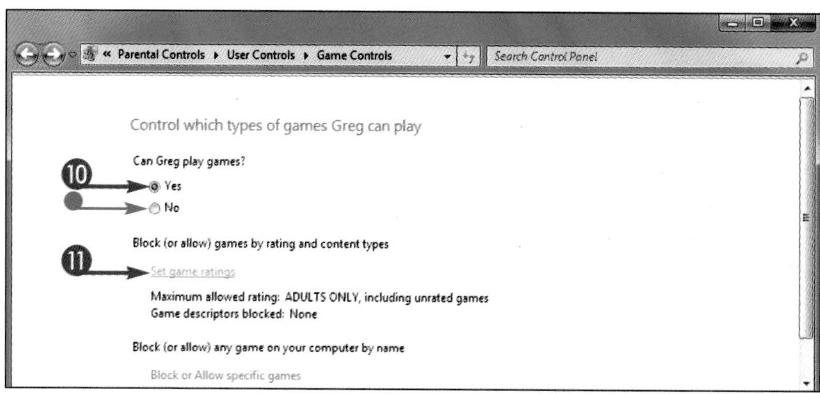

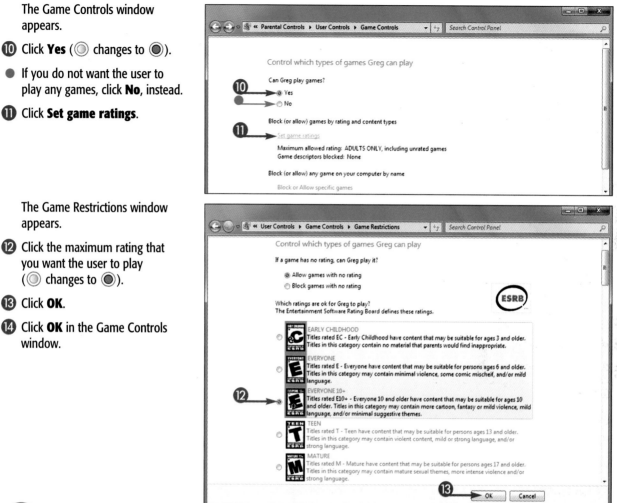

The Game Restrictions window appears.

⑫ Click the maximum rating that you want the user to play (◎ changes to ◉).

⑬ Click **OK**.

⑭ Click **OK** in the Game Controls window.

TIPS

### Can I block a specific game?

Yes. In the Game Controls window, click **Block or Allow specific games** to display the Game Overrides window, which shows all the games installed on your computer. For the game you want to block, click the **Always Block** option (◎ changes to ◉), and then click **OK**.

### Can I prevent my kids from running certain programs?

Yes. In the User Controls window, click **Allow and block specific programs** to display the Application Restrictions dialog box. Click ***User* can only use the programs I allow** (where *User* is the name of the user). In the list, click the check box for each program you want the user to be able to run (☐ changes to ☑). Click **OK**.

# Delete Your Browsing History

To ensure that other people who have access to your computer cannot view information from sites you have visited, you can delete your browsing history.

**See the tip on the next page to learn more about browsing history.**

## Delete Your Browsing History

1. Click **Safety**.
2. Click **Delete Browsing History**.

***Note:*** *You can also press* Ctrl + Shift + Delete.

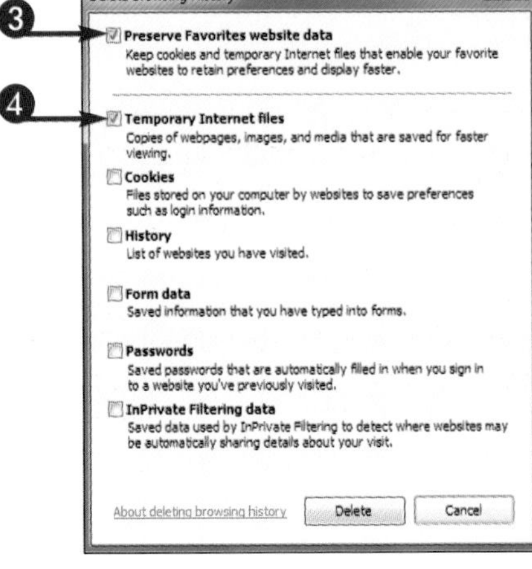

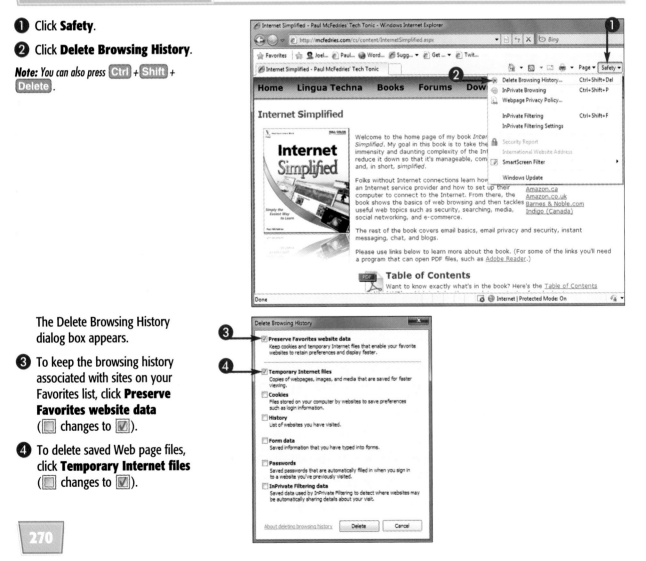

The Delete Browsing History dialog box appears.

3. To keep the browsing history associated with sites on your Favorites list, click **Preserve Favorites website data** (☐ changes to ☑).
4. To delete saved Web page files, click **Temporary Internet files** (☐ changes to ☑).

5 To delete cookies files, click **Cookies** (☐ changes to ☑).

6 To delete the list of Web sites you have visited, click **History** (☐ changes to ☑).

7 To delete saved form data, click **Form data** (☐ changes to ☑).

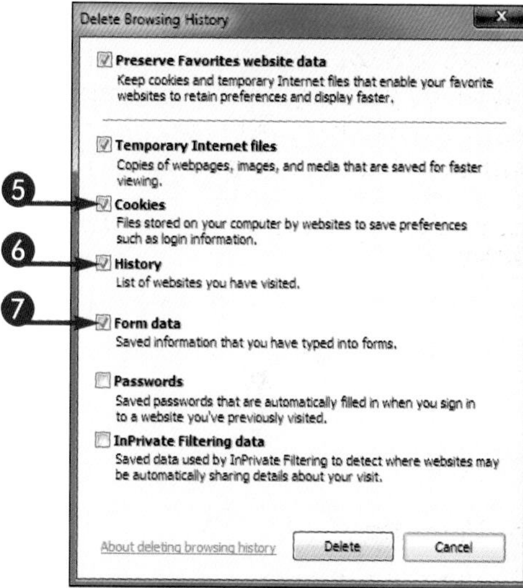

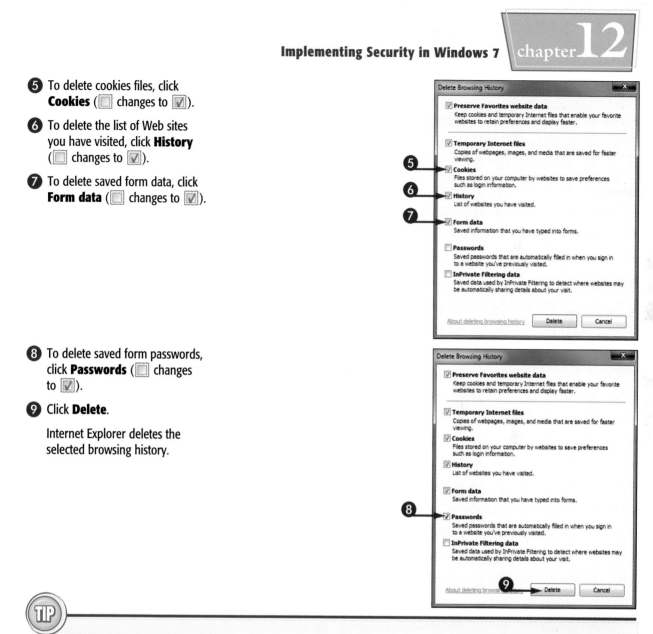

8 To delete saved form passwords, click **Passwords** (☐ changes to ☑).

9 Click **Delete**.

Internet Explorer deletes the selected browsing history.

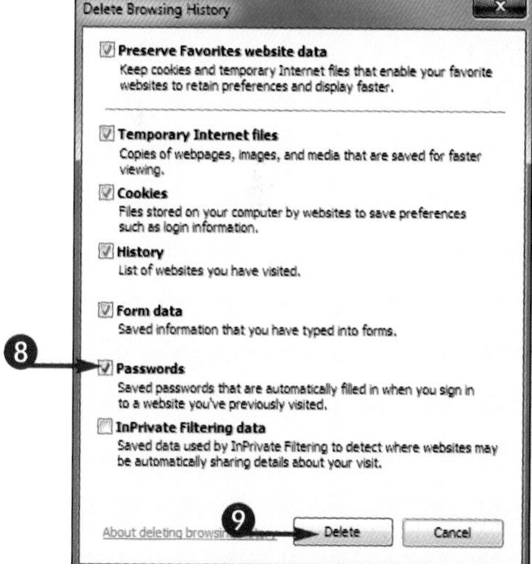


TIP

### What is browsing history?

Internet Explorer maintains a list of the sites you visit, as well as copies of page text, images, and other content so that sites load faster the next time you view them. Internet Explorer also saves text and passwords that you have typed into forms, and *cookies*, which are small text files that store information such as site preferences and site logon data.

Saving this history makes surfing easier, but it is also dangerous because other people who use your computer can just as easily visit or view information about those sites. This can be a problem if you visit financial sites, private corporate sites, or some other page that you would not want another person to visit. You reduce this risk by deleting some or all of your browsing history.

# Browse the Web Privately

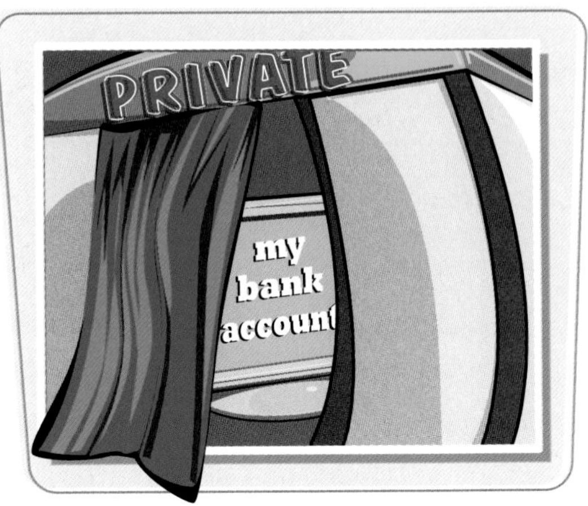


**If you visit sensitive or private Web sites, you can tell Internet Explorer not to save any browsing history for those sites. When you activate the InPrivate Browsing feature, Internet Explorer stops saving browsing history when you visit Web sites.**

**Internet Explorer also turns off third-party toolbars and other add-ons that you have added to the browser.**

## Browse the Web Privately

❶ Click **Safety**.

❷ Click **InPrivate Browsing**.

***Note:*** *You can also press* Ctrl + Shift + P.

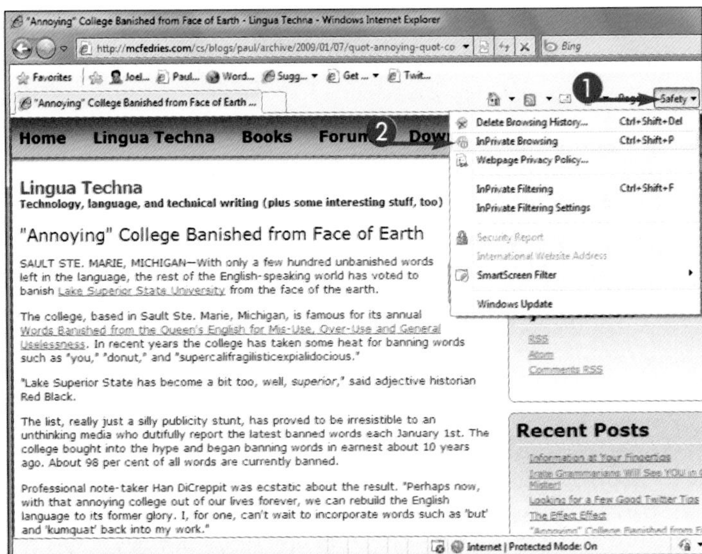


A new Internet Explorer window appears.

- [InPrivate] appears in the title bar.
- The InPrivate indicator appears in the address bar.

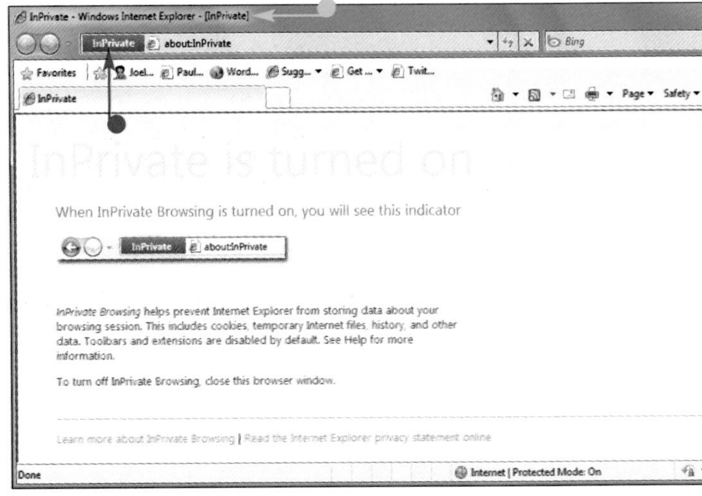

3 Surf to and interact with Web sites as you normally would, such as the banking site shown here.

4 Click **Close** (X).

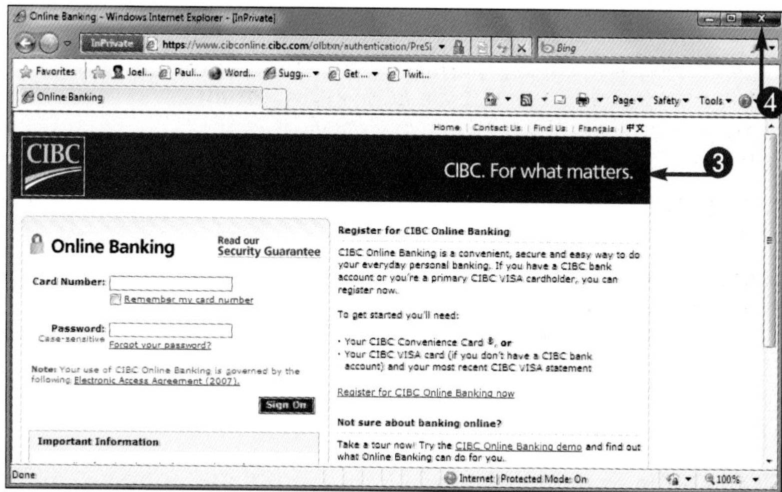

Internet Explorer closes the InPrivate Browsing window.

- Internet Explorer retains no history of your InPrivate Browsing session. For example, none of the addresses you typed appear in the Address list, shown here.

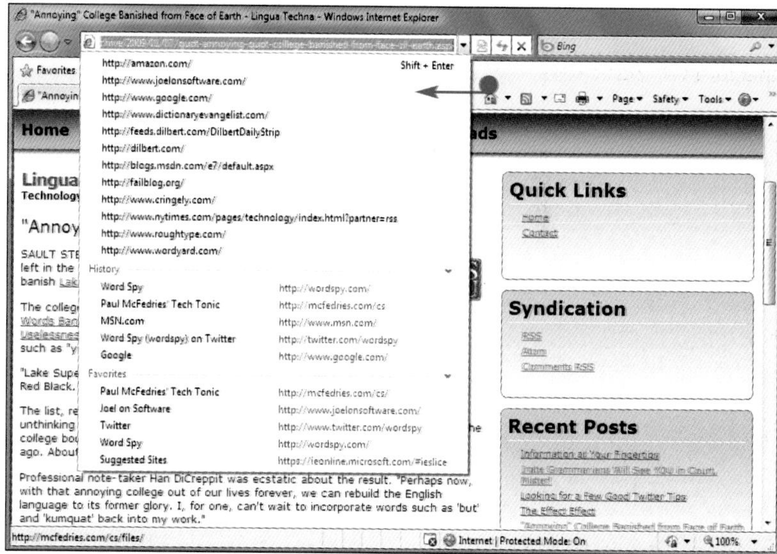

TIP

### What does InPrivate Filtering do?

Some Web sites load content such as ads and maps from a third-party site. If a particular third-party company provides data for many different sites, that company could conceivably build up a profile of your online activity. InPrivate Filtering looks for third-party sites that provide data quite often to the places you visit, and will begin blocking those sites' content so that they cannot build up a profile of your activity. To turn on this feature, click **Safety** and then click **InPrivate Filtering** (or press Ctrl + Shift + F).

# Set the Junk E-mail Protection Level

You can make junk messages easier to manage by setting the Windows Live Mail junk e-mail protection level. You can set a higher level if you receive many junk messages each day, or you can set a lower level if you receive very few junk messages.

**The higher the protection level, the more aggressively Windows Live Mail checks for junk e-mail. All suspected junk messages get moved to the Junk E-mail folder. If a legitimate message is moved to Junk E-mail by accident, you can mark the message as not junk.**

## Set the Junk E-mail Protection Level

### SET THE JUNK E-MAIL PROTECTION LEVEL

1. Click **Menus** (📋).
2. Click **Safety options**.

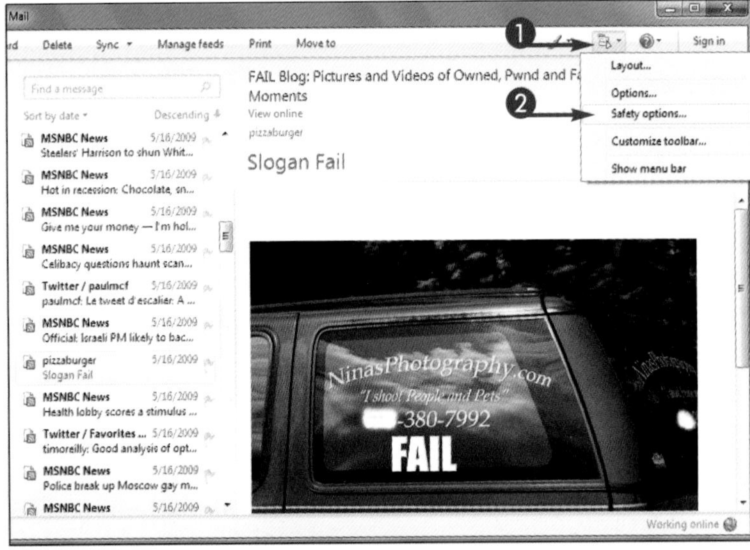


The Safety Options dialog box appears.

3. Click the **Options** tab.

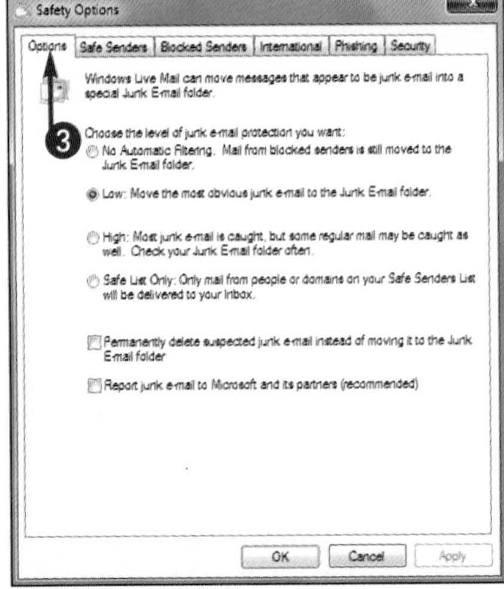

4. Click the protection level you want (◯ changes to ◉):

   Click **No Automatic Filtering** if you receive very few junk messages each day.

   Click **Low** if you receive a moderate number of junk messages.

   Click **High** if you receive many junk messages each day.

5. Click **OK**.

   Windows Live Mail puts the new protection level into effect.

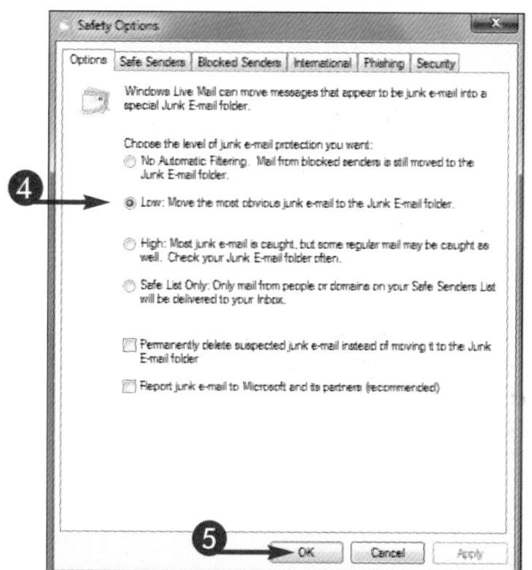


## MARK A MESSAGE AS NOT JUNK

1. Click the Junk E-mail folder.
2. Click the message.
3. Click **Not junk**.

   Windows Mail returns the message to the Inbox folder.

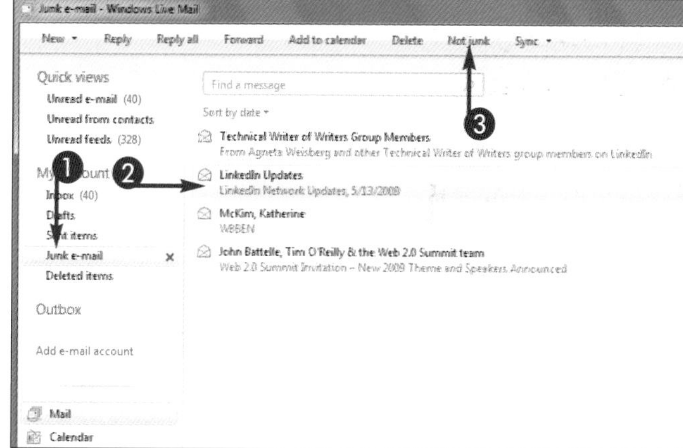


## TIPS

### What is a false positive?

A false positive is a legitimate message that Windows Live Mail has mistakenly marked as spam and moved to the Junk E-mail folder. If you select the High protection level, you run a greater risk of false positives, so you should check your Junk E-mail folder more often to look for legitimate messages.

### How does the Safe List Only protection level work?

Safe List Only means that Windows Live Mail treats every message as junk, unless the sender's e-mail address is on your Safe Senders list. To populate this list, follow Steps **1** and **2**, click the **Safe Senders** tab, click **Add**, type an address, click **OK**, and repeat as necessary. Alternatively, right-click a legitimate message, click **Junk e-mail**, and then click **Add sender to safe senders list**.

# Block a Person Who Sends You Junk Mail

You can reduce the amount of junk mail — also known as *spam* — you have to deal with by blocking those people who send you such messages. Windows Live Mail automatically moves existing and future messages from that person to the Junk E-mail folder.

**You can block a sender by either using an example message from that person, or adding the person's e-mail address directly.**

## Block a Person Who Sends You Junk Mail

### BLOCK A SENDER USING A MESSAGE

1. Right-click the junk e-mail message.
2. Click **Junk e-mail**.
3. Click **Add sender to blocked senders list**.

   Windows Live Mail adds the sender's e-mail address to the list of blocked senders.

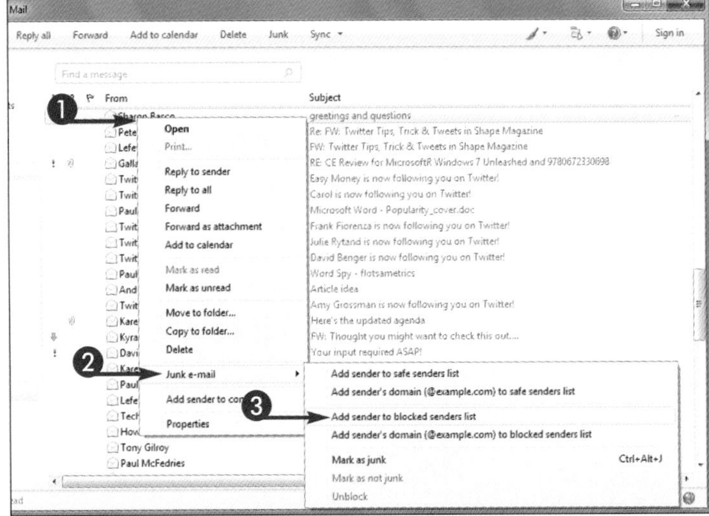

### BLOCK A SENDER BY HAND

1. Click **Menus** (□).
2. Click **Safety options**.

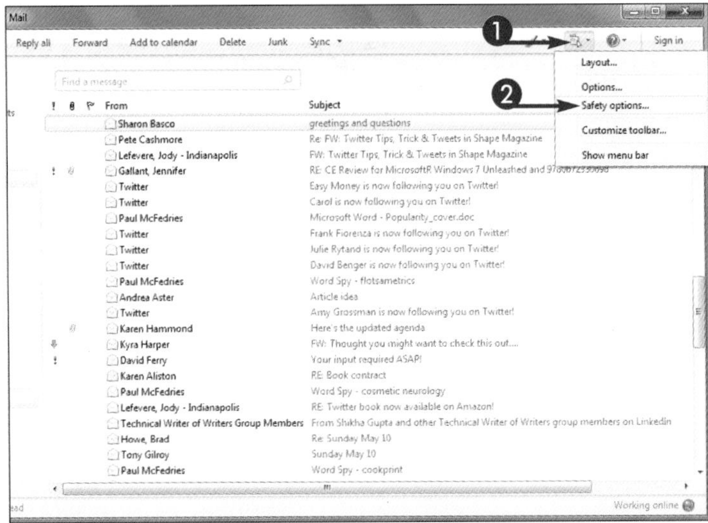

The Safety Options dialog box appears.

3. Click the **Blocked Senders** tab.
4. Click **Add**.

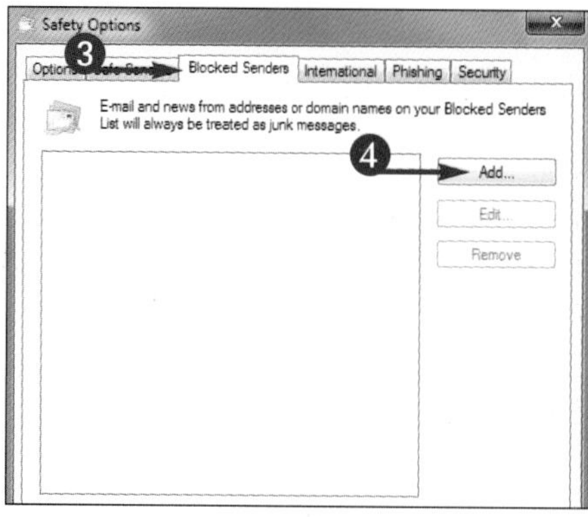


The Add Address or Domain dialog box appears.

5. Type the sender's address.
6. Click **OK**.

- Windows Mail includes the address on the list of blocked senders.

7. Follow Steps **4** to **6** to add more addresses.
8. Click **OK**.

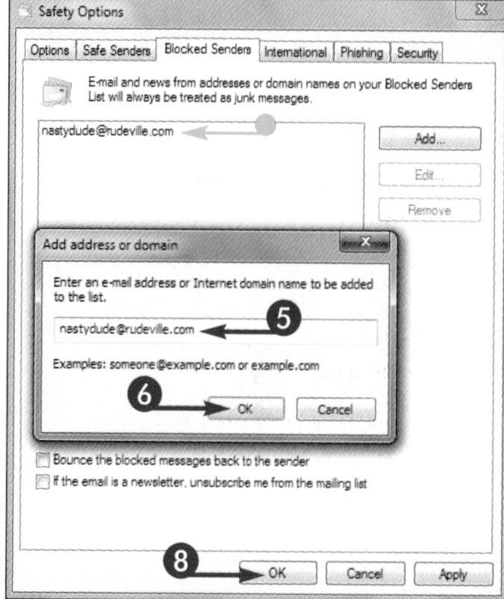

**How do I take someone off the blocked senders list?**

If you add someone by mistake, you should take that person off the blocked senders list as soon as possible. Follow Steps **1** to **3** to display the Block Senders tab, click the person's e-mail address, click **Remove**, and then click **OK**.

**I get lots of unwanted messages from a particular country. Can I block messages from that country?**

Yes, in most cases. Messages sent using a foreign address usually include a country code as part of the address. These so-called top-level domains include ru for the Russian Federation, cn for China, and kr for South Korea. To block a country, follow Steps **1** and **2** to display the Safety Options dialog box, click the **International** tab, click **Blocked Top-Level Domain List**, click the check box beside the country (☐ changes to ☑), and then click **OK**.

CHAPTER

13

# Customizing Windows 7

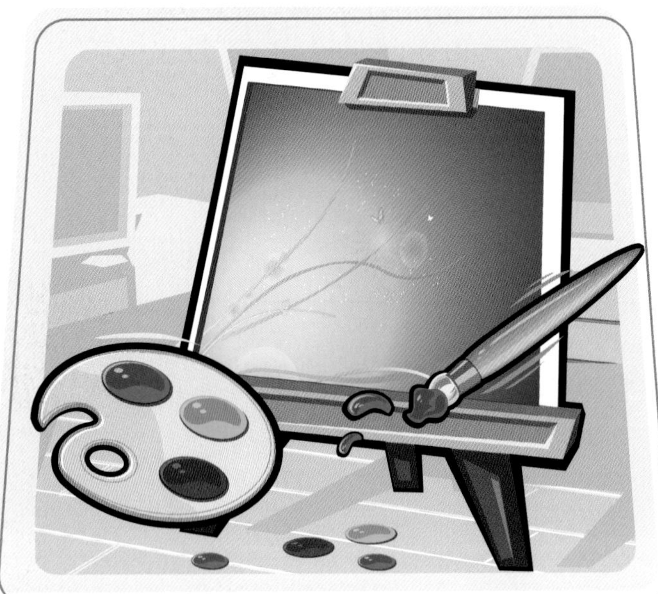

Windows 7 comes with a number of features that enable you to personalize your computer. Not only can you change the appearance of Windows 7 to suit your taste, but you can also change the way Windows 7 works to make it easier to use and more efficient.

# Open the Personalization Window

To make changes to many of Windows 7's display options, you need to know how to open the Personalization window.

## Open the Personalization Window

1. Click **Start**.
2. Click **Control Panel**.

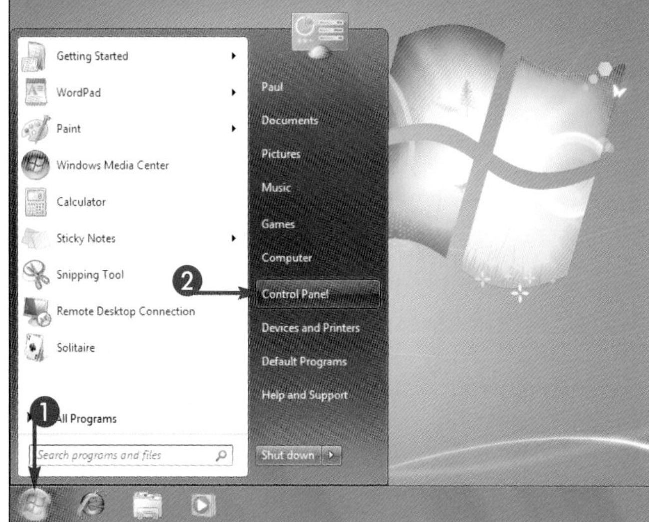


The Control Panel window appears.

3. Click **Appearance and Personalization**.

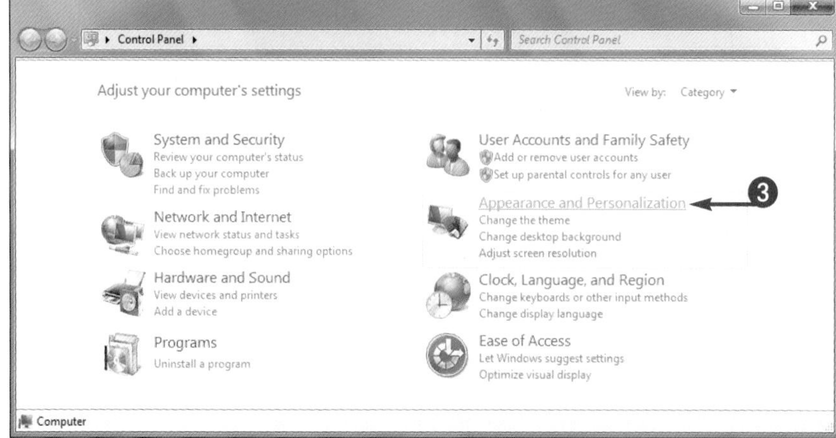

The Appearance and Personalization window appears.

4 Click **Personalization**.

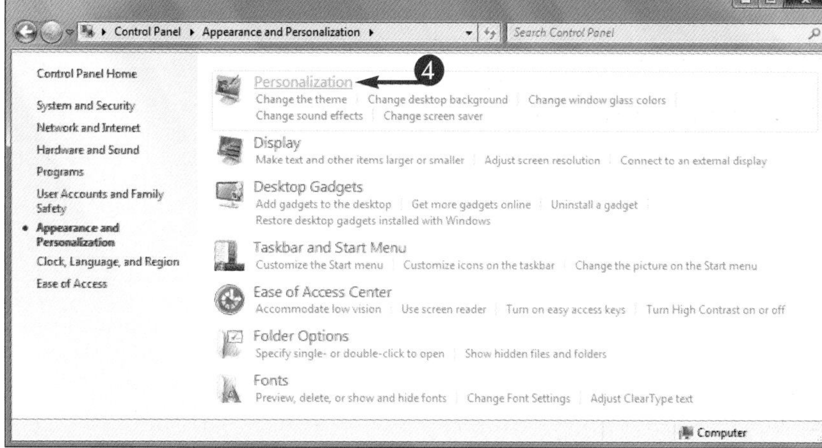

The Personalization window appears.

5 Click the **Close** button (✕) when you are finished working with this window.

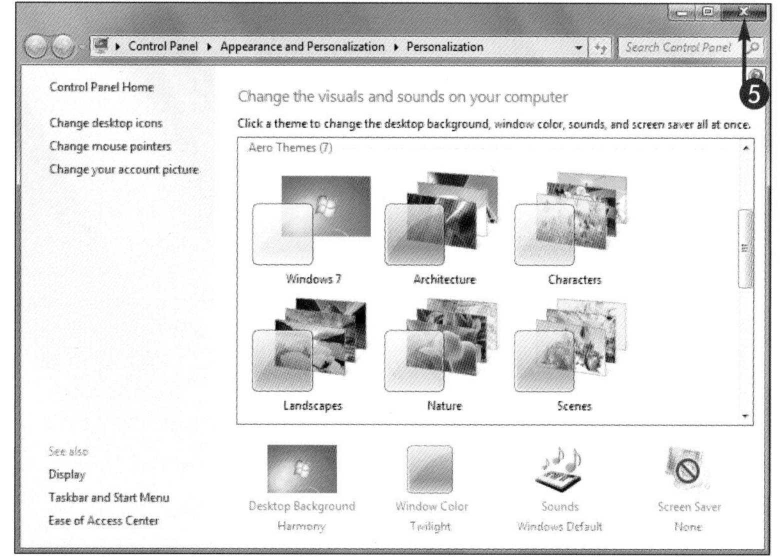

## TIP

**Is there a quicker way to open the Personalization window?**

Yes. Follow these steps:

1 Right-click an empty section of the desktop.

2 Click **Personalize**.

The Personalization window appears.

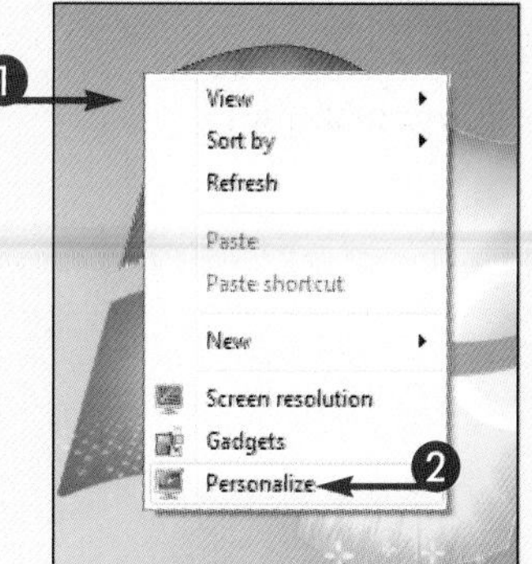

# Change the Desktop Background

For a different look, you can change the desktop background to display either a different image or a specific color.

**You can also display multiple desktop images as a slide show. See "Set Up a Desktop Slide Show," later in this chapter.**

## Change the Desktop Background

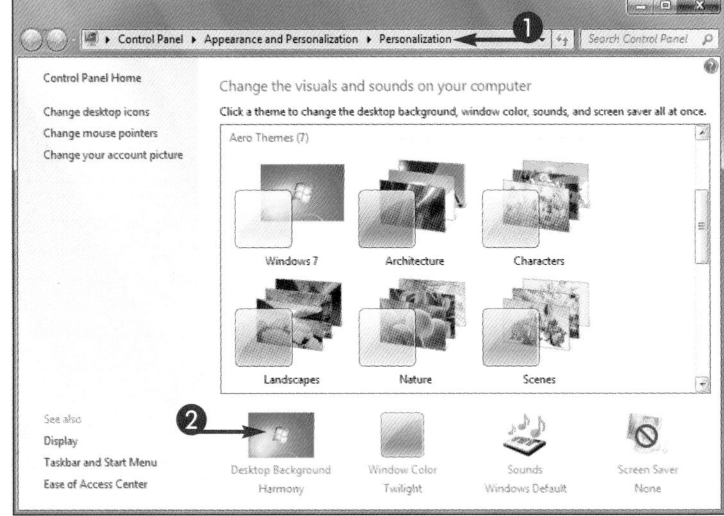


1. Open the Personalization window.

***Note:** See the "Open the Personalization Window" section earlier in this chapter.*

2. Click **Desktop Background**.

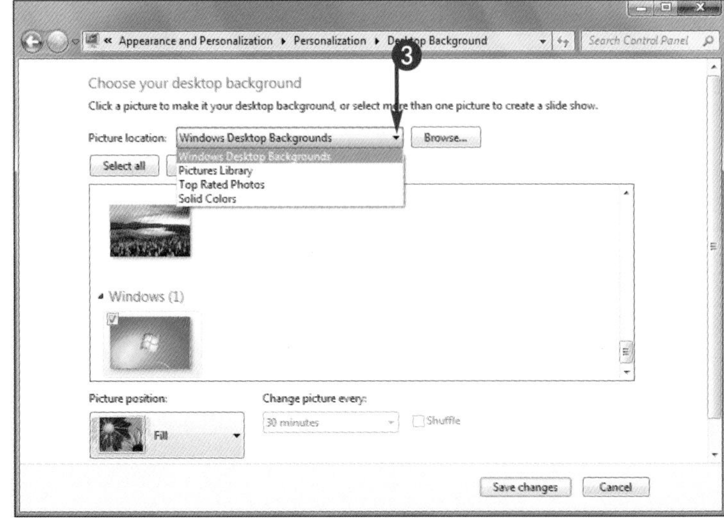


The Desktop Background window appears.

3. Click the **Picture location** ▾ and then click the background gallery you want to use.

***Note:** If you have your own image that you would prefer to use as the desktop background, click **Pictures Library** in the list. You can also click **Browse** and then use the Browse dialog box to select the file.*

- Windows 7 displays the backgrounds in the selected gallery.

4. Click **Clear all**.
5. Click the image or color you want to use.
6. Click the **Picture position** and then click the positioning you want.

***Note:*** *See the tip, below, for an explanation of each option.*

7. Click **Save changes**.
8. Click the **Close** button (X).

The picture or color you selected appears on the desktop.

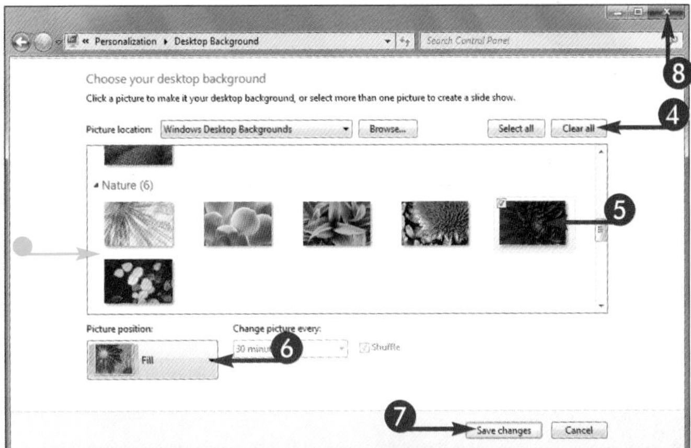

### What is the difference between the five Picture position options?

- **Fill**: Displays a single copy of the image extended on all sides so it fills the entire desktop. As it extends the picture, Windows keeps the ratio of width to height the same, so this usually means that part of the image gets cut off.
- **Fit**: Displays a single copy of the image extended until either the width of the picture fits the width of the screen, or the height of the picture fits the height of the screen. Use this position if you want to display all of the image without distortion and without cutting off any of the image.
- **Stretch**: Displays a single copy of the image extended on all sides so it fills the entire desktop. In this case, Windows does not keep the ratio of the width to height, so your picture may end up a bit distorted.
- **Tile**: Displays multiple copies of the image repeated so they fill the entire desktop. Choose this option for small images.
- **Center**: Displays a single copy of the image in the center of the screen. This is a good choice for large images.

# Set Up a Desktop Slide Show

You can add visual interest to your desktop by configuring Windows 7 to display a slide show of images as the desktop background. This means that Windows 7 changes the desktop background automatically at a preset time interval.

## Set Up a Desktop Slide Show

1. Open the Personalization window.

***Note:*** *See the "Open the Personalization Window" section earlier in this chapter.*

2. Click **Desktop Background**.

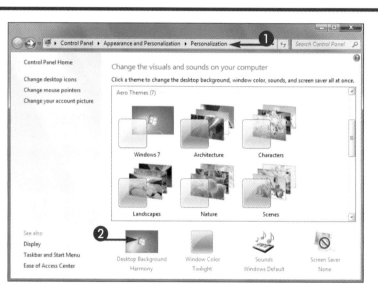

The Desktop Background window appears.

3. Click the **Picture location** ▾ and then click the background gallery you want to use.

***Note:*** *If you have your own image that you would prefer to use as the desktop background, click* ***Pictures Library*** *in the list. You can also click* ***Browse*** *and then use the Browse dialog box to select the file.*

- Windows 7 displays the backgrounds in the selected gallery and selects all the images.

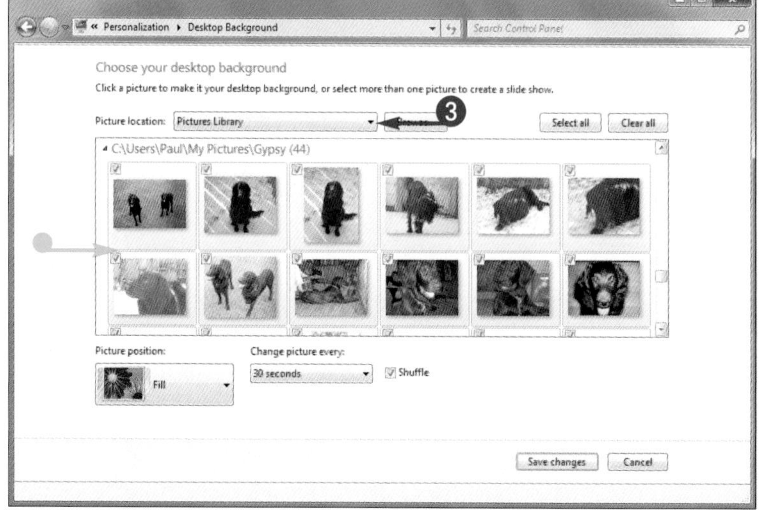

If you want to use all the images in the gallery, skip to Step **6**.

4. Click **Clear all**.
5. For each image you want to include in the slide show, position the mouse over the image and click the check box (☐ changes to ☑).

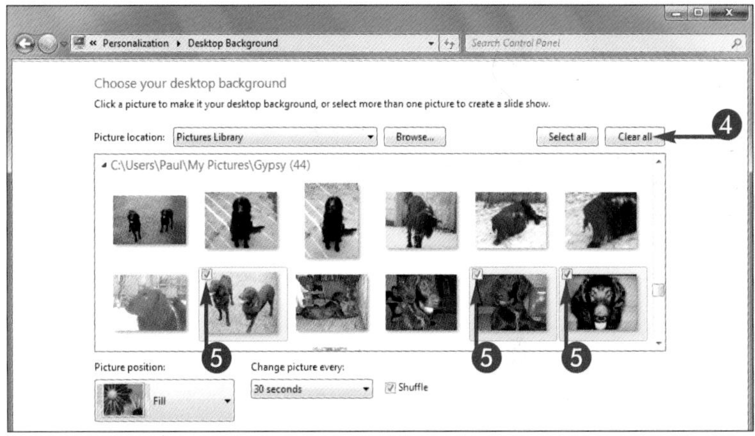


6. Click the **change picture every** ▾ and then click the time interval between pictures.
7. To display the pictures in random order, click **Shuffle** (☐ changes to ☑).
8. Click **Save changes**.

Windows 7 displays the first picture on the desktop and displays new images using the interval you selected.

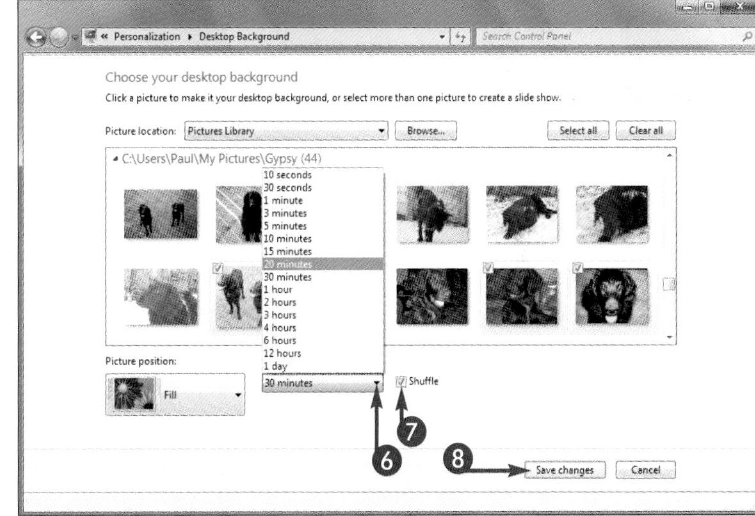

### Can I control the playback of the desktop slide show?

Yes, but Windows 7 gives you only very limited control over the playback. For example, if you do not like the currently displayed image, right-click the desktop and then click **Next desktop background**. Windows 7 immediately changes the background to the next image in the slide show. Unfortunately, you cannot pause the slide show or return to a previous image.

### Are there more background images available online?

Yes, Microsoft has a large number of desktop background images available on its Web site. In the Personalization window, click the **Get more themes online** link, and then click the **Desktop backgrounds** tab in the Web page that appears. For each background you want to use, click the **Download** link to open the picture in Internet Explorer, click **Page**, and then click **Save As**.

# Set the Screen Saver

You can set up Windows 7 to display a *screen saver*, a moving pattern or series of pictures. The screen saver appears after your computer has been idle for a while.

**If you leave your monitor on for long stretches while your computer is idle, the unmoving image can end up temporarily "burned" into the monitor's screen. A screen saver prevents this by displaying a moving image.**

## Set the Screen Saver

1. Open the Personalization window.

*Note:* *See the "Open the Personalization Window" section earlier in this chapter.*

2. Click **Screen Saver**.

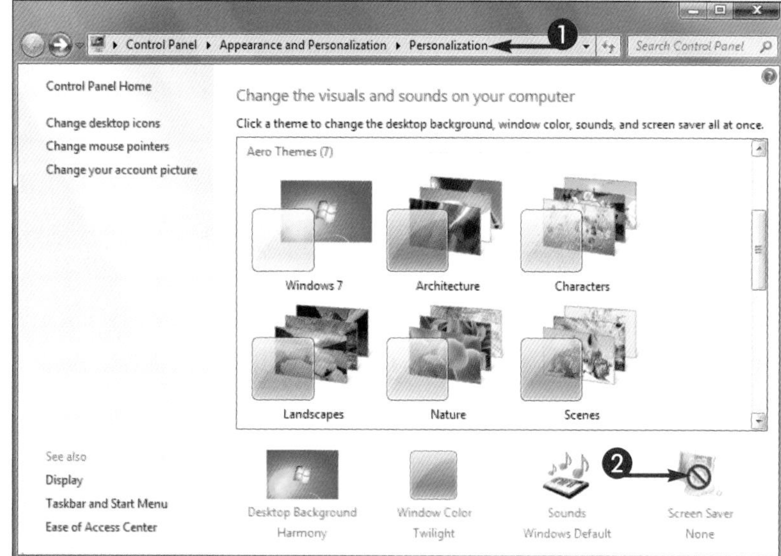


The Screen Saver Settings dialog box appears.

3. Click the **Screen saver** ▾ and then click the screen saver you want to use.

- A preview of the screen saver appears.

*Note:* *Not all screen savers can display the small preview. To see an actual preview, click* ***Preview****. When you are done, move the mouse or press a key to stop the preview.*

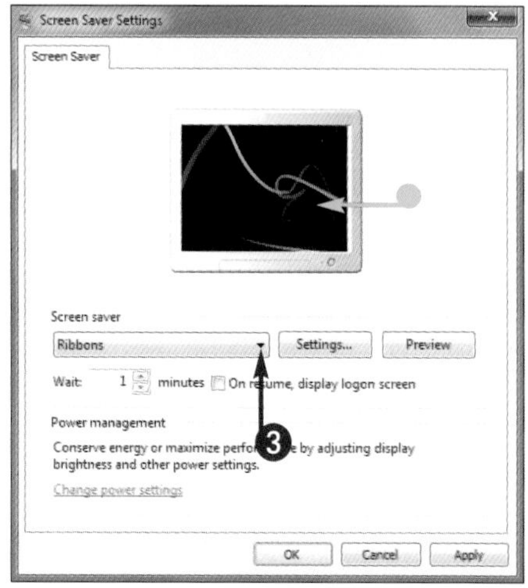

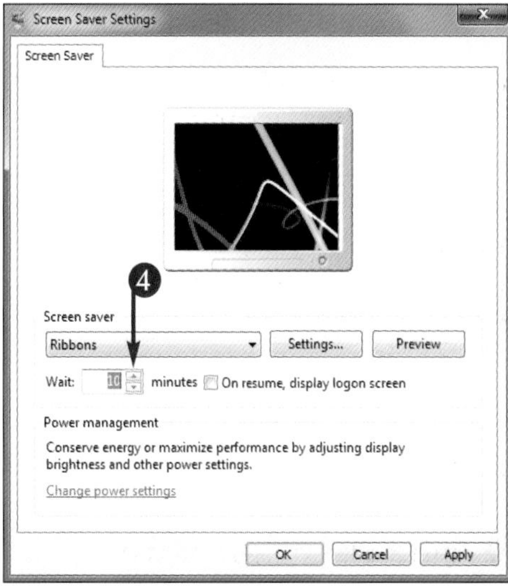


4 Click the **Wait** to specify the number of minutes of computer idle time after which the screen saver appears.

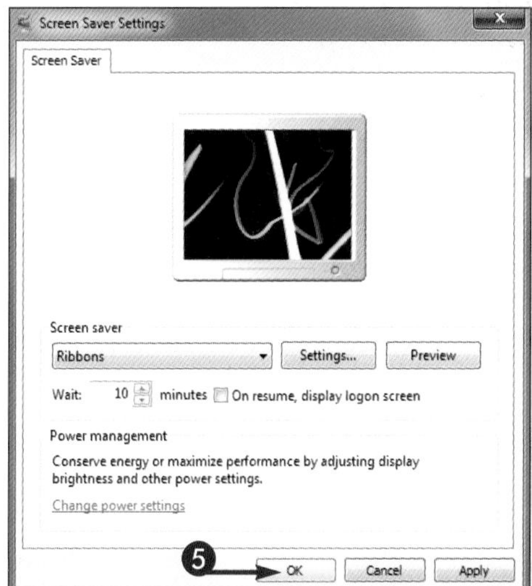


5 Click **OK**.

The screen saver appears after your computer is idle for the number of minutes you specified in Step **4**.

***Note:*** *To interrupt the screen saver, move the mouse or press* Shift *on the keyboard.*

**Can I use a screen saver to hide my work while I am away from my desk?**

Yes. By itself, the screen saver's pattern automatically obscures the screen. However, another person can interrupt the screen saver to see your work. To prevent this, first assign a password to your Windows 7 user account, as described in the "Protect an Account with a Password" section in Chapter 12. In the Screen Saver tab, click the **On resume, display logon screen** check box (☐ changes to ☑). This means that anyone who interrupts the screen saver can see your work only if he or she knows your password.

# Change the Windows 7 Color Scheme

You can personalize your copy of Windows 7 by choosing a different color scheme, which Windows 7 applies to the window borders, taskbar, and Start menu.

**You can also customize the Windows 7 look by toggling the transparent glass effect on and off, setting the color intensity, and even creating your own colors.**

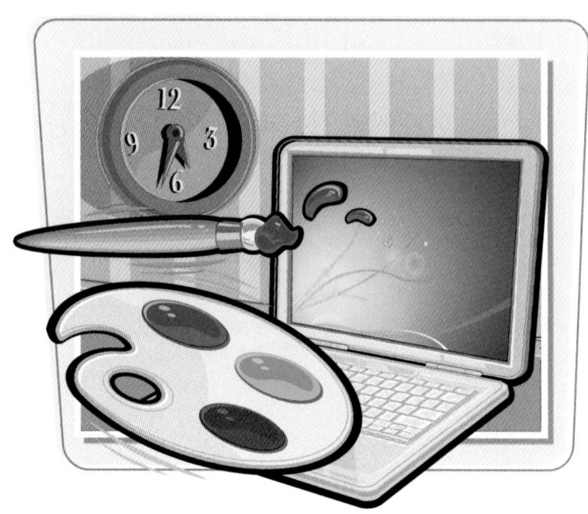


## Change the Windows 7 Color Scheme

1. Open the Personalization window.

***Note:*** *See the "Open the Personalization Window" section earlier in this chapter.*

2. Click **Window Color**.

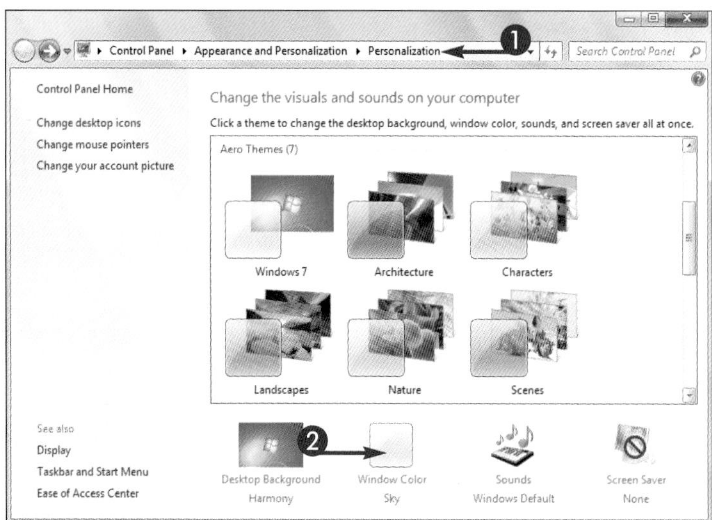


The Window Color and Appearance window appears.

***Note:*** *If you see the Window Color and Appearance dialog box, instead, see the tip on the next page.*

3. Click the color you want to use.

- Windows 7 changes the color of the window border.

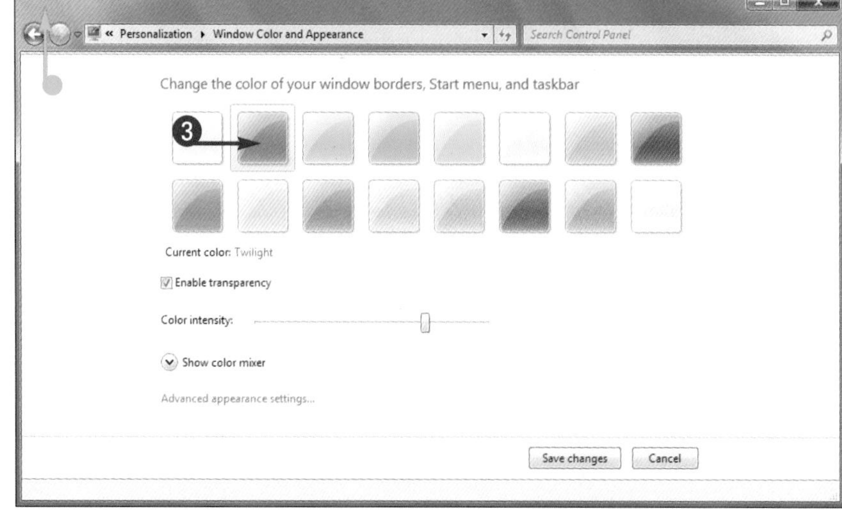

4 If you do not want to see the glass effect, click **Enable transparency** (☑ changes to ☐).

5 Click and drag the **Color intensity** slider to set the color intensity.

- Windows 7 changes the transparency and intensity of the window border.

6 Click **Show color mixer**.

- The color mixer sliders appear.

7 Click and drag the **Hue**, **Saturation**, and **Brightness** sliders to set your custom color.

8 Click **Save changes**.

Windows 7 applies the new color scheme.

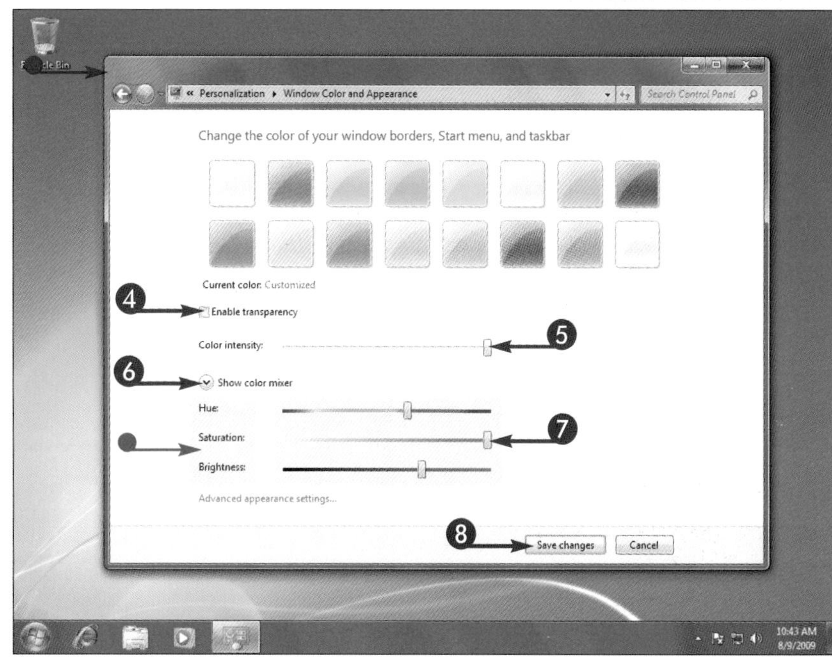


TIP

### Why do I see the Window Color and Appearance dialog box instead of the Window Color and Appearance window?

On systems with lower-end graphics cards or little graphics memory, Windows 7 is unable to use high-end effects such as transparency and color intensity. On such systems, you follow these steps to set the color scheme:

1 In the Item list, click the interface object you want to customize.

2 Click ▾ in each Color list and select a color or colors for the item.

3 If the item includes text, use the Font, Size, Color, Bold, and Italics controls to format the text.

4 Repeat Steps **1** to **3** to customize other items.

5 Click **OK**.

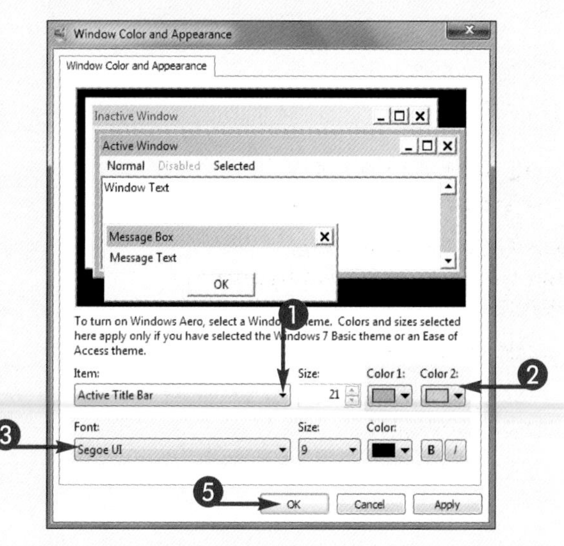

# Save a Custom Theme

After you have customized the desktop background, screen saver, and color scheme, you can save all of these changes as a custom theme.

**After you have saved the custom theme, you can reapply it at any time if you make changes in the Personalization window and want to restore your previous look.**

## Save a Custom Theme

1. Open the Personalization window.

***Note:*** *See the "Open the Personalization Window" section earlier in this chapter.*

2. In the My Themes section, click **Unsaved Theme**.

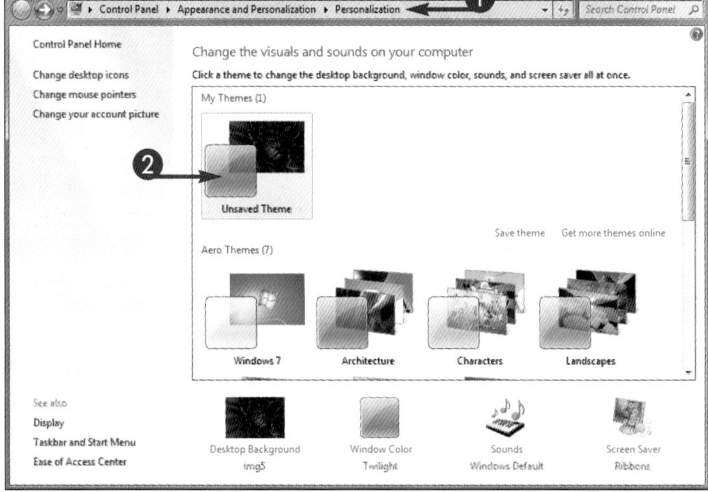


3. Click **Save theme**.

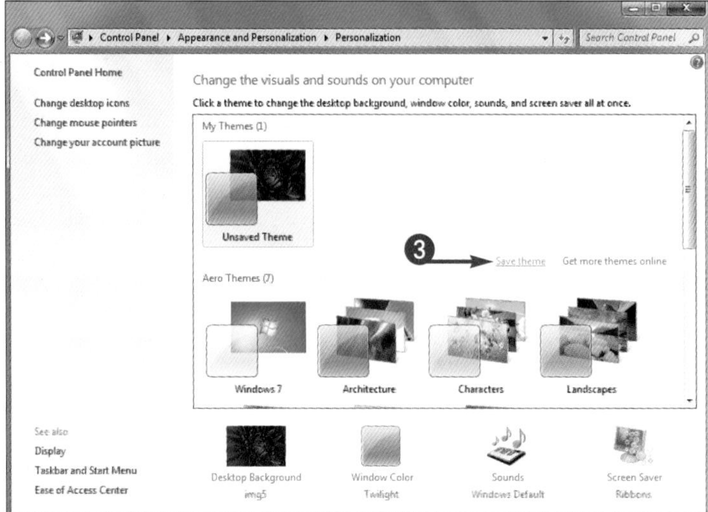

The Save Theme As dialog box appears.

4 Use the Theme Name text box to type a name for your theme.

5 Click **Save**.

- Windows 7 saves your theme.

***Note:*** *To reapply your theme later on, open the Personalization window and then click your saved theme.*

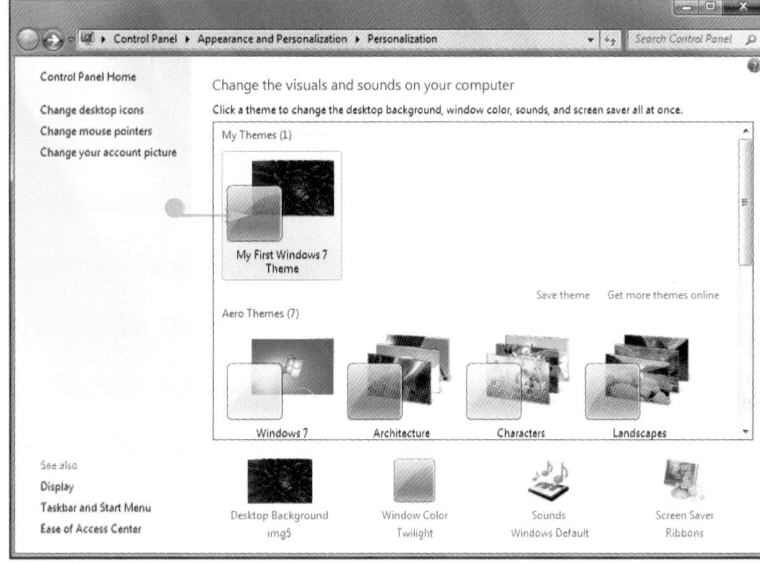

### How do I include custom sound effects in my theme?

Open the Personalization window and then click **Sounds** to open the Sound dialog box with the Sounds tab displayed. Click an item in the **Program Events** list and then click a sound effect in the **Sounds** list. Repeat this for each Windows event you want to customize, and then click **OK**.

### How do I include custom mouse pointers in my theme?

Open the Personalization window and then click **Change mouse pointers** to open the Mouse Properties dialog box with the Pointers tab displayed. Click a pointer in the **Customize** list, click **Browse**, use the Browse dialog box to click a pointer, and then click **Open**. Repeat for each pointer you want to customize, and then click **OK**.

# Apply a Theme

Instead of tweaking the desktop background, screen saver, and color scheme individually, you can change all of these at once by applying a theme.

**Each theme also includes its own set of desktop icons, sound effects, and mouse pointers.**

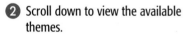

## Apply a Theme

1. Open the Personalization window.

***Note:*** *See the "Open the Personalization Window" section earlier in this chapter.*

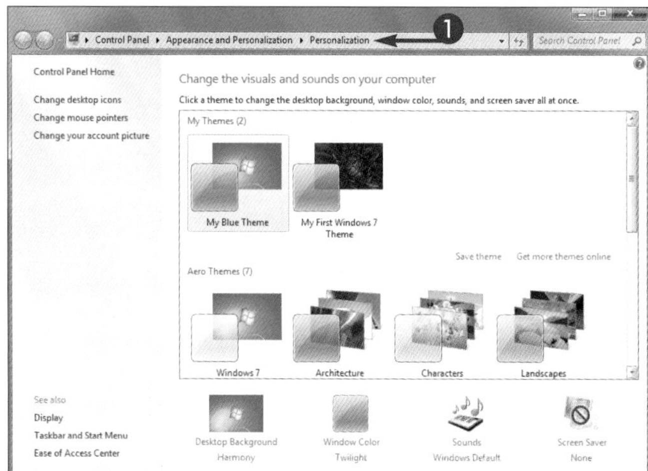


2. Scroll down to view the available themes.

- Aero Themes use transparency effects, color intensity, and high-resolution background images.
- Basic and High Contrast Themes use simple effects or high-contrast effects suitable for people with impaired vision.

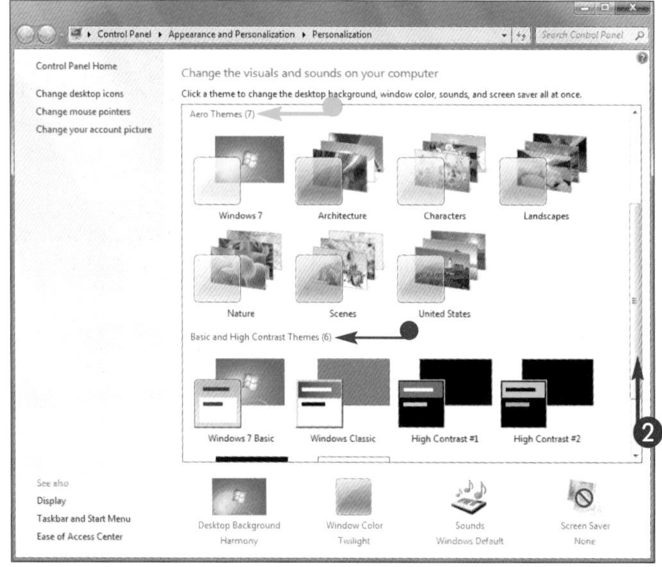

3 Click the theme you want to use.

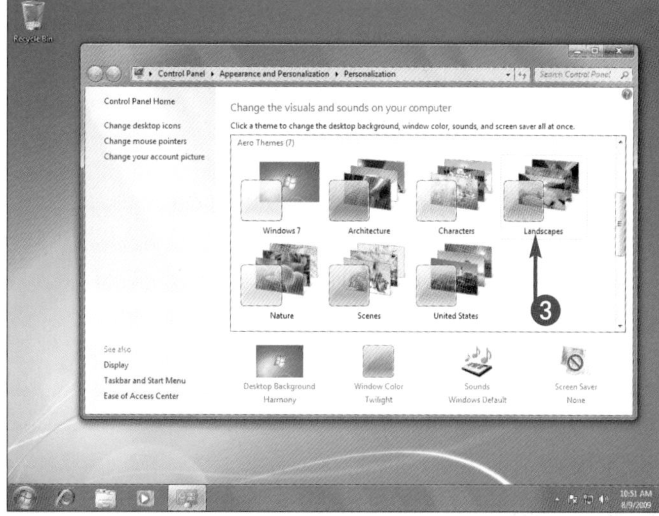

- Windows 7 applies the theme.

4 Click **Close** (☒).

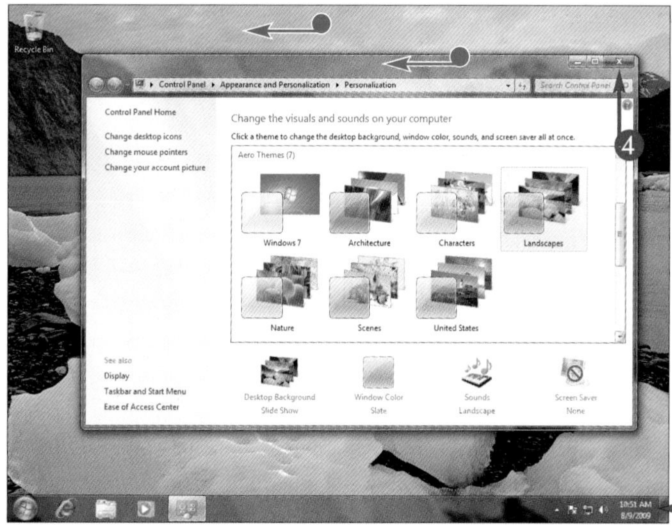

**TIP**

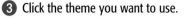

### Are there more themes available online?

Yes, Microsoft has a number of themes available on its Web site. In the Personalization window, click the **Get more themes online** link, and then click the **Themes** tab in the Web page that appears. Locate the theme you want to use, click the **Download** link, click **Open**, and then click **Allow** when Internet Explorer asks for confirmation. Windows 7 applies the theme and adds it to the Personalization window's My Themes section.

# Add a Gadget to the Desktop

You can make the Windows 7 desktop more useful by adding gadgets to it. A *gadget* is a small program such as a clock or calculator that performs a specific function.

**You can also keep your desktop tidy by removing any gadgets that you do not use.**

## Add a Gadget to the Desktop

### ADD A GADGET TO THE DESKTOP

1. Right-click the desktop.
2. Click **Gadgets**.

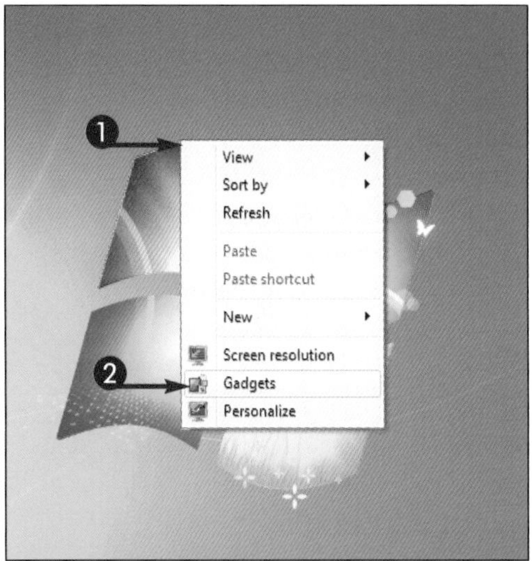


The Gadget Gallery appears.

- To see a description of any gadget, click **Show details** and then click the gadget.

3. Double-click the gadget that you want to add.

- Windows 7 adds the gadget to the desktop.

4 Repeat Step **3** to add more gadgets to the desktop.

- You can click this link to view and download more desktop gadgets on Microsoft's Web site.

5 Click the **Close** button (X).

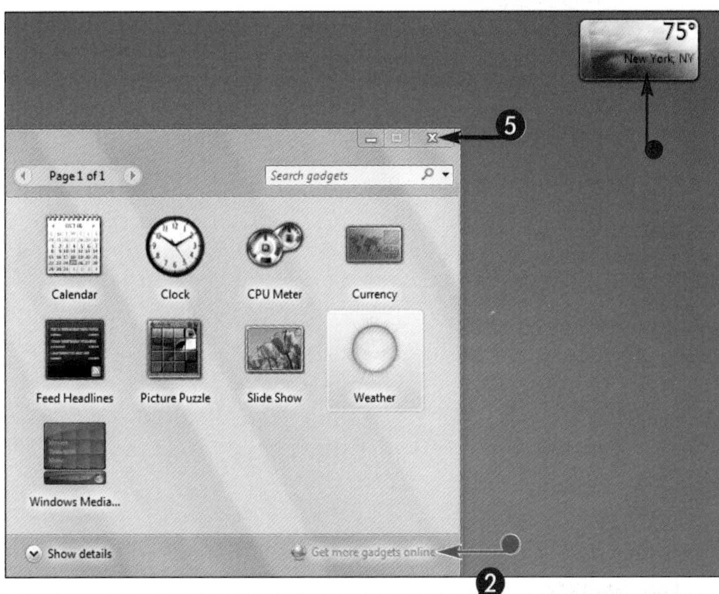


### REMOVE A GADGET FROM THE DESKTOP

1 Position the mouse over the gadget.

- The gadget controls appear.

2 Click the **Remove** button (X).

***Note:** You can also right-click the gadget and then click **Close gadget**.*

### How do I work with the gadgets once they are in the desktop?

Windows 7 gives you many ways to manipulate the gadgets:

- Click and drag a gadget around the desktop to change its position.
- Click the **Larger size** icon (⧉) to view a larger version of the gadget. (This icon is available only on some gadgets.)
- Click the **Options** icon (🔧) to view the gadget's properties.

# Customize the Start Menu

You can personalize how the Start menu looks and operates to suit your style and the way you work. For example, you can turn off the lists of recently used documents and programs for privacy.

**You can also control the items that appear on the right side of the menu, and you can customize the number of recent programs that appear on the Start menu and the number of items that appear in jump lists.**

## Customize the Start Menu

1. Right-click **Start**.
2. Click **Properties**.

The Taskbar and Start Menu Properties dialog box appears with the Start Menu tab displayed.

3. If you do not want Windows 7 to list your recently used programs, click here (☑ changes to ☐).
4. If you do not want Windows 7 to list your recently used documents, click here (☑ changes to ☐).
5. Click **Customize**.

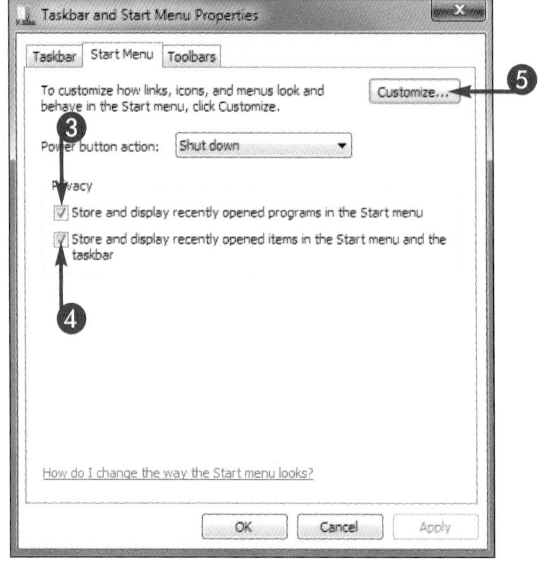

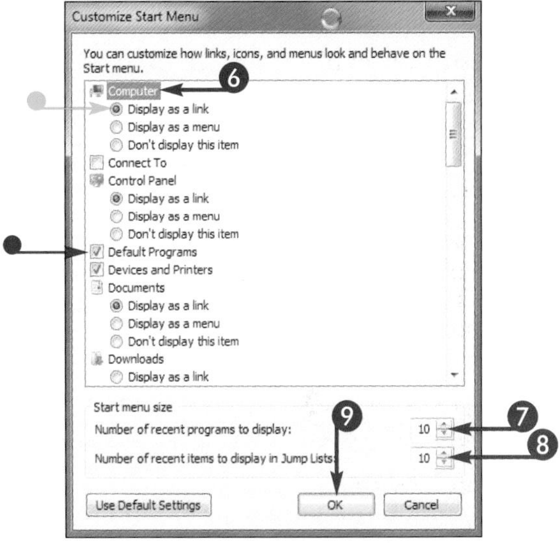


The Customize Start Menu dialog box appears.

6. Use the Start menu items list to control the icons that appear on the right side of the Start menu.

- Some items have several option buttons that control how they appear on the Start menu; click the option you want (◯ changes to ◉).
- Some items have check boxes that determine whether the item appears (☑) or does not appear (☐) on the Start menu.

7. Click ⬍ to change the maximum number of your recent programs that can appear on the Start menu. (Select a number between 0 and 30.)

8. Click ⬍ to change the maximum number of the recent items that can appear in jump lists. (Select a number between 0 and 60.)

9. Click **OK**.

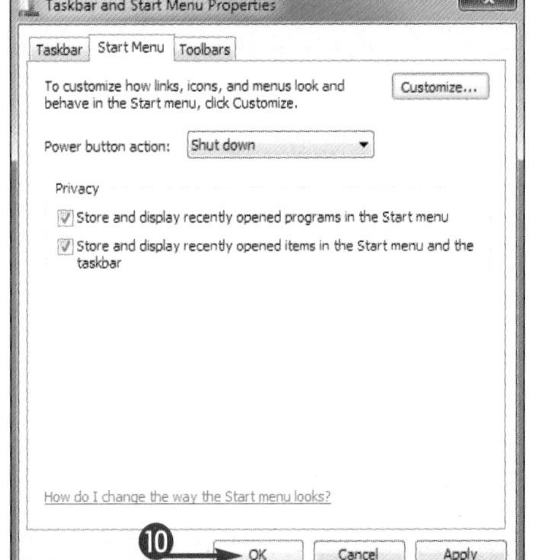


10. Click **OK**.

Windows 7 puts your new Start menu settings into effect.

### Can I remove a program that appears on my Start menu's list of most often used programs?

Yes. Click **Start** to open the Start menu, and then right-click the program that you want to remove. In the shortcut menu that appears, click **Remove from this list**. Windows 7 removes the program's icon from the Start menu.

### Can I add a program permanently to the Start menu?

Yes, you can *pin* a program so that it always appears at or near the top of the Start menu. Click **Start** to open the Start menu, and then right-click the program that you want to pin. In the shortcut menu, click **Pin to Start Menu**. The program's icon now appears in the top part of the menu, above the list of frequently used programs.

# Customize the Taskbar

You can personalize how the taskbar operates and looks to make it more efficient and suit your working style.

**For example, you can unlock the taskbar for moving or resizing, temporarily hide the taskbar, and display smaller icons on the taskbar.**

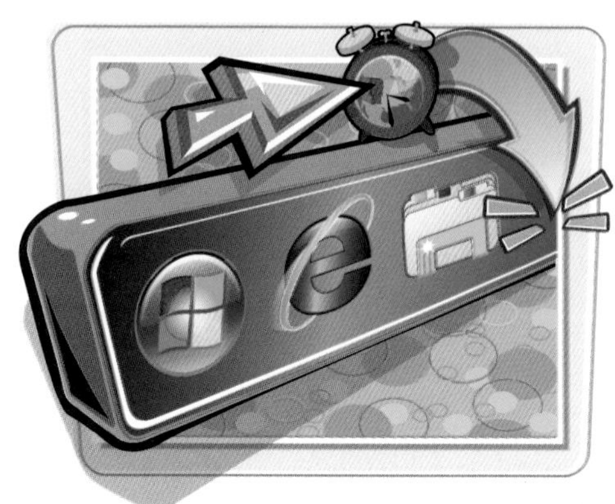

## Customize the Taskbar

- You can click and drag a taskbar icon to move it to a different location.

1. Right-click an empty section of the taskbar.
2. Click **Properties**.

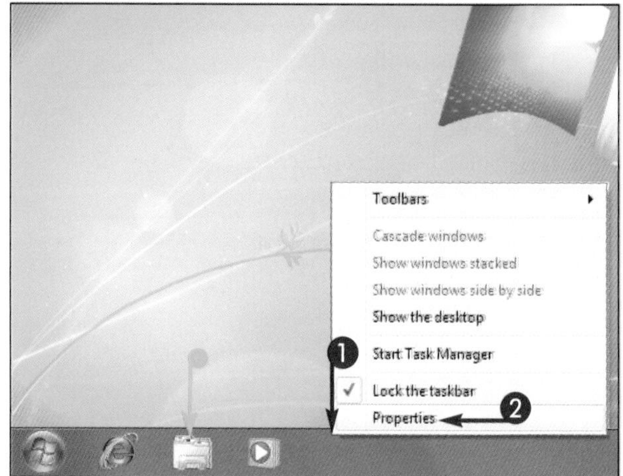


The Taskbar and Start Menu Properties dialog box appears with the Taskbar tab displayed.

3. Click **Lock the taskbar** (☑ changes to ☐) to unlock the taskbar.

***Note:*** *Unlocking the taskbar enables you resize the taskbar.*

***Note:*** *To quickly lock and unlock the taskbar, right-click an empty section of the taskbar and click* ***Lock the taskbar****.*

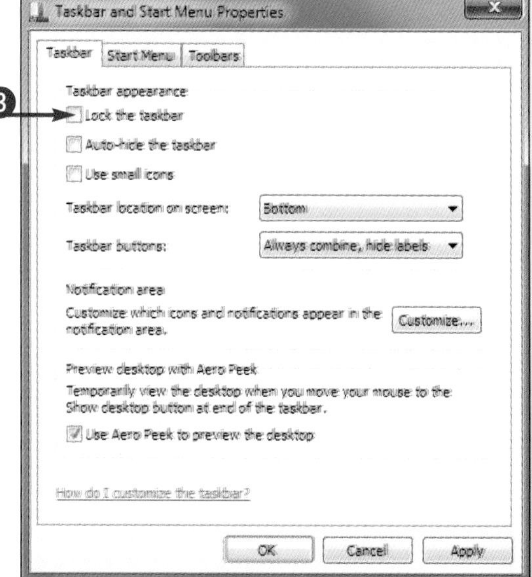

4 Click **Auto-hide the taskbar** (☐ changes to ☑) to hide the taskbar when you are using a program.

***Note:*** *Auto-hiding the taskbar gives you more room on the desktop to display your program windows.*

***Note:*** *To display the hidden taskbar, move the mouse to the bottom edge of the screen.*

5 Click **Use small icons** (☐ changes to ☑) to use smaller versions of the taskbar icons.

***Note:*** *Switching to smaller icons enables you to fit more icons on the taskbar.*

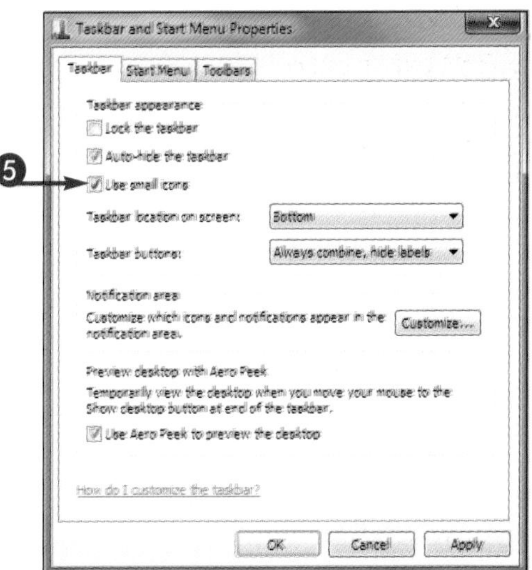

## TIPS

### How do I resize the taskbar?

To resize the taskbar, first make sure you have followed Steps **1** to **3** (and then clicked **OK**) to unlock the taskbar. Click and drag the top edge of the taskbar up to get more taskbar rows. If you later find that the taskbar is too big, click and drag the top edge of the taskbar down to get fewer taskbar rows.

### What is Aero Peek?

Aero Peek is a new Windows 7 feature that enables you to temporarily hide all your open windows to see the desktop. This is useful if you have gadgets on the desktop that you want to quickly view. When you activate the **Use Aero Peek to preview the desktop** check box (☐ changes to ☑), position your mouse pointer over the right edge of the taskbar to view the desktop.

continued

# Customize the Taskbar *(continued)*

**To further personalize your taskbar, you can change the taskbar location, group taskbar buttons, and customize the notification area icons.**

## Customize the Taskbar *(continued)*

6. Click the **Taskbar location on screen** ▼ and then click the location you prefer: Bottom, Left, Right, or Top.

7. Click the **Taskbar buttons** ▼ and then click the grouping option you prefer.

***Note:*** *See the tip on the next page to learn about the various grouping options.*

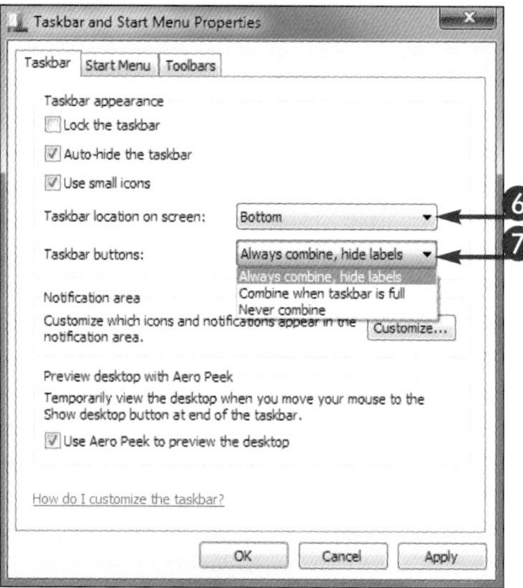


8. Click **Customize**.

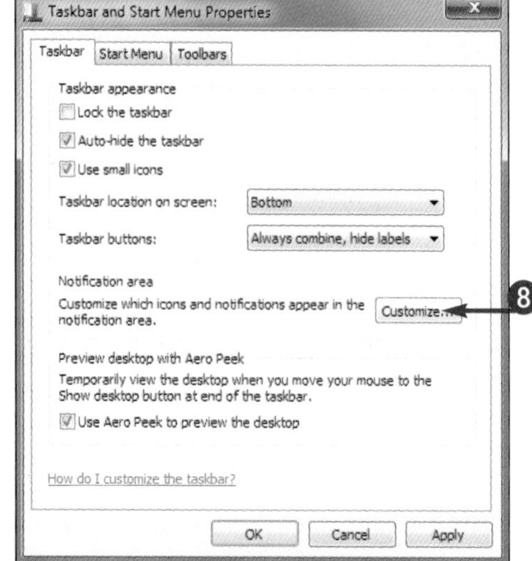

The Notification Area Icons window appears.

9 For each notification area icon, click ▾ and then click the setting you prefer.

***Note:** See the tip below to learn about the various settings.*

- If you choose to hide one or more notification area icons, you can click here to display the hidden icons.
- You can click this link to turn the system icons on or off.

10 Click **OK**.

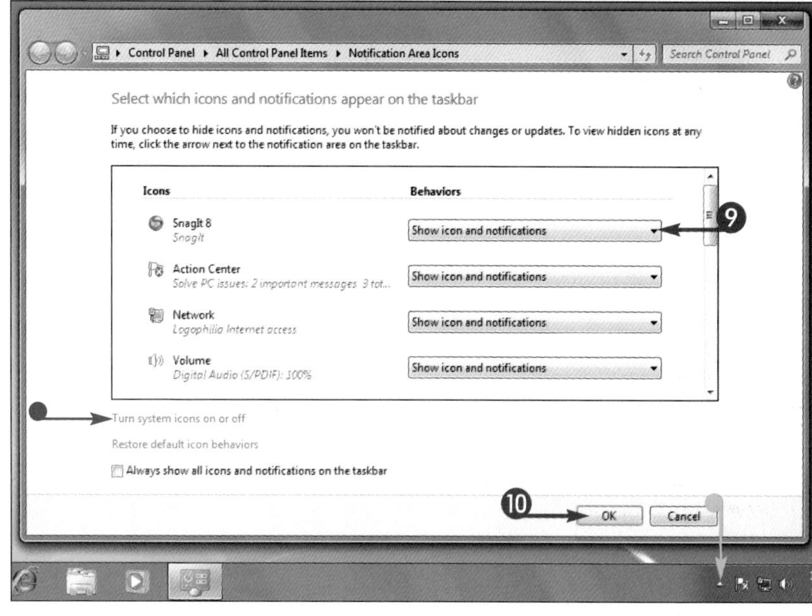


11 Click **OK**.

### What do the different taskbar grouping options mean?

Grouping taskbar buttons means showing only a single button for a program that has multiple windows open. To switch to one of those windows, click the taskbar button and then click the window name. **Always combine, hide labels** means that Windows 7 always groups buttons; **Combine when taskbar is full** means that Windows 7 waits until the taskbar is full before grouping; and **Never combine** disables grouping.

### What do the different options for the notification area icons mean?

These options control whether the icon appears in the notification area and whether you see messages from the icon's program. Choose **Show icon and notifications** to see both the icon and its messages; choose **Only show notifications** to hide the icon but still see the messages; or choose **Hide icons and notifications** to hide the icon and not show the messages.

CHAPTER

14

# Maintaining Windows 7

To keep your system running smoothly, maintain top performance, and reduce the risk of computer problems, you need to perform some routine maintenance chores. This chapter shows you how to delete unnecessary files, check for hard drive and other device errors, back up your files, and more.

# Check Hard Drive Free Space

You can check how much free space your hard drive has. This is important because if you run out of room on your hard drive, you cannot install more programs or create more documents.

**Of particular concern is the hard drive on which Windows 7 is installed, usually drive C. If this hard drive's free space gets low – say, less than 20 percent of the total hard drive space – Windows 7 runs slowly.**

## Check Hard Drive Free Space

1. Click **Start**.
2. Click **Computer**.

***Note:** You can also check the free space on CDs, DVDs, memory cards, or flash drives. Before you continue, insert the disc, card, or drive.*

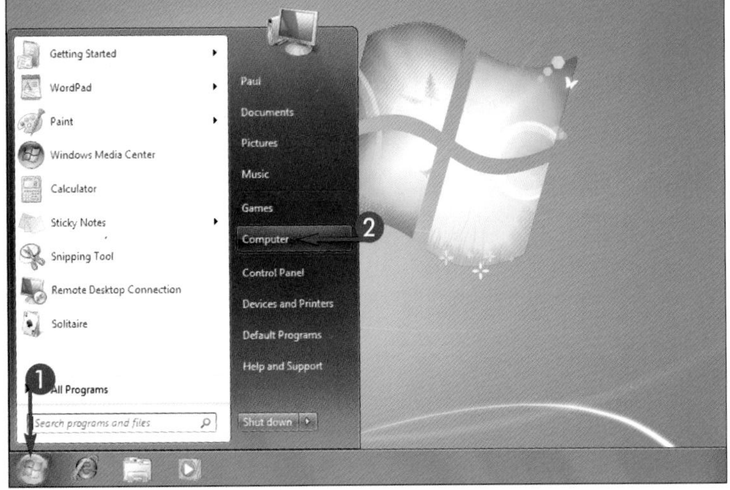


The Computer window appears.

3. Click the **View** icon.
4. Click **Tiles**.

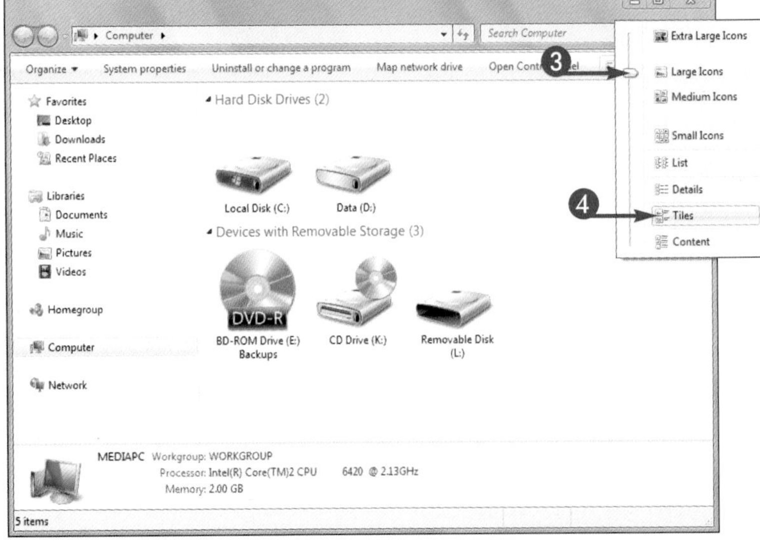

- Information about each drive appears along with the drive icon.
- This value tells you the amount of free space on the drive.
- This value tells you the total amount of space on the drive.
- This bar gives you a visual indication of how much disk space the drive is using.

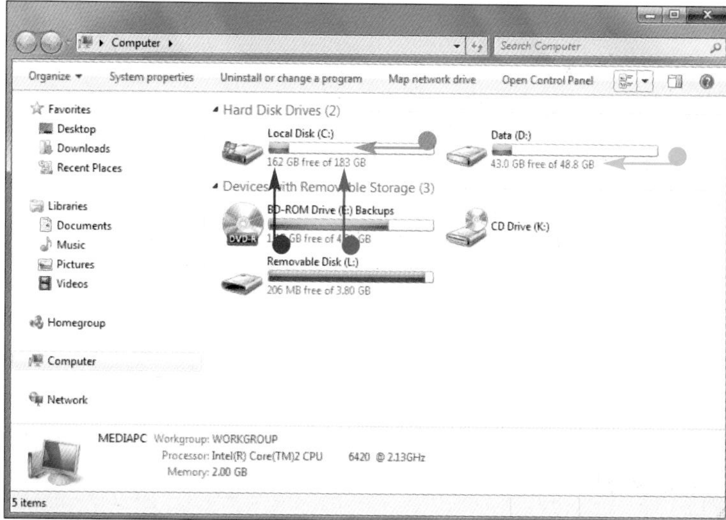

- The used portion of the bar appears blue when a drive still has sufficient disk space.
- The used portion of the bar turns red when a drive's disk space becomes low.

5 Click the **Close** button (X) to close the Computer window.

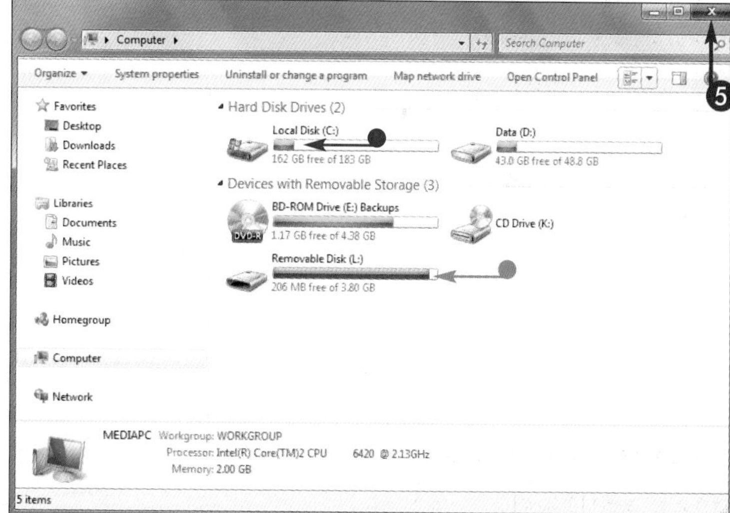

TIPS

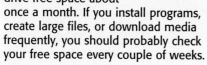

### How often should I check my hard drive free space?

With normal computer use, you should check your hard drive free space about once a month. If you install programs, create large files, or download media frequently, you should probably check your free space every couple of weeks.

### What can I do if my hard drive space is getting low?

You can do three things:

- **Delete Documents**. If you have documents — particularly media files such as images, music, and videos — that you are sure you no longer need, delete them.
- **Remove Programs**. If you have programs that you no longer use, uninstall them (see "Uninstall a Program" in Chapter 2).
- **Run Disk Cleanup**. Use the Disk Cleanup program to delete files that Windows 7 no longer uses. See the next section, "Delete Unnecessary Files."

# Delete Unnecessary Files

To free up hard drive space on your computer and keep Windows 7 running efficiently, you can use the Disk Cleanup program to delete files that your system no longer needs.

**Run Disk Cleanup any time that your hard drive free space gets too low. If hard drive space is not a problem, run Disk Cleanup every two or three months.**

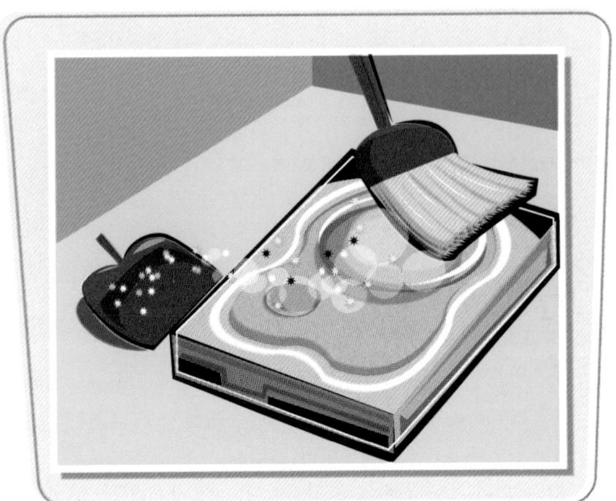

## Delete Unnecessary Files

1. Click **Start**.
2. Click **All Programs**.

*Note: When you click* ***All Programs****, the command name changes to Back.*

3. Click **Accessories**.
4. Click **System Tools**.
5. Click **Disk Cleanup**.

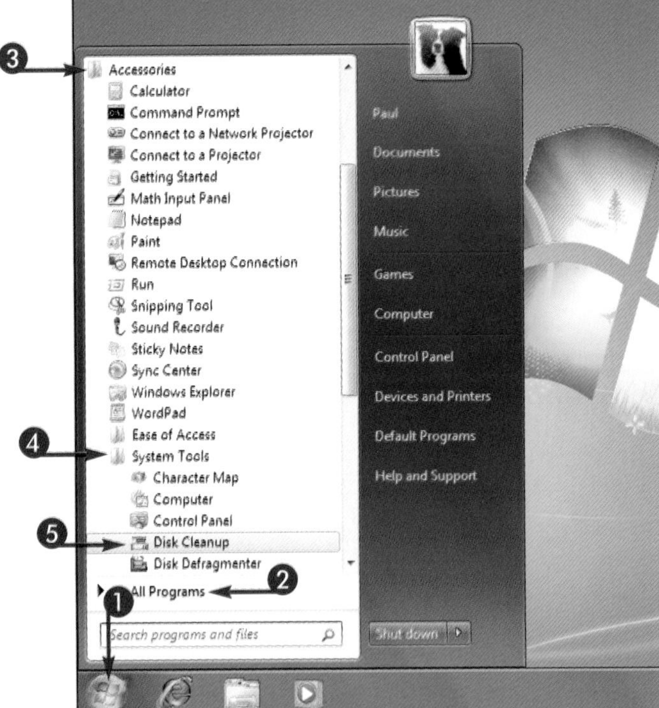


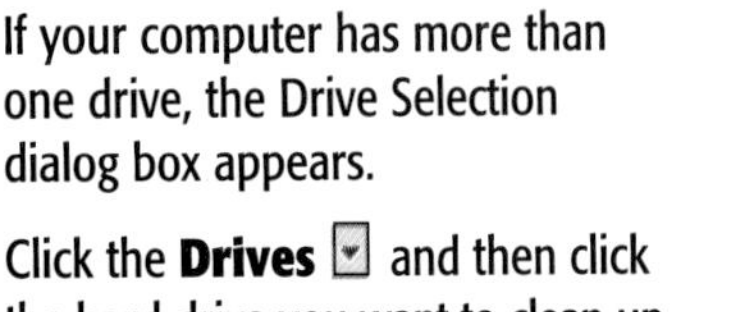

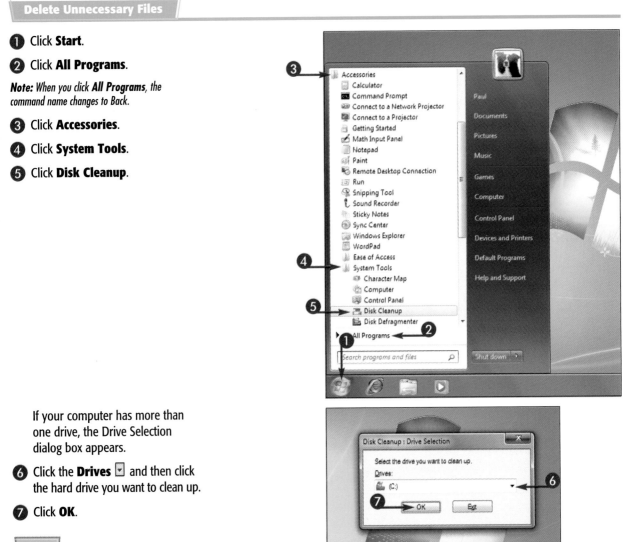

If your computer has more than one drive, the Drive Selection dialog box appears.

6. Click the **Drives** ▾ and then click the hard drive you want to clean up.
7. Click **OK**.

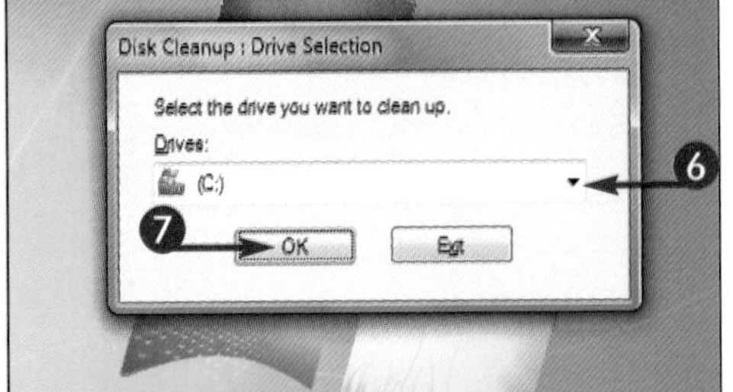

The Disk Cleanup dialog box appears.

- This area displays the total amount of drive space you can free up.
- This area displays the amount of drive space the activated options will free up.

8 Click the check box (☐ changes to ☑) for each file type that you want to delete.

- This area displays a description of the highlighted file type.

9 Click **OK**.

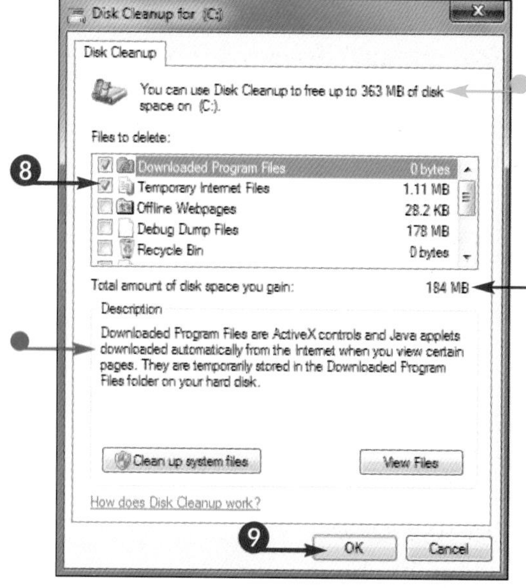


Disk Cleanup asks you to confirm that you want to delete the file types.

10 Click **Delete Files**.

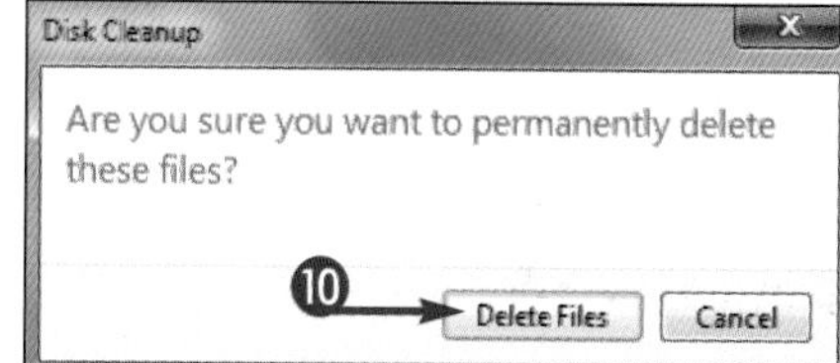

### What types of files does Disk Cleanup delete?

It deletes the following file types:

- **Downloaded Program files**: Small Web page programs downloaded onto your hard drive.
- **Temporary Internet files**: Web page copies stored on your hard drive for faster viewing.
- **Offline Web pages**: Web page copies stored on your hard drive for offline viewing.
- **Recycle Bin**: Files that you have deleted since you last emptied your Recycle Bin.
- **Temporary files**: Files used by programs to store temporary data.
- **Thumbnails**: Miniature versions of images and other content used in folder windows.

# Defragment Your Hard Drive on a Schedule

You can make Windows 7, and your programs, run faster, and your documents open more quickly, by defragmenting your hard drive on a regular schedule.

**Most files are stored on your computer in several pieces, and over time, those pieces often get scattered around your hard drive. Defragmenting improves performance by bringing all those pieces together, making finding and opening each file faster.**

## Defragment Your Hard Drive on a Schedule

1. Click **Start**.
2. Click **All Programs**.

*Note: When you click **All Programs**, the command name changes to Back.*

3. Click **Accessories**.
4. Click **System Tools**.
5. Click **Disk Defragmenter**.

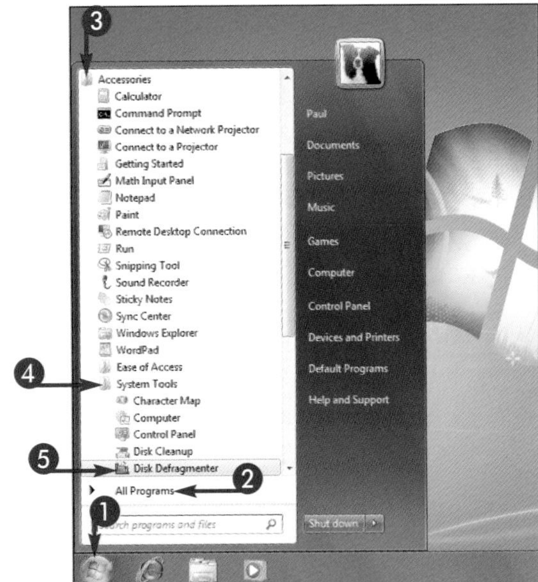


The Disk Defragmenter window appears.

6. Click **Configure schedule**.

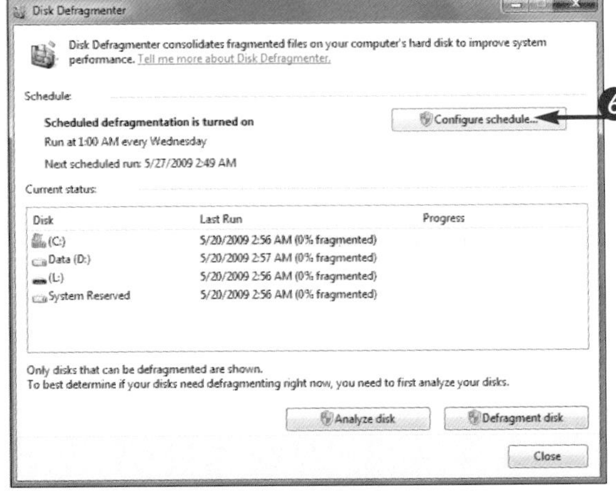

The Disk Defragmenter: Modify Schedule dialog box appears.

7 Click **Run on a schedule (recommended)** (☐ changes to ☑).

8 Click the **Frequency** ▾ and then click the frequency with which you want to defragment (Daily, Weekly, or Monthly).

9 Click the **Day** ▾ and click either the day of the week (for a Weekly schedule) or the day of the month (for a Monthly schedule).

10 Click the **Time** ▾ and then click the time of day to run the defragment.

11 Click **OK**.

- The new schedule appears here.

- If you want to defragment your drives now, click **Defragment disk**.

12 Click **Close**.

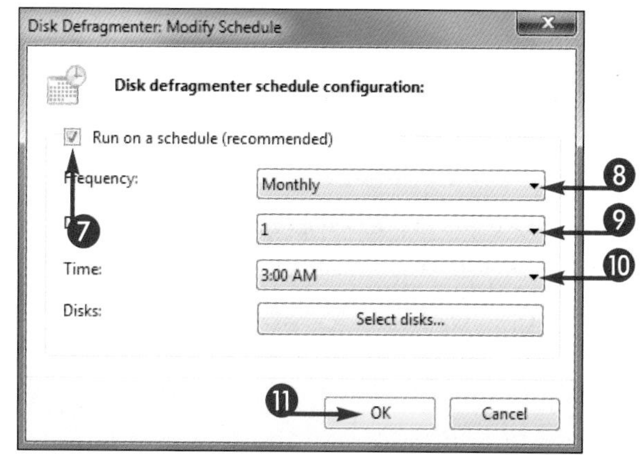


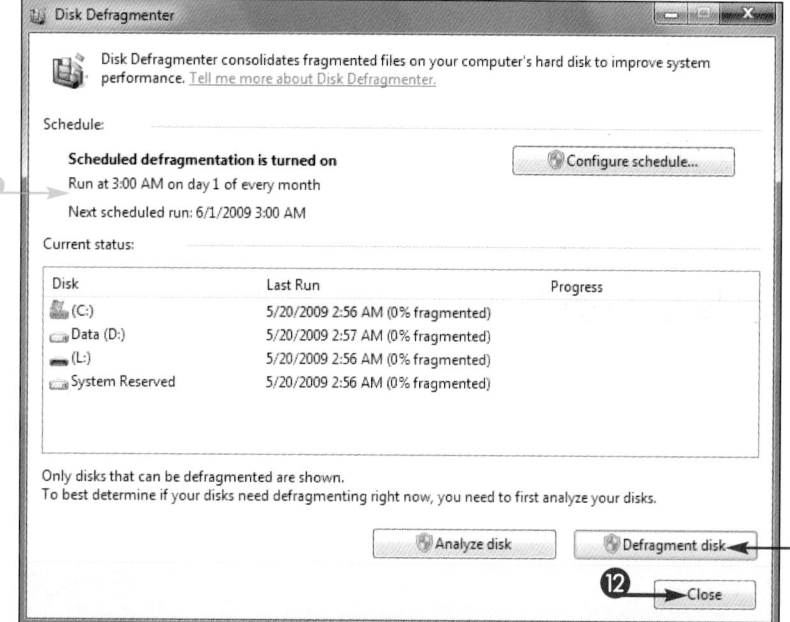

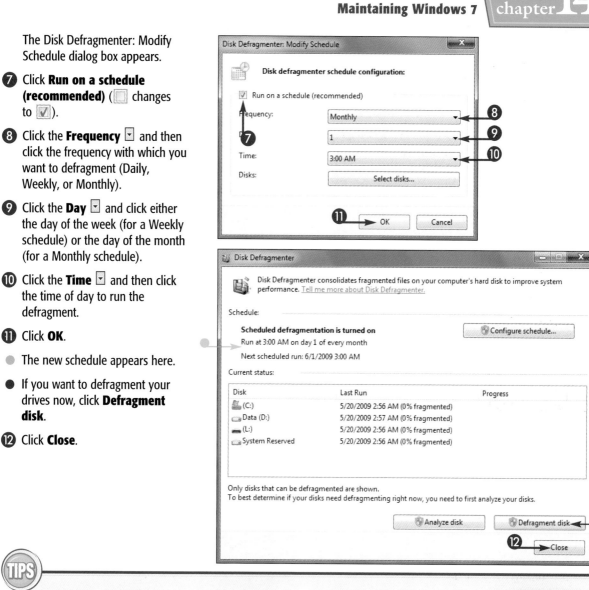

## TIPS

### How often should I defragment my hard drive?

This depends on how often you use your computer. If you use your computer every day, you should defragment your hard drive weekly. If you use your computer only occasionally, you should defragment your hard drive monthly.

### How long will defragmenting my hard drive take?

It depends on the size of the hard drive, the amount of data on it, and the extent of the defragmentation. Budget at least 15 minutes for the defragment, and know that it could take more than an hour.

# Check Your Hard Drive for Errors

Because hard drive errors can cause files to become corrupted, which may prevent you from running a program or opening a document, you can use the Check Disk program to look for and fix hard drive errors.

## Check Your Hard Drive for Errors

1. Click **Start**.
2. Click **Computer** (not shown).

   The Computer window appears.
3. Click the hard drive that you want to check.
4. Click **Properties**.

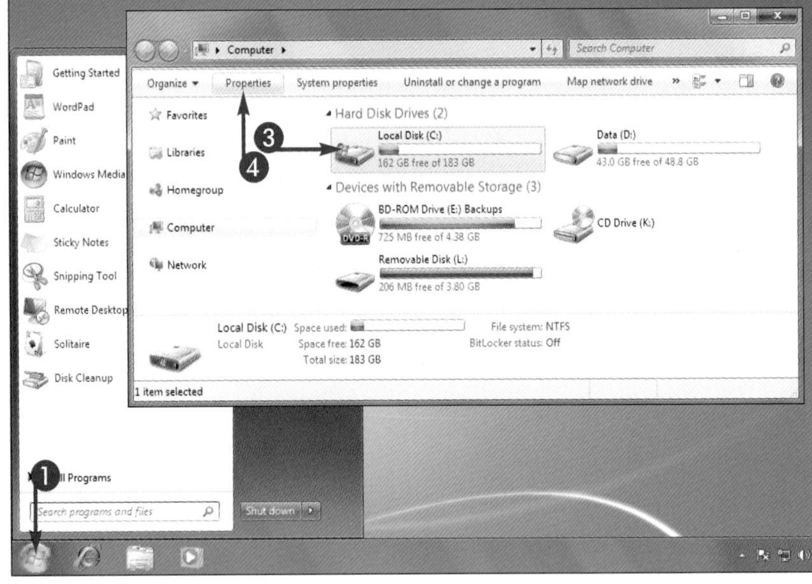

The hard drive's Properties dialog box appears.

5. Click the **Tools** tab.
6. Click **Check now** to open the Check Disk dialog box.

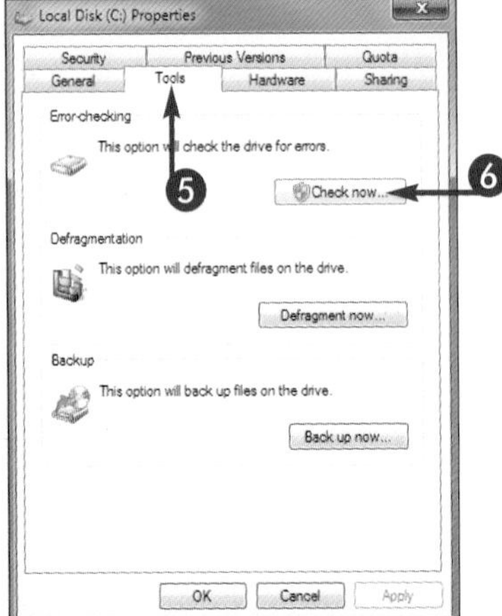

7 If you want Check Disk to fix any errors it finds, click **Automatically fix file system errors** (☐ changes to ☑).

8 If you want Check Disk to look for bad sectors, check **Scan for and attempt recovery of bad sectors** (☐ changes to ☑).

9 Click **Start**.

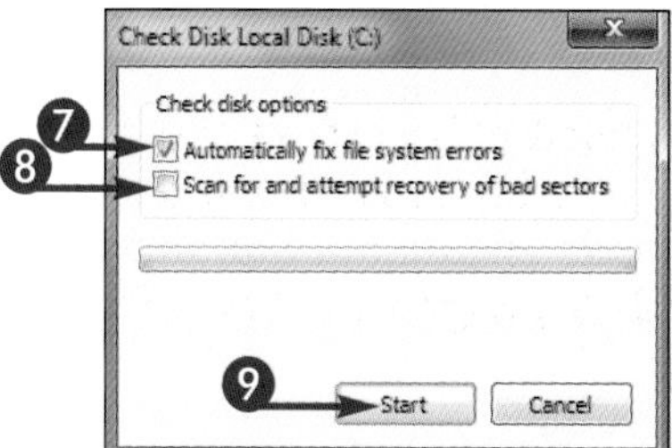


If you are checking the drive where Windows 7 is installed, Check Disk asks whether you want to check the disk the next time you start your computer.

10 Click **Schedule disk check**.

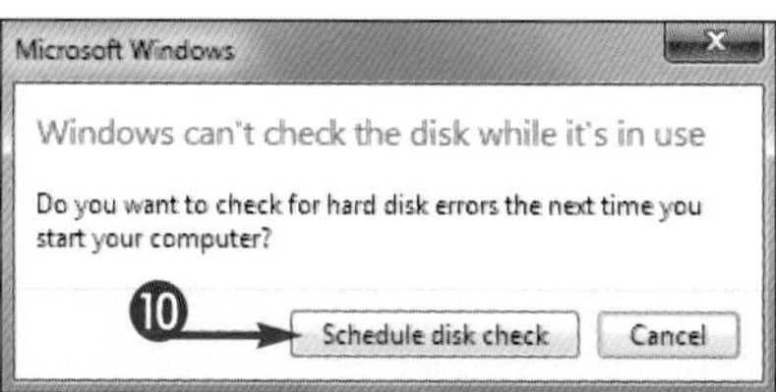


11 Click **OK**.

Windows 7 checks your hard drive the next time you start your computer.

***Note:** If Check Disk finds any errors and you did not click the **Automatically fix file system errors** option in Step **7**, follow the instructions provided by the program.*

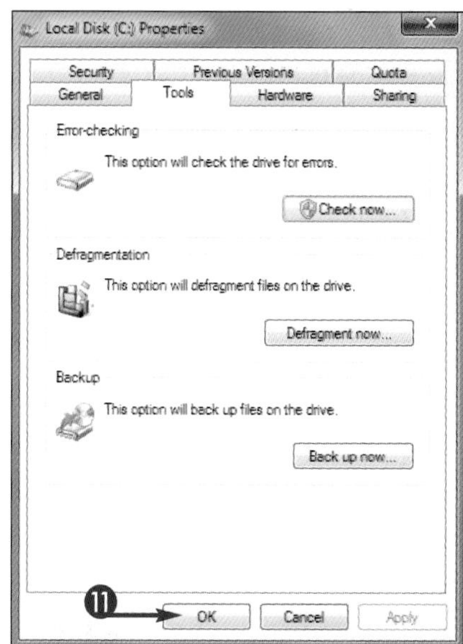


## TIPS

### What is a "bad sector"?

A *sector* is a small storage location on your hard drive. When Windows 7 saves a file on the drive, it divides the file into pieces and stores each piece in a separate sector. A bad sector is one that, through physical damage or some other cause, can no longer be used to reliably store data.

### How often should I check for hard drive errors?

You should perform the basic hard drive check about once a week. Perform the more thorough bad sector check once a month. Note that the bad sector check can take several hours, depending on the size of the drive, so perform this check only when you will not need your computer for a while.

# Check Your Devices for Errors

You can use Windows 7's new Devices and Printers feature to check your installed devices for errors. You can also use Devices and Printers to troubleshoot your problem devices.

## Check Your Devices for Errors

### CHECK FOR DEVICES WITH ERRORS

1. Click **Start**.
2. Click **Devices and Printers**.

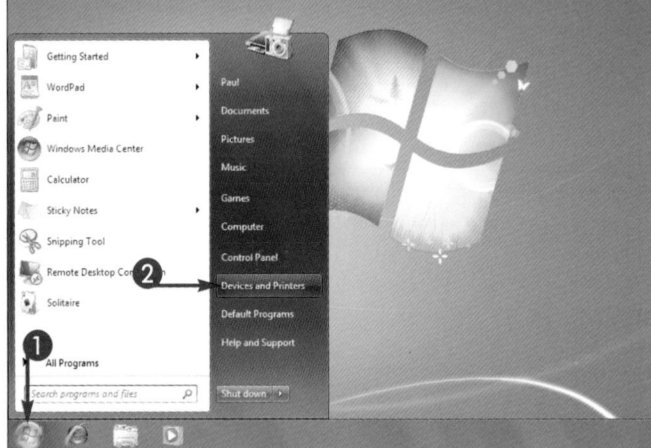


The Devices and Printers window appears.

3. Examine the device icons for errors.

- Windows 7 indicates devices with errors using this icon (![warning icon]).

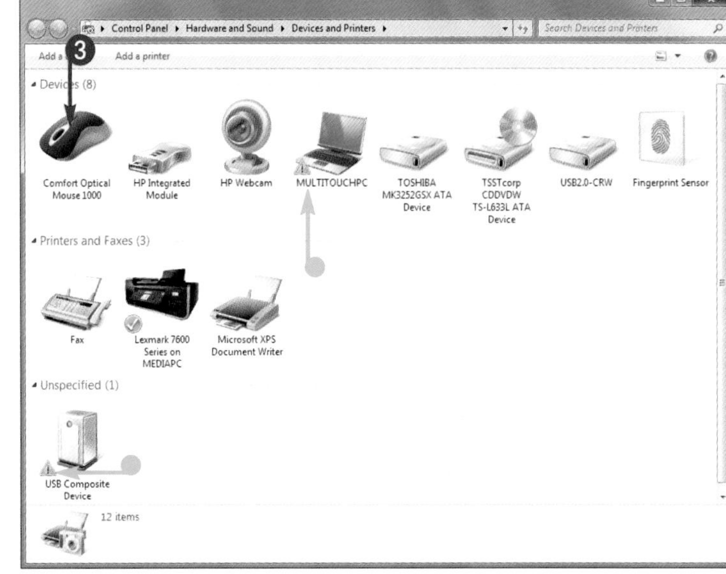

## BEGIN DEVICE TROUBLESHOOTING

1. Click a device that has an error.
2. Click **Troubleshoot**.

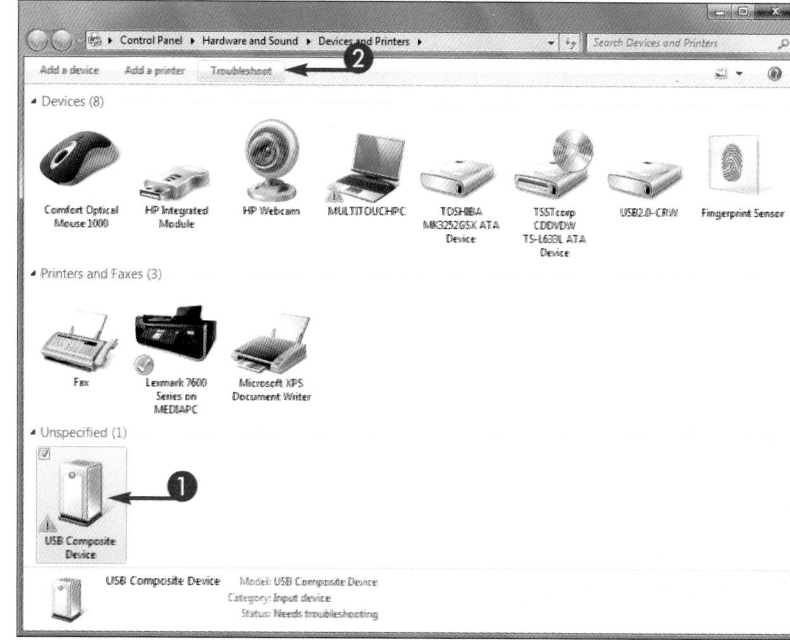


The Devices and Printers troubleshooting wizard appears and displays the first fix.

3. Click **Apply this fix**.

   Devices and Printers 7 applies the fix. If this did not solve the problem, Devices and Printers displays the next fix.

- If you are certain this fix is not the solution, click **Skip this fix**, instead.

4. Repeat Step **3** until the problem is resolved.

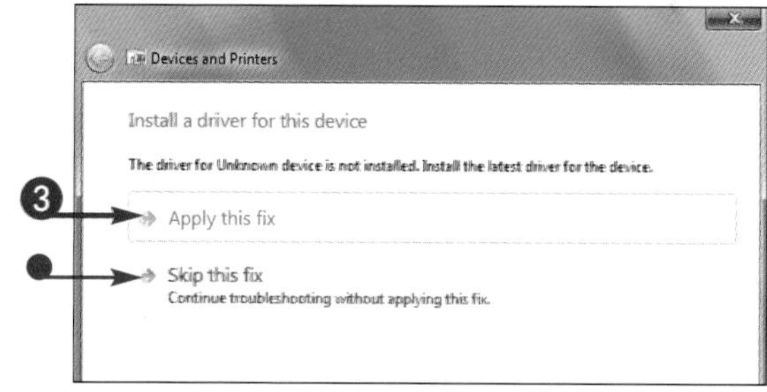

### What is a device driver?

A device driver is a small program that Windows 7 uses to communicate with a particular device. Many hardware problems are the result of either not having a device driver installed, or having an incorrect driver installed. Many devices come with discs that have the correct device driver, so you should insert that disc when troubleshooting. You can also obtain the latest device driver from the manufacturer's Web site.

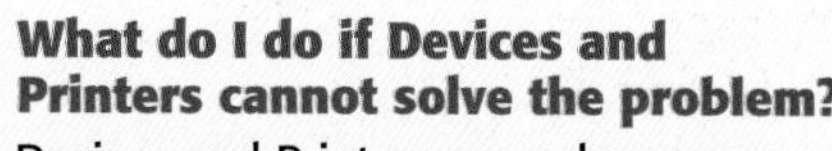

### What do I do if Devices and Printers cannot solve the problem?

Devices and Printers can solve many types of device problems, but not all of them. For example, if your device is broken or defective, there is nothing that Devices and Printers can do to fix it. In that case, you need to either return the device to the manufacturer for repair or replacement, or take it to a local computer shop for fixing.

# Create a System Restore Point

If your computer crashes or becomes unstable after you install a program or a new device, Windows 7's System Restore feature can fix things by restoring the system to its previous state. To ensure this works, you need to set restore points before you install programs and devices on your computer.

**Windows 7 automatically creates system restore points as follows: every week (called a *system checkpoint*); before installing an update; and before installing certain programs (such as Microsoft Office) and devices.**

## Create a System Restore Point

❶ Click **Start**.

❷ Right-click **Computer**.

❸ Click **Properties**.

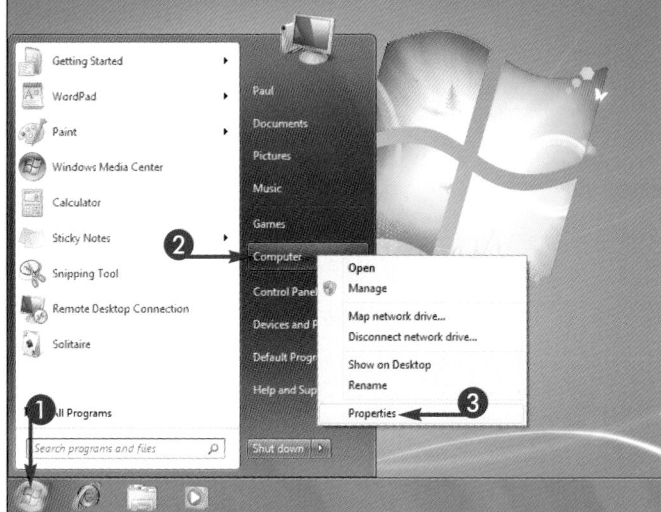

The System window appears.

❹ Click **System protection**.

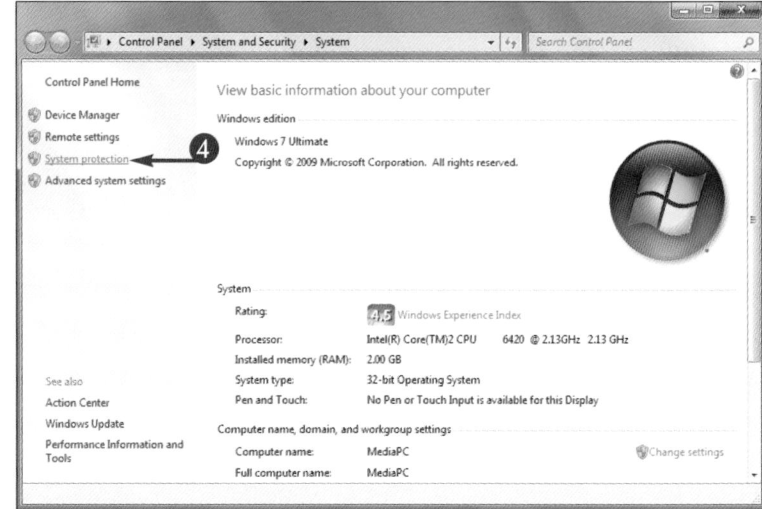

The System Properties dialog box appears.

- The System Protection tab is already displayed.

5. Click **Create**.

The Create a Restore Point dialog box appears.

6. Type a description for your restore point.
7. Click **Create**.

System Restore creates the restore point.

Windows 7 tells you the restore point was created successfully.

8. Click **Close**.
9. Click **OK** to close the System Properties dialog box.

**When should I create a restore point?**

To be safe, you should create a restore point before you install any software, whether you purchased the program at a store or downloaded it from the Internet. You should also create a restore point before you add any new hardware devices to your system.

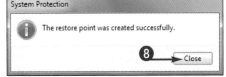

# Apply a System Restore Point

If your computer becomes unstable or behaves erratically after you install a program or device, you can often fix the problem by applying the restore point you created before making the change.

**When you apply a restore point, Windows 7 reverts your computer to the configuration it had when you created the restore point.**

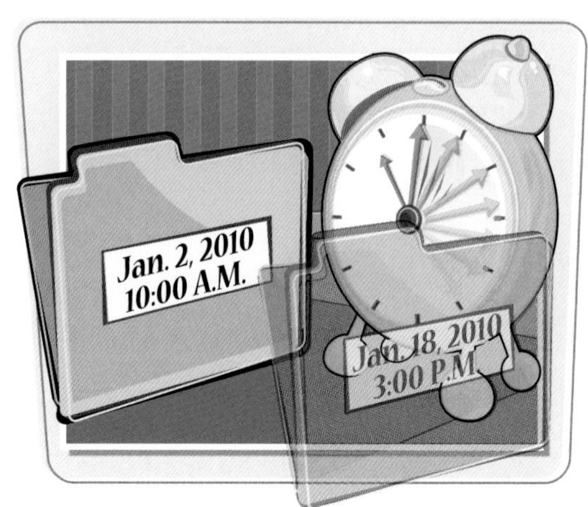


## Apply a System Restore Point

1. Save all your open documents and close all your open programs.
2. Click **Start**.
3. Click inside the Search box and type **system restore**.
4. Click **System Restore**.

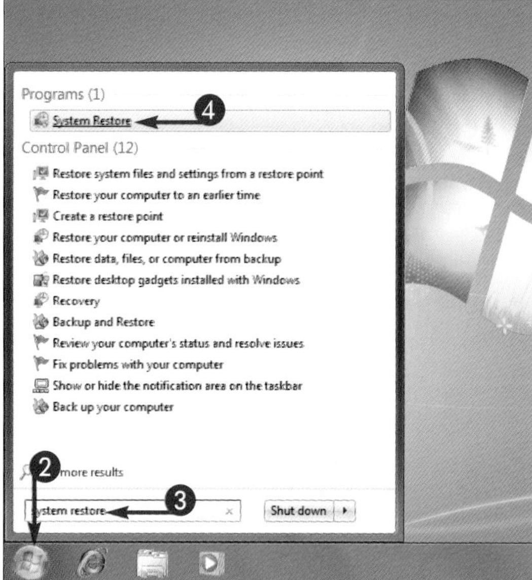


The System Restore window appears.

- System Restore might show the most likely restore point here. If this is the restore point you want, or if you do not see a restore point, skip to Step **8**.

5. Click **Choose a different restore point** (◎ changes to ◉).
6. Click **Next**.

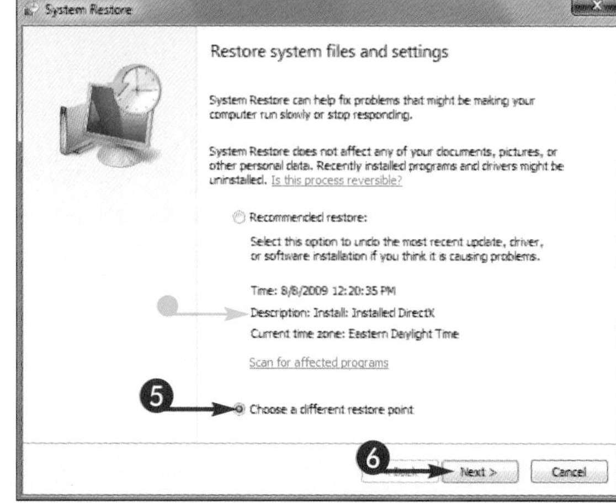

The Choose a Restore Point window appears.

7. Click the restore point you want to apply.
8. Click **Next**.

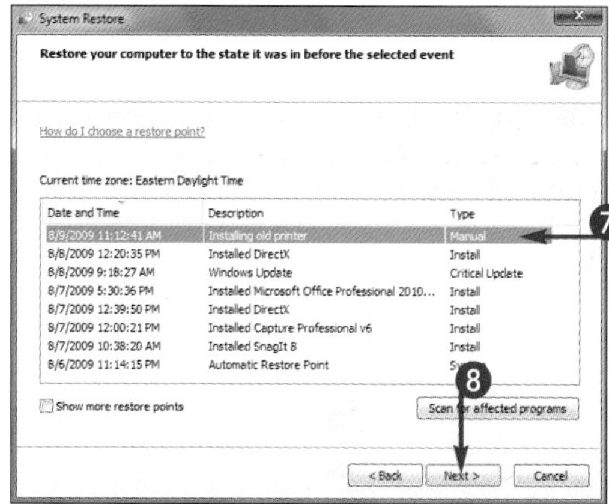


The Confirm Your Restore Point window appears.

9. Click **Finish**.

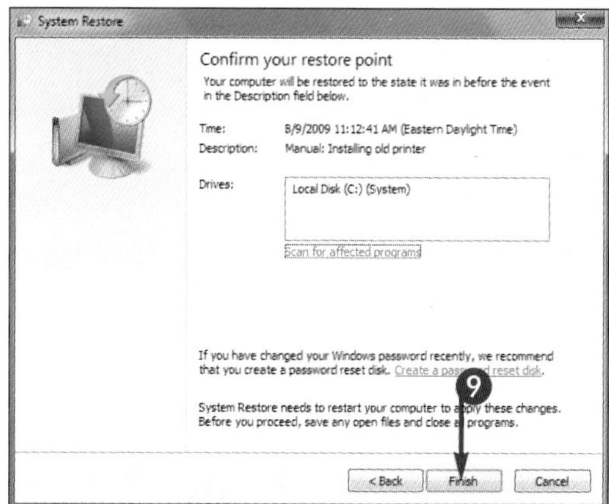


System Restore asks you to confirm that you want to restore your system.

10. Click **Yes**.

System Restore applies the restore point and then restarts Windows 7.

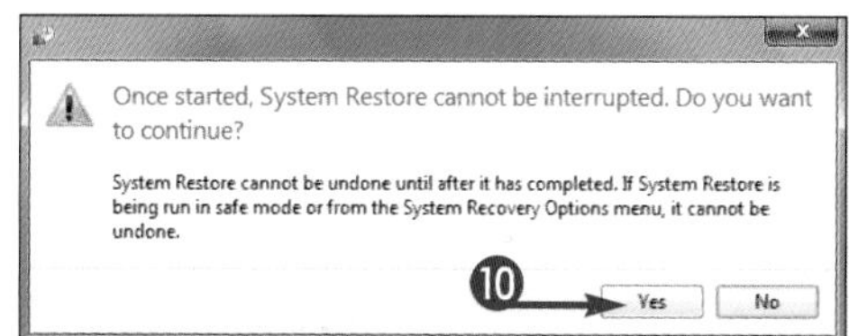

### Will I lose any of my recent work when I apply a restore point?

No, the restore point only reverts your computer's configuration back to the earlier time. Any work you performed in the interim — documents you created, e-mails you received, Web page favorites you saved, and so on — is not affected when you apply the restore point.

### If applying the restore point makes things worse, can I reverse it?

Yes. Follow Steps **1** to **6** to display the list of available restore points on your computer. Click the **Restore Operation** restore point, and then follow Steps **8** to **10**.

# Back Up Files

You can use the Windows Backup program to make backup copies of your important files. If a system problem causes you to lose one or more files, you can restore them from the backup.

**In the Windows Backup program, you can back up to a recordable CD or DVD drive, to another hard drive on your system, or to a network location.**

## Back Up Files

1. Click **Start**.
2. Click **All Programs**.

***Note:*** *When you click **All Programs**, the command name changes to Back.*

3. Click **Maintenance**.
4. Click **Backup and Restore**.

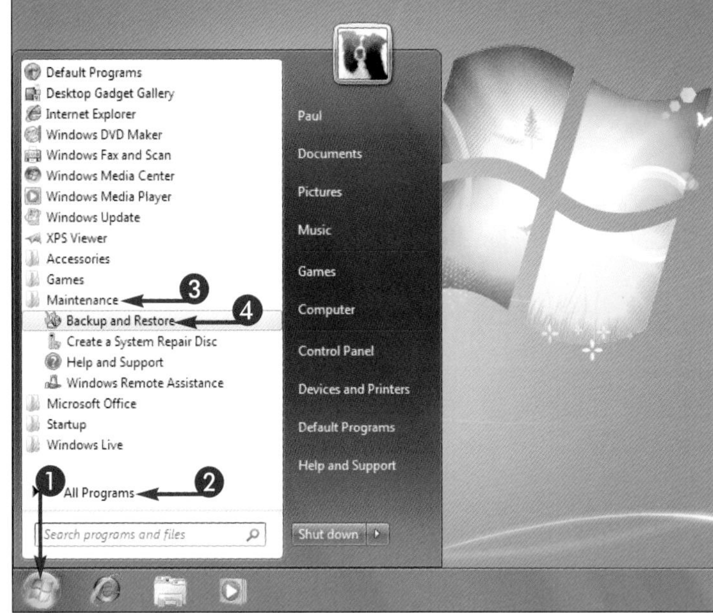


The Backup and Restore window appears.

5. Click **Set up backup**.

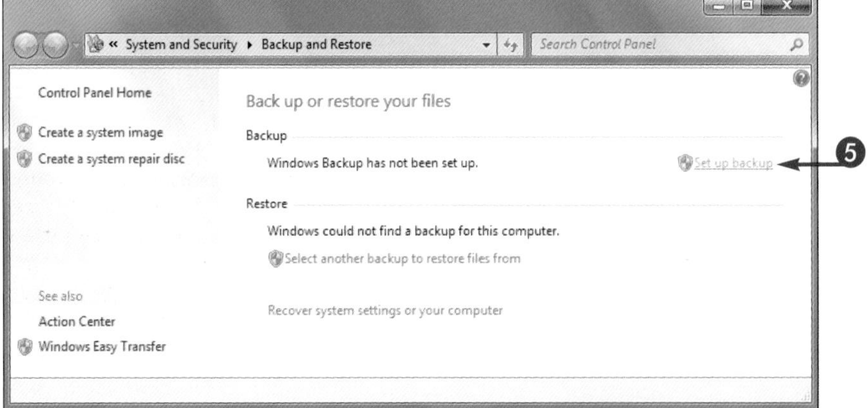

The Set Up Backup dialog box appears.

6. Click the drive where you want to store the backup.

- For a network backup, click **Save on a network**, click **Browse**, click the network folder, and then click **OK**.

7. Click **Next**.

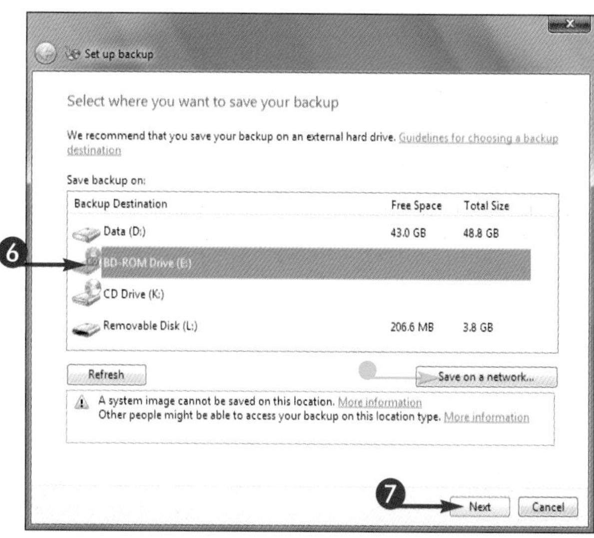


BD-ROM Drive (E:)
CD Drive (K:)
Removable Disk (L:)

The What Do You Want to Back Up? dialog box appears.

8. Click **Let Windows choose (recommended)** (◯ changes to ◉).

- If you want to specify what to include in the backup, click **Let me choose** (◯ changes to ◉), instead, and then make your selections in the next dialog box.

9. Click **Next**.

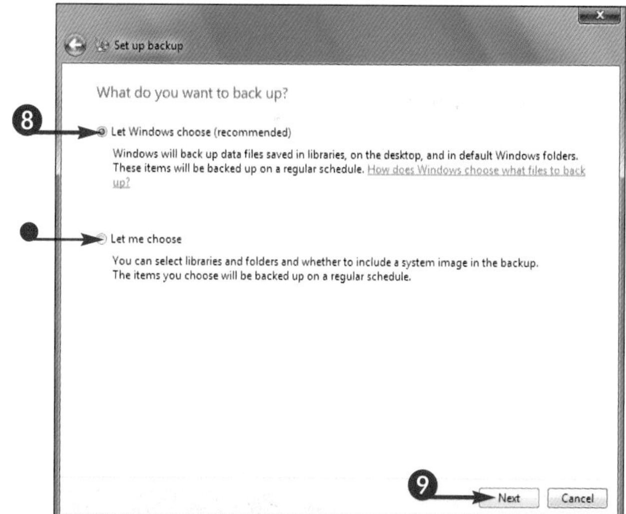

Set up backup
We recommend that you save your backup on an external hard drive. Guidelines for choosing a backup destination
Save backup on:
Backup Destination
What do you want to back up?
Let Windows choose (recommended)
Windows will back up data files saved in libraries, on the desktop, and in default Windows folders. These items will be backed up on a regular schedule. How does Windows choose what files to back up?
Let me choose
You can select libraries and folders and whether to include a system image in the backup. The items you choose will be backed up on a regular schedule.
A system image cannot be saved on this location. More information
Other people might be able to access your backup on this location type. More information
Next
Cancel


TIPS

### I just created some important documents. Can I back up right away?

Yes. First you must complete the steps in this section to perform at least one backup and set your backup configuration. Now, whenever you need to perform a backup, follow Steps **1** to **4** to display the Backup and Restore window, and then click **Back up now**.

### What is a system image?

A system image is an exact copy of your entire system. This type of backup includes not only your documents, but also your programs, your Windows 7 configuration, and all the Windows 7 files. If your computer crashes and will no longer start, you can use a system image backup to restore the entire system. If you back up to another hard drive or a network drive, a system image is automatically included in the backup.

continued

# Back Up Files *(continued)*

By default, Windows Backup backs up the files in your Windows 7 library, as well as the library files for the other users on your computer.

**Note that you only need to run through these configuration steps once. After you have configured your initial backup, Windows Backup runs automatically once a week.**

## Back Up Files *(continued)*

The Review Your Backup Settings dialog box appears.

⑩ Click **Save settings and run backup**.

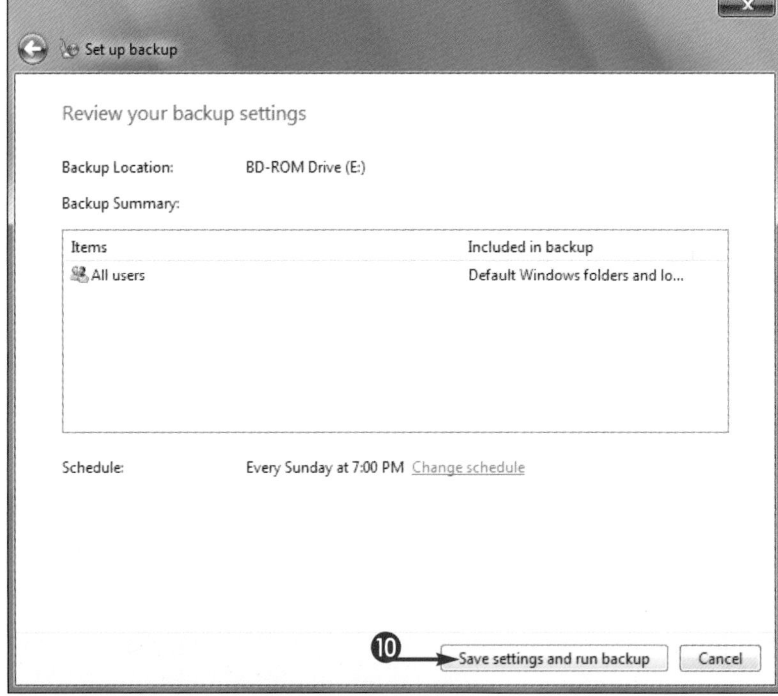


If you are backing up to a CD or DVD, Windows Backup asks you to insert a blank disk.

⑪ Insert a blank disc in the drive.

⑫ Click **OK**.

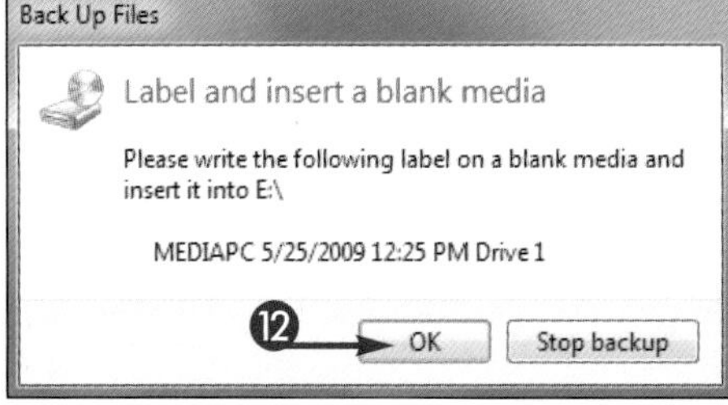

Windows Backup asks if you are sure you want to format the disc.

13 Click **Format**.

Windows Backup formats the disc and resumes the backup.

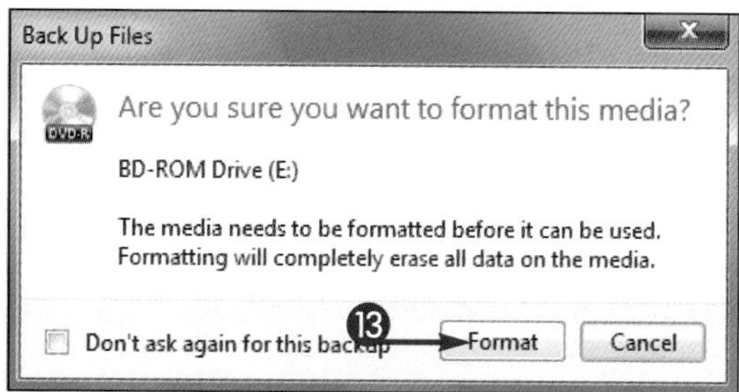


If the medium you are backing up to becomes full, the Label and Insert a Blank Media dialog box appears.

14 Remove the full medium, replace it with a new one, and then click **OK**.

***Note:*** *If your backup requires multiple media, you should give each medium a label, such as Backup 1, Backup 2, and so on.*

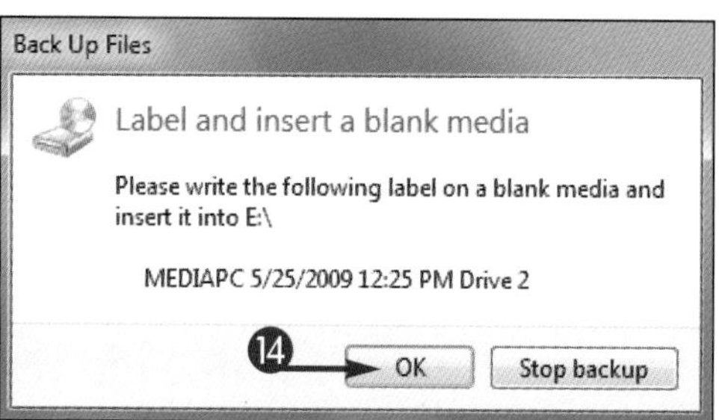


When the backup is done, the Windows Backup Has Completed Successfully dialog box appears.

15 Click **Close**.

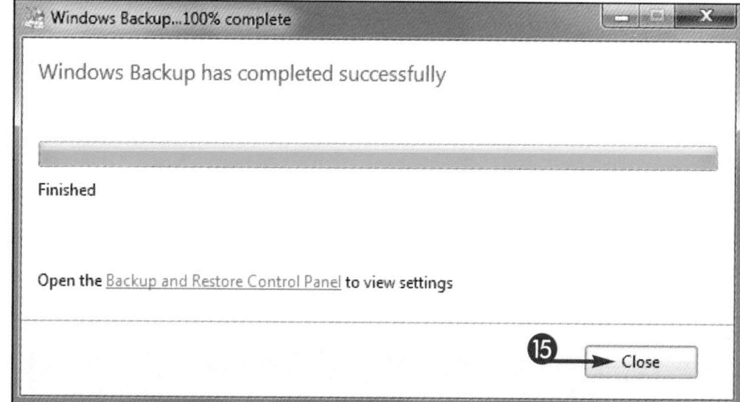


## TIPS

### How often should I back up my files?

By default, Windows Backup performs a weekly backup, which is fine for most users. If you use your computer every day to create important business files, you should consider performing backups daily; more occasional users might consider monthly backups. To change the schedule, follow Steps **1** to **4**, click **Change settings**, click **Next**, click **Next**, and then click **Change schedule**.

### Can I change my backup configuration?

Yes. Follow Steps **1** to **4** to display the Backup and Restore window, click **Change settings**, and then follow Steps **5** to **9** to adjust your configuration. In the final Set Up Backup dialog box, click **Save settings and exit**.

# Restore Backed-Up Files

You can restore a file from a backup if the file is lost because of a system problem or because you accidentally deleted or overwrote the file.

## Restore Backed-Up Files

1. Click **Start**.
2. Click **All Programs**.
3. Click **Maintenance**.
4. Click **Backup and Restore**.

   The Backup and Restore window appears.

5. Click **Restore my files**.

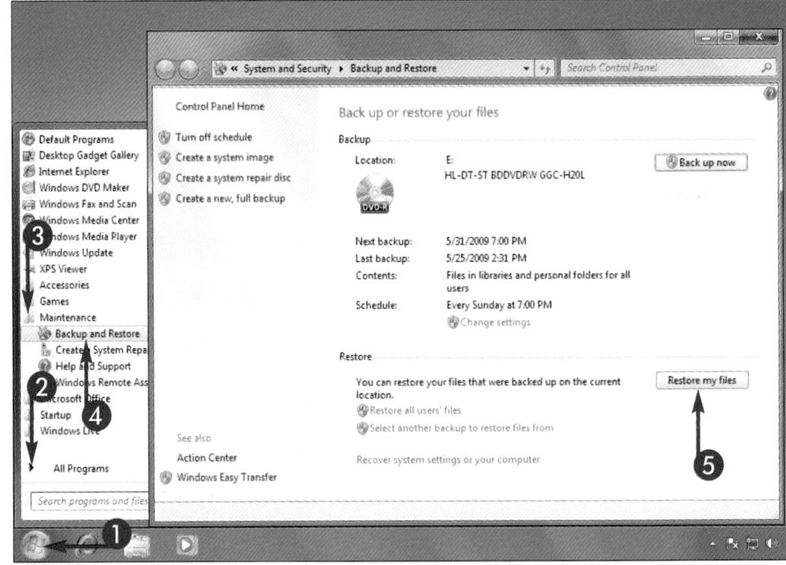


The Browse or Search Your Backup for Files and Folders to Restore dialog box appears.

6. If you backed up using a removable medium such as a CD, DVD, or memory card, insert the medium that contains the backups.
7. Click **Browse for files**.

- If you want to restore an entire folder, click **Browse for folders**, instead.

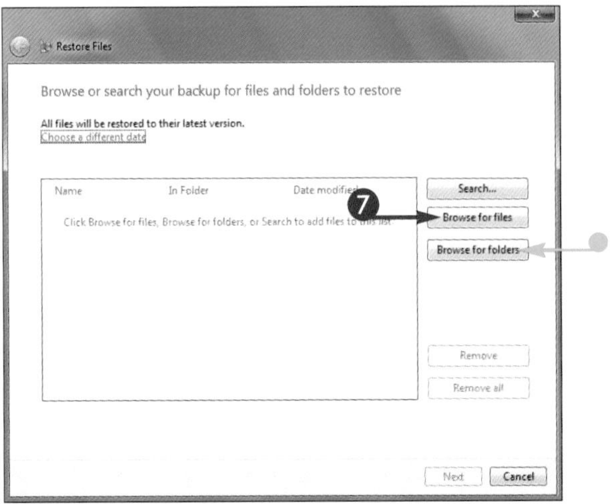

The Browse the Backup for Files dialog box appears.

8 Open the folder that contains the file you want to restore.

9 Click the file you want to restore.

*Note: To restore multiple files from the same folder, press and hold Ctrl and click each file.*

10 Click **Add files**.

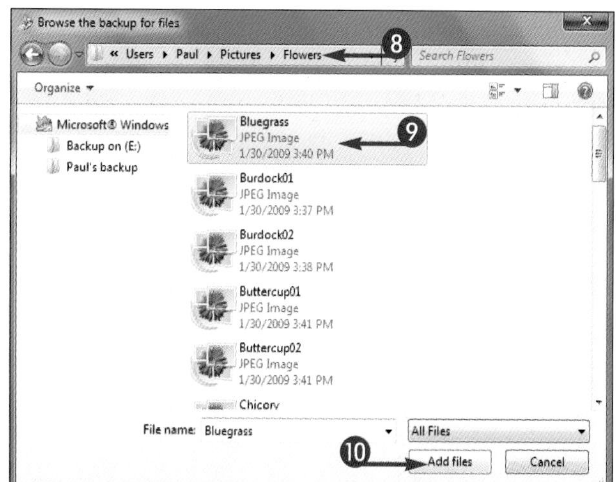

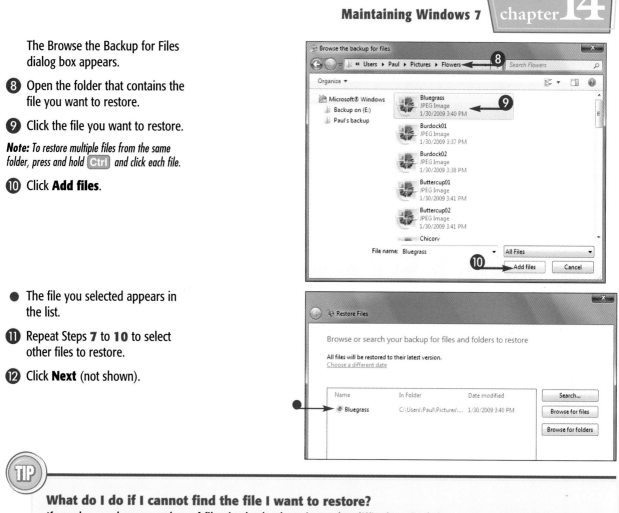

- The file you selected appears in the list.

11 Repeat Steps **7** to **10** to select other files to restore.

12 Click **Next** (not shown).

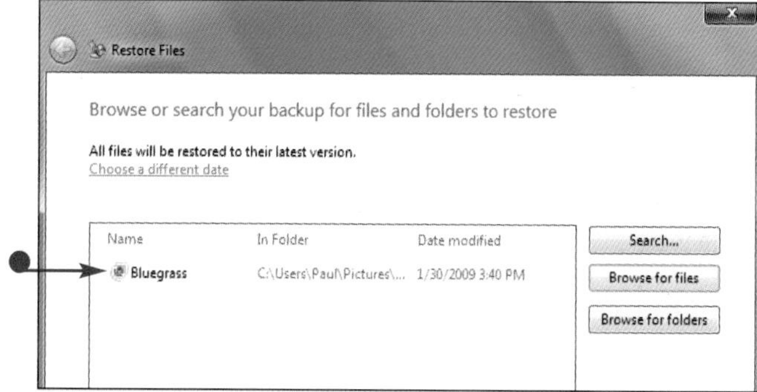


## TIP

### What do I do if I cannot find the file I want to restore?

If you have a large number of files in the backup, it can be difficult to find the one you need. Follow these steps:

1 Follow Steps **1** to **5** to display the Browse or Search Your Backup for Files and Folders to Restore dialog box.

2 Click **Search**.

3 In the Search for Files to Restore dialog box, type some or all of the file name.

4 Click **Search**.

5 Click the file to restore (☐ changes to ☑).

6 Click **OK**.

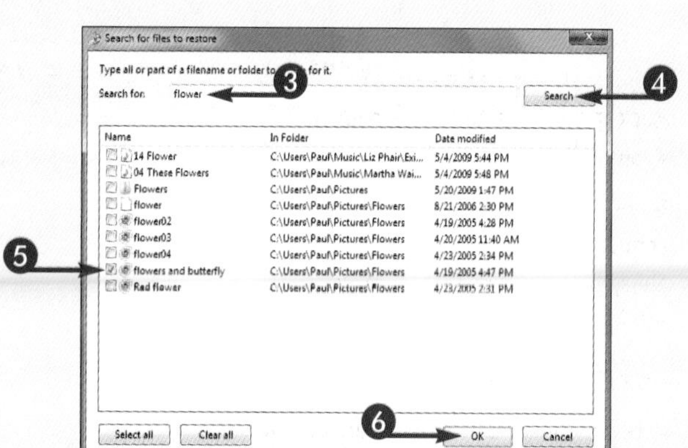


continued

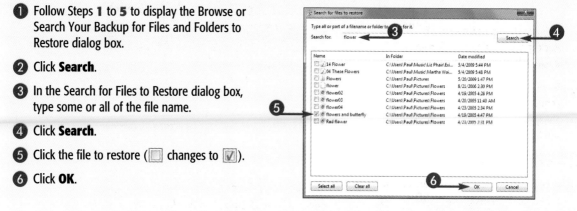

# Restore Backed-Up Files *(continued)*

You can restore all of the backed-up files or you can restore just one or more of the backed-up files. You can also restore the files in their original locations or in a different location.

## Restore Backed-Up Files *(continued)*

The Where Do You Want to Restore Your Files? dialog box appears.

⓭ Click **In the original location** (◎ changes to ◉).

- If you prefer to restore the file to another folder, click **In the following location** (◎ changes to ◉), instead, and then click **Browse** to choose the location.

⓮ Click **Restore**.

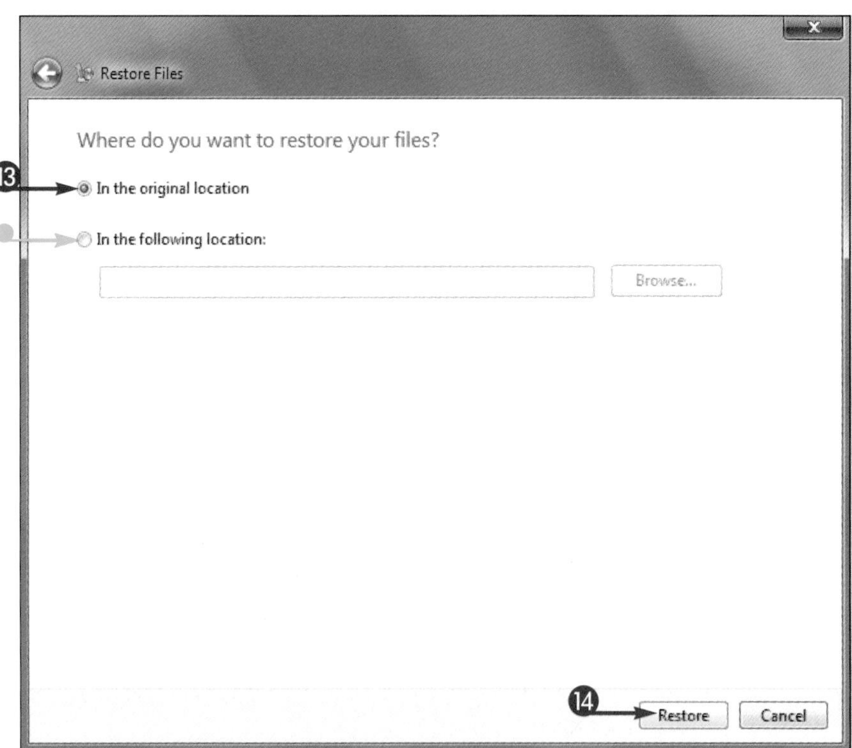


If you do not have the correct backup media inserted, Windows Backup prompts you to insert the correct disc or drive.

⓯ Insert the requested media.

⓰ Click **OK**.

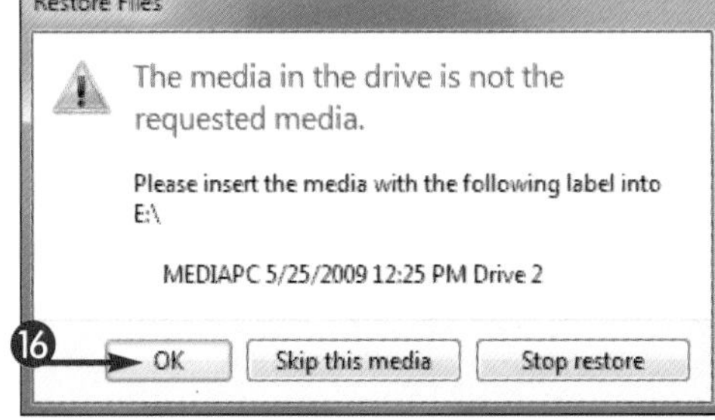

If a file with the same name exists in the original location, you see the Copy File dialog box.

17 If you want Windows Backup to handle all conflicts the same way, click **Do this for all conflicts** (☐ changes to ☑).

18 Click **Copy and Replace**.

- If you want to keep the original, click **Don't copy**, instead.
- If you want to see both files, click **Copy, but keep both files**, instead.

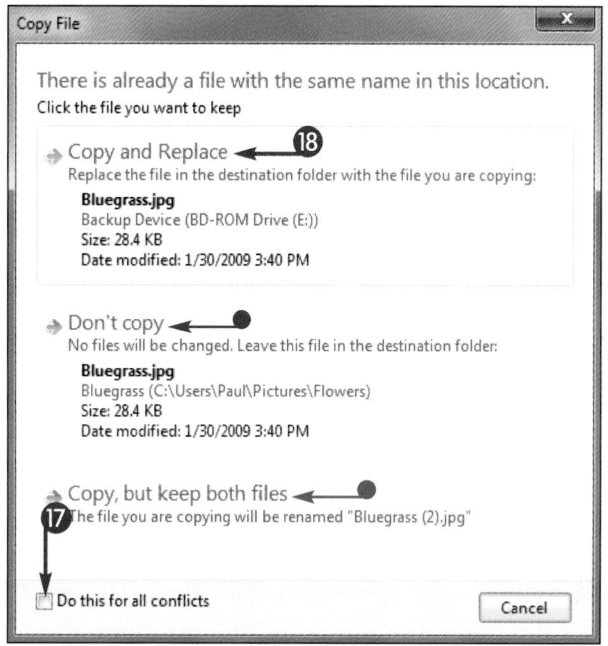

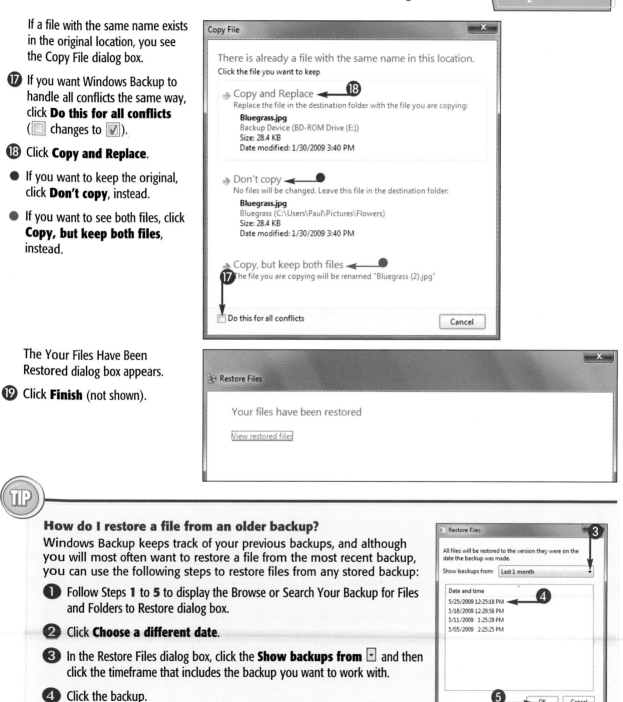

The Your Files Have Been Restored dialog box appears.

19 Click **Finish** (not shown).

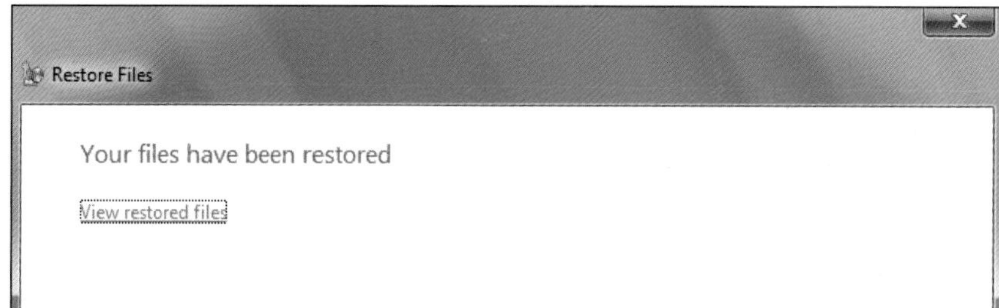

## How do I restore a file from an older backup?

Windows Backup keeps track of your previous backups, and although you will most often want to restore a file from the most recent backup, you can use the following steps to restore files from any stored backup:

1. Follow Steps **1** to **5** to display the Browse or Search Your Backup for Files and Folders to Restore dialog box.
2. Click **Choose a different date**.
3. In the Restore Files dialog box, click the **Show backups from** ▾ and then click the timeframe that includes the backup you want to work with.
4. Click the backup.
5. Click **OK**.

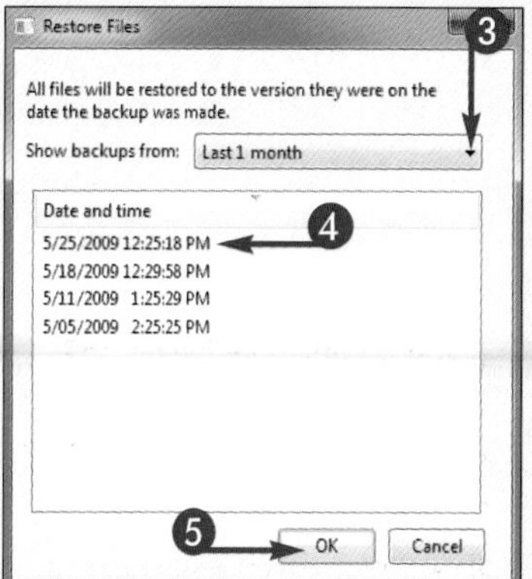

# Index

## D

# Index

## G



## H



## I

# Index

# Index

## T

# Index

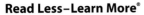

Read Less–Learn More®

Visual®

# There's a Visual book for every learning level...

## Simplified®

**The place to start if you're new to computers. Full color.**

- Computers
- Creating Web Pages
- Digital Photography
- Internet
- Mac OS
- Office
- Windows

## Teach Yourself VISUALLY™

**Get beginning to intermediate-level training in a variety of topics. Full color.**

- Access
- Bridge
- Chess
- Computers
- Crocheting
- Digital Photography
- Dog training
- Dreamweaver
- Excel
- Flash
- Golf
- Guitar
- Handspinning
- HTML
- iLife
- iPhoto
- Jewelry Making & Beading
- Knitting
- Mac OS
- Office
- Photoshop
- Photoshop Elements
- Piano
- Poker
- PowerPoint
- Quilting
- Scrapbooking
- Sewing
- Windows
- Wireless Networking
- Word

## Top 100 Simplified® Tips & Tricks

**Tips and techniques to take your skills beyond the basics. Full color.**

- Digital Photography
- eBay
- Excel
- Google
- Internet
- Mac OS
- Office
- Photoshop
- Photoshop Elements
- PowerPoint
- Windows

# ...all designed for visual learners—just like you!

## Master VISUALLY®

**Your complete visual reference. Two-color interior.**

- 3ds Max
- Creating Web Pages
- Dreamweaver and Flash
- Excel
- Excel VBA Programming
- iPod and iTunes
- Mac OS
- Office
- Optimizing PC Performance
- Photoshop Elements
- QuickBooks
- Quicken
- Windows
- Windows Mobile
- Windows Server

## Visual Blueprint™

**Where to go for professional-level programming instruction. Two-color interior.**

- Ajax
- ASP.NET 2.0
- Excel Data Analysis
- Excel Pivot Tables
- Excel Programming
- HTML
- JavaScript
- Mambo
- PHP & MySQL
- SEO
- Ubuntu Linux
- Vista Sidebar
- Visual Basic
- XML

## Visual Encyclopedia™

**Your A to Z reference of tools and techniques. Full color.**

- Dreamweaver
- Excel
- Mac OS
- Photoshop
- Windows

## Visual Quick Tips

**Shortcuts, tricks, and techniques for getting more done in less time. Full color.**

- Crochet
- Digital Photography
- Excel
- Internet
- iPod & iTunes
- Knitting
- Mac OS
- MySpace
- Office
- PowerPoint
- Windows
- Wireless Networking

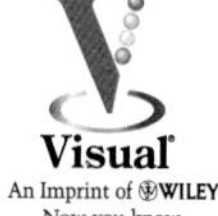


**For a complete listing of Visual books, go to wiley.com/go/visual**